Frontier Military Series
XII

Brevet Brigadier General
FREDERICK WILLIAM BENTEEN

Harvest of Barren Regrets
The Army Career of
Frederick William Benteen
1834-1898

by
CHARLES K. MILLS

THE ARTHUR H. CLARK COMPANY
Glendale, California
1985

To
KAROL ASAY
of Paris, Texas
for her extraordinary contributions

Contents

Illustrations

Sources of the illustrations are identified by the following abbreviations:
cbnm — Custer Battlefield National Monument, Crow Agency, MT
jmc — John M. Carroll, Bryan, TX
lc — Library of Congress, Washington, DC
na — National Archives, Washington, DC
usamhi — U.S. Army Military History Institute, Carlisle Barracks, PA
usma — U.S. Military Academy, West Point, NY

Maps

Virginia to Missouri

Frederick William Benteen was born Sunday, 24 August 1834 in the Virginia port city of Petersburg.

His father, Theodore Charles Benteen, had been born in Baltimore, Maryland in 1809 and about 1830 had married Caroline Hargrove (born there 1810). The Benteens were of Dutch/English extraction, their forebears on the Continent originally came from Germany — according to family tradition. The Benteen family had resided in Baltimore since coming to the New World before the American Revolution. They were merchants, moderately prosperous, Lutherans, Democrats, and conservative.

Sometime after their first child, a daughter, was born in October 1831, Theodore C. ("Charley") and Caroline Benteen left Baltimore for Petersburg, Virginia, the "Cockade City," about 20 miles south of Richmond. The rest of the Benteen clan remained in Baltimore; a younger brother of Charley's, Frederick Damish Benteen, acquired a modest amount of fame publishing sheet music. (One of the young composers he took a chance on was a hitherto unknown shipping clerk from Pittsburgh named Stephen Collins Foster.)

Charley Benteen's line of work was a bit more prosaic. He was a paint and painting supplies purveyor who also sold his services putting his supplies to use. To categorize him as a *house painter* as did the census takers of the 19th century is to form an inaccurate impression of him, his business, and his status in the community. Today, a man doing work such as Charley Benteen did in Petersburg in the early 1830s would be described as a paint and hardware contractor.

Frederick William was the oldest surviving son. He had been preceded by a sister, Henrietta ("En") Elizabeth, in 1831; and he was followed in February 1837 by a younger brother, Theodore ("Theo") Charles, Junior.

By 1840, Charley Benteen had prospered. He owned slaves and was able to send his oldest son to a private academy. Years later, Frederick Benteen was to refer to this academy as the "Petersburg Military Institute"; however, the Petersburg Military Institute did not exist until 1910 and then lasted for only a year. What Benteen was referring to was undoubtedly the Petersburg *Classical* Institute, which featured some military training. (For that matter, it *may* have been known locally — though unofficially — as the Petersburg Military Institute.)

In October of 1841, tragedy struck. Benteen's mother died, leaving a 32-year-old husband, a ten-year-old daughter, and two sons aged seven and four. Unfortunately, there is no way of knowing for certain the extent of the impact his mother's early death had on Benteen's formative personality. Nothing of a documentary nature exists. But the sudden deprivation of a mother at such an early age, even in an era of grim mortality statistics, cannot be ignored. Fred Benteen grew up essentially motherless.

In the spring of 1849, following the marriage of Henrietta, Charley Benteen packed up his earthly goods and two sons and departed for St. Louis, Missouri. The Benteens were not the only Americans on the move that year. The Gold Rush was on in full swing. Never before had there been such a mass disruption of American society and never since has there been one to rival it. St. Louis, the erstwhile French fur trading post, had been transformed into a leading center for processing and shipping agricultural and manufactured goods. Its population was about 50,000 by the time Charley Benteen arrived to settle down and establish a partnership with two men: Alexander and Hugh Carswell. Benteen & Carswell sold paint and glass supplies to the steamboats that plied the Mississippi River trade. Somewhere along the way, Charley Benteen acquired a second wife. Her name was Beulah Kane and she had three small children from a previous marriage.

Frederick W. Benteen, out of school by age 16, worked for his father for several years. He eventually established himself as an independent sign painter, beginning the normal process of breaking with his progenitor, a process that in his case was hastened and aggravated by the American Civil War. Through his father, he became acquainted with a family in Philadelphia called Norman. His father apparently pursued a young woman named Anita Norman, while Fred Benteen took an interest in her younger sister: Catharine Louisa Norman (born 5 March 1836). Both Norman girls were children in a large family that migrated to St. Louis sometime after the death of their father, Henry Norman, in 1856. Benteen's acquaintance with "Kate" Norman, a staunch supporter of the Union, was to have a profound effect on his future.

According to the bare military records, Frederick William Benteen entered the Army as a first lieutenant on 1 September 1861. In order to put this into perspective, however, a (very brief) background sketch is needed.

With the election of Abraham Lincoln in the fall of 1860, the factions polarized. Southern, slave-holding states began to talk of secession and to take serious acts in furtherance of that end. The spark that ignited what came to be called the Civil War, it is generally acknowledged, was Confederate artillery fire on Fort Sumter in April 1861. Four months earlier, out-going President Buchanan had dispatched a relief expedition to Sumter, which had been forced to turn back for fear of starting a war. The principal vessel in this relief convoy was called the *Star of the West* and numbered among its passengers a young West Point first lieutenant named Charles R. Woods, who would later play an important role in the military career of Frederick William Benteen.

Benteen asserted late in his life that the war "was started by a number of politicians who had been defeated in the national election and were sore on that account." For a man living in Missouri in 1860-1861, such a conspiracy theory, however simplistic, was reasonable. The majority of Missourians were Union in sentiment in 1861, though the state politicians, in the main, were sympathetic to the Confederate cause. When it became obvious that secession was spreading, Missouri supporters of Abraham Lincoln swung into action. They were concentrated in St. Louis, deriving most support from the German and Hungarian immigrants in that city, and in the extreme north and south of the state, well away from the Missouri River valley. The acknowledged Union leader was Francis Preston Blair, Jr. Frank Blair was determined that U.S. Army installations in Missouri should not fall into the hands of the pro-Confederate politicians as so many Federal arsenals had in the Deep South. To this end, he enlisted the support of Captain Nathaniel Lyon, commanding officer of the St.

Louis Arsenal. With like-minded volunteers such as John McA. Schofield, an ex-artillery lieutenant, the Blair/Lyon faction succeeded in
disarming the pro-Confederate militia and establishing Federal control
over St. Louis.

The first significant conflict of the war in Missouri was the battle
of Wilson's Creek (10 August 1861). It was Benteen's first taste of
combat. His exact status there has been obscured. He was not an
officer until 1 September. He apparently was not an enlisted man
either. He claimed much later that he went to the Wilson Creek as
a "sight-seer," but that is a misleading oversimplification. Wilson's
Creek was over 220 miles from his home in St. Louis and the railroad in those days went only as far as Rolla, less than halfway between the two points. Furthermore, the battle was begun deliberately
by the Union forces after an all-night march brought them onto an
unsuspecting Confederate encampment. There were no "sight-seers"
at Wilson's Creek. Since Benteen was certainly not in the Confederate camp, he could only have reached the battlefield in the company
of Union forces. Finally, by his own admission, he had been "setting
up" (i.e., training) Union volunteers for some time prior to the battle.
When he mustered in as an officer in September, a notation was made
to date his service from mid-*July*. What Benteen may have been trying to convey with his preposterous "sight-seer" comment was that
he was not formally a member of the Union cause on 10 August, but
he was unquestionably with Union volunteers. Whether or not he
fired a weapon on that day is debatable, but he was certainly in a
position to do so and, what is more, he had put himself into that
position deliberately. His comment about drilling the troops suggests
that his role may have been that of an unenrolled drillmaster. Apparently, he was knowledgeable about military drill as a carryover from
his Petersburg academy days, though he may well have been a member of a marching club or unofficial militia unit from St. Louis.

Whatever Benteen's precise status there, the battle of Wilson's
Creek was a very important one for him. He came away from it determined to fight for the Union. The battle also involved some individuals who would have an important influence on his life and career
for many years to come.

2

Wilson's Creek

The Union forces in Missouri spent the late spring and most of the summer of 1861 maneuvering for advantage over the pro-Confederate forces. Commanded by Nathaniel Lyon, who had been promoted from captain to brigadier general overnight, the forces of Frank Blair and the Union drove on central Missouri. Using railroads and steamboats skillfully, they succeeded in establishing control over the vital Missouri River valley and, by doing so, compelled the Confederates to rally in the southwest corner of the state — in counties hostile to slavery and secession. But Lyon's victories of early summer had the negative effect of driving the various Confederate factions together into one massive encampment. And, on 9 August 1861, Lyon discovered that the Confederates were about ten miles southwest of Springfield in a heavily wooded area bisected by Wilson's Creek. Over the objections of Major John McA. Schofield, whom Lyon had appointed his chief of staff, Lyon and his brigade commanders hatched a scheme to attack the Confederates from two directions. The plan, which Lyon credited to Colonel Franz Sigel (who had been an officer in the German Army), called for a splitting of forces and a two-pronged assault on the estimated 22,000 Confederates at dawn 10 August. Sigel was to take a force of slightly more than 1200 men and assault the encampment from the southeast. Lyon was to take the balance (about 3700 men) and assault simultaneously from the northwest. Their respective points of release (lines of departure, in modern infantry jargon) were about three miles apart. They were attacking a force that outnumbered them about five to one.

Lyon's small army marched out of Springfield at 5:00 in the evening on 9 August, split as pre-arranged, and marched about ten miles in the dark until they came in sight of the bonfires that marked the Confederate encampment. About 4:00 in the morning of 10 August 1861 Lyon's skirmishers encountered Confederate sentries and the fight was on. Sigel was late getting into position and Lyon's force tackled the enemy by themselves for the first hour or more. Lyon placed a small battalion of Regular Army infantry companies on his left flank, across Wilson's Creek from his main body. They bore the brunt of the early fighting. There were some Missouri mounted volunteers with the isolated battalion. One of these was a young captain named William D. Bowen.

Sigel's brigade, late arriving, heard the firing, swept across Wilson's Creek and advanced slowly north along its west bank. They halted after advancing less than a mile. Rumors persisted for years afterward that the halt was caused because Sigel's mostly German troops left their ranks to plunder some of the tents they had overrun. Whatever the reason, Sigel did not move forward more than a half mile in the next three hours.

When the Confederates finally reorganized to counterattack Sigel's brigade, precious time (essential to the success of such an audacious plan) had been lost. Furthermore, the Confederates were not wearing the gray or butternut uniforms that later in the war became their standard dress. Many were wearing blue uniforms, identical to those worn by Lyon's and Sigel's men. In the confusion over identity, the Confederates marched right up to Sigel's ill-disciplined line and delivered a series of devasting vollies. Sigel's men fled.

The commanding officer of the small Regular Army cavalry squadron attached to Sigel's brigade was Captain Eugene A. Carr of the 1st (later 4th) Cavalry. He conferred with a much-demoralized Colonel Sigel and related: "It was then decided to move south. . . till we could go out and circle round the enemy towards Springfield." Sigel's troops did just that. They circled to the southwest and passed around the battlefield behind Lyon's brigades who were fighting desperately. This retreat left an indelible impression in the minds of the participants of the battle. Benteen later remarked that he had been appalled by the conduct of the "Dutch troops," implying that he had been with Sigel's brigade. On the other hand, he may well have not actually witnessed the retreat, but merely heard it discussed (and cussed) around campfires long after the battle was over.

The immediate effect of Sigel's precipitous departure was on Lyon's hard-pressed troops. The Confederates turned on Lyon with a fury. Lyon himself, twice wounded, personally led a counterattack and was killed. The situation was desperate. In one volunteer regiment, the surgeon (a man named Florence M. Cornyn), gave up trying to treat the wounded and seized up a musket, firing it just like any private in the line. In this same regiment, a young Irish-born lieutenant named Thomas Hynes was leading his men with the coolness of a veteran officer. Hynes was, in fact, Lyon's own former first sergeant and was seeing action for the first time as a volunteer officer. Another veteran sergeant was an acting company commander in the Regular Army dragoon company protecting Lyon's rear. His name was Myles Moylan.

Because of men such as Cornyn, Hynes, and Moylan, the lines held even though Lyon was dead. Major Schofield learned of Lyon's death and took it upon himself to seek out the next senior officer. There were some volunteer colonels still on their feet at that time, but Schofield went directly to the ranking Regular Army officer, Major Samuel D. Sturgis of the U.S. 1st (later 4th) Cavalry. Sturgis assumed command of Lyon's brigades.

"Buckskin Sam" Sturgis was a 39-year-old West Pointer who had seen action in the Mexican War and some minor Indian campaigns. He was a rather dour, tobacco-chewing old-line cavalry officer of a decidedly conservative nature. Sturgis decided to retreat. No sooner had the decision been communicated to the companies when the Confederates launched an all-out assault. Skillfully, Sturgis re-deployed to meet the threat and his weary troops beat off the attack. Finally, about 11:30 on the morning of 10 August, Sturgis's men began an orderly withdrawal to Springfield. By 5:00 that evening the last stragglers had reached Springfield and the preliminary figures were in. Out of a combined force (Lyon's *and* Sigel's) of less than 5000, Sturgis could account for 1235 casualties: 223 killed outright, 721 wounded, and 291 missing. Ironically (and unbeknownst to Sturgis at the time), the Confederates had fared even worse, suffering at least 3000 casualties. The retreat, wrote Major Schofield years later, "was undoubtedly an error. . . It was only necessary to hold our ground, trusting to the pluck and endurance of our men, and the victory would have been ours."

In fairness to Major Sturgis, however, this view was not held at the time. The surviving officers agreed on a retreat to Rolla. Colonel Sigel, the ranking officer, commanded for the first two days — until a delegation led by Major Schofield "demanded a change." The march to Rolla was demoralizing. Provisions had been low to begin with and Sigel exercised no real control over the march, necessitating additional hardships. "Major Sturgis, in compliance with the demand, assumed command."

Frederick William Benteen was a keen observer of events. By the time he arrived in Rolla, he had made up his mind. "A man with my views could no longer withhold offering his services, and life, if necessary, for the preservation of his country," he later said. "I then commenced my services in the cavalry."

He was 27 years old, but looked about 10 years younger. His face was large, round, and smooth-shaven. (He grew a scraggly mustache from time to time, but never sported a beard.) This, coupled with his large, round, blue eyes, gave him a distinctive cherubic appearance. One reporter who described him in 1879 remarked that he might have been mistaken for an overgrown drummer boy. Benteen was tall (5'10½") and broad-shouldered. He had a large torso, long muscular arms, and huge hands. As subsequent events proved, he was formidable in combat, including the hand-to-hand variety. Physically, Frederick W. Benteen was impressive.

3

Bowen's Battalion

Major Samuel D. Sturgis's battered, bickering command arrived at Rolla 19 August after an eight-day march through central Missouri. Almost at once, the bulk of the troops were placed on trains and sent to St. Louis for the necessary refitting and reorganization. A few of the survivors of Wilson's Creek remained at Rolla and Benteen was one of these.

His decision to accompany Union troops had generated a family crisis. Because of this, Benteen had refused "many and many" offers of a commission from the infantry companies he had drilled in the summer. His father, a strong secessionist, was quite vehement on the subject of Benteen's siding with the Union faction. "When Benteen told his family that he was going with the Union Army his father told him: 'I hope the first god damned bullet gets you'." But, Benteen had pulled away from his father some time before and was furthermore very much influenced by his girl friend, Kate Norman, "who brought pressure on him to support the Union." The fight at Wilson's Creek had decided him.

Benteen was "horrified" by the spectacle of defeat and retreat and thought that the "Union deserved better troops than they had." He decided to stay and offer his services as an officer, knowing full well that "the prayers of my nearest kin were being offered up that I might get so badly wounded that I could render no service." His first opportunity to render his service came at Rolla a few days later.

The post at Rolla consisted of six regiments, five of which were infantry units that had not seen action. The sixth was the 1st Missouri Volunteers, which was in the process of being converted to an artillery unit to be known as the 1st Missouri Light Artillery. Surgeon Cornyn and Lieutenant Thomas Hynes were members of this organization. The commanding officer at Rolla was Colonel John B. Wyman, who was attempting to raise a battalion of cavalry. The recruits for this new cavalry battalion came from the survivors of Wilson's Creek. Benteen was one of them.

By 1 September, the fledgling battalion consisted of 234 men organized into three companies of approximately seventy men each — with the overflow assigned to a yet unorganized fourth company. Colonel Wyman, commanding the 13th Illinois Volunteers (from Dixon, Illinois), wanted the new battalion assigned to his regiment. However, as the bulk of the recruits were from Missouri, they resisted amalgamation with an Illinois unit and remained separate from — but attached to — Wyman's command.

On 1 September, the 67 members of C Company of this new (as yet unnamed) cavalry battalion held an election of officers. William D. Bowen, the captain who had fought with the Regulars on the left flank at Wilson's Creek, was elected its captain and commanding officer. Frederick W. Benteen was elected first lieutenant and a man named Daniel W. Ballou was elected second lieutenant.

This new cavalry unit, in keeping with standard cavalry organization at the time, was authorized 100 enlisted men per company to be led by three officers: a captain, a first and second lieutenant. The original first lieutenant of C Company, a man named Fisher, had resigned. Benteen took his place as a result of the election and commenced drilling his new charges.

Mounted troops in America were rarely employed as true cavalry in the Continental manner. Rather, they were invariably used as *mounted infantry* who rode to the scene of an engagement, dismounted, and then fought on foot. But, there were assignments peculiar to the cavalry branch that justified the expense and time it took to train cavalry troopers and their mounts. First, "mounted units performed tactical reconnaisances, pursued enemy infantry after a victory, and covered friendly infantry after a defeat." Second, "Cavalry was often used to cover the flanks of the main lines of infantry on Civil War battlefields. This employment of cavalry was common most of the war in both theaters." Third, "cavalry units were sometimes held in the rear of infantry units, where they served as file closers, to prevent straggling and desertion." Finally, "mounted troops were sometimes used to screen infantry movements and help achieve tactical surprise. . . The mobility and flexibility of cavalry made it the arm most capable of confusing and misleading the enemy."

The four primary missions of the cavalry given above can be summarized as follows: screen, shield, police, and mask the infantry. Frequently, cavalry units (especially smaller ones) found themselves *being* the infantry. To make this transition, they dismounted and moved forward to engage the enemy on foot, leaving their horses in the hands of the "horse-holders." Standard practice was to leave one man in four behind with his own horse and the horses of three of his comrades. Sometimes, the ratio was one horseholder to *two* fighting men, which seriously reduced the fighting effectiveness of the unit (the horseholders, naturally, being out of action). There were occasions in Benteen's Civil War career when the ratio of dismounted men to horseholders was eight to one, but such occasions were quite rare and never possible with small units such as Benteen's new company at Rolla.

Because of the relative complexity of cavalry evolutions (as compared to infantry maneuvers), more training was required of would-be cavalrymen. The conventional wisdom at the time was that it took two years to turn a soldier into a fully-qualified cavalryman. Obviously, Benteen and his men did not have two years. So, they crammed as much training as they could into a month and hoped that combat and campaigning would iron out the wrinkles. Benteen had certainly picked one of the most challenging jobs imaginable for that time and place.

Once in the field, they learned that in addition to their combat roles cavalrymen were often called on to perform such unglamorous roles as mounted messengers, escorts to wagons and senior officers, and servers of writs and warrants (police work on horseback). Still, an inordinate amount of their training was devoted to learning the pure *cavalry charge*. All cavalrymen had to learn the use of the saber and all carried the *arme blanche* (as it was called) in the units with which Benteen was associated, but they rarely got a chance to use them.

By 1 October, the cavalry battalion had been filled up. The fourth company, designated Company D, had been organized and another election was held. Captain William D. Bowen of C Company was promoted to major and made commanding officer of the battalion which was formally designated the 1st Battalion, Missouri Cavalry. First Lieutenant Benteen was elected captain commanding C Company. Daniel W. Ballou was promoted by election to first lieutenant of the same company and the adjutant of the post at Rolla, Edwin M. Emerson, was elected second lieutenant. The 1st Battalion, Missouri Cavalry was still attached to Colonel Wyman's 13th Illinois Volunteers.

Election of officers was a standard practice until later in the war. Men were made officers by the men they would lead in combat and the supervision of such elections was the responsibility of the U.S. Mustering Officer for the state. In Missouri in 1861, the U.S. Mustering Officer was Major Schofield.

DUTCH HOLLOW

Benteen's first taste of action as an officer was at a little field called Dutch Hollow near the present-day town of Wet Glaize, close to the geographical center of the state of Missouri. Colonel Wyman was leading a column consisting of his own 13th Illinois, preceded by Major Bowen's 1st Battalion, Missouri Cavalry, and followed by a similar cavalry battalion called the Fremont Hussars. About 8:00 in the morning of 13 October 1861, Bowen's skirmishers discovered a large body of irregular Confederate cavalry about three miles ahead of the column. Major Bowen immediately deployed three of his companies. B Company swung out in a line on the right hand side of the road, C Company (Benteen's) swung out on the left side, and Bowen led A Company straight down the road toward the enemy. The Confederates retreated for about three miles before they drew up a line to meet Bowen's three companies. Bowen charged with A Company (about 40 men) and caused the Confederates to retreat "in great confusion" for about a half a mile.

At Dutch Hollow, the retreating Confederates were reinforced by another unit estimated at 600 or more and counterattacked Bowen's lead company (A), forcing him to fall back on Companies B and C. The Confederates then began an attack on Bowen's left flank (Benteen), but were driven back by two volleys delivered by Benteen's dismounted company. In the meantime, Bowen had sent back to the main column for support and Major Clark Wright came galloping up with two companies of Fremont Hussars. The Union reinforcements were sent swinging around the left of the Confederate position, a forested ridge about a half mile south of Bowen's deployed companies. Major Wright remained with Bowen's B Company in the center, while Bowen, leading A and C Companies, charged toward the Confederate right flank. Colonel Wyman hurried six infantry companies forward at a run, reaching the battlefield about 45 minutes later. Bowen's two companies were not successful in breaking the Confederate line, but Wright's two companies on the right flank managed to break in amongst them with a saber charge.

As the Confederates turned to deal with Major Wright's companies, Colonel Wyman arrived with the infantry. Five of the infantry companies (and Bowen's B Company) launched a foot assault on the Confederate center. The Rebels did not wait to meet it, but "commenced a rapid retreat." The infantry was unable to keep up with the retreating Confederates, so Colonel Wyman ordered Bowen and Wright to pursue with the cavalry until dark. The cavalry companies chased the Confederates across fields for about 12 miles, killing 12, wounding 17, and taking eight prisoners. The Fremont Hussars that had not been engaged in the battle were detailed to bury the bodies at Dutch Hollow. They buried 66. The Union troops lost one man killed and two wounded. Bowen's companies lost no one, not even a horse. It was an auspicious beginning.

The battle of Dutch Hollow was a resounding Union victory, but it was merely a minor skirmish in the context of the entire war. The Confederates, led by a colonel named William W. Summers (who was captured), were simply no match for Wyman's command, which when concentrated outnumbered them three to one. The interesting aspect to this battle is that Wyman's command was never completely concentrated and the burden of the fighting was borne by the five cavalry companies engaged. It was a cavalry battle, primarily. The Confederate horsemen fled before Wyman's infantry and were decimated in the process. The cavalry pursuit destroyed the Confederates as a fighting unit.

The following day at Linn Creek, Major Wright's battalion of Fremont Hussars led the column and charged a Confederate encampment. The fighting was over before either Wyman's infantry or Major Bowen's cavalry could arrive on the scene. Colonel Wyman reported that he was "embarrassed" with 88 prisoners as a result of that lop-sided skirmish.

In both of these battles, Wyman's Union troops were not fighting regular Confederates, but irregulars of the bushwhacker sort. Neither battle was much of a contest, though both contributed to the Union domination of central Missouri.

The net result of the battles of Dutch Hollow and Linn Creek was that Colonel Wyman and his attached cavalry units were avoided for at least six weeks. They occupied small towns in the south central portion of the state and spent their time patrolling and continuing to train their men. Benteen's military career settled down into a familar routine: reveille, stables, drill, meals, patrols, escorts, taps, and more of the same. The men of his company, Missourians almost to a man, were given ample opportunity to learn their new trade without harassment from Confederates or guerrillas. It was almost idyllic while it lasted.

The war rudely intruded again in the early morning hours of 3 December 1861 just outside the sleepy hamlet of Salem about 20 miles south of Rolla. Major Bowen had been sent with a patrol of 40 men to round up some witnesses for a military trial in Rolla. Upon hearing that Confederate guerrillas were active in the Salem area, Colonel Wyman directed Bowen to take an additional 80 men, which was done, borrowing from all four companies. (The 120 men thus assembled represented slightly less than half of the battalion.) They rounded up their witnesses on the afternoon of 2 December and went into camp, planning to move back to Rolla in the morning.

At 4:00 in the morning, a Confederate force of about 300 men rode up to within two miles of Bowen's camp and infiltrated through the woods. They emerged from the woods among the tents of A Company and opened fire. Captain Benteen was sleeping about 500 yards away when the shooting started. He awoke, rallied his own men and some men from Captain Ing's B Company, and launched a counterattack on foot. The skirmish was hot for a time, but Benteen was driving them back when Major Bowen brought D Company up in support about 20 minutes later. D Company, commanded by Captain Martin H. "Hal" Williams, charged on horseback through the Confederates and drove them from the camp.

Major Bowen reported that he had suffered 12 casualties, including four killed, while inflicting 36 casualties, including 16 dead, on the guerrillas. It was the first blooding of the war for Benteen's new unit. Two days later, Major General Henry W. Halleck, the senior officer in the West, wired a congratulations to Major Bowen. "Please receive my thanks to yourself and your command for their gallant conduct on that occasion," he said, "I hope soon to hear that it has been repeated." It *would* be repeated.

Immediately after receiving General Halleck's wire, Bowen and his men were in the saddle again in pursuit of the guerrilla band

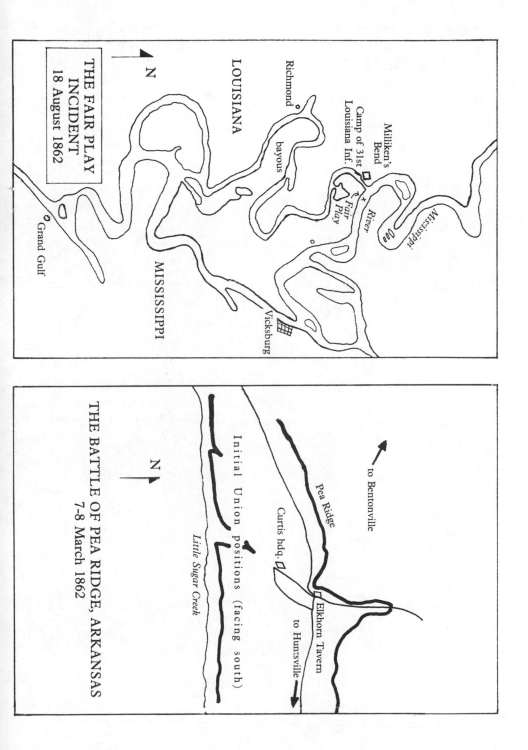

THE FAIR PLAY
INCIDENT
18 August 1862

N

LOUISIANA

Richmond

bayous

Milliken's
Bend

Camp of 31st
Louisiana Inf.

Fair
Play

River

Mississippi

MISSISSIPPI

Grand Gulf

Vicksburg

THE BATTLE OF PEA RIDGE, ARKANSAS
7-8 March 1862

N

Initial Union positions (facing south)

Little Sugar Creek

Pea Ridge

Curtis hdq.

Elkhorn Tavern

to Bentonville

to Huntsville

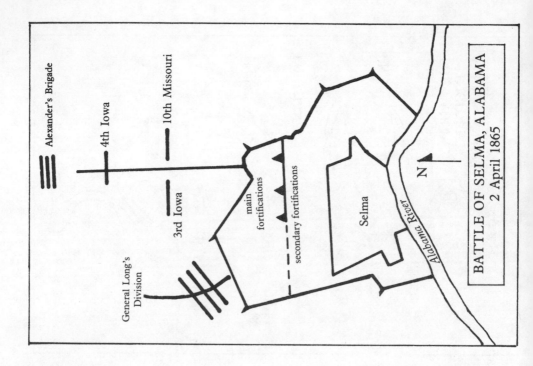

Alexander's Brigade

4th Iowa

10th Missouri

3rd Iowa

main
fortifications

secondary fortifications

General Long's
Division

Selma

Alabama River

N

BATTLE OF SELMA, ALABAMA
2 April 1865

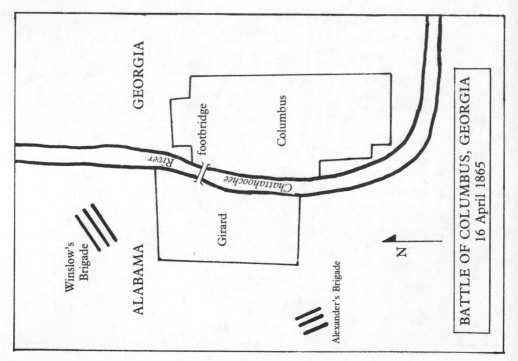

GEORGIA

footbridge

Columbus

River

Chattahoochee

Winslow's
Brigade

ALABAMA

Girard

Alexander's Brigade

N

BATTLE OF COLUMBUS, GEORGIA
16 April 1865

that had surprised them. They swept through Missouri's rough Current Hills for four solid days, accompanied by reinforcements from their own battalion and a company of Fremont Hussars. They made sporadic contact with the enemy, falling back on Salem only after they had run out of forage and provisions. They brought in 20 prisoners, which prompted Major Bowen to pen an amusing post script to his report on the scout to Colonel Wyman in Rolla.

"Will you please inform me what I will do with the prisoners," he wrote. "I think if half of them were kicked and let go it would be the best thing we could do with them, for they are already near scared to death."

Bowen's 1st Battalion, Missouri Cavalry, remained in Salem until the end of the year, not seeing any more action. Fred Benteen, however, discovered a serious problem at home and requested a ten day furlough to attend to personal business. He applied to Major Bowen on 29 December. Bowen endorsed the request as did Colonel Wyman, who offered to let him "quarter in Rolla." General Halleck approved the request on 1 January 1862 and Benteen departed for St. Louis and New York on his personal business.

Here is the pertinent part of Benteen's letter of request:

I have a sister (and the only living relative in the United States whom I have not seen for many years) residing in New York City, whose husband, since I joined the Army, has been cruelly mistreating her. Unfortunately, she is of a very weakly constitution, and not able to endure the privations she has been forced to undergo much longer. Of this fact I was uninformed until a few weeks ago.

It is her wish and my desire to have her in St. Louis, where I can be in more direct communication with her. If I knew of anyone in N.Y. that would attend to it in the manner I should wish, I would be satisfied, but its being of rather a private nature dislike to publish it where it can be avoided, so prefer attending to it in propria persona. . .

If it is impolitic or impossible to grant my request, I shall be compelled to resign, as the greatest measure of my happiness is constituted in the well doing of my sister.

The sister, Henrietta ("En") Fairbanks, was duly brought with her three "almost infant" daughters from New York to St. Louis.

Benteen's furlough was not entirely consumed in protecting his older sister from an abusive husband. On Tuesday, 7 January 1862, Frederick William Benteen and Catharine Louisa Norman were married at St. George's Episcopal Church in St. Louis by the Reverend

Dr. Berkely, pastor of the church. The witnesses were: Miss Norman's mother, Elizabeth Lowrey Norman, and one of her sisters, Marcella K. Norman.

Catharine Louisa Norman Benteen, called Kate by her family and also "Pinkie" or "Frabbie" by her new bridegroom, was just weeks shy of her 26th birthday. She was to remain Mrs. Fred Benteen for the next 44 years, bearing his five children and accompanying him wherever possible throughout the next 36 years of their married life.

The newlyweds did not have an extended honeymoon. Fred Benteen was back in Rolla three days later. Kate settled into a house in St. Louis to wait out the war. And, the war was heating up, especially in Missouri. The new Confederate commander, Major General Sterling Price, was gathering a large army in Arkansas and the Indian Territory to invade Missouri. The new commanding general of the Union forces in Missouri was 57-year-old Brigadier General Samuel R. Curtis.

Curtis had resigned his commission in the Regular Army in 1832, just a year after graduating from West Point, to devote himself to engineering. He had served as a volunteer colonel during the Mexican War and, by 1850, had settled down to become the city engineer of St. Louis. He later moved to Keokuk, Iowa, where he became an engineer, lawyer, and a successful candidate for the U.S. Congress in 1858 and 1860. He resigned from Congress in the summer of 1861 to accept a commission as a brigadier general and it was in this capacity that he returned to St. Louis after a hiatus of ten years.

Curtis was determined to stop the Confederate invasion before it started and to that end, he deployed the forces at his disposal into southwestern Missouri. Among those forces was the 1st Battalion, Missouri Cavalry, now officially known as Bowen's Battalion.

INVASION OF ARKANSAS

On 29 January 1862, General Curtis moved from Rolla to a little town called Lebanon about halfway between Rolla and his objective, Springfield. There, he organized what was to become the Army of the Southwest into four divisions and began deploying it toward Springfield.

Bowen's Battalion was not assigned to any of the four divisions, but rather was kept at General Curtis' headquarters as a bodyguard and escort for the general and his staff. Four mountain howitzers were issued to the battalion and A Company under Captain J.W. Stephens was converted from a pure cavalry to a horse artillery company. The other three companies, besides escorting General Curtis and his staff, provided security for the four mountain howitzers. This meant that when the howitzers were deployed, it was the men from these companies who dug entrenchments, carried water, and performed a host of other duties, the most significant of which was protecting the artillerymen from enemy infantry and cavalry.

The first taste of action for General Curtis and his troops was at Springfield. The lead elements of the Army of the Southwest entered Springfield on 12 February 1862 at about 10:00 in the morning. They were practically unopposed, though Bowen's Battalion got a chance to try out its new howitzers "on a heavy picket of the enemy, concealed partially from view by the thick brush." "After two rounds," Major Bowen reported laconically, "the rebels disappeared." That evening (8:00 p.m.), Bowen's Battalion was called to the front after some heavy firing had been heard. By the time they arrived on the scene, the Rebels were gone.

General Curtis did not linger in Springfield, the site of Lyon's travail six months before, but kept his four widely scattered divisions moving generally south by west toward known concentrations of Confederate troops in the Boston Mountains just over the Arkansas border.

On 14 February, Bowen's Battalion, leading the headquarters column, stumbled into a minor Confederate camp near Crane Creek, Missouri. Major Bowen unlimbered his howitzers and let fly with ten shells, inflicting 24 casualties. He sent his mounted men storming through the camp, but recalled them when it appeared that a larger Confederate force was moving up on his flank. They withdrew without casualties, bringing away 30 prisoners, including the guerrilla leader who had attacked their camp at Salem two months before.

Major Bowen had come to rely heavily on Captain Benteen and his C Company. On 16 February, it was a patrol from Benteen's company under Lieutenant Ballou and Sergeant-Major Evans that discovered Confederate positions along Sugar Creek in northwestern Arkansas. Major Bowen hurried forward with reinforcements and commenced a running fight with the Confederate rear guard. He used his four howitzers liberally, throwing shell and canister at suspected enemy positions "concealed by the brush" and kept it up until "they fled."

During the Civil War, howitzers such as the weapons Major Bowen and his Battalion employed were basically muzzle-loading, wheel-mounted weapons. Each had to be served by a crew of four to six men. They fired a variety of projectiles instead of a single leaden ball. One of these varieties was called *shot*. Shot was essentially a giant ball, analagous to the musket ball. It was made of cast iron and, obviously, was not intended to be wasted on individual soldiers. It was used for battering, for knocking holes in fortifications and so forth. The "shell" that Major Bowen used was a hollow ball packed with powder that exploded either on impact or when ignited by a time fuse. *Shell* was used with great effect against concealed troops and horses or concentrations of the same. There was a special shell that was used more often than the type described above. Technically, it was called *spherical case*. It was a hollow shell filled with a mixture of powder *and* musket balls. And it was fired as (and frequently reported as) shell. It was better known by its nickname, inspired by its developer's name: *shrapnel*. The "shell" that Major Bowen reported using was probably shrapnel. Finally, there was *canister*. This was sometimes called *grapeshot* and was essentially a big tin can filled with cast iron balls, fired like a giant shotgun shell. Canister, or grapeshot, had an extremely limited range and was invariably employed against dense concentrations of the enemy at close range.

Whatever combination of these various projectiles Civil War artillerymen used was kept in a large wooden chest, which was mounted in a wagon called a *caisson*. Horse artillery units generally used a specially constructed vehicle called a *limber*. Two-wheeled limbers, besides having ammunition chests, had devices for hooking the howitzer (with its two wheels) and towing the resultant combination behind a team of horses. Normally, each chest in the caisson or limber was capable of carrying 32 rounds of ammunition in any combination of the varieties described. Both caissons and limbers generally held four such chests. Major Bowen indicated that he was served by 24 round "pack caissons," which was a local improvisation. When the ammunition was used up, it was necessary to move the howitzer back to the rear or to have a resupply brought forward.

The following day of the pursuit along Sugar Creek, 17 February 1862, a Confederate battery (a stand of guns numbering two or more) began to return harassing fire. Major Bowen moved two howitzers forward and led his three cavalry companies in an attack that stalled about 200 yards from the Confederate battery. The Rebel guns pulled back. Major Bowen was wounded in the right wrist in this engagement, but led his battalion forward to a position on a bluff overlooking Sugar Creek and held it against heavy fire until larger howitzers moved forward and took up the fight.

Two days later, Major Bowen sent two of his howitzers with Capt. Ing's B Company on a scout to Huntsville, Arkansas. They were gone almost two weeks.

Before Ing returned, Captain Benteen's company at Sugar Creek was given a special assignment. They had been providing escort to officers of General Curtis' staff on a daily basis for some time, but now were ordered to detach 20-30 men to provide a special escort to Curtis' staff officer responsible for subsistence (rations) for an indefinite period of time.

The Commissary of Subsistence on Curtis' Army of the Southwest staff was Captain Philip H. Sheridan of the U.S. 13th Infantry, an outspoken, combative 32-year-old West Pointer. His job was to travel around the countryside gathering food and grain for the army in the field. In northwestern Arkansas in March of 1862, this assignment, while not exactly glamorous, was a very dangerous one as the woods and hills were filled with Rebel troops and sympathizers.

It has long been an army tradition to unload inept and otherwise undesirable members of any command onto detached service details so as to be rid of them and meet the requirements of military orders at the same time. Benteen did not do this. He gave Captain Sheridan 28 of the best men he had and placed the detail under the command of his "efficient" second lieutenant, Edwin M. Emerson. Sheridan was delighted with his escort and especially 2Lt. Emerson. This single act of unexpected courtesy on Benteen's part was to pay dividends until the end of his military career 25 years later.

While Eddy Emerson and the detachment were on their way back to Missouri assisting Captain Sheridan, General Curtis was concentrating his four divisions along the north bank of Sugar Creek. With his staff and escort, he had taken up residence in a house owned by a family named Pratt, located about halfway between his line on the bluffs and a large escarpment to the north known locally as Pea Ridge. The weather turned bad. It snowed on 5 March, covering the ground and the wind was cold and blustery.

To the south of Curtis' new positions, the Confederates had been reinforced with regiments from Texas and the Indian Territory. The commanding general of the Confederates was an ex-governor of Missouri, Major General Sterling Price. The newcomers, led by the same General McCulloch that Lyon had faced at Wilson's Creek, made the combined force total more than 16,000. (Curtis had about 10,000.)

On 4 March, in the Boston Mountains south of Fayetteville, Major

General Earl van Dorn arrived and assumed command of the entire Confederate army. He immediately set in motion a plan to swing wide to the west, screened by the mountains, and come in from behind Pea Ridge, north of Curtis' line. Van Dorn planned to assault at daylight on 7 March 1862.

Brigadier General Samuel R. Curtis spent most of the day entrenching along the small bluffs overlooking Sugar Creek on 6 March. The ground was almost frozen and difficult to dig, but the Union troops made do with wooden breastworks created with axes and saws from the surrounding trees. The four divisions of the Army of the Southwest were strung out in numerical order from west to east. The first two divisions were commanded by Brigadier General Franz Sigel, the same Sigel who had done so poorly at Wilson's Creek. The third division was commanded by an Indiana colonel with the embarrassing name of Jefferson C. Davis. (He was *not* related to the President of the Confederacy.) The fourth division was commanded by Colonel Eugene A. Carr of the 3rd Illinois Cavalry, the same Carr who as a captain had fought with Sigel at Wilson's Creek.

About 2:00 that afternoon (6 March), General Sigel's pickets near the town of Bentonville were attacked by a large Confederate force. Sigel managed to get his troops back to the Union lines above Sugar Creek without any damage. General Curtis was made very uneasy by this new development and dispatched cavalry companies around his lines to reinforce the pickets. He sensed that the Confederates were swinging around his right flank by way of Bentonville. As the night wore on, sounds and reports made Curtis even more uneasy. By early morning, he had convinced himself that the Confederates were not merely trying to slip around his right flank by way of Bentonville, but were actually marching behind his entire army beyond Pea Ridge. Accordingly, he called a conference of his division commanders and proposed to swing his entire army around 180 degrees to meet the new (perceived) threat. But, the move was to be made by stages, with Sigel's divisions remaining on Sugar Creek, Carr's division fortifying Elkhorn Tavern, and Davis' division between the others, facing Pea Ridge.

Elkhorn Tavern was a small stage stop at the foot of Pea Ridge where two major roads intersected. One road ran east to Huntsville and west along the foot of Pea Ridge to a little hamlet called Leetown. The other road, the so-called Telegraph Road, ran almost straight north and south. Several miles north, it intersected the road behind Pea Ridge that went to Bentonville.

Carr's position proved the critical point in the Union line. The pickets were driven in by a wave of screaming Confederates who swarmed down off the high ground and assaulted Elkhorn Tavern. Colonel Carr, hurrying his 4th Division into place, had barely arrived when, to his left, Colonel Davis's 3rd Division opened up on the Rebels.

General van Dorn, the Confederate commander, had attempted to launch a two-pronged assault. General McCulloch and several high-ranking Confederates were killed by Davis's assault. Their troops, leaderless and ill-disciplined, were unable to recover the initiative.

In the meantime, Colonel Carr was receiving the second prong with one small division. The troops attacking him, led by Sterling Price, steadily drove Carr back. The 4th Division had two brigades, one of which was commanded by Colonel Grenville M. Dodge; the other, by Colonel William Van Dever, and they were hard pressed all morning long. Carr sent to General Curtis for reinforcements, but Curtis, unable — or unwilling — to extricate any reinforcements for his right flank, responded with instructions for Carr to "persevere." Carr did. He was wounded several times himself, once badly, and lost over 700 men in the process of persevering. He kept sending pleas to Curtis for help. Curtis, harrassed, ordered the only reserves he had available to go to Carr's relief: Captain Benteen's C Company and the two remaining howitzers from A Company.

At noon, Major Bowen led the reinforcements into the fight, stationing them on the eastern slope of Pea Ridge at the extreme left of the line between two regiments of Van Dever's Brigade. Benteen sighted one gun; Bowen, the other. After firing all the ammunition they had, Bowen's troops fell back. Re-supplied, they took up a position about 300 yards south of Elkhorn Tavern on either side of the telegraph road and threw shrapnel into the packed ranks of advancing Confederates, enabling Carr to re-form his shattered brigades. It was not enough.

The Confederates, having a decided advantage in numbers, steadily pushed Carr's division back until they had gained control of Elkhorn Tavern and the crossroads there. Bowen was compelled to withdraw his howitzers when the Confederate artillery found the range and began shelling them. Out of a force that did not number a hundred to begin with, he lost six men. As he pulled back, reinforcements from another division were hurrying forward. Benteen later remembered that he had "withstood three separate and fierce charges from the whole of General McIntosh's Indian Brigade, and by holding the rebels in check sufficient time was given Brig. Genl. Eugene A. Carr to change his front and form his brigade(s) in the rear of Elk Horn Tavern, and save the day at that point, and had that point been lost, the battle had been lost!"

The fighting kept up until long after dark with no ground gained or lost. General Curtis, after a considerable delay, was able to move Sigel's other division up to reinforce Carr. The next morning, 8 March 1862, Curtis counterattacked all along his new front, gaining the heights of Pea Ridge. The Confederates held the crossroads stubbornly as Curtis massed his artillery. Then, they vanished.

Actually, the survivors had moved east from Elkhorn Tavern on the road to Huntsville. A small group retreated north toward the Missouri line. Curtis, mistaking the small group for the main body, sent his cavalry in pursuit. The only uncommited element of Bowen's Battalion, D Company under Captain Williams, pursued for about four miles, taking ten prisoners and a wagon. The rest of the Confederate army fled east and then south. In three days time, they had completed a circuit of the Union Army, fought (and lost) a desperate, bloody battle — the largest fought west of the Mississippi to that time.

On 9 March 1862, Bowen's Battalion was attached to Colonel Cyrus Bussey's 3rd Iowa Cavalry for a raid on Confederate stragglers near Bentonville, southwest of the battlefield. It was the first association of Bowen's men with the 3rd Iowa, but it was not to be the last. The 3rd Iowa was a well-led unit that won many honors through the course of the war. Its adjutant that day, John W. Noble, would become an important associate of Benteen's in the years to come.

The battle of Pea Ridge (especially Elkhorn Tavern) was a very costly battle for both sides. In retrospect, it saved Missouri for the Union because the Confederate high command in Richmond, concluding that the troops surviving could best be used elsewhere, removed them across the Mississippi. Arkansas was left open to a Union occupation.

Just as the Confederate high command had decided to transfer men, so did the Union leadership. General Curtis moved his command back into Missouri to be closer to his lines of supply and to reorganize for the occupation of Arkansas. He established his army headquarters just east of the present-day town of Forsyth, south of Springfield. There, on 18 April 1862, Captain Benteen ran afoul of his superiors.

Major Bowen, having been wounded at Sugar Creek and debilitated

by the strenuous campaigning, was granted a 30-day leave of absence
to recuperate, beginning 12 April. A week later, his temporary replacement, Captain Stanford Ing of B Company, preferred charges against
Benteen for: 1) "disrespectful behavior towards his commanding
officer" and 2) "conduct prejudicial to good order and military discipline." Both charges specified the same offense.

Here is what had happened: General Curtis' son, Henry Zarah
Curtis, the acting assistant adjutant of the Army of the Southwest,
issued a special order detailing a man named Weaver from Benteen's
company to report to headquarters as an orderly. Benteen snatched
the order from Captain Ing's hands and wrote on it: "*Corporal* Weaver
declines the polite invitation to leave his mess, and feels highly insulted at his rank being not attended to." He flipped the order over
and added: "Adjutant, Corporal Weaver cannot and shall not come,
nor do I recognize the right of any one to detail the men of my Co.
by name — they have taken of some of the best of them and if they
want them all, my resignation is at their service. The company is small
enough, without furnishing servants for Staff Captains, as one of
them is at present."

Benteen was a soft-spoken man. This fact has been remarked on
by all his acquaintances who left written records of their impressions.
He had developed a rather convoluted style of speech and behavior
that caused him to be described as "courtly." When angered, he re-
sorted to sarcasm rather than raising his voice. While he was quite
capable of forming friendships and seemed to enjoy belonging to
various groups, he remained at the core his own man. The feuds
within Bowen's Battalion (and subsequent units he served in) were
almost proverbial. Benteen remained aloof. He developed an unfortunate tendency to bottle up his aggravations and appear to be genial
on the outside while seething with rage on the inside. Occasionally
in his career, he was unable to hold back his contempt. When he
exploded, it was always spectacular.

It may well be that the angry response of Benteen's was verbal
in the beginning, but that Captain Ing insisted on the reply in writing. In any case, Benteen *wrote* the angry reply on an official order
from the Army Headquarters.

The charges drawn up and signed by Captain Ing were somewhat
heated and illogical, but perhaps typical for a field army without
much time or use for legal niceties in a time of war. There is no
record of a court-martial or *any* punishment, for that matter. From

the way the charges were written up, it seems unlikely that any punishment beyond a verbal reprimand was called for in any case.

The next day Bowen's Battalion was in the saddle and under way on a raid into Arkansas with the 3rd Illinois Cavalry. They raided a saltpeter manufactory near a crossing on the White River called Talbot's Ferry. Whether or not Benteen went along is debatable. He was not mentioned by name in the report, but neither were any of the others.

Whatever the outcome of Benteen's clash with Zarah Curtis (and Ing), he *was* present when the Army of the Southwest captured Batesville, Arkansas on 4 May 1862. Ten days later he commanded his company in the attack on Cotton Plant, Arkansas. On 29 May, he and the rest of Bowen's Battalion were involved in a little fight called Kickapoo Bottom (near Sylamore, Arkansas). There they killed 10 Rebels and captured another 25, without a single loss. Two weeks later, Benteen's nemesis, Captain Ing, resigned his commission.

None of these small skirmishes in Curtis' invasion of Arkansas were of major importance. The Confederate high command had written Arkansas off. The only opposition came from local bands, semi-guerrilla in nature and no match for the victors of Pea Ridge. Curtis' army was driving through Arkansas in a generally southeast direction, making full use of waterways, particularly the White and Black rivers. They were driving toward the Mississippi River in conjunction with Major General Ulysses S. Grant's drive into northern Mississippi on the other side of the river.

On 12 June 1862, part of Benteen's company under Lieutenant Ballou accompanied part of the 9th Illinois Cavalry on an escort that beat off an attack on the wagon train they were escorting and launched what the commanding officer of the 9th Illinois described as "the finest cavalry charge I ever witnessed." Bowen's contingent lost no one and the Confederates lost 28 in this little skirmish which took place at Waddell's Farm near Village Creek, Arkansas.

Four days after Lieutenant Ballou's fight at Waddell's Farm, the entire company was re-united for a two-day scout from Army Headquarters at Batesville to determine the character of the little organized opposition that existed between the White and Little Red rivers. The scout was commanded by the colonel of the 4th Missouri Cavalry, George E. Waring, Jr., a renowned sanitary engineer before and after the war. Besides four companies of his own 4th Missouri, Colonel Waring also had a portion of Bowen's Battalion (Benteen's company and two howitzers), two companies from two other cavalry units and four companies from the crack 4th Iowa Cavalry. (This was Benteen's first association with the 4th Iowa Cavalry, but it would not be his last. His Civil War career would be very closely bound to the fortunes of the 4th Iowa, the celebrated "Black Coat" Cavalry.)

Colonel Waring broke his large command into three separate columns, sending Benteen's contingent to a place called Hilcher's Ferry. The three columns returned after two days bearing "a good amount of negative information from every direction." They learned little, except for rumors placing Confederate forces south of the Little Red and small guerrilla bands of 10-12 men north of that river. "The scout was very hard on horses of the command," Colonel Waring concluded, "and I regret that its result was of so little positive value."

On 3 July 1862, Bowen was promoted to lieutenant colonel.

With northern Arkansas under Union control, General Curtis cast his eyes south. He conceived a brilliant idea: launching amphibious/commando raids deep into Confederate territory. He reasoned that "the navy and army, moved to any point on the Mississippi River, makes a new and unexpected base, from which the troops can dash into the country. . . carrying death and desolation." He asked for naval transportation for a force of 10,000 men, intending to make marines out of his Army of the Southwest by raiding up and down the Mississippi from steamboat transports. The Navy could only provide enough transportation for a single brigade and Curtis had to content himself with a limited, but spectacular, expedition known to history as the Woods' River Expedition. Benteen's C Company was one of the two cavalry companies chosen to accompany the expedition. The command's first exploit was the *Fair Play* incident.

4

The *Fair Play* Incident

On 31 July 1862, the Confederate commanding general at Vicksburg, Mississippi, ordered a professional river pilot named Plummer to seize a luxury steamboat called the *Fair Play* for use in transporting quartermaster stores from Mississippi to the fragmentary forces in Louisiana and southern Arkansas. Plummer found the *Fair Play* berthed in the Sunflower River and brought her to Vicksburg. A man named J.M. White was appointed captain of the boat and she steamed up and down the river between Greenville and Vicksburg, carrying Confederate war supplies. Her chief engineer, apparently, was Theodore C. "Charley" Benteen.

On 16 August 1862 an Army/Navy task force departed Helena, Arkansas, intending to raid and reconnoiter down the Mississippi River as far as Vicksburg. General Ulysses S. Grant, with his much larger Army of the Tennessee in northern Mississippi, was attempting an approach to Vicksburg from the north. General Curtis was unable to actually capture Vicksburg, but launched the flotilla to provide intelligence for an inevitable advance on that vital river port from another direction.

The flotilla was organized as follows:

Colonel Charles R. Woods
(76th Ohio Infantry), commanding

2 TRANSPORTS: *McDowell* & *Rocket*
with selected troops from the 58th & 76th Ohio Infantry regiments, the 4th Ohio Battery, and two companies (C & D) from Bowen's Battalion, Missouri Cavalry.

4 ARMORED RAMS: *Switzerland* & *Monarch* & *Sampson* & *Lioness*
with special Army troops commanded by Lieu-
tenant Colonel Alfred W. Ellet (which later
formed the nucleus of the famed Mississippi
Marine Brigade).

3 GUN BOATS: *Benton* & *Mound City* & *General Bragg*
with selected Navy personnel under Lieutenant
Commander S. Ledyard Phelps.

A *ram* was essentially an iron- and oak-reinforced steamboat brimming with artillery pieces and was the invention of one Charles Ellet,
brother of Lieutenant Colonel Alfred W. Ellet. Charles Ellet had been
killed at Memphis four months before, but his ideas and inventions
were carried on by his son and younger brother. A ram could provide
fire support for shore parties, engage enemy gun boats and transports
by gunfire, or as its name implies, *ram* them amidships and cause
them to sink.

Bowen's Battalion contributed about 100 cavalrymen from two companies and two of their own howitzers. Lieutenant Colonel Bowen
was present in command of the cavalry. Colonel Charles R. Woods,
the same man who had been turned back from Fort Sumter in the
ill-fated *Star Of The West* a year and a half before, was the overall
commander of the expedition. Captain Frederick W. Benteen commanded about 40 men from his own C Company.

In the evening of 17 August 1862, Confederate quartermaster personnel in Vicksburg loaded the *Fair Play* with muskets, ammunition,
and other military stores and dispatched Captain White to Milliken's
Bend, Louisiana to unload them. The boat proceeded on its way and
came to anchor in the Bend about 11:00 that night. Captain White
went ashore to visit his own house. (He lived in Milliken's Bend.)
The rest of the crew went to sleep on board, with the sole exception
of the first mate, William Waggener, who took it upon himself to
stand watch.

Colonel Woods' River Expedition made good progress. They stopped
once about 40 miles below Helena and, after gathering some local
intelligence, moved on. They stopped a second time near Laconia,
Arkansas, where local resistance melted when the escorting gunboats
hove into view. They continued steadily down the river.

About midnight, Captain White returned to the *Fair Play* for some
ice, saying that someone in his house was ill. He wanted to know
what Waggener was doing up and, when the First Mate told him

that there were no other watchmen, White agreed that it was a good idea to keep someone on watch. He told Waggener to keep "some wood in the furnace" and expressed a lack of concern for the safety of the big steamer, saying that there were pickets and couriers all up and down the river and that any approach by Union gun boats would be announced in plenty of time. (The pilot, Plummer, later complained that he had warned White about the folly of running guns after dark, but that the captain had expressed no concern.) A short while later, Waggener was visited by the Confederate government agent responsible for the arms and stores: a man named Kennard. Waggener asked Kennard if the supplies were to be unloaded. Kennard replied that he would have 300 men on board in a few minutes and that he was returning to shore to get wagons to transfer the supplies to the railroad at Richmond, Louisiana, nine miles away. The Confederate 31st Louisiana Infantry regiment was billeted on shore about 300 yards from the boat and Waggener assumed that Kennard was going to organize them in getting the supplies ashore. But, Kennard never returned and the Confederate soldiers (and the *Fair Play's* crew except for Waggener) slept on.

About 1:00 in the morning of 18 August 1862, the Union flotilla came steaming around Milliken's Bend, seeking whom they might devour. Waggener, on board the *Fair Play*, saw their lights and roused the crew. The flotilla was coming directly toward the tempting prize, slowly. To the great disgust of Waggener, Pilot Plummer, and many of the others on board, the engineers reported that there was not enough steam up to run away. Plummer overheard someone ask the elder Benteen, "Charley, how much steam have you got?" Benteen's disgusted reply was: "There is not enough to turn the wheel over." Plummer and most of the others, including a few passengers aboard, abandoned ship to avoid capture. Charley Benteen and the engineers made a frantic effort to fire up.

Actually, eight of the nine boats in the Union flotilla missed the *Fair Play*. They were preoccupied with the bonfires of the Confederate army encampment. But, the gun boat *Benton* spotted the steamer dead in the water and, within minutes, Lieutenant Commander Phelps' tars swarmed aboard, capturing Charley Benteen and some of the others at pistol and cutlass point. On shore, the Rebel soldiers fled without bothering to take down their tents.

It took Phelps better than two hours to complete an inventory of the *Fair Play* and relay word of his fantastic success to the other boats. But, by 4:00 in the morning, the entire flotilla was anchored off Milliken's Bend, marvelling at the unexpected capture and trooping ashore. Colonel Woods took command. His infantry prowled through the abandoned Rebel camp and the cavalry readied their horses for an inland pursuit.

Lieutenant Colonel Bowen got anxious when he received no orders. His cavalrymen milled around uncertainly as Woods' infantry plundered the camp. Finally, after waiting 20 minutes for orders that never came, Bowen dispatched a 10-man column down each of two roads discovered. Lieutenant Daniel W. Ballou of C Company (Benteen's) took the road to Vicksburg. Lieutenant John D. Crabtree of D Company took the road to Richmond.

Less than an hour later, Lieutenant Crabtree sent back an urgent call for reinforcements. He had discovered a large body of retreating Confederates who were too much for his little 10 man patrol. Bowen got permission to lead out with the balance of his cavalry (approximately 80 men that included Captain Benteen). Colonel Woods told Bowen to go ahead and raid the town of Richmond, that the infantry supports would be up as fast as they could come. Bowen's force linked with Lieutenant Crabtree just as the enemy began to withdraw. "Pursuing them rapidly," Bowen reported, "we took quite a number of prisoners, shotguns, rifles, &c., scattering their forces in every direction." Lieutenant Colonel Ellet, left back at Milliken's Bend with his rams, said that the total number of prisoners taken on the boat and by Bowen's cavalry was "about 40."

Bowen's party pushed on. Within a mile of Richmond, they discovered a large group of Confederates concealed in a corn field to their right. Bowen concluded that the Rebels were trying to ambush him and trotted forward his two howitzers. He threw "a few shell, and the enemy moved off rapidly in the direction of the town." When Bowen arrived at the railroad depot at Richmond, he found the retreating Confederates had again rallied. He halted his advance, trotted forward his howitzers again, and opened fire. The Confederates fled.

Bowen "then proceeded to destroy the depot, which contained a large amount of sugar and other stores for the use of the army." He "also destroyed the telegraph and several cars remaining on the railroad." Colonel Woods brought his infantry up on the run, but they were too late to see any action. The Confederates had fled towards Tallulah. After a short rest, the entire raiding party marched back slowly under a burning sun to the boats nine miles away.

Frederick W. Benteen in 1863

Florence M. Cornyn

Edward Hatch

Navy Lieutenant Commander Phelps had completed his inventory of the *Fair Play*. The captured cargo included "about 1200 new Enfield rifles and 4000 new muskets, with accouterments complete, a large quantity of fixed ammunition for field guns, mountain how-itzers and small arms." A year later, the Confederate government settled with the owners of the *Fair Play*, Joshua Wiley and Malcolm Cameron, to the tune of $25,000. The damages awarded were for the loss of the steamboat through negligence while it was in the service of the Confederacy. The *Fair Play* was indeed an expensive boat and remained a Federal prize for the rest of the war.

The non-military prisoners were eventually released at Helena — with the exception of Theodore Charles Benteen. He remained a prisoner for the duration of the war. About 1875, while his son was in Dakota Territory, he was informed by his young grandson that "papa" was responsible for his capture. The elder Benteen had not been aware that his son was present at his capture, apparently, and was totally ignorant of (and baffled by) the circumstances surrounding his incarceration. He spent a sleepless night pondering the information inadvertently blabbed by his grandson (then seven years old) and wrote to Captain Benteen explaining that the family secret had been spilled. "Some little boys talk too damn much," he concluded gruffly. Frederick Benteen's reply was unrecorded.

The family secret regarding the incarceration of the elder Benteen remains a secret to this day. But, from the circumstances surrounding the incident, the conclusion is obvious: Fred Benteen interceded with someone in authority at Helena and had his father put away for the duration of the war. He commanded a company that provided an escort to General Curtis' staff and was certainly familiar with men who were empowered to confine his father to prison. There is no shortage of candidates for the "connection." The Judge Advocate General for the Army of the Southwest at that time was Captain John W. Noble of the 3rd Iowa Cavalry. The Provost Marshal of the District of Eastern Arkansas at that time was Captain Edward F. Winslow of the 4th Iowa Cavalry. Both men were close friends and associates of Frederick William Benteen throughout the war and for years afterward.

5

The 9th Missouri Cavalry

The Woods' River Expedition left Milliken's Bend on the evening of 18 August 1862 and headed for the mouth of the Yazoo River above Vicksburg. Infantry troops were sent ashore at Haines' Bluff and a Confederate battery was destroyed there. Further up the Yazoo went the rams, almost to Lake George, but "nothing more of any importance was learned." The flotilla steamed back down the Yazoo, then up the Mississippi, landing briefly at Wilton, Louisiana to cut a telegraph line before moving on to Greenville, Mississippi.

At Greenville on 23 August, Captain Benteen went ashore for the first time since Milliken's Bend. Lieutenant Colonel Bowen marched his cavalry about a mile east of the river until he came to a fork in the road. Confident that there were Rebels nearby, he placed his howitzers and the bulk of his troops at the crossroads and sent two detachments, one led by Lieutenant Crabtree, the other by Captain Benteen, down each of the two roads to reconnoiter. Twenty minutes later, Colonel Woods sent orders to fall back on the boats. Bowen rallied his two reconnaisance parties and rejoined the infantry closer to the river. The Confederates were drawn up before them. Woods ordered Bowen to advance.

Bowen chased the Confederates for about two miles and, just as he was deploying to reverse an ambush, the gun boat *Benton* opened fire on the concealed ambush party, coming dangerously close to Bowen's advancing troops in the process. The pursuit along the river ended abruptly and the cavalrymen returned to the boats.

Two days later, Lieutenant Colonel Bowen got a chance to exorcise his frustrations from the Greenville fiasco. The flotilla pulled in near

Bolivar, Mississippi. They were acting on information received that the Confederates had crossed the Mississippi there in great numbers a week before. They were looking specifically for rumored flatboats and supply wagons. Colonel Woods' infantry had little difficulty getting ashore, but Bowen's cavalry were unable to get their horses off the boats because the banks were too steep. Bowen, on his own iniative, ordered the boat captain to advance about a half mile up the river where the banks were low enough to land the horses. The cavalrymen had no sooner gotten their horses ashore when they were attacked from two directions. Bowen ordered Benteen to block the river road and the Confederates bearing down on them from the north. Lieutenant Crabtree from D Company drew the assignment of trying to hold the enemy advancing from the east directly against the river bank. Both Benteen and Crabtree were able to hold off the advancing enemy by deploying their own men on foot. They held long enough for Bowen to get the howitzers off the boats and into position. Bowen fired up the last of his ammunition and was immediately supported by the 4th Ohio Battery and the gun boats on the river. The Confederates withdrew and Bowen pursued about two miles inland before it dawned on him that the force he was chasing with his 100 cavalrymen numbered over 3000. He lost three men to fire from an ambush and considered himself lucky to have gotten off so easily. After being joined by the infantry regiments of Colonel Woods, he advanced (thus supported) another half mile and then retired to the boats. Lieutenant Commander Phelps reported that some of the Confederates had been driven from *rifle pits*. Lieutenant Colonel Ellet credited the fire of the gun boats for the victory, and while they certainly contributed enormously, it was the intrepidity of Bowen's Battalion that made the difference.

The weary, but victorious, commandos arrived back at Helena on 31 August, boats laden with prisoners from Milliken's Bend and Bolivar and guns taken from the top of Haines' Bluff. General Curtis was very pleased, regretting only the inability to win a more complete victory at Bolivar. He attributed the lack of complete success there to an insufficiency of numbers. "I ought to have transportation for 10,000 men," he complained to General Halleck.

As soon as the flotilla landed at Helena, Captain Benteen availed himself of a leave of absence to go to St. Louis. Before he could return, Bowen's Battalion had been transferred to Benton Barracks in north St. Louis for reorganization. They were no longer Bowen's Battalion.

General Grant's assault in northern Mississippi had stalled. In the east, the Army of the Potomac had fought the bloodiest one-day battle in American history at Antietam Creek. All over the North there was a desperate need for more troops. General Halleck, now ensconced in Washington as Commander-in-Chief, decided to reorganize the Army. One of his targets was the small *ad hoc* cavalry units such as Bowen's Battalion that existed all over the Union Army. In Missouri, Bowen's had such sister organizations as: the Benton Hussars, Merrill's Light Horse, the Fremont Hussars, the Hollan Horse, and Wood's Battalion, not to mention the small infantry units of less than regimental strength that proliferated.

Lieutenant Colonel Bowen was ordered to take officers and enlisted men from other fragmentary units and to form them into an eight-company cavalry regiment to be known as the 9th Missouri Cavalry Regiment. Accordingly, the four companies of Bowen's Battalion became A-D of the new 9th. Four additional companies, E-H, were created from the new troops.

Some of the new men were to have a profound effect on Benteen's career. The most important association begun at this point was with William J. DeGress, who became a second lieutenant in the new E Company. DeGress, a German-born man Benteen's own age, had served as an enlisted man in the Regular Army Mounted Rifles for five years. Discharged in New Mexico Territory just as the war was beginning, he remained there as a volunteer aide-de-camp to the departmental commander. DeGress was badly wounded at the battle of Valverde in January of 1862, but his valor there (and his experience as a Regular Army enlisted man) qualified him for a commission in the volunteers. Benteen and DeGress became fast friends.

DeGress's commanding officer was Captain Robert B.M. McGlasson, a former lieutenant in an infantry unit. McGlasson was a tough, competent officer who hailed from Nokomis, Illinois, and was to become a valued asset to the new unit, noteworthy for his reputation for battlefield courage and leadership. F Company had as its first lieutenant a young medical doctor named Elisha M. Jennings from Punjaub, Missouri. Jennings left behind a series of letters to his girlfriend that provide the best insight into the unit Benteen eventually commanded. A regimental history was never written, and Jennings' letters provide the only clues to this murky period in Benteen's career.

Not only were new faces added to the organization; some old faces disappeared. Tragically, Benteen's brilliant young second lieutenant,

Eddy Emerson, who had so impressed Captain Sheridan, died after a brief illness on 19 October 1862 at Benton Barracks. The week before, Lieutenant Edward Madison, the artillery specialist from A Company, resigned. The second lieutenant in the artillery company seemed especially jinxed. Lieutnant Bushnell, the original officer in this position, drowned in August of 1862. His replacement, Lieutenant Robinson, resigned in November. But, the new unit kept busy working the "bugs" out of the new organization.

Benton Barracks, being right in St. Louis, was a handy location for Fred Benteen. His new wife lived less than three miles away and even with the inevitable hard work involved in shaking down the new command, Benteen was able to slip away to see Kate.

6

The 10th Missouri Cavalry

Ten miles to the south of Benton Barracks was a larger, more modern cavalry post: Jefferson Barracks. There, a new unit called the 28th Missouri Volunteers was in the process of becoming the 10th Missouri Cavalry. They were engaged in activities identical to Bowen's 9th Missouri Cavalry.

The commanding officer of the new 10th Missouri was 33-year-old Colonel Florence M. Cornyn, the same man who as a surgeon had fought at Wilson's Creek. He had most recently been a surgeon in the 1st Missouri Light Artillery and, as such, had distinguished himself at the battle of Shiloh in April 1862. Cornyn, an Ohio-born medical doctor from St. Louis, evidently found inflicting wounds more to his tastes than sewing them up. "A redheaded Irishman, absolutely fearless," commented a contemporary. At both Wilson's Creek and Shiloh, he had been highly commended for valor on the battlefield. At Wilson's Creek, he had seized up a musket; at Shiloh, he had placed an artillery battery and directed its fire. His sponsor, Frank Blair, thought that Cornyn could be put to better use in the Union cause than as a surgeon. Cornyn received permission to recruit an infantry regiment: the 28th Missouri Volunteers. Once he had gathered enough men to form a regiment, he received permission to transform it into a six-company cavalry regiment. His lieutenant colonel was Thomas Hynes, the same Hynes who had fought so well as a lieutenant at Wilson's Creek.

In December of 1862, Bowen's 9th and Cornyn's 10th were amalgamated into a single regiment: the 10th Missouri Cavalry. There is only fragmentary documentation in existence detailing the political maneuverings involved in the amalgamation of the two regiments, unfortunately. But what does exist is very interesting.

On 26 November 1862, Lieutenant Colonel Bowen wrote a rather emotional letter to General Curtis objecting to prospects of service with (or under) one Lieutenant John T. Price, the most recent U.S. Mustering Officer for the state of Missouri. Lieutenant Price was apparently offered command of the *9th* Missouri with the rank of full colonel.

"If he had acted towards me as a gentleman or a soldier," Bowen told General Curtis, "I would have stood by him to the last; but it has been and is now his object to sacrifice me to gratify his own ambition." Bowen went on to specify Price's offenses: "bringing those false charges against me" and "threatening me in your presence." He concluded by entreating Curtis "to prevent my being associated in a regiment with my bitter enemy," threatening to resign if Curtis could not find it in his power to prevent the association.

Bowen had a considerable amount of influence with General Curtis, having commanded the general's bodyguard for almost a year. Lieutenant Price was duly assigned to the *1st* Missouri Cavalry as a lieutenant colonel. The same day that Bowen was spared the agony of having to associate with his bitter enemy, General Curtis ordered the 9th and 10th Missouri Cavalry regiments to be consolidated. In Special Orders 218, dated 4 December 1862, the Adjutant General of the state of Missouri further directed Bowen to consolidate *six* of his companies with the six companies of Cornyn's new regiment. Colonel Cornyn, being Bowen's superior in rank, was designated the new commanding officer. A week later, the Adjutant General promulgated Special Orders 224 which specified which two of Bowen's eight companies were to be divested: Companies G & H. They were sent to Rolla to become Companies L & M of the 3rd Missouri Cavalry.

The amalgamation produced a flurry of resignations in the 9th Missouri, including the adjutant and *all* of the officers of the artillery company (A). Significantly, all of the resignees ended up in the 11th Missouri Cavalry with higher ranks six months later, suggesting that personalities may not necessarily have been involved.

Cavalry regiments, beginning in July 1862 (and for many years thereafter) were authorized 12 companies of three officers and 60-100 enlisted men each. Regiments of cavalry were commanded by a colonel, assisted by a lieutenant colonel and three majors. Florence M. Cornyn was the full colonel of the 10th Missouri Cavalry. There was never any question of that. The Special Orders 218 that directed the consolidation reduced Cornyn's lieutenant colonel, Thomas Hynes, to major. William D. Bowen was designated the new lieutenant colonel of the 10th Missouri Cavalry. As a sop, Major Hynes was made the senior major. Frederick W. Benteen was promoted from command of C Company to second major of the regiment. The third majority went to William H. Lusk, one of Cornyn's men. Benteen's captaincy in C Company was taken by his friend William J. DeGress two days later.

The flurry of resignations from A Company created more openings and, within a week, Captain DeGress was assigned to A Company. He decided, however, that his wounds were bothering him too much to accept and resigned his commission. He left to open a store in Newport, Kentucky. A week later, DeGress's vacancy in C Company was filled by making Lieutenant Daniel W. Ballou a captain and the position DeGress refused in A Company was given to Captain Duncan McNichol.

Lieutenant Elisha M. Jennings' off-hand remarks to his girl friend suggested that there was some tension in the new regiment between Bowen's men and Cornyn's men. The amalgamation was a shotgun marriage from the start and, apparently, William D. Bowen had used up his favors with General Curtis in getting away from John T. Price. Benteen wrote later that Colonel Cornyn moved the regiment to Memphis, Tennessee "by permission of General Grant." Politics were unquestionably involved. General Frank Blair was in Memphis and Cornyn seemed anxious to get away from Missouri and join the more active campaign east of the Mississippi. The new, 1200 man regiment "left for the South by detachments as fast as transportation could be furnished them." General Curtis tried to intercept the detachment commanded by Lieutenant Colonel Bowen at Columbus, Kentucky, on 12 January 1863, but Bowen ignored the order and pushed on to Memphis.

The entire 10th Missouri Cavalry moved from Memphis to Grant's forward post at Corinth, Mississippi, on 7 February. It took them eight days to make the 90-odd miles that separted the two towns, "the weather being very severe, roads bad, and the country destitute of forage."

By hook or crook, the regiment was no longer part of the Army of the Southwest. It was assigned to Major General Ulysses S. Grant's massive Army of the Tennessee, which was being reorganized for a renewed attack on Vicksburg. Specifically, the 10th Missouri Cavalry belonged to the District of Corinth (which became the Union XVI Corps) under the command of Major General Stephen A. Hurlbut. It was assigned in Corinth to the 2nd Division that was commanded by Brigadier General Grenville M. Dodge, the same Dodge who as a colonel had commanded a brigade that Bowen and Benteen had supported at Pea Ridge. General Dodge, later to become famous as the chief engineer on the Union Pacific Railroad construction project after the war, was no stranger to Benteen. Dodge had also commanded at Rolla in the fall of 1861 alternately with Colonel Wyman of the 13th Illinois.

Shortly after the regiment arrived at Corinth, General Dodge made Colonel Cornyn his chief of cavalry. Cornyn was thus elevated to the command of a *brigade* that included his own 10th Missouri Cavalry, the 7th Kansas Cavalry (Jennison's Jayhawkers), the 15th Illinois Cavalry, the 9th Illinois Mounted Infantry, and a fledgling organization of two companies known as the 1st Alabama Cavalry. Lieutenant Colonel Bowen became the acting commander of the 10th Missouri.

The new regiment got its first taste of action within three days of its arrival in Mississippi. Colonel Cornyn led the entire brigade out of Corinth on 18 February for a raid on Tuscumbia, Alabama. The raid was intended to harrass Confederate Major General Earl van Dorn's rear guard there and develop intelligence about the surrounding countryside.

The first day out, an incident occurred that was to affect Benteen's career dramatically, though he was not personally involved. Major Hynes and Lieutenant Colonel Bowen got in a fight, resulting in Hynes' arrest "on trivial charges." Hynes was sent back to Corinth.

Here is what happened: Colonel Cornyn had assigned Major Hynes one wing of the 10th Missouri. The first night out, Hynes left his wing and crossed a creek to camp with other officers more to his liking. He did not report his absence to Lieutenant Colonel Bowen, who became aware of the dereliction the next day when A Company encountered difficulty crossing the same creek. Bowen, noticing the difficulty, asked Hynes how he intended to cross the howitzers. Hynes churlishly replied: "I do not know sir. I do not command it." Bowen snapped back: "You certainly have command of the four squadrons in the left of the column." "I know my place in column, sir," Hynes replied angrily, "I shall not take orders given to me in such manner."

William D. Bowen was unquestionably a tactless, hot-headed young officer. Hynes was still steaming about his reduction in rank and being forced to serve under an officer with less experience in military matters. Inevitably, the little heated exchange grew into court-martial charges. Bowen accused Hynes of "disrespectful conduct towards his superior officer," "disobedience of orders," and "neglect of duty." Colonel Cornyn, having specifically assigned Hynes the responsibility for the howitzers in question, had no choice but to back Bowen, arrest Hynes, and prefer the charges.

Curiously, Hynes was later acquitted of all but "neglect of duty," but by the time his court-martial rolled around, Bowen had tacked on an additional charge of an unrelated nature stemming from another incident in their running feud. Hynes *never* returned to duty as senior major and the effective second-in-command of the 10th Missouri was Major Benteen from that day forward.

In addition to fighting amongst themselves, the 10th Missouri also found time to fight with van Dorn's Confederates. Cornyn's brigade stormed into Tuscumbia on 22 February and drove the enemy about six miles, capturing "several prisoners, one piece of artillery, a large number of small arms, and over one hundred thousand dollars worth of rebel property."

"Colonel Cornyn succeeded in bringing all his captured property safe into Corinth, although the brigade had to move with heavy trains over mountains and through swamps." The raid proved an unqualified success and also offered a chance to shake down the new command. It brought Colonel Cornyn and his officers to the favorable attention of such senior officers as General Hurlbut, who commended them "for their gallant performance of severe duty."

In the middle of April, General Grant was stuck on the west bank of the Mississippi opposite Vicksburg very near where Woods' River Expedition had captured the *Fair Play*. He was determined to cross the river, but wanted to bluff as many Confederate troops as possible out of his way before moving. He was counting on Hurlbut's XVI Corps to draw away as many Confederates as they could with a series of interrelated cavalry raids. The first of these raids, though planned and led by another department, was called Streight's Raid. It was an attempt on the part of one Colonel Abel D. Streight with four regiments of mule-mounted infantry to draw off the Confederate cavalry leader, Nathan Bedford Forrest. The raid's route was across northern Alabama; its objective, deep into Georgia. Hurlbut's troops, covering the corner of Alabama, Tennessee, and Mississippi, were to draw off as many pursuers as possible with another raid (less ambitious) that has gone down in history as Dodge's Expedition to Courtland. Simultaneously, General Hurlbut sent three regiments straight down the length of Mississippi, a spectacularly successful cavalry raid known to history as Grierson's Raid.

Colonel Cornyn was given the unenviable task of providing a smoke screen for two other raids, both of which would be remembered far longer than his efforts. On 14 April 1863, Cornyn's cavalry brigade was ordered out of Corinth. For two days they marched, preceding the balance of General Dodge's 2nd Division. On the morning of 17 April, Dodge ordered Cornyn to charge across Steminine's Ford and pursue the enemy on the other side. Cornyn did so with such alacrity that a serious problem arose that had an unfortunate effect on his brigade.

Dodge had ordered Cornyn to pursue only 3½ miles, but Cornyn got carried away and advanced so rapidly that some of his artillery pieces fell behind by three miles. The Confederates, under Brigadier General Philip D. Roddey, took advantage of the strung-out column and swept around to attack the trailing artillery pieces. Cornyn heard the gunfire in his rear and turned back. He ordered one James Cameron, a captain commanding the incomplete 1st Alabama Cavalry, to turn about and lead a charge against the Rebels attacking the rear. Cameron replied that his men had fired their muskets and, having no sabers or revolvers, had nothing to attack with.

"So Cornyn told him he was a damn coward," reported Lieutenant Jennings. Stung, Captain Cameron ordered a charge. His unarmed men drove off a Confederate force that had temporarily captured two artillery pieces. Cameron and his men suddenly stopped and, in doing so, allowed the retreating Confederates a chance to turn about and pour a withering fire into Cameron's ranks. Cameron and two of his men were mortally wounded. As Cameron lay dying on the field, he said: "I wonder if Colonel Cornyn thinks I am a damned coward now."

The reaction was not sympathetic to Colonel Cornyn. General Dodge felt that Cornyn had brought on near disaster by running too far ahead of his artillery and being too slow to come to their relief. Cornyn blamed Cameron for a hesitant charge. But, Cameron's dying declaration branded Cornyn a dictatorial tyrant in the eyes of many. "That has ruined Colonel Cornyn here," Lieutenant Jennings told his girl friend.

Cornyn, oblivious to the undercurrents, paraded his entire brigade in front of the enemy as a bluff. Roddey's Confederates, heavily reinforced by then and outnumbering Cornyn three to one, were not fooled. They launched a screaming attack on horseback and Cornyn was compelled to retreat behind Dodge's infantry. The infantrymen were able to repulse Roddey.

The following day Cornyn was again ordered to advance with his cavalry brigade. This time, he stayed within the limits of his brief and returned to General Dodge without seeing any action. Dodge took the balance of the 1st Alabama Cavalry away from Cornyn and gave it to another brigade.

The next day, Sunday 19 April 1863, Colonel Cornyn again moved out in a generally easterly direction. He dispatched Captain Patrick Naughton of H Company down a small byroad with orders to scout it thoroughly.

"If you get surprised," Cornyn told Naughton, "I will be very much surprised at you."

Captain Naughton was not surprised. In fact, his little detour led him right into the camp of General Roddey where 1200-1500 Confederate cavalry awaited. Naughton hesitated, then drove forward. The Confederates, well aware that Cornyn's brigade was looking for them with blood in their eyes, concluded that Naughton was the advance of Cornyn's brigade and fled.

Colonel Cornyn, in the meantime, had skirmished with a small holding force at a certain Widow Barton's Plantation near Dickson Station, Alabama. They were unable to entice the Rebels to attack them, so returned to their camp on Bear Creek.

They remained in camp four days. Friday, 24 April, General Dodge once again put his division in motion toward Tuscumbia, Alabama. Colonel Cornyn's cavalry was to the right (south) flank of the advancing column and, "owing to the difficult nature of the road and the greater distance travelled. . . did not reach Tuscumbia until after the infantry and the main body." General Dodge told Cornyn to take his weary cavalrymen on through the town and push on to the east in the direction of Leighton, Alabama. Cornyn followed the embankment of the Memphis and Charleston Railroad, destroying the track as he went along. He encountered Confederate skirmishers right away and pursued them about four miles east. There, Cornyn found the main enemy force and, characteristically, engaged it. The Rebels retreated about a mile, taking up new positions in some woods on either side of the railroad tracks. Lieutenant Colonel Thomas P. Herrick of the 7th Kansas Cavalry commanded the Union cavalry troops on the left side of the railroad embankment and tracks. Lieutenant Colonel Bowen commanded the troops on the right side. The center was commanded by Colonel Cornyn and kept in reserve as "chargers." Major Benteen, it seems almost certain from the context of the reports, was in the center, or reserve, section.

Colonel Cornyn sent Lieutenant Colonel Herrick forward to develop the positions for his chargers, but the enemy fled. Cornyn kept up pursuit. A mile further east, the Confederates made another stand. Cornyn kept his reserves back and sent his right and left flank forward to feel out the positions. Once again, the Rebels withdrew before Cornyn's reserve had been committed. They pulled back to an abandoned slave quarters and commenced firing with artillery pieces. Cornyn brought his own howitzers forward and engaged in an artillery duel that lasted about twenty minutes.

The Confederates fell back yet again. Cornyn kept pushing closer. The next stand he came to, he had to use the 10th Missouri Cavalry in a pistol charge along with his howitzers. The enemy abandoned the little town of Leighton and Cornyn pushed right on through. Here he learned that the force he was up against was from four different Confederate commands, including Brigadier General Nathan Bedford Forrest's, numbering perhaps 3500 men. (Cornyn had less than 900.)

Nonetheless, he kept up pursuit until he came to a large plain about four miles east of Leighton. Here the enemy's "line of battle seemed to extend from horizon to horizon." With night coming on, Cornyn boldly went into camp in plain view of the watching Confederates and sent back a messenger to General Dodge requesting reinforcements, especially artillery. He placed pickets and ordered the rest of his men to sleep under arms. Incredibly, he was not attacked during the night.

At daybreak 25 April, Cornyn received orders to return post haste to Tuscumbia. He did, arriving before noon. Cornyn was very quick to obey orders to fall back after the fiasco beyond Steminine's Ford the week before. He had displayed an audacity in the advance to Leighton and beyond that was almost incredible, but had become sensitized (understandably) to orders for limits of advance and recall.

The next day he took the 10th Missouri and part of the 7th Kansas north from Tuscumbia to raid a little town called Bainbridge. General

Dodge wanted the means of crossing the Tennessee River there destroyed. Cornyn found nothing worth destroying and returned to Tuscumbia before dark.

On 27 April 1863, General Dodge's entire expeditionary force moved to Town Creek, Alabama. The cavalry was discomfitted when their camp there was shelled, but did little active fighting. Two days later, they scouted to the east and south and, gathering forage, commenced the march back to Corinth.

General Dodge's expedition to Courtland was a success. His primary task had been to draw troops away from Colonel Streight and this he had done admirably. Unfortunately, Colonel Streight and his entire command was captured under humiliating circumstances by General Forrest three days later at Lawrence, Alabama, near the Georgia state line. Dodge's next mission came to him while still on the march back to Corinth. The other raid that had been designed to draw Confederates away from the Mississippi River, Grierson's Raid through central Mississippi, was encountering much greater success than expected. Colonel Edward Hatch, Grierson's principal subordinate, had doubled back and eluded his pursuers. He reached safety on 26 April, the same day Cornyn was looking for boats to to burn in Bainbridge, but the telegraph lines were down and the mounted messengers took some time getting through to General Dodge.

On 1 May 1863, four days after Colonel Hatch was safely back at LaGrange, Tennessee, Colonel Cornyn was ordered to draw ten days rations and lead a raid toward Tupelo, Mississippi to link with Hatch. Cornyn got the assignment at Burnsville, a little whistlestop on the railroad between Corinth and the Alabama state line. He immediately led out with his brigade toward Tupelo, about 50 miles south.

Cornyn's men arrived at Tupelo on 5 May. They saw no sign of Hatch, of course, but encountered more than 2000 Rebels, stirred up by Grierson's Raid. In approaching the east side of the town from the north, they found they had to march through a "dense and almost impassable swamp" called the Dismal Swamps. At its western edge, Cornyn's brigade came to a bridge. Major Benteen was ordered to dismount several companies of the 10th Missouri and secure the bridge. The "gallant Major Benteen" did just that and kept his dismounted skirmishers in front of the rest all the way around the eastern edge of Tupelo. Then, in a field south of Tupelo, Benteen discovered a large force estimated at 600 drawn up before him. Cornyn dismounted the 7th Kansas (who were armed with Colt's revolving rifles) and ordered them to charge on foot. Benteen's skirmishers mounted and, joined by the rest of the 10th Missouri (all under the leadership of Lieutenant Colonel Bowen), galloped at the ranks of Confederates as the rapid fire from the 7th Kansas broke them up. The 10th Missouri charged, "driving them in all directions."

An hour and a half later, as Cornyn was withdrawing along the west edge of Tupelo, a large force of Confederates advanced "with yells." Cornyn placed his howitzers on the brow of a hill and began to pour canister, then grapeshot, into the ranks of the advancing Confederates, who fled. The Union cavalry pursued.

Cornyn's brigade remained in Tupelo until 11:00 that night. They had lost one killed, five wounded and three missing. They also had 81 prisoners, three of them officers, 150 weapons, over 600 horses, and what Cornyn described as "immense quantities" of coats and blankets. There was a brief conference of all the field grade officers (majors and above) in which the question of finding Hatch was discussed. Cornyn decided to move back toward Corinth.

Two days later a messenger reached them near Booneville and instructed them to come on in to Corinth as the lost (Colonel Hatch's) command had been found. Cornyn's weary brigade reached Camp Sweeney near Corinth on 8 May 1863. The 10th Missouri was especially singled out for praise and Major Benteen was cited for his "gallant assistance" throughout the campaign. From that day on, the 10th Missouri was known throughout northern Mississippi and Alabama as the "Fighting Tenth."

The 10th Missouri Cavalry and its sister regiments in Colonel Cornyn's cavalry brigade got to stay at Camp Sweeney for almost three weeks. Their tents were gradually being replaced with semi-permanent log cabins. Their stables were gradually being enclosed. Walkways were being constructed to keep the men from having to wade through northern Mississippi mud. The troops relaxed and enjoyed mail from Missouri that had finally caught up with them.

Mail was important to Civil War soldiers as in all wars. It was especially important to men from Missouri in the spring of 1863; for, while the state had been saved for the Union by General Curtis' victory at Pea Ridge over a year before, the countryside was full of guerrillas of the breed that produced William Quantrill, Jesse James, and Bloody Bill Anderson. Lieutenant Jennings was especially concerned about a rumored guerrilla attack near his girl friend's home.

The knowledge that they were fighting in a part of the country foreign to them while their own kin in Missouri were not safe made them a little harder than the average Union soldier. The Fighting Tenth had quite a reputation for wreaking havoc and before the month of May was out, got a chance to prove that they had earned it.

Their numbers had diminished since leaving St. Louis with 1200 men. They were unable to put more than 500 men in the saddle by late May. They had largely solved the problem of lack of horses with their spectacular fight at Tupelo, but disease and french leave had taken its toll. During the war, they lost a total of 54 men killed in action. They lost 298 to disease.

Also, General Grant's staff had asked for the loan of a single company from Cornyn's brigade to be employed in headquarters escort duty around Vicksburg. Significantly, the company selected was C Company under Captain Daniel Ballou, Benteen's old company. Ballou left Corinth on 27 April and did not return to the regiment until October. Other companies and details were parceled out to various assignments, sapping the strength of the 10th Missouri notice-ably. Major Benteen could take scant pride in reflecting that his old company was considered the best in the regiment. To all intents and purposes, they were lost.

Tuesday, 26 May 1863, at 10:00 in the morning Cornyn's brigade left Corinth for a raid on Florence, Alabama. They did not take the direct approach to the south and east. Florence was on the north bank of the treacherous Tennessee River. The cavalrymen marched north to Hamburg Landing, Tennessee, and boarded steamboats to be ferried across the river. It took them from 6:00 that evening until 1:00 the following afternoon to get across the river.

Once across, they marched all through the night, stopping but once, until they reached a little town called Rawhide. At the crossing, Cornyn had detached a small party under a Captain Carmichael of the 15th Illinois Cavalry to march north, hoping that maneuver would confuse the enemy spies and scouts. It did. Cornyn's main column caught the garrison at Florence completely by surprise. The 10th Missouri swept through the town without stopping. The 9th Illinois Mounted Infantry was detailed to go house to house looking for contraband. They "found in Florence some 5000 rounds of canister and 30,000 rounds of ammunition for small arms." These were destroyed. "The few wagon shops in the place were engaged in making artillery wheels, and the blacksmith shops doing other Government work, and were burned." Colonel Cornyn's men discovered "immense tan yards in that vicinity, and the largest in the Southern Confederacy." "These were destroyed, and all their contents with them. The contents were worth more than the cost of the establishments and their entire machinery" Several old houses were burned and others booby-trapped by placing shells in the corners and covering them with combustible materials to discourage close pursuit. "If the enemy attempted too close a pursuit," Colonel Cornyn reported, "they would hear from us in a manner that would be disastrous to them."

At first light on 29 May, the brigade began a slow march of destruction back toward Corinth. They destroyed every corn crib they came to, they burned a large cotton factory containing over 300 looms that employed 2000 workers, and they burned about 200,000 bushels of corn. They captured 69 prisoners, another 200 horses, and brought away about 300 Negro slaves. They lost only one man killed, returning to Corinth on 1 June. They had burned all the bridges they had crossed.

July 1863 was a memorable month for Frederick W. Benteen.

On 4 July Grant took Vicksburg. In Pennsylvania, the Army of the Potomac finally defeated Robert E. Lee for the first time at Gettysburg. In St. Louis, Kate Benteen gave birth to a baby girl, the couple's first child. She was named Caroline Elizabeth Benteen after her two grandmothers. And, on 7 July, Major Benteen was involved in the cavalry clash at Iuka.

The fight at Iuka on 7 July should not be confused with the battle of Iuka fought by General Grant in September of 1862. The 7 July 1863 fight was a (relatively) minor cavalry engagement, but it was, in the words of Lieutenant Jennings, "the hottest this Regiment has ever been engaged in."

Lieutenant Colonel Bowen was in arrest. It was part of what Jennings described as a "continual war amongst the officers of this Regiment." Bowen and Cornyn were constantly feuding and placing one another in arrest. In early July it was Bowen's turn to be arrested, which meant that Major Benteen was the acting commanding officer of the 10th Missouri Cavalry.

General Dodge decided on another raid to the southeast. He ordered Cornyn to get his brigade onto the road to Burnsville by 4:00 in the morning on 7 July. For "some reason, as yet unexplained," Dodge complained, Cornyn "failed to move until 5:30." While Cornyn was getting his brigade on the road, a Confederate cavalry regiment raided the government corrals near Glendale just outside Corinth. They initially stole over 600 horses, but were able to make off with only about 240. Had Cornyn been on the road at the appointed time, he would have run smack into the raiders.

Colonel Cornyn lost no time once acquainted with the news. He hurried his brigade in pursuit, advancing about 23 miles by 2:00 in the afternoon. Then, atop a small hill just 1¼ miles north of Iuka, he found the raiders drawn up in a line of battle across a road with a dense woods between their hastily erected barricades and the foot of the hill where Cornyn's skirmishers were rapidly deployed.

Because of the thickly forested area between the Rebel lines and his cavalrymen, Cornyn could not bring his artillery to bear effectively on the enemy. He dismounted the 10th Missouri and sent them up the slope of the hill, three companies on the left hand side of the road, four companies on the right side. Major Benteen was in command of the assault.

In order to make his artillery effective, Cornyn had to move them through the forested area and up the hill to within a few hundred yards of the Confederate position. He managed to get his howitzers in position, but dared not fire them too long as the enemy had the range. When the return fire got so hot that the gunners could no longer face it, Colonel Cornyn ordered Major Benteen to storm the hill. Benteen led the 10th up the hill in the face of a withering fire that Cornyn described as: "a tremendous and destructive volley of musketry, as severe, for the time it lasted, as any I have ever had the fortune to witness." (Cornyn, of course, had been at Wilson's Creek and Shiloh.)

The 10th Missouri had only recently been issued a new carbine that loaded from the breech. It gave them increased firepower (even though the weapons were *not* repeaters) by the simple fact that they were able to load and fire on the run, instead of stopping to ram a ball down the muzzle after every shot.

And run they did. Benteen was in front, in the middle, and was one of the first to mount the barricades. Captain Henry G. Bruns of G Company, who was running beside him, was shot through both lungs and killed instantly. The others kept up the advance, cheering in the manner peculiar to the Civil War: "Hurrah! Hurrah! Hurrah!" and firing their Gibbs .52 caliber carbines as fast as they could load them. An exultant Elisha Jennings told his girl friend: "Our bullets and shells was too much for mortal men to stand, so they broke and fled in disorder."

Years later, Benteen still got emotional about the desperate charge he had led that day. "The regiment I was commanding unhesitatedly charged a Brigade of rebels who were behind breastworks," he said, "and although the three nearest men to me were instantly killed, one of them being a Captain, still there was no faltering, and our guidons were planted on those works, and they stayed there!"

Cornyn placed his wounded in ambulances and fell back about six miles. The next morning he started back slowly for Corinth. As it turned out, there were only four killed and eight wounded in the brigade, all 10th Missouri men. Three of the four dead had fallen beside Benteen, but he was not hit.

For the first time in his career he received a commendation that singled him out. It wouldn't be the last time. "Major F.W. Benteen, commanding the Tenth Missouri Cavalry," Colonel Cornyn wrote, "was where a leader should be, in the front, and, by his coolness and great tact and skill, did much toward gaining the day."

Major Thomas Hynes's court-martial had concluded in May. He was found guilty of neglect of duty and a second charge of "breach of arrest." He immediately appealed, still in arrest, and waited out the mills of military justice grinding slowly in Memphis. Eventually, the reviewing authorities got around to publishing their findings: Major Thomas Hynes was to be "cashiered." Curiously, his court-martial findings were published in the same general orders as another officer's, a man as yet unknown to Benteen, but who would become a very important associate in his post-war career. Captain Joseph G. Tilford of K Company, 3rd U.S. Cavalry had gotten himself into trouble much like Hynes. The difference was that Tilford was drunk. Ordered to his quarters in arrest, he refused to go until threatened with force. Once in his quarters, he left. He was brought back and then back again and again, four times in all. Told that he was violating his arrest on one of these occasions, he muttered: "I don't care." The court-martial board found him guilty of all offenses specified and decreed dismissal from the service. The reviewing authorities ordered further punishment remitted. Tilford was released and restored to duty.

The difference in the two cases seems to be in the penitence (or lack of it) expressed. Major Hynes, convinced that he had been wronged by a vengeful, vindictive superior, fought his case tooth and nail. (In fact, he continued to fight it well into the 1890s.) Captain Tilford, on the other hand, was a 35-year-old West Pointer with fifteen years service experience. And, he was demonstrably drunk when he acted in his disobedient manner. *His* court-martial board recommended clemency; Hynes' did not.

In August 1863, the fate of Major Hynes was still a question mark. *Both* Colonel Cornyn and Lieutenant Colonel Bowen were in arrest. In fact, Cornyn was being tried by court-martial. Both he and Bowen were in the rooms where courts-martial were held in Corinth on 10 August 1863.

"Cornyn thought he was a great fist fighter," Jennings explained, "and had frequently said that he just wanted to get a lick or two at Bowen." At about 11:00 that morning. Cornyn and Bowen exchanged some unremembered words. Cornyn suddenly roared, "Stand back!" and pushed the restraining arms of other officers aside. He advanced on Bowen and struck him twice in the face and then clinched with him. The other officers pulled him away. As they did so, Bowen drew his revolver. Cornyn saw it and went for his own. He never got a chance to fire it.

As Jennings, an eyewitness, reported: they "went to shooting." Bowen's first shot missed and hit the floor. His second struck Cornyn in the right thigh, shattering the bone and rupturing the femoral artery. The third shot passed through his body. Mortally wounded, Cornyn turned in an attempt to flee. Bowen's fourth and final shot struck him in the right hip, ranged downward and came out his groin. He was dead before he hit the floor.

The next day, Lieutenant Jennings, drawing on his medical skill, performed an autopsy. In the practice of the day, he gutted the dead man and filled the abdominal cavity with salt. The body of Florence M. Cornyn was then placed in a metallic burial case and shipped, under escort, to St. Louis for burial. Lieutenant Colonel Bowen was arrested and sent to Memphis on a charge of murder.

The reaction throughout the regiment was mixed. Many of the officers hated Cornyn with a passion. One of them was heard to say that he would not have spoken to Bowen had he *not* shot Cornyn after being punched in the face. Benteen's reaction at the time has been lost. Years later, he said of Cornyn: "God seldom made a better man." A modern authority has written: "Except for a strong tendency to rashness, which cannot be accounted a serious fault in a cavalryman, Cornyn was a competent tactician and a capable leader."

The immediate effect of the Bowen-Cornyn duel was to make Major Frederick W. Benteen the *de facto* commanding officer of the

10th Missouri Cavalry. His quiet, gentlemanly manner was just what the dissension-ridden regiment needed. As an officer by election, he was unusually sensitive to the feelings of the enlisted men, who time and again repaid his kindness and essential humanity with loyalty and fond recollections of him. As he explained his system many years later: "I started in with my troop to make friends and soldiers of them. I would treat them like men, and everybody else had to; so they got to love me."

He was not as easy-going with his fellow officers, especially his superiors.

The body of Florence Cornyn went north on the steamboat *Mary Forsyth*, escorted by Captains Sherman Underwood (K Co.) and Patrick Naughton (H Co.). The party reached St. Louis on 16 August 1863. The following afternoon, the remains were taken to the house of General Frank Blair.

In the meantime, larger events dictated the reassignment of the 10th Missouri. The loss of Colonel Cornyn not only made a new commanding officer of the regiment necessary, especially with Bowen in arrest, but it also was necessary for General Dodge to find a new brigade commander. However, after Grant had won his hard-fought victory at Vicksburg, the Union high command began to transfer elements from his Army of the Tennessee to the other localities where they were needed more. These transfers did not occur at once, but rather over a long period of time. Grant's victorious army was basically divided into two sections: the main body around Vicksburg, and the support troops (under General Hurlbut) concentrated along the Tennessee-Mississippi state line from Memphis to Corinth. Only one complete regiment of cavalry had been present with General Grant at Vicksburg: Colonel Edward F. Winslow's 4th Iowa Cavalry. The rest of Grant's cavalry were small detachments much like C Company of the 10th Missouri under Captain Ballou. The bulk of the cavalry assigned to Grant's Army of the Tennessee were concentrated in Hurlbut's XVI Corps. With the fall of Vicksburg, General Grant set his sights east. Beginning in late August, the bulk of the troops from Memphis to Corinth along the state line were infantry. The cavalry was transferred unit by unit to the Vicksburg area and reassigned there to the Union XVII Corps under Major General James B. McPherson.

For the 10th Missouri, the change of station came suddenly. They had four companies under Captain Williams out on a raid to Henderson, Tennessee when their newly-assigned division commander, Brigadier General Benjamin H. Grierson, rather peremptorily ordered Major Benteen to "move immediately," not to wait for the four companies (who would follow upon their return) and to "ship all extra baggage by railroad."

By 27 September 1863, the bulk of the 10th Missouri was at Yazoo City, Mississippi.

7

Winslow's Brigade

Lieutenant Colonel Bowen was left behind, in arrest, at Memphis. He was kept under guard at a military prison camp near there, but was frequently allowed to go into town with an escort officer to confer with his attorney. On the evening of 14 September, he bought a raffle ticket for a cake, and, to the embarrassment of his escort and jailers, won the cake the next day. The authorities were not amused.

On 22 September 1863, a new colonel was appointed to command the 10th Missouri: Colonel Andrew J. Alexander, Frank Blair's chief-of-staff (and Mrs. Blair's cousin). Colonel Alexander never joined the regiment, though, content instead to occupy the staff position. Major Benteen remained the commanding officer in fact if not in name.

On 14 October, Lieutenant Colonel Bowen's court-martial was finished. Despite predictions of his supporters, he was not acquitted. He was sentenced to be dismissed from the service for murder. That same day, his old regiment began another expedition. They had a new brigade commander: Colonel Winslow of the 4th Iowa.

Edward F. Winslow was 25 years old, a transplanted New Englander from one of America's oldest families. He had moved from Maine to Mount Pleasant, Iowa, in 1856, seeking a find employment as a bank clerk. Instead, he became a railroad construction engineer and worked for the St. Louis, Vandalia & Terre Haute Railroad. When the war broke out, he raised a company of cavalrymen at Ottumwa, Iowa, that became F Company of the justly-famed 4th Iowa Cavalry. He was made its captain and joined General Curtis in Arkansas where he was detached to serve as Provost Marshal.

In February of 1863 he was promoted to major and given command of the 4th Iowa, which was assigned to General Grant opposite Vicksburg. When that town fell on 4 July, Winslow was made a full colonel and chief of Grant's cavalry.

In September, Colonel Winslow had taken his 4th Iowa north on a spectacular raid to Grenada. They were joined there by some troops that had been in Cornyn's brigade and proceeded north to Memphis. Winslow, to the great delight of Major General William T. Sherman (General Grant's right hand man), had succeeded in capturing virtually every railroad car and engine between Vicksburg and Memphis. When he returned by boat to Vicksburg, Winslow was appointed commanding officer of the cavalry forces in General McPherson's XVII Corps. The forces consisted of five regiments. Three of them were woefully understrength: the 4th, 5th, and 11th Illinois. The other two were more complete: the 10th Missouri under Major Benteen and Winslow's own 4th Iowa under Major Alonzo B. Parkell.

On 14 October 1863, Winslow's cavalry command led out on an expedition toward Canton, Mississippi. The commanding officer of the expedition was General McPherson, who had two infantry divisions totalling about 6500 men besides Winslow's 1500 cavalrymen. At 5:30 in the morning they crossed the Big Black River east of Vicksburg and headed toward the town of Brownsville. The infantry took a very direct route northeast. Winslow's cavalry was kept south of the main column and slightly ahead so as to develop any opposition that might be encountered.

They skirmished with a scratch force of Confederate cavalry on both sides of Brownsville but encountered no serious opposition until 16 October on the road from Brownsville to Livingston, about halfway to Canton. Confederate cannon fire forced Winslow to withdraw from his position four miles east of Brownsville until he could be reinforced by an infantry brigade. He left Major Benteen with the infantry brigade and sought another road. The cannon fire did not let up all that day. 'The Tenth Missouri Cavalry was under fire of enemy's cannon for six hours." They lost only two men during the entire expedition, but fifty of their horses were killed or wounded.

Winslow's force, in the meantime, had closed to within three miles of Livingston and destroyed a mill and wagon shop. Unable to dislodge a superior enemy force, they withdrew. General McPherson's entire column marched back toward Vicksburg, crossing Messinger's Ferry on 24 October.

Colonel Winslow in his report singled out Major Benteen and four other officers "as being valuable and gallant officers." Commenting on the fight at Livingston which did not involve Benteen, Winslow demonstrated his droll sense of humor by relating "the conduct of curious personages, who fled to the rear when the situation became uncomfortable because of enemy's shells. They gave self-originated orders while going to the rear."

Immediately upon his return from the field, Major General James B. McPherson found a letter waiting for him from Major Thomas Hynes, who had ensconced himself in Vicksburg's Washington Hotel in partial compliance with orders to join his regiment on the Big Black River east of Vicksburg. The letter was dated 21 October and asserted in part: "I have been ordered to report to Major Benteen 'under arrest,' an order which under all circumstances is most repugnant to me, as he is junior to me in the Regt. and further I am reliably informed a *personal enemy* of mine."

General McPherson granted Hynes's request to remain in Vicksburg under arrest until his case had been decided. Actually, Hynes had been dismissed from the Army, but the court-martial proceedings and sentence had been mislaid and were not to be found for another seven months. Meanwhile, he remained (on paper) the senior major of the regiment, but his request brought to General McPherson's notice the situation in the 10th Missouri Cavalry. Simultaneously, Major Benteen requested a leave of absence which was also granted.

Benteen left Vicksburg for St. Louis 27 October to visit his wife and see his three-month-old daughter, Caroline, for the first time. In his absence, the junior major, William H. Lusk, commanded the regiment, ably assisted by Captain Martin H. Williams of D Company who was designated acting major. Benteen returned 15 November.

The 10th Missouri spent the first ten days of December engaged in the operations against Natchez to the south. They saw no action. On 9 December, Benteen promoted a private in F Company to regimental sergeant-major. The man, John L. Walsh, a middle-aged Irishman, was especially close to Benteen for the remainder of the war and after. The rest of December and all of January 1864 found them in camp on the Big Black preparing for General Sherman's raid on Meridian.

In the fall of 1863, the Confederates had won a bloody victory at Chickamauga Creek in Georgia, only to throw away their dubious gains at Chattanooga in November. Sherman returned to Mississippi determined to expand Union control in the Mississippi Valley before undertaking his march into Georgia.

Sherman's raiding force consisted of infantry from General McPherson's XVII Corps and one division of cavalry from that same command under Brigadier General Benjamin H. Grierson. One of Grierson's brigades was Winslow's.

Winslow's cavalry crossed the Big Black at 6:30 in the morning of 3 February, headed east toward Jackson and their ultimate goal Meridian, 120 miles due east of Vicksburg. At the same time a larger cavalry force under Brigadier General William Sooy Smith left Corinth, headed south. The two commands were to converge on Meridian, the last major rail center in Mississippi still under Confederate control.

Winslow's cavalry brushed aside Confederate pickets the first day out and did not meet organized resistance until the next day near Bolton. There, the 10th Missouri was dismounted and sent forward to attack the enemy positions. Major Benteen led the dismounted attack which resulted in the enemy being "driven immediately from his positions with some loss." The cavalry continued to advance.

On the 5th, Colonel Winslow discovered a Confederate column three times the size of his own attempting to hurry into the town of Jackson to meet McPherson's infantry column from behind its defenses there. He dismounted the 4th Iowa and seized a hill overlooking the approach and sent the 10th Missouri thundering into the town while he supported their mounted charge with artillery. Benteen's 10th Missouri "advancing at a gallop closely pursued through the line of fortifications and into Jackson." Winslow sent other regiments south and north of the city simultaneously and all drove the Confederates out. The advance was so rapid that the Rebels did not have time to burn a pontoon bridge across the Pearl River east of town. The valuable bridge was captured intact by Benteen's 10th Missouri, saving the slow-moving infantry from unnecessary delay when they finally caught up.

The next day Winslow's cavalry brigade moved north in the direction of Canton and found nothing but abandoned wagons, dead mules, and other indications of a hasty flight on the part of the Confederates. They then swung east, crossed the Pearl River and found themselves once again in the advance of McPherson's XVII Corps. They skirmished outside Morton on 9 February, on Ontagoloo Creek on 10 February, and on Chunky Creek on 12 February. They captured over a hundred small arms in a skirmish west of Meridian on the 13th and drove the Rebel defenders out of Meridian on the 14th.

Sherman's army arrived at Meridian and began a methodical destruction. The eminent Civil War scholar Bruce Catton, in describing this event, observed: "The 10th Missouri, it was said, took particular pleasure in the work; it contained men who had been driven from their homes by Confederate guerrillas, and they were out to get even." In fact, this was the only mention that Catton ever made of the 10th Missouri. They *were* notorious for pillage. "Meridian was thoroughly sacked."

Winslow's brigade, minus the 11th Illinois (and the only other officer in the brigade who was senior to Benteen), was sent northeast to harry the retreating Confederates. They found a hospital at Lauderdale Springs, but no sign of William Sooy Smith's cavalry. They kept ranging further north, looking for signs of Smith and burning anything that seemed remotely useful to the Confederate military. Before crossing the Pearl River north of Philadelphia, one of the 10th Missouri's officers, Lieutenant Jacob Greenwood of L Company, was placed in arrest for firing the home of a civilian. Greenwood was the only officer in the regiment ever taken to task for an act of pillage. He was dishonorably discharged a few months later, but a year later he managed to have the record amended to an honorable discharge, though he never served again.

The brigade kept pushing north. Winslow reported that he "sent two messengers eastward," implying that they never got through. They may not have. One definitely did not. He was William Spicer of the 10th Missouri. Private Spicer volunteered to ride northeast in a Confederate uniform to see if he could get through to General Smith. He left Kosciusko on the evening of 23 February. Unfortunately, the second Confederate patrol he encountered had among its members a former neighbor of his. "A drumhead court martial was held in the middle of the road. The verdict was soon reached, and Spicer was hanged to a near-by tree."

At Canton, Colonel Winslow suddenly took sick and was excused by General Sherman. Winslow headed back to Vicksburg, leaving command of the brigade in the hands of Major Frederick W. Benteen. On the 27th, Winslow's (now Benteen's) Brigade started back for Vicksburg in the rear of McPherson's XVII Corps. Almost at once the rear was assailed by three brigades of Confederate cavalry, believed to be men from Nathan Bedford Forrest's command. Under

Benteen's leadership, the brigade deployed and drove the Confederates back. General McPherson, alarmed by the commotion in the rear, hurried back. But, by the time he arrived Benteen's men had put the harrassing Rebels to flight. McPherson, the handsome curly-haired *Beau Sabreur* of the Union Army, was delighted. "Splendid, Benteen!" he boomed, patting the gallant major on the back in the presence of other officers, "*You* never get sick and I always know where to find you!"

Benteen's handling of the rear guard was indeed splendid. Each time the pursuing Confederates would close in, Benteen's small brigade (10th Missouri, 4th Iowa, and 5th Illinois) would drive them away. The infantry brigades would from time to time deploy to meet the threat as a precaution, but as Benteen later recalled: "it got to be said, 'It is of no use for us to get off the road. Benteen can take care of that batch if you just let him alone!' and the prediction was not a fallacy."

The entire force arrived back at Vicksburg on 2 March 1864. Upon his return, Benteen found that he had been promoted to lieutenant colonel on 27 February with rank to date from 14 February. The authorities had finally been advised of Lieutenant Colonel Bowen's dismissal and had appointed Benteen to fill that vacancy. The status of Major Hynes was mooted. Captain Williams was promoted to major, filling Benteen's old slot.

In April 1864 there was another reorganization. Winslow's Brigade was reconstituted to consist of three regiments: the 10th Missouri Cavalry (under Lieutenant Colonel Benteen), the 3rd Iowa Cavalry (under Colonel John W. Noble), and the 4th Iowa Cavalry (under Lieutenant Colonel John H. Peters). This new organization was to remain unchanged until the end of the war.

On 1 May, the brigade arrived at their new station: Memphis, Tennessee. The next day, they engaged Confederates at Bolivar, Tennessee, impressing Colonel Joseph Karge of the 2nd New Jersey Cavalry "with the celerity and ease with which they could capture earthworks."

Ten days later, the final act of the Major Hynes feud began. Lieutenant Colonel Benteen sent to Vicksburg for the balance of the regiment still there and the "books, papers and records of (the) regiment." Major Hynes, released from arrest and commanding the stay-behinds at Vicksburg, "refused to send them." Benteen spent the better part of two months attempting to get action, making two trips in person to Vicksburg to accomplish this. By the time he succeeded in getting action, Major Hynes' court-martial findings had been published. The unlucky Hynes was dismissed from the Army. He repaired to St. Louis to begin a thirty-year struggle to clear his name. He never succeeded.

Meanwhile, Benteen's regiment, reduced to about 200 men, went off on an expedition to Guntown, Mississippi with the rest of the brigade and a large infantry force. The expedition was commanded by Brigadier General Samuel D. Sturgis, the same man who had commanded the retreat from Wilson's Creek in 1861. On Friday, 10 June 1864, Sturgis encountered Confederate General Nathan Bedford Forrest about six miles from Guntown at a place called Brice's Crossroads. The result was a disaster for the Union troops there.

Benteen was not present, being involved in getting his men and records from Vicksburg. The skeleton 10th Missouri Cavalry was commanded by Major Hal Williams. And, by all accounts, it was Winslow's Brigade that kept the disaster from becoming a complete rout. Sturgis tried at first to blame Colonel Winslow, but seeing that others present (especially Winslow's immediate superior, General Grierson) were crediting Winslow with saving what little was saved, asked for a court of inquiry.

"In view of the fact that my campaign has ended disastrously, and will be severely and perhaps unjustly criticised and misrepresented," Sturgis wrote his commanding officer on 14 June, "I would respectfully request. . . that an investigation of the cause of failure be made as early as practicable, and while the officers are now here and their evidence can be secured." His request was granted.

Benteen, in the midst of recovering his regimental records, returned to Memphis long enough to promote Sergeant-Major Walsh to adjutant (first lieutenant) of the regiment. The previous adjutant, Jeremiah Young, was promoted to captain commanding K Company. John L. Walsh remained Benteen's adjutant throughout the Civil War.

In July, Winslow's Brigade (still minus Benteen) accompanied Major General Andrew J. Smith on a similar expedition to Tupelo. It had happier results for the Union cause. Smith found Forrest on 14 July near Tupelo and defeated him badly. Again, the small 10th Missouri Cavalry was commanded by Major Williams. He commended Captains Frederick R. Neet and Robert McGlasson "for prompt assistance rendered at all times" as well as Lieutenant Van B. Stoddard for rallying a picket line that had been driven back and Walsh's successor as sergeant-major, Edmond Bates Kanada, "for efficient discharge of duty."

Upon return to Memphis, the court of inquiry for General Sturgis was held. The outcome was of no moment, for General Sherman had already absolved Sturgis of blame, commenting: "That Forrest is the very devil!" Colonel Winslow was circumspect in his testimony, careful not to impugn Sturgis' conduct. Major Abial R. Pierce of the 4th Iowa was not so kind. Writing to the Adjutant General of Iowa, he bluntly declared: "I am sorry to have to say that the officers and men of my command have no confidence in the general commanding the expedition." Benteen unquestionably heard the inevitable discussions of Sturgis' conduct and the impression left in his mind, hardly favorable, was to have a long-lasting effect.

Benteen in the meantime had finally succeeded in getting the balance of the regiment and its books, papers, etc. out of Vicksburg. Unfortunately, on 21 July their transport, the steamboat *B.M. Runyan,* struck a snag in the river near Greenville, Mississippi "and in fifteen minutes went to pieces." No lives were lost, but the regiment was stripped of "wagon train, much quartermaster and ordnance property; in fact, nearly everything but hope."

A week later, Lieutenant Colonel Benteen was forced to face another grim fact of the Civil War. His 10th Missouri consisted of 3-year volunteers and many of them from the old Bowen's Battalion were due for discharge. Since March of that year, President Lincoln had authorized units who were successful in retaining a certain percentage of their 3-year men to have added to their unit designation the term 'Veteran.' Both the 3rd and 4th Iowa became Veteran Volunteer Cavalry regiments. The 10th Missouri men did not reenlist in sufficient numbers. This is not a reflection on their patriotism or on Benteen's leadership. There were rumblings to the south of Missouri in the summer of 1864. General Sterling Price was organizing an army of Confederate cavalry to invade the state and the fact was pretty well known. The men, understandably, wanted to go home and see their loved ones for the first time since December 1862. Confederate guerrilla bands had been roaming with seeming impunity throughout the state and the men wanted to get back and see to things on the home front. Cornyn's men were not eligible for discharge. Bowen's old companies (A, B, C, & D) were.

Because the regimental papers had been lost on the *Runyan,* this necessitated "their being ordered to St. Louis for muster out, copies of muster in rolls and descriptive books being on file at the Adjt. Gen. of State's Office." Benteen asked for and received permission to march Companies A, B, C, & D to St. Louis. They departed 1 August.

PRICE'S RAID

As Benteen was marching four companies of his regiment north to muster out, the commanding general of the few Confederate troops west of the Mississippi had come to a decision. On 4 August 1864, he authorized Major General Sterling Price to form an organization of about 12,000 men to be known as the Army of Missouri. Price's Confederate army was to consist almost entirely of cavalry in three divisions: the first under a general named Fagan, the second under a future governor of Missouri — John S. Marmaduke, the third under the incomparable Brigadier Joseph O. "Jo" Shelby.

General Price, a tall, white-haired, 300-pound ex-governor of the state of Missouri, was given three objectives. First, he was to capture St. Louis if he could. Second, whether succeeding in St. Louis or not, Price was to seize Jefferson City at least long enough for the new Confederate governor, Thomas C. Reynolds, to be inaugurated there. Third, Price was to capture Kansas City and especially Fort Leavenworth with all its military stores on the other side of the Missouri River.

The Confederates had high, but not unrealistic, hopes for the raid. They expected to harrass the Union Army, embarrass the Union government in St. Louis, and by so doing influence the November elections. They also planned to do some recruiting amongst their sympathizers. They planned to replenish their stores with plunder from Federal installations. In fact, fully a third of Price's men went on the raid virtually unarmed, counting on a quick victory or two to net enough weapons to go around. And, in the end, they decided to raid in Kansas on the way back for reasons similar to their reasons for raiding Missouri.

As it happened, it took Price and his cavalry "army" almost six weeks to get organized and cross the Missouri state line near Doniphan. In the meantime, the new Union commanding general in Missouri, Major General William S. Rosecrans, had plenty of time to prepare. He had too much time. He responded by scattering his meager forces around the state in small garrisons, a tactic familiar nowadays as the strategic hamlet concept. It did not work very well in 1864.

Benteen did not stay long in St. Louis. He had come and gone before Rosecrans had received any definite word on the impending Price Raid. Most of the men in the first four companies had mustered out. Eight of the officers left the regiment and only six new ones were appointed in their place. The appointments were significant. Sergeant-Major Kanada was appointed a first lieutenant in A Company. To compensate L Company for its loss of Lieutenant Greenwood, Benteen appointed Leslie R. Norman from St. Louis to be its new first lieutenant. Leslie was Kate Benteen's younger brother. Benteen's friend, William J. DeGress, was appointed a first lieutenant, then captain, in B Company.

DeGress had resigned his commission in December of 1862 and set out for Kentucky to open a store. Three months later, he was arrested and confined in St. Louis's Myrtle Street Prison, charged with murder and defrauding the government. DeGress remained in prison for nearly a year before the slow wheels of justice finally turned and his court-martial was held. The murder charge was related to an incident in the fall of 1862 when the troops under his command shot and killed a fleeing prisoner, a civilian who was a suspected Confederate guerrilla. The defrauding the government charge stemmed from his resignation after accepting a captaincy in the new 10th Missouri Cavalry. His court-martial acquitted him of all charges and he was released. He immediately volunteered to serve as a general's aide on Sherman's march to Atlanta and was wounded again outside the Georgia city. When Benteen turned up in St. Louis, DeGress was once again available for service in the 10th Missouri. His wounds were still bothering him, though, and he accepted Benteen's offer with the proviso that he be placed on detached service in an office. For the rest of the year 1864, DeGress supervised clerks in reconstructing the lost regimental records and served as the regimental recruiting officer in St. Louis.

Upon his return to Memphis, Benteen found a reorganization problem facing him. The regiment was authorized 1200 men by law. They had never been able to assemble more than 600 of those men for any one expedition. By late summer of 1864, they couldn't muster 300. Benteen was able to take advantage of the emergency in Missouri and the bounty system to raise his total strength by recruiting to 322 by October. This figure included the sick, the wounded, and those on detached service. By way of contrast, the other two regiments in Winslow's Brigade seldom had less than 500 men and the

4th Iowa Cavalry had at times more than 900. The 10th Missouri was the smallest regiment in the brigade and would remain so until the end of the war.

At the same time, Benteen's small regiment began receiving a new weapon: the seven-shot Spencer repeating carbine. Not all received the new repeater that summer and fall. They continued to be armed with a mixture of weapons that included their old Gibbs carbines, the newer Sharps carbine, and a limited issue of Hall carbines. *All* were breechloaders, however, and the new Spencers gave them firepower that more than made up for their lack of numbers. From the journal entries of Captain Charles F. Hinricks of L Company (Leslie Norman's commanding officer), it seems that perhaps a third of the regiment had Spencers by October. They did not *all* receive Spencers until January of 1865.

As Price's army advanced slowly north through Arkansas, the Union commander of that state became alarmed and asked for reinforcements. He was given a division of infantry from Major General A.J. Smith's command and a small division of cavalry consisting of Winslow's Brigade and Colonel Joseph Karge's Brigade. Colonel Winslow commanded the division, while a lieutenant colonel of the 3rd Iowa commanded Winslow's Brigade. The reinforcements left Memphis bound for Little Rock on 2 September 1864.

The march across east Arkansas nearly destroyed them as a fighting unit. They saw no action, of course, but were following in the wake of Price's marauding Confederates in an area of the country already devastated by three years of war. There was not enough forage in the area to feed Winslow's 1300 horses as what was left had already been appropriated for Price's 12,000+ horses. Inevitably, Winslow's horses fell out and had to be abandoned. He moved slowly north by east on the trail of Price.

General Price crossed into Missouri on 19 September and a week later fought a very bloody battle at the rail head near Pilot Knob. Though his Army of Missouri outnumbered Pilot Knob's defenders about six to one, they were repulsed. Price had elected to try a frontal assault against the advice of his subordinates, principally Jo Shelby, and had been greeted by entrenched Federals supported with artillery. After giving Price a terrific pounding, the outnumbered defenders withdrew. Price hurried on to St. Louis, arriving at its outskirts three days later. St. Louis had been reinforced by A.J. Smith's infantry while Price had delayed at Pilot Knob, learning the folly of frontal assault on prepared defenses. Price was reluctant to try more of the same at St. Louis. He decided to bypass St. Louis and swing west toward his second objective, Jefferson City, the state capital.

On 5 October, Winslow's cavalry, almost totally dismounted by then, reached Cape Girardeau on the Mississippi River.

Price's Confederates raced the scattered Union forces to Jefferson City and lost. After skirmishing with small forces on its outskirts, Price decided against an attack on the capital. His reasons were the same as those for avoiding his first objective: Federal troops in position and his own distaste for bloody, head-on assault. While Price would probably not have been able to take St. Louis under the circumstances, he *might* have been able to take Jefferson City, but he was convinced that he could not. Confederate "governor" Reynolds was furious.

The main reason for assigning command of the army to Price was that Sterling Price was a household word in Missouri and had come to symbolize the Confederate cause in that state. He had a reputation for being a brave and fairly competent commander in the field, but as events were to prove, cavalry tactics were not his forte. He was of the old school and set in his ways, believing that an army on the march must have a supply train and that this supply train had to be defended at all hazards. His cavalry officers were unable to convince him otherwise. This obsession with a wagon train would prove Price's undoing.

Winslow's Brigade trooped aboard steamboats at Cape Girardeau on the 7th and began ferrying to St. Louis. They arrived by detachments on the 8th, 9th and 10th and went into camp at Benton Barracks. Lieutenant Colonel Benteen had very little time to visit his wife, as his time was occupied refitting and remounting his men. Fortunately for them, Benton Barracks was close enough to a major remount station of the Union Army to enable the men of Winslow's Brigade to draw 500 new horses and effectively put themselves back into the saddle. The men were also issued new clothing, blankets, coats, and other accoutrements. They even drew some more Spencer repeaters.

On 7 October, Major General Alfred Pleasonton arrived in Jefferson City to take charge of the Union forces in the state. Pleasonton's most recent assignment had been as commanding general of the cavalry of the Army of the Potomac, but he had been relieved of that duty in March under questionable circumstances and sent West. General

Rosecrans, his superior, saw him as the salvation of the emergency. Pleasonton was a West Point professional, a tall sarcastic bachelor who was in fact a gifted leader of cavalry troops. His relief in the East had been politically inspired; there was nothing wrong with his ability. (One of the aides he brought with him was a young Michigander named George W. Yates.)

As Pleasonton surveyed the conditions in Missouri from Jefferson City, he saw that Price would never be defeated by the militia troops who were trying so hard to tie down all the scattered garrisons. As soon as he learned that Winslow's troops were in St. Louis, Pleasonton sent for them. Winslow's men had been in action against Confederate regulars for years. They were accustomed to hard marches and hard fighting. Understandably, Pleasonton was anxious to have their services.

Winslow's 1st Brigade (Karge's) left St. Louis on steamboats at 5:00 in the evening of the 10th, headed for Jefferson City. The 2nd Brigade (Winslow's own) left the following evening on horseback. They marched slowly, taking especial care of their horses so as to avoid the problem that had aborted their march through Arkansas and Missouri.

While Pleasonton at Jefferson City was gathering his cavalry for a pursuit, Price was at Boonville, about 40 miles northwest, meeting with some local guerrilla leaders that included William Quantrill, George Todd, and Bloody Bill Anderson. Price was shocked when Anderson's men rode in with scalps dangling from their saddle pommels and ordered the irregulars to remove them. He seemed embarrassed by his new associates, but determined to use every resource. He was headed west toward his third objective, Kansas City.

Near Kansas City, Union forces were gathering to meet him. Major General Samuel R. Curtis was in command of the department that included Kansas, Nebraska and large chunks of Indian Territory. Despite the fact that a Colorado regiment had massacred a band of Cheyenne Indians earlier and sparked a bloody Indian war, Curtis had only 4000 men available with which to meet Price. He asked the governor of Kansas to call out the state militia. The governor refused.

The situation was ludicrous on the surface, but not untypical of political-military relations during the Civil War. General Curtis, who had commanded Benteen in 1862 in the Army of the Southwest, had been relieved from command in Missouri for squabbling with *that* governor. President Lincoln, in ordering the relief of command, had commented that he did it only because he lacked the Constitutional authority to relieve the governor. Stiff, competent General Curtis did not suffer fools gladly and did not thrive in his new environment. To make matters worse, his son Zarah Curtis (the same Zarah Curtis who had locked horns with Benteen a year and a half before) had been killed by Quantrill's men in Kansas and the father understandably wanted little to do with that state.

But Governor Carney of Kansas was not just being pig-headed. He simply did not believe that an emergency existed. He found the timing very suspicious, for one thing. Elections were to be held the first Tuesday in November and Carney felt that the emergency was a ploy on the part of his political enemies to call out the militia and draw them away from the polls just before the election. Price's arrival at Boonville changed his mind. He agreed to call out a portion of the militia. After some squabbling, he agreed to call out the entire militia, but insisted that they remain within the borders of the state of Kansas. It took all of General Curtis' rapidly diminishing patience and considerable negotiating skill to get Carney to let Kansas state troops deploy in Missouri.

Again, Carney was not being unrealistic. The Kansas-Missouri feud was a legendary one. It was also a bloody one. The border area had spawned such men as Quantrill on the Confederate side and Doc Jennison of Jayhawker fame on the Union side. Sending Kansas troops into Missouri, including a new regiment of Jennison's Jayhawkers, was almost certain to trigger bloody reprisals in Kansas. Carney was reluctant to stir up more trouble than he already had, but he became convinced of the seriousness of the emergency and went along with the drastic measures.

By 20 October 1864, Major General Curtis was able to deploy a thin line of Kansas troops along the Little Blue River east of Kansas City, Missouri. The following day, Price's Confederates drove them back and captured the town of Independence. Curtis, having finally located Price's army, drew up his troops around the little village of Westport, south of Kansas City. He was waiting for Price to make the first move and hoping that Pleasonton's pursuing column would arrive in time to join the fight. If they did not, Curtis was prepared to pull back.

WESTPORT

Pleasonton's cavalry roared through Independence, narrowly missing a golden opportunity to swallow up Price's precious wagon train.

They halted about 10:30 at night on the 22nd and waited for the moon to rise. Karge's Brigade had been decimated by detachments hither and yon. Fragments of only two of his regiments remained: the 4th Missouri Cavalry and the 7th Indiana Cavalry, about 200 men in all. They were attached to Winslow's Brigade.

The day before had been windy and cold, the early morning air was positively chilly. There was even ice in the creeks. Men and horses alike blew out streams of vapor as they stamped restlessly, waiting for the coming light and the battle it was sure to bring. General Curtis had drawn his much enlarged Army of the Border up south of Westport. His main force faced directly south between the Big Blue River and the state line. He had a secondary force that was actually stationed across that line in Kansas. His defensive position looked like the letter L tipped over to the right. General Price's Confederate positions were just south of Curtis' and arranged in an identical L shape. The stem of Price's L faced Curtis, enfiladed (unbeknownst to them) by Curtis' troops across the state line. The base of Price's L covered the approaches to the Big Blue River. Confederate Major General John S. Marmaduke's troops formed this base. They were on the west side of the Big Blue facing east. "Marmaduke had stationed his entire division of some 2700 men and two batteries of artillery in a wooded area above a low cliff that with its trees and a few houses would provide good protection for his excellent defensive position."

General Pleasonton at Independence (northeast of Westport) had intended to swoop down on Price's rear as soon as the moon was up and shedding enough light to illuminate the roads. His lead brigade was a Missouri Militia unit and they fumbled their assignment badly. Pleasonton, in great disgust, sent Colonel Winslow's Brigade on ahead to locate the enemy.

Winslow's scouts found a crossing of the Big Blue called Byram's Ford which placed them on the flank (southeast) of Price's army directly opposite Marmaduke's position. Pleasonton then sent one of the militia units forward to cross the river. Then, he waited and waited. And, waited. Finally, when the gunfire from near Westport was plainly audible to the west and the sun was almost up, he hurried forward to find out why his division was not moving. He found the militia general in a conference, his command still unmoved. Angrily, Pleasonton relieved him on the spot and turned to his veterans to lead the way. Colonel Winslow was ordered to cross the ford and

attack Price's right rear. Simultaneously, Pleasonton sent another
militia brigade further south to find Price's wagon train.

Price and Curtis were engaged in a desperate fight, neither knowing for certain when or where Pleasonton would arrive. Curtis had
sent messengers and knew that Pleasonton was coming. Price had
a division watching the river and also knew something was coming.
The delay caused by the militia general's inability to move his troops
against Marmaduke almost gave Price enough time to defeat Curtis,
but Curtis' men, encouraged by the prospects of imminent reinforcements, stubbornly held their ground.

Colonel Winslow had dismounted part of his own 4th Iowa Cavalry on a hill overlooking the ford site and turned over his artillery
to the commander of that detachment, Captain Edward Dee. He
ordered them to shell the hill on the west side of the river about 900
yards from the water's edge where the Confederate defenders seemed
to be concentrated. Captain Dee's dismounted men were sent forward
to a wooded ravine just east of the river and ordered to fire at the
defenders so as to pin them down. Winslow then ordered the recalcitrant militia brigade across the river. To the militia's surprise, Marmaduke had placed skirmishers along the river's edge some 900 yards
in advance of his main hilltop position. The militiamen were badly
shot up trying to cross and might not have made it at all had not
Captain Dee decided to push his dismounted troopers across the river.
Dee's 4th Iowa men swam across the river and emerged, dripping
and shivering, but firing their Spencers. The Confederate skirmishers withdrew about 200 yards and the brief respite gave the militiamen a chance to ford the river without being massacred in the process.

Winslow sent the 10th Missouri, the 3rd Iowa, and the balance
of his brigade across the river. They crossed, formed in a line in front
of the Rebel hill, and dismounted. Under a heavy fire they drove
the skirmishers back and worked their way forward to the rocks
at the base of the hill. Captain Dee's detachment was on the right
(north), flanked on their left by the 7th Indiana and 4th Missouri.
The 10th Missouri was in the middle, flanked by the 3rd Iowa to the
south. The rest of the 4th Iowa was on the extreme left flank adjacent
to a small road that led to the top of the hill. Winslow tried to get
the militia brigade to charge up the road, but Confederate artillery
fire drove them back repeatedly.

Then, Colonel Winslow was shot in the left leg. His troops were
scrambling up through the rocks and trees and meeting with very

little success. Another militia brigade had finally crossed the river and was forming up behind Winslow's men. General Pleasonton joined the fray.

Winslow turned over command of his brigade to Lieutenant Colonel Benteen and withdrew back across the river to seek medical attention. Benteen "by dint of great urging and exertion of authority" succeeded in getting his men moved forward up the rocky, tree-lined bluffs. By about noon, after an hour of heavy fighting but little progress, the Union troops had just about been stalemated at the foot of the hill.

Suddenly, unaccountably, the 4th Iowa detachment closest to the road (under Major Abial R. Pierce) broke through in a "wild wave." They swarmed up the ravine next to the road and, in effect, enfiladed the Rebel lines on top of the hill. The Confederates pulled back to meet the new threat and Benteen's own 10th Missouri, taking advantage of the sudden lull in the firing above them, clawed their way to the top of the bluffs, followed simultaneously all along the line by the rest of Winslow's brigade.

In fact, they came so fast that the Confederates could not form a second line in time to stop them. Benteen's men bounded over the top of the hill and rushed across the open ground, driving the Confederates until "the grayclads ceased their resistance and fled westward across the prairie." General Pleasonton joined the chase, leading the artillery forward from the ford to new positions covering the retreating Confederates.

"Rebels! Fire! You damned asses" he kept shouting over and over.

Winslow's (now Benteen's) Brigade halted and waited for their horses to be brought forward. Pleasonton took up the chase with the reserves from the other militia brigade. Benteen mounted his men and followed the flow of the action until he came to a cornfield. "I took the responsibility upon myself," he later reported, "to halt my command in a large cornfield and take a few minutes to feed" the horses. Ahead of him the running battle flared with renewed violence and he hurried his brigade forward toward the sound of the guns.

What had happened is this: Marmaduke's division had ceased to exist as an organized unit that day, but as they streamed back in a panicky retreat from Pleasonton and two brigades of Missouri militia, they collided with another division that was falling back south, away from Curtis' men. The other division, commanded by a general named Fagan, was withdrawing from Curtis in response to the sounds of firing where Marmaduke's men had been. General Price, realizing that Pleasonton had penetrated his right rear, ordered a withdrawal Fagan's men, in executing that withdrawal, found themselves backing into Pleasonton and his militia brigades. The Rebels turned and charged.

General Curtis missed an opportunity to end the battle at that point. But, his men were exhausted and had no way of knowing that one little extra push would effectively crunch Fagan's men between two units. They held back, weary, thankful, and waiting for the white smoke to clear a little. Fagan's men drove Pleasonton's militia brigades back. This was the "battle raging" that Benteen reported as having decided him to abandon feeding and push on, perceiving "there was work to be done."

Benteen wasted a few minutes trying to rally the demoralized militia, then ordered his brigade to charge. The 10th Missouri led the mounted charge that hit Fagan on his left flank. The Confederates charge became a rout as Benteen's men drove "the enemy far beyond the battleground, beyond Missouri, and into Kansas." Benteen's charge at Westport drove across the rear of what had been Price's lines and, had it taken place a few minutes sooner, would have trapped Jo Shelby's brigade. As it was, Shelby's men were the last to retire and did so in good order.

Far to the south, Pleasonton's third militia brigade, sent to find the wagon train, had been held up by the Confederate rear guard, and so the wagon train escaped. General Shelby's men protected the rear of Price's army as it moved south along the Kansas border. Pleasonton halted just over the state line to join with Curtis' men and trade congratulations. General Curtis finally sent Colonel Jennison's Jayhawkers ahead in pursuit, but the Confederates were long gone. One of the lieutenants in Jennison's 15th Kansas Cavalry was a man named David W. Wallingford, who would be discharged in less than a year for an act of pillage only to be restored and given a commission in the post-war Army.

MINE CREEK

The victorious commanders, Major Generals Samuel R. Curtis and Alfred Pleasonton, had a conference in a farmhouse in Kansas about 2:30 in the afternoon of that fateful day, 23 October 1864. They had just fought the battle that would go down in history as the Gettysburg of the West. Though admittedly smaller than its eastern counter-

part, the battle of Westport was much more decisive in the immediate
sense than was the battle of Gettysburg. And, Pleasonton and Curtis
made plans for a follow-up that Gettysburg lacked. It wasn't easy.
Curtis was hot for a pursuit, but Governor Carney of Kansas (who
was also present) argued for a release of the Kansas militia so that
they could return home in time to vote. Pleasonton made a pursuit
possible by agreeing to accompany Curtis. Curtis disbanded part of
the Kansas militia on the spot and ordered the pursuit to begin.

The next morning the pursuit got underway in earnest. The delay
had given the Confederates a good 12-hour head start, but, encum-
bered by their wagon train loaded with plunder from the raid in
Missouri, they had made only 33 miles. Pleasonton's division moved
briskly, the militia brigades in the lead. Benteen, in the rear, commented: "That day we marched over a desolate country, where even
water was scarce, at a speed that necessarily kept the rear at a trot,
and bivouacked, without forage for our jaded horses, a distance of
at least forty-two miles." To make matters even more miserable for
all concerned, it rained on the night of the 24th.

Tuesday, 25 October 1864, "broke and gave promise of a dull and
dreary day." Benteen's Brigade was ordered to the front of the pursuing column with orders to charge the enemy wherever encountered.
Benteen formed them into a column with the 10th Missouri Cavalry
(Major Lusk) leading, followed by the 4th Iowa Cavalry (Major
Pierce), the 3rd Iowa Cavalry (Major Jones), and trailed by the
remnants of the 7th Indiana and 4th Missouri (jointly commanded
by Major Simonson).

After three hours of marching, the skies had cleared and the sun
burst forth. Benteen had mounted skirmishers far in advance searching the prairie horizon for signs of the retreating Confederates. As
they neared a slight rise to their left, the brigade was galvanized
when the skirmishers came galloping back to report the enemy drawn
up in a line of battle across a stream called Mine Creek about 80 miles
south of Westport. At the same time, one of General Curtis' staff
officers hurried over and told Benteen that one of the militia brigades
was formed on his right (the Rebels' left) but was too weak to make
a charge alone.

Benteen reported: "I at once determined to form on the left of this
brigade, especially as a few more paces brought us in view of the
line of rebels; seeing the position in which he had his artillery, I
immediately surmised that the rebel commander had commited a fatal

blunder, and resolved to capture it." He sent one of his officers over to the militia brigade to inform them of his plan to charge and to request them "for God's sake" to join in the charge. He swung his brigade into a column of regiments in line. That is to say, they were organized in the same order they had been formed in that morning, the diffierence being that each regiment was formed in line rather than in column. This meant that the second regiment in the column (the 4th Iowa Cavalry) overlapped the first regiment (the 10th Missouri Cavalry) by quite a bit. The 4th Iowa was almost twice the size of the leading regiment. This arrangement proved fortuitous.

By 9:45 in the morning the Rebel line facing Benteen on the north side of Mine Creek was made up of what had been Marmaduke's and Fagan's divisions. They numbered about 7000 men. Benteen's Brigade had about 1300 and the militia brigade to his right about that same number. Jo Shelby's division was south of Mine Creek hurrying the wagon train to safety. The Confederate artillery arrangement north of Mine Creek was unusual and this is what prompted Benteen's comment about the "fatal blunder." Most of the Confederate guns were concentrated in the middle of the road. There were a few pieces on each end of the Rebel line — and *nothing* in between but mounted Confederates. The guns in the center could not support the guns on the flanks without firing down their own lines — and vice versa. There were no dismounted troops to support these guns aside from their crews. (Mounted troops are virtually useless while stationary.) Mine Creek, with a marsh and a "thick grove of trees" on its north bank, was *behind* them, giving no room for maneuver. Their only hope under the circumstances was to launch a quick charge, but Benteen's men were bearing down on them.

The Confederate arrangement at Mine Creek was admittedly sloppy, but not without some justification. The leading Union pursuers to that point had been militia, who had stopped to deploy every time the Confederates made a stand. The Confederates had every reason to believe that the troops moving up toward their impromptu line would stop and deploy, giving them ample time to cross the creek and continue their retreat unmolested.

Benteen's veterans had increased from a trot to a gallop and closed the distance. To their right, the militia brigade remained stationary, uncommitted. Benteen ordered the trumpeters to sound the charge and the cavalrymen thundered ahead. Then, it happened.

Benteen's leading regiment, his own 10th Missouri, froze. They had come within rifle range of the Confederates and were beginning to catch some fire. "Again and again, Benteen ordered the charge, and many of his regiment made brave efforts to overcome the singular balk. Some got forward a little farther, but the line could not be moved. He persisted most heroically in trying to break the unfortunate situation. He rode directly in front of his men, within pistol shot of the enemy, hatless, white with passion, waving his sword and shouting the order to charge."

Major Abial Pierce's 4th Iowa, with nowhere else to go, swept around the stalled 10th Missouri, in some cases riding right through them, and reached the Confederate lines quicker than it takes to tell. The rest of the brigade followed Pierce's example. "Then began a fierce hand-to-hand fight," Benteen reported, "one that surpassed anything for the time it lasted I have ever witnessed." By all accounts, it was a wild melee, the Union cavalrymen swinging sabers and firing pistols. Their horses collided with the stationary horses of the Confederates. "I cut eight rebels from their horses with my own saber," Major Pierce boasted. The artillery pieces were especially vulnerable. With screaming, charging, saber-wielding Union cavalrymen all around them, they were abandoned. Their crews dived into the creek and scrambled through the thick grove of trees. Some of Benteen's men dismounted and began pumping their Spencers into the fleeing ranks. Some of the wagons in the rear of the train caught fire. Ammunition for the artillery pieces exploded.

One of Marmaduke's brigades fled without firing a shot, leaving a gaping hole in the center of the line. The militia brigade on Benteen's right, seeing how well things were going, joined in enthusiastically. Benteen himself had the right skirt of his long blue overcoat shot off when he took his thoroughbred mare *over* one of the Rebel guns. "Bonny Brown Bess" (as he called her) "took the first of the enemy's guns at the muzzle and cleared the trail of the piece" in one gigantic bound.

On the left flank, two of Major Pierce's companies were unable to reach the Confederate lines because of a ravine north of the creek. To get around it, they had to swing wide to the left (east) and sweep in behind the Confederate lines. General Marmaduke believed at first that they were Shelby's men come to rescue him. The 4th Iowa men charged the Confederate right flank in the rear, causing a complete collapse. The center had been broken when one of Marmaduke's brigades had vanished. The sudden appearance of Companies A and

K of the 4th Iowa in their rear broke the right flank. That left only the left flank, which was being assailed by the militia brigade. "The rebel line was routed along its whole length within a few minutes for the long infantry rifles with which many of the troops were armed were difficult to reload on horseback and therefore almost useless in a cavalry fight." From that point on, the fight degenerated into a general brawl involving thousands of individual combatants. There were no longer any lines or organization, just several thousand men fighting for their lives.

"The thousands of Confederates driven back from the line feverishly attempted to cross the fords which quickly became jammed with panic-stricken horsemen trying to flee." Many of them in their haste to escape threw away their weapons. What had taken General Price a month of raiding to accomplish was literally thrown away in a matter of minutes. Many of the Confederates would leave the state the same way they had entered it: without weapons. Mine Creek in 1864 was deep and had a swift current. Moreover, its south banks were especially slippery. Scores of Rebels were crushed by falling horses or drowned in the treacherous current or trampled by pursuing horses. The main ford had been completely blocked by stalled and burning wagons.

The whole charge had lasted less than 20 minutes. The Union troops swept across Mine Creek in hot pursuit. "In the bend of the creek, only a few acres in extent, 300 Confederates were killed or wounded and about 900 were captured." As the Union troops sped after the retreating foe, one of the wounded men from the 3rd Iowa Cavalry captured a man who turned out to be General Marmaduke. Another Rebel general was captured trying to cross the creek on a borrowed horse. His captor was also from the 3rd Iowa Cavalry. (Both 3rd Iowa men won Medals of Honor for their feats that day.) As a rule, though, the men of Benteen's Brigade did not bother with prisoners. They simply told unarmed and surrendering men to go to the rear and kept up the pursuit. "Eight artillery pieces and two stands of colors were also taken, besides numerous wagons, small arms, and other equipment and supplies."

General Jo Shelby came up to help stem the tide, but he was unable to organize anything between the distaster at Mine Creek and the Little Osage River eight miles further south. The Confederates rode as if the Hound of Hell was after them. Thomas C. Reynolds, the Confederate "governor" of Missouri, had this explanation for the disaster: "The enemy, not mounted riflemen but real cavalry using the saber, charged our lines. It matters little to inquire which company or regiment first gave way; the whole six large brigades, were in a few minutes utterly routed, losing all their cannon."

At the Little Osage River eight miles to the south, General Shelby with help from the famed "Swamp Fox" of southeastern Missouri, Brigadier General M. Jeff Thompson, got set to meet the advancing Union troops. They had a while to wait. Benteen's Brigade was halted near a farmhouse about a mile south of Mine Creek, where they dismounted to rest their horses. Casualties were amazingly light. Benteen could report seven killed and just over 30 wounded in his brigade. The Confederates, by contrast, had at least 120 killed and about twice that many wounded. In addition, the Confederates had lost about 900 to enemy capture, a rough figure which probably includes most of the wounded.

It was nearly 2:00 in the afternoon before any Union troops challenged Shelby's rear guard on the Little Osage. Benteen's men were in the rear once again, flushed with their stupendous victory. Pleasonton hurried one of the unengaged militia brigades forward. They were forced to deploy against Shelby and thus lost valuable time even though Shelby's men did not put up much of a fight.

Price's wagon train stalled at the Marmaton River almost at the Missouri state line and Shelby was once again forced to deploy his men and the fugitives from Mine Creek into a line to slow up pursuit. It was 3:30 before anyone molested him. The unarmed men were pressed into line and stood plainly visible to create a false impression of great strength. The militia brigade pursuing was impressed by Shelby's defences and called for help. Benteen's weary brigade marched about 12 miles to their relief. Their horses were beginning to falter. Indeed, their first charge against Shelby's position on the Marmaton petered out because the horses could not be made to gallop. Benteen "felt it would be more than useless to continue," so ordered a halt. His ammunition was nearly depleted, but he boldly formed a line of battle. Major Pierce of the 4th Iowa was wounded seriously in the foot during the aborted charge and was unable to ride a horse. The brigade waited in front of Shelby's line for reinforcements.

No reinforcements came and, as the sun went down, Benteen's men watched in frustration as the Confederates leisurely withdrew across the Marmaton and headed back into Missouri. It was equally frustrating for the Confederates, though. M. Jeff Thompson's cavalry had to be dismounted to push the wagons up the high bank on the south side of the river. Once safely across, they halted.

General Price came up and ordered the wagons burned.

The destruction of the wagons south of the Marmaton River in the early hours of 26 October 1864 was a fitting climax to Price's Raid and an ironic one. The wagons had been the cause of the disaster. All of the serious fighting done after Boonville and especially the defeats at Westport and Mine Creek were brought on by Price's insistence on protecting his slow-moving train. The losses at Westport (and in the minor skirmishes that led up to it) have never been accurately reported. They probably exceeded 4000, however, and added to another 1500 lost in the pursuit to the Marmaton, effectively reduced Price's Army of Missouri to half the strength of the army that had invaded Missouri a little over a month before. Price failed to take St. Louis, Jefferson City, *or* Kansas City. He may have influenced the fall election for all that — in favor of Lincoln. And, as a matter of fact, Governor Carney was defeated in the elections that followed in spite of his militiamen's being home in plenty of time to vote.

Sterling Price came under a lot of criticism for his raid from the Confederate authorities and especially from the weary men who had to burn the wagons. But, he was not the only one being criticized. Generals Curtis, Pleasonton, and even Rosecrans were severely chastised for letting Price get away at all. In fact, General Grant (the Commander-in-Chief by then and engaged in the siege of Petersburg) relieved Rosecrans and Curtis after the campaign. General A.J. Smith, whose infantry never got a chance to fight Price, threatened to arrest General Pleasonton for failing to delay Price long enough for the infantry to catch up.

But, there were no recriminations in Benteen's Brigade. They moved slowly, proudly, into Fort Scott, Kansas on the morning of the 26th and waited there until assigned once again to General Curtis' command.

THE PURSUIT OF PRICE

The same day that Benteen's Brigade arrived at Fort Scott, General Pleasonton took one militia brigade to Warrensburg in Missouri about 60 miles northeast of the Mine Creek battlefield. Benteen's men were assigned to General Curtis and ordered to continue the pursuit of Price. Benteen left Scott at 10:00 in the morning of the 27th. On

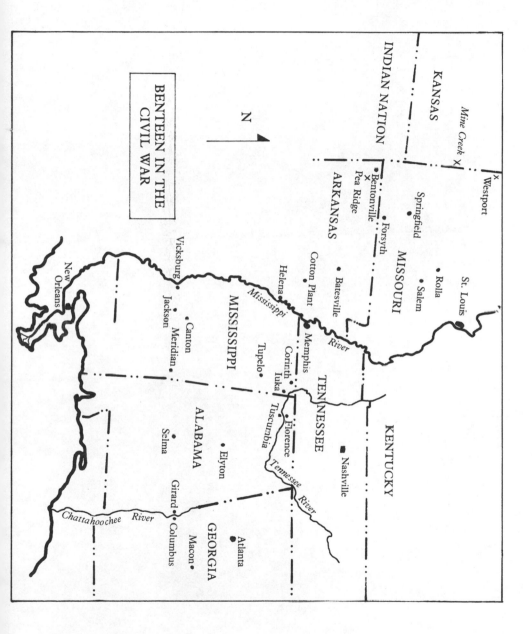

BENTEEN IN THE
CIVIL WAR

N

KANSAS

Mine Creek X

INDIAN NATION

X Westport

ARKANSAS

Bentonville
X
Pea Ridge

Springfield

Salem

Rolla

St. Louis

MISSOURI

Forsyth

Batesville

Cotton Plant

Helena

Vicksburg

Mississippi

New
Orleans

Jackson

River

Canton

Memphis

Meridian

MISSISSIPPI

Tupelo

Corinth

Iuka

TENNESSEE

KENTUCKY

Nashville

ALABAMA

Tuscumbia

Florence

Selma

Tennessee River

Elyton

Girard

Chattahoochee River

Columbus

Macon

Atlanta

GEORGIA

Edward F. Winslow

John W. Noble

the evening of the 28th, he reported to Curtis that he would camp at Carthage, Missouri about 60 miles southeast of the Marmaton battle-field. He related: "I met a great many stragglers coming back from your command, who all agree in relating that you have discontinued the pursuit, Price being out of striking distance." He was wrong in surmising that Curtis had given up pursuit. His horses, Benteen reported, were "very much jaded" and had found no forage the previous night.

The next evening, Benteen wrote Curtis reporting that he had finally found forage for his horses and adding that he wished to know "in writing" whether or not he was to continue to pursue or return to Memphis via Springfield, Missouri. Curtis had already wired General Halleck, Grant's chief of staff in Washington, that he was left with only Benteen's Brigade and deemed it "improper to continue a pursuit in another Department" (Arkansas). He stated that he would return to his own command (Kansas).

General Grant intervened and instructed Curtis to continue the pursuit to the Arkansas River. Curtis duly advised Benteen of the new orders, adding "as long as horses can stand on their feet they must be considered fit for duty." The following day, 31 October, Curtis told Benteen to scout the area around Cassville, Missouri (in the southwestern corner of that state) and find Price's trail which had apparently been lost.

Benteen found the trail and followed it into the Indian Nation (modern Oklahoma). There, on 6 November, his patience wore thin and he angrily responded to a request from the adjutant of Pleasonton's cavalry division in Missouri for a report by stating that he was *not* a "portion of the forces of the Department of the Missouri, but a transient brigade stationed at Memphis." He went on to "request" that his brigade be considered independent and that orders come only from General Curtis of the Army of the Border.

Two days later, General Curtis had caught up with Benteen in the general vicinity of present-day Muskogee, Oklahoma. There, General Curtis drafted a letter to the Union governor of Missouri (Willard P. Hall (stating in part: "I have had the cooperation of a Brigade of Cavalry commanded by Lieutenant Colonel F.W. Benteen of the 10th Missouri Cavalry, who has exhibited the most fearless and distinguished success in the field of battle. . . . I hope you will aid me in securing for him a Brigadier's commission, which he well deserves — and is most competent to fill."

As Curtis' letter went to the governor, Benteen's Brigade was being transferred (on paper) to yet another command. The men on the march with Benteen from the Indian Nation back to St. Louis, as well as the fragments of those same regiments still in Memphis under the command of the wounded Colonel Winslow, were assigned to the Cavalry Corps, Military Division of the Mississippi. This new organization was under the command of a 27-year-old West Pointer named James Harrison Wilson. Major General Wilson's command consisted of seven cavalry divisions, virtually all of the cavalry units west of the Appalachians. "Red" Wilson, a former staff officer of General Grant's as well as an experienced cavalry division commander, was attempting to pull six of his scattered division together to face an impending Confederate attack on Nashville, Tennessee. (The seventh division was marching through Georgia with General Sherman.)

On 23 November, Governor Hall forwarded General Curtis' letter of recommendation to re-elected President Lincoln, adding that Benteen "has at all times been a most faithful and loyal citizen." He also declared: "I visited his regiment at Vicksburg, Miss. last spring, and heard him spoken of by all in the highest terms, indeed, I have seen few men who impress me more favorably than he has done." Governor Hall concluded his letter to the President by endorsing Curtis' recommendation and closed, saying: "I have made him a Brigadier General of the Enrolled Militia of Missouri. I most sincerely hope you will promote him."

About the same time that Governor Hall was penning his flattering remarks, Benteen and his command were limping into St. Louis. The command was broken down almost completely by the 1800 mile expedition. Benteen reported that he had not got "a horse to St. Louis," but that he had received another 1100 horses upon arrival. He reported to his new superior, General Wilson, that while the portion of the brigade under Colonel Winslow in Memphis would move by 6 December, his own immediate command in St. Louis could not possibly board steamboats before the 7th.

True to his word, he was ready to board with his command on the 7th and wired that information to General Wilson. He wanted to know if he should proceed straight to Nashville or go by way of Louisville, Kentucky. Wilson's superior ordered Benteen to go up the Cumberland River to Clarksville, Tennessee.

As Benteen's men were steaming south down the ice-clogged Mississippi River, Colonel Winslow was promoted to Brevet (temporary) Brigadier General. The next senior officer in the brigade, Colonel John W. Noble of the 3rd Iowa Cavalry, was not promoted at that time. Naturally, Benteen was not promoted either. There simply were not enough men in the brigade to warrant three generals. And, there were no more brigades in Wilson's cavalry corps needing commanding officers. In fact, one of Wilson's brigade commanders was Colonel A.J. Alexander, the same man who had been given the titular command of Benteen's 10th Missouri a year before. As soon as Alexander was promoted to brigadier general, Benteen would have been eligible for promotion to colonel. But, the 10th Missouri had less than 600 men and thus did not warrant a full colonel. Benteen remained a lieutenant colonel until the end of the war.

Two days out of St. Louis, Benteen's men had to be taken off the boats because of the ice on the river. One of the boats had blown up. They marched overland to Cairo, Illinois, arriving 17 December. The expected attack on Nashville had taken place on 15 December and had been decisively defeated, eliminating any need for Benteen's cavalry at Clarksville. After some delay, they proceeded to their new station: Chickasaw Landing on the north bank of the Tennessee River in the northwest corner of Alabama.

8

Wilson's Raid

Major General James Harrison Wilson was forced to give up two of his six remaining cavalry divisions for an operation against Mobile, Alabama, but succeeded in assembling the other four along the Tennessee River and began to drill them in preparation for a spring raid through central Alabama. For lack of horses, one division, commanded by Brigadier General Edward Hatch (the same man for whom Benteen and the 10th Missouri had hunted near Tupelo in May 1863), did not accompany the rest of the expedition. The 4th Division of the Cavalry Corps, Military Division of the Mississippi was commanded by Brigadier General Emory Upton, an intense 25-year-old West Pointer who had been seriously wounded twice in battle with the Army of the Potomac. Upton, who would eventually write the Army's manual on tactics, had two brigades in his division. The first was Brevet Brigadier General Edward F. Winslow's: Colonel John W. Noble's 3rd Iowa Cavalry (948 men), Lieutenant Colonel John H. Peters's 4th Iowa Cavalry (872 men), and Lieutenant Colonel Frederick W. Benteen's 10th Missouri Cavalry (551 men). The second brigade was commanded by Brevet Brigadier General Andrew J. Alexander. (General Upton would later marry Mrs. Alexander's sister.)

"All that winter Wilson's troopers had been undergoing an intensive training program, designed to bring the corps to its highest possible level of combat efficiency." They performed mounted and dismounted drills, practiced with the saber and stood in line to be issued the 7-shot Spencer repeating carbine. Wilson's 23 cavalry and mounted infantry regiments thus had unprecedented firepower. Rains and swollen creeks postponed the start of the raid, which was to coincide with Grant's final offensive against Petersburg.

Finally, on 22 March 1865, the three divisions under General Wilson's personal command were able to march. Captain Charles F. Hinricks, a 37-year-old German immigrant commanding L Company (10th Missouri), kept a very detailed diary of the raid. He reported that on the second day out (23 March) Captain William J. DeGress, commanding a division foraging party, had a skirmish with Confederate guerrillas, capturing 75. The divisions were split up because the country through which they marched had been scoured of forage for three years. Upton's 4th Division alone followed the same general line of march that Colonel Cornyn had followed in 1863 during his daring raid toward Courtland. They turned away from the Memphis and Charleston Railroad just west of Tuscumbia (another old 10th Missouri battleground) and struck out through the pitch pine woods of northwest Alabama toward the little town of Jasper. They crossed several rivers and streams without bridges, always a dicey proposition with Civil War era cavalry. On one occasion, crossing the Black Warrior River, Hinricks related: "A band was playing & whenever a boy would reach shore in safety the boys would send up a shout. Lots of mules & horses were drowned, but only a few men, however hundreds of them got a good dunking, but saved themselves, by holding to the tails of the animals." There was frost on the ground in the mornings and it rained heavily at night. The men of the 10th Missouri rode with wet clothing and blankets, resignedly.

On 28 March Upton's division reached Jasper only to find that one of the other divisions had beaten them to the place. They hurried on to Elyton (now Birmingham) and destroyed the iron works there. After Elyton, the route became almost directly south, headed for their main objective: Selma. They crossed the Cahaba River by rebuilding the flooring of a partially destroyed bridge with railroad ties. By 31 March, they had reached Montevallo.

"At sunrise, the 10th Missouri Cavalry was in the saddle & by itself underway, on a mission of destruction." About five miles south of the town near the hamlet of Brierfield, Lieutenant Colonel Benteen captured an iron works called the Bibb Naval Furnace with a portion of his regiment and held it against a superior force of Brigadier General Philip D. Roddey's Confederates sent there expressly to defend it. Benteen considered this "the boldest act of his life." Others agreed that it was audacious under the circumstances. Captain Hinricks reported: "Had we but known our situation at the time, we might have wished ourselves away from there, for our whole command did not number over 300 men & it was divided into two squadrons several miles distant, in order to destroy the works. And yet the enemy had between 6 & 7000 there & allowed us without opposition to destroy a million & ½ worth of property." Benteen's Fighting Tenth retired to Montevallo. They unsaddled and were attempting to indulge in a much-earned rest when General Roddey, reinforced, suddenly attacked Montevallo. Benteen's pickets were driven in, but Colonel Noble's 3rd Iowa galloped to their rescue, driving the Confederates back. Actually, the main thrust of Roddey's attack had fallen on a division further to the west, but was beaten back there too. The retreating Confederates used every rail fence between Montevallo and Randolph to slow up the pursuit and the going was rough. "This is a most cruel fighting," Hinricks complained. General Upton reported that 100 Confederates were captured at the battle of Montevallo. That night, Lieutenant General Nathan Bedford Forrest took personal command of the Rebel forces and prepared for a fight south of Randolph near the crossroads called Ebenezer Church.

General Upton's division was sent on by-roads to the east, hoping to flank the retreating defenders of Alabama and leaving the main advance to another division. They almost missed the battle of Ebenezer Church on 1 April. Forrest had managed to get a line formed to meet the fast-moving Union cavalry divisions and the brunt of the fighting was borne by another division while Upton's meandered around Forrest's right flank. About 4:00 in the afternoon, General Alexander's brigade rolled up Forrest's right flank by marching in from the east, followed by Winslow's Brigade. Benteen and his 10th Missouri saw little action that day, being in the rear of this left hook. General Winslow reported that his brigade arrived "just as the engagement was being decided" and pursued Forrest's men for about five miles. They nonetheless managed to capture two artillery pieces and 300 prisoners.

(That same day, in Virginia, General Grant finally managed to crack the Petersburg defenses. Major General Philip H. Sheridan, the same Captain Sheridan for whom Benteen had provided an escort in 1862, broke the Confederate lines at Five Forks, a battle that was the beginning of the end for General Robert E. Lee.)

Winslow's brigade went into camp less than twenty miles from their primary objective: Selma. They had been in motion through Alabama a scant ten days and had covered over 300 miles, an incredible record for speed. The Confederates, even led by the redoubtable

Forrest, simply could not concentrate their troops in time. That night (1 April) a story went around the campfires of Winslow's men that partially explains the ruthlessness of the Union troops in Selma the next day. Hinricks reported:

> The boys say that the enemy in the beginning of the engagement took 8 men & one Captain prisoners & afterwhile when we pushed them & they found that they could not carry them off, they deliberately shot them down like dogs. One poor fellow of the lot was shot 3 times & supposed to be dead & he fell in our hands again & made the statement. I suppose this matter will be properly investigated & if found correct, I have no doubt we will retaliate to a fearful extent, as many of our boys now swear that they will not bring in a prisoner. Tomorrow will be a warm day, I think.

Selma, Alabama, was considered the last bastion of the Confederacy. It had not been hitherto subjected to the hardships other major cities in the South had undergone. It was a rail head, a place where two major railroad lines intersected. It was also a manufacturing center, boasting employment of over 10,000 men. It had one of the largest arsenals in the Confederacy, a giant complex of 24 buildings, and a large naval gun foundry. Selma was a food and supply center for the Confederate army and the people of the Deep South. There were other factories, almost all engaged in war production: ten foundries and iron works, a nitre works, a powder mill, and shops producing edged weapons, shovels, leather gear, ammunition boxes, and many articles of apparel including uniforms.

Selma's defenses rivalled those of Richmond and Petersburg. A large parapet surrounded the city on three sides, protected by rifle pits, a ditch and a wall. Trees had been cleared for some distance in front and redoubts studded with artillery pieces commanded the approaches. There was a shorter, incomplete second line closer to the city itself. The Alabama River protected Selma from the south. On 2 April 1865, Selma seemed impregnable.

SELMA

Major General Wilson's three divisions had been effectively reduced to two. Casualties had been minimal, but detachments had sapped Wilson's strength by almost a third. One whole brigade was off on a separate mission. The remainder were used up guarding the train, captured bridges, prisoners, and so forth. As his troops moved south toward Selma, they were organized into two divisions. Brigadier General Eli Long commanded the right (west) division; Brigadier

General Emory Upton's 4th Division was on the left (east) flank. Wilson decided to storm Selma as soon as he could get his two divisions to the parapet together. He had one stroke of good fortune that had some effect on the outcome: his skirmishers captured a British-born engineer who had helped build the Selma positions. Furthermore, this engineer was quite willing to give General Wilson all the details he knew. He even drew a sketch.

General Wilson sat down with his staff and principal subordinates and hatched a bold plan. General Long was to swing in from the northwest on what was known as the Summerfield Road. Long's thrust was intended to be diversionary, to pin down as many defenders as possible. The main thrust, by Upton's 4th Division, was to be delivered straight north-to-south on what was known as the Range Line Road. The divisions moved out about 9:00 in the morning, 2 April 1865. They did encounter some opposition along the way, but were unbothered by it. They spent most of their time burning cotton and moving south.

Both divisions arrived within sight of the defenses about 2:00 p.m. General Upton had General Winslow's Brigade in the lead. In accordance with their plan, two regiments, the 10th Missouri and the 3rd Iowa, were dismounted and sent forward through a wooded area to fall into line at its edge facing the Selma defenses. One man in eight was left behind the wooded area to hold the horses. Colonel Peters' 4th Iowa Cavalry deployed, still mounted, on the road further back, out of range. General Alexander's Brigade, also mounted, remained far in the rear as a reserve for the main assault.

Captain Hinricks of L Company lay beside Colonel Benteen, talking about the prospects. Hinricks repeated some camp gossip to the effect that there were another two Union divisions deployed around the city to assist in the assault. Benteen, Hinricks ruefully recalled, "undeceived me at oncet & told me that all we could depend upon were our stout hearts and our Spencer carbines."

The attacking Union cavalrymen may have been slightly outnumbered. In any case, the Confederates were behind stout defenses of a kind Benteen's men had rarely encountered in almost four years of combat. By all the rules of conventional war, a frontal assault would have been suicide. "I must say," Hinricks confided, "that Col. Benteen had rather made me feel a little downhearted," adding: "of course, I kept what I knowed to myself & tried to look as cheerful as possible."

Forrest's defenders weren't idle. They had engaged the Union men with artillery and small arms as soon as they spotted the intruders, but no one was hit, according to the reports. They were less than a mile from the parapet.

Then it happened. About 5:00 p.m. one of Forrest's cavalry units that had been unable to get to Selma in time suddenly turned up in the *rear* of General Long's division. Long deployed two regiments to meet the unexpected threat and then decided to go ahead and launch his diversionary attack, even though Upton had not signalled that he was ready yet. To the surprise of everyone (including future historians), Long's men actually got on top and over the parapet in what was supposed to be a holding action. Upton heard the shooting and concluded (correctly) that Long had jumped the gun. He ordered the 10th Missouri and 3rd Iowa forward.

Benteen's men moved out slowly, closing the distance. When they were within a thousand yards of the parapets, General Wilson and his staff suddenly galloped up behind them.

"Go in boys! Give them hell!" they shouted. "We have the town already. General Long has the city. We are all right. Give them hell!"

Hinricks remembered: "From that moment, there was no more holding back." Benteen's men broke into a jog and advanced through a maelstrom of whistling shells and bullets. "Their rifle pits were constantly wrapped in a blue cloud," said Hinricks, "and at intervals their artillery would puff out white smoke and fire." The fire became terrific, but Benteen's men pushed on. "To our greatest astonishment, our skirmishers bounded ahead, scaled the works & waved their hats in triumph." They went to work at once clearing gaps for the mounted men who were moving up from behind at a trot. The 4th Iowa Cavalry thundered through the makeshift holes and poured into Selma. General Alexander's Brigade was right behind. Forrest's men simply folded up. The dismounted men stormed through the incomplete secondary line of forts and rifle pits while the mounted men, for the most part, simply went around. Prisoners began to arrive in droves. General Forrest himself escaped, swimming a mule across the Alabama River to the south. In less than an hour his force had ceased to exist as a fighting unit. The 10th Missouri had not lost a single man.

Inevitably, fires broke out in the captured city. By dark, "the whole horizon was illuminated. The boys were at work in town." For years afterward there were horror stories about the rapacity of the invading Yankee hordes. Private homes were broken into, fires started, civilians assaulted, and treasures plundered. Some of the stories were undoubtedly true. The fight had not lasted long enough to exhaust most of the men. The allegations about murdered Union soldiers were fresh in their minds. In front of their eyes was the infamous Selma Stockade, "where in former times so many of our unfortunate boys lingered away their lives." But, the consensus of historians has been that Selma was very kindly treated in comparison with Richmond, Petersburg, Atlanta and other captured towns. General Wilson has been generally credited with humanity and restraint. He made admirable efforts to minimize the damage to civilians and their property. General Winslow was placed in charge of the captured town. "After the first night Wilson and Winslow were quick to provide protection to those requesting it." The military targets were not spared, though. In the ensuing days, General Winslow made a concerted effort to destroy anything remotely useful to the Confederate war machine.

The victorious Union cavalrymen camped around the town, most of them too excited to sleep. General Upton reported the capture of thirteen guns, 1100 prisoners, and five battle flags, the latter exclusively the work of the 4th Iowa Cavalry. (Three men from the 4th Iowa won Medals of Honor for their work that day.) Upton's figures did not include the guns captured in the city factories or the captures of the other division. Winslow's inventory alone took up a whole page of his six page report covering the three-month campaign. According to him, there were almost a hundred artillery pieces and siege guns at various stages of completion destroyed after the battle. Ammunition seized was estimated at more than a million rounds. Considering the comparative odds at the outset and the peculiar circumstances, it was perhaps the most lop-sided victory of the Civil War.

The capture of Selma and the magnitude of the victory there was obscured throughout much of the 19th century. It got little play in the papers of the day for two simple reasons: one, the only reporters present were Southern; and two, that same day, Grant took Richmond. To these must be added a third reason accounting for the obscurity the battle of Selma had endured to this day. General Wilson had one particularly powerful enemy: Vice-President Andrew Johnson. Wilson, as chief of cavalry in Tennessee the year before, had seized some horses belonging to Johnson and would not succumb to political pressure. His post-war career suffered accordingly.

Frederick Benteen was aware of the magnitude of the victory. Its

obscurity affected *his* post-war career. He could never be convinced
that his accomplishments there (and at other places) were not equal
to or greater than the more heavily-publicized exploits of men with
whom he would later come in contact. Selma in particular (and
Wilson's Raid in general) left an indelible impression in his mind.

Benteen's men were astonished at their own success at the time.
Said Captain Hinricks: "I do not believe that had we seen, when we
made the assault, the extent of the defenses before us our hearts
would have failed us. Thank God we were ignorant." Historians have
offered many explanations for the unparalleled victory. By all the
standard measurements, the opposing forces were equal. The Union
troops, to be sure, had momentum, audacity, and a record of success
to that point. Benteen had never been in a losing battle himself,
though some of his men had. But, these intangibles must be balanced
by the formidable defenses of the city. The late S.L.A. Marshall would
not have been surprised by the explanation for the victory at Selma.
Nor would discerning military historians who have accepted Marshall's tactical ideas. The decisive factor was in a word: *fire-power*.
Not only were Wilson's Union cavalrymen armed, to a man, with
sabers and pistols, they had *repeating* carbines. The Confederates
had few, if any, repeaters to compare with the Spencers. The Union
cavalry very simply had a seven to one advantage in fire-power. This
advantage, used by audacious cavalry leaders such as Wilson, Upton,
Winslow, and Benteen, made the difference.

"In short," Captain Hinricks concluded, "it was one of the greatest
victories of the war."

The following day, Winslow's Brigade (commanded by Colonel
Noble) went on a scout to the west of the city. Winslow himself
remained in Selma supervising the destruction. His brigade was gone
for three days. Upon their return, they took turns going into the captured city to see the sights. On 8 April, Lieutenant Leslie Norman
went into town and got in very serious trouble. He "got drunk and
tractened to shoot General Winslow," reported his scandalized company commander, Captain Hinricks. "He was court-martialed that
night. Colonel Benteen, his own brother-in-law was one of the court."
(Three weeks later, Leslie Norman was allowed to resign his commission "for the good of the service.")

The next night, the 10th Missouri Cavalry crossed a makeshift
pontoon bridge over the Alabama River, headed for points south and
west. Hinricks remembered that event vividly. "The surrounding

buildings were fired to give us light. I crossed safely with my Co. about 10 o'clock p.m. The picture I beheld beggars all description. It was one of the grandest imagineable. In front was the dark river, which the bridge crossed. To our right were the burning buildings. To our left were the woods and in the rear the remains of the Arsenal and other public buildings. Part of the walls and the high chimneys stood yet. Here were a crowd of negroes of both sexes, of all colours and ages. There a crowd of confederate prisoners with their guards and besides the approaching column of mounted men. All of which and everything illuminated by the burning buildings. I cannot describe it but it was beautiful. We crossed and bade Selma and its 15 mile Breastworks farewell and encamped about 3 miles on the other shore."

(Earlier that day, unbeknownst to Benteen's men, General Robert E. Lee had surrendered his army to General Ulysses S. Grant at Appomattox Court House in Virginia.)

The following morning at daybreak, Wilson's two divisions headed east toward the Georgia state line. Winslow's Brigade was shy six companies of the 3rd Iowa Cavalry, who had remained in Selma with their Major George Curkendall as the town's Provost Marshal. The marching cavalrymen moved steadily east into the plantation-and-palmetto country of southeast Alabama. At one point, Captain Hinrick's troops stopped to banter with an aged Negro slave.

"Sambo," they asked him, "where is your massa?"

'Sambo said, 'Lord massa, the last this nigger seen of old massa was last Monday. Old Massa. . . headed down to big swamp, crying 'All done gone, Selma gone, Richmond gone too'." Hinricks' men were startled by the intelligence. "This was the first information we received about the fall of Richmond," Hinricks declared.

On 12 April Wilson's men rode unopposed into Montgomery, the first capital of the Confederacy. They had anticipated a fight, but found instead a parade. They were well received by the populace, to their surprise. "I think they were not sorry to see their chivalry driven off," Hinricks wrote, "and their town filled with the vandals from the north." The 10th Missouri stayed at Montgomery for a day.

The following day, 14 April, they took up their eastward march. They were getting cocky and a little careless. The opposition *was* rather faint-hearted. Benteen's Fighting Tenth did not bother to deploy when confronted by barricades, they simply charged. On one occasion that day, their aggressiveness netted a bridge the fleeing

Confederates were not able to burn in time, intent instead on getting out of the way. "The negroes said they went by, not running but flying, & bareheaded, throwing away their guns as they went. We heard further from a white lady that some of them cried when their captain tried to rally them for another stand."

(That night in Washington's Ford Theater, President Lincoln was shot.)

The next day, the triumphant raiders rode through the little town of Tuskegee, again astonished at the reception from erstwhile Confederates. "We saw here white ladies standing in the rain, waving their handkerchiefs, & *hurraying for Lincoln*. This is the first time that this happened (to) us. The boys cheered them as they passed."

The following day they were within striking distance of Columbus, Georgia.

Columbus was a major manufacturing center for the Confederacy throughout the war. It was not quite as major as Selma, but large and tempting nonetheless. While Columbus did have some iron works, an arsenal, and a navy yard (including a gun boat still in dock), its primary industry was textiles. They produced clothing and uniforms. There was a tannery there, some flour mills, and small local shops that specialized in such military accoutrements as bayonets, belt buckles, saddles and harnesses.

By 16 April 1865, the city's defenses were concentrated on the east side, the direction of their most recent threat: Sherman's March through Georgia. Sherman had, of course, bypassed Columbus and additional defenses were hastily erected along the western edge of its sister city across the Chattahoochee River, Girard (now Phenix City), Alabama. The river separated the two towns, spanned by no less than five bridges. Two of the bridges were railroad bridges, one was merely a foot bridge. Girard had little of commercial or military importance, but in order to cross the river into Columbus, Wilson's men had to fight their way through Girard.

COLUMBUS

About 2:00 in the afternoon, Wilson's two divisions arrived at Girard. General Long's division was kept in reserve and General Upton's division was deployed for the assault. As at Selma, General Wilson received vital information about the defenses before him from a citizen, who also provided a sketch.

Brigadier General Emory Upton sent a regiment from General

Alexander's Brigade through Girard at a gallop to see if they could seize one of the railroad bridges. They nearly took it, but were driven off by a Confederate counterattack launched from Columbus across the river. The bridge was set afire.

Simultaneously, General Upton had sent the bulk of the 10th Missouri under Captain Jeremiah F. Young (K Company) three miles north to seize another bridge near Clapp's Factory. This attempt at an easy victory was also foiled. Again, the Confederates burned the bridge just as Young's men were reaching it. Upton, somewhat frustrated, elected to advance through the northern part of Girard to strike at one of two other bridges not yet burned. These were defended by semi-concealed strongpoints just west of the river. Though Upton's men were ignorant of their extent, they had a pretty good idea where the forts were located. Upton ordered General Alexander to draw his brigade up in strength along the southwest approach and sent orders to General Winslow to launch the main assault. General Winslow could not be found.

When Winslow was finally located and his tangled-up regiments sorted out, it was after 5:00 p.m. The sun was rapidly setting behind them and the attack that been ordered could not be launched before dark. The alternative was to wait until morning, but General Wilson, brimming with confidence, ordered Upton to go ahead and launch the attack after dark. Upton was delighted.

The assault force was in position northwest of Girard by 8:00 p.m. "Leading the assault were six dismounted companies of Col. John W. Noble's Third Iowa." (The other six were garrisoning Selma under Major Curkendall.) The remainder of Noble's regiment, "guided through the dark by the white line of the Summerville Road, would strike the outer Confederate defensive positions before it encountered the main rebel line. Lieutenant Colonel Benteen's Tenth Missouri and Lt. Col. John H. Peters' Fourth Iowa, both units mounted, were in reserve and ready to ride in support of Noble's lead troops."

Upton's plan was certainly audacious. While small units had fought at night throughout the Civil War, nothing of this magnitude had ever before been attempted in darkness. The defenders of Columbus/Girard numbered more than 3000 and, thus, outnumbered Winslow's attacking brigade well over three to one. On the other hand, they *were* spread out, covering both towns and all approaches. And, they were not first-class Confederate troops of the kind Benteen's men had been facing all through the war. They were local militia, for the most part, buttressed by fragments of regular units scattered throughout Georgia and Alabama. Their commanding officer was a Prussian colonel named Leon von Zinken, but "General" Howell Cobb, lieutenant governor of Georgia, was also present. The long delay between 2:00 and 8:00 p.m. had played havoc with their nerves. They seemed to be of the opinion that the Yankee invaders were: 1) either trying to circle around, crossing the river up or down stream, to come in from the east, or 2) waiting to bring up artillery to shell them into submission. For these reasons, they were reluctant to reinforce the forts that were Winslow's targets.

Colonel Noble's dismounted men swept through the outer defenses easily. General Upton, watching, believed that the main defenses had fallen and ordered the 10th Missouri to take the 14th Street footbridge with a mounted charge. It was nearly calamitous. Benteen's men rode right by the main defenses. The withering fusillade that greeted them wrecked their formation and Benteen lost control of his galloping men in the dark.

However, two of his companies (commanded by Captain Robert McGlasson) made it to the bridge, "nearly three-quarters of a mile distant, securing it with about fifty prisoners," reported General Winslow. "This detachment passed in front and to the rear of the enemy's lines unhurt, but the officer, Captain R.B.M. McGlasson, finding his position untenable, released the prisoners and rejoined his regiment with loss of one man killed." What Winslow was referring to was McGlasson's incredible ride *around* the Confederate positions in the dark, a feat that nearly netted the bridge in the bargain. Amazingly, McGlasson's first lieutenant, Ferdinand Owen, actually crossed the bridge with a small party and attacked a Confederate battery on the other side of the river before being recalled.

"The remainder of the Tenth Missouri was now directed to prepare to fight on foot," Winslow went on in his report. "This command had, however, been thrown into much confusion by the enemy's fire, being only about 100 yards in front of their best position. The officers had done all they could, but the confusion was almost unavoidable."

Captain Hinricks' description of this phase was most graphic:

The enemy now commenced from 2 forts to treat us with shell & canister. 3 horses of my co. were killed; 2 men struck with canister. They came by the basket full. Several officers asked me to hunt for Col. (Benteen) & inform him of our whereabouts. We tried to retrace our steps, but were so mixed up that we took a

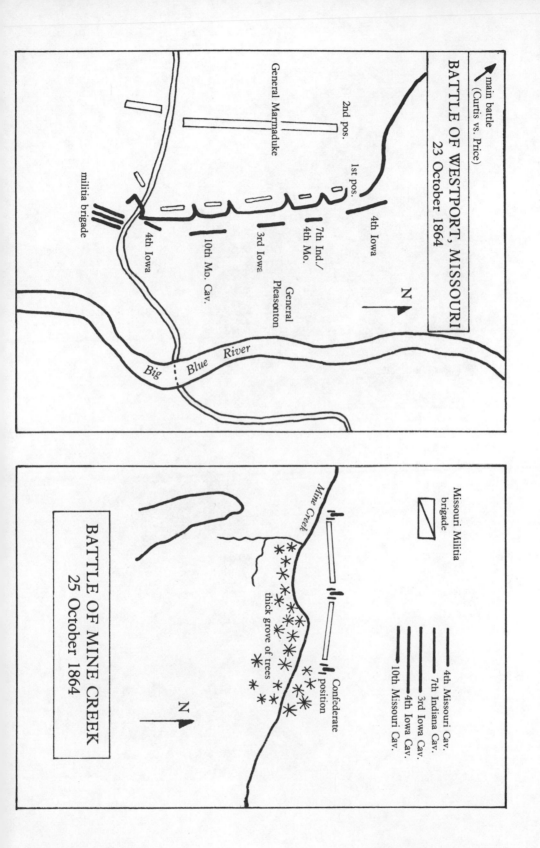

BATTLE OF WESTPORT, MISSOURI
23 October 1864

main battle
(Curtis vs. Price)

N

General Marmaduke

2nd pos.

1st pos.

militia brigade

4th Iowa

4th Iowa

10th Mo. Cav.

3rd Iowa

7th Ind./
4th Mo.

General
Pleasonton

Big   Blue   River

Missouri Militia
brigade

4th Missouri Cav.
7th Indiana Cav.
3rd Iowa Cav.
4th Iowa Cav.
10th Missouri Cav.

BATTLE OF MINE CREEK
25 October 1864

N

Mine Creek

thick grove of trees

Confederate
position

James H. Wilson

Frederick W. Benteen in 1865

road leading directly to the fort of the enemy. We did not discover this until the enemy, who had from that fort ceased firing,
sent a ½ doz. shells whizzing over our heads. We were within 60
yards of the fort & had I but known the situation at that time, I
should not have hesitated a moment to attack — even without
orders. We reformed again & were halted within less than 125
steps of the muzzles of the rebel guns. We were hardly reformed
when a solid shot struck right between us. The men stood. A second shell struck and exploded within 4 feet of my horse, covering
myself & my Comp(any) with mud. The most of the men broke
& as I could not talk to them for fear that the enemy would send
us more such customers, I found myself left with ½ doz. men.

Generals Wilson, Upton and Winslow, watching the make-shift
plan unravel before their eyes, acted with dispatch. "The flashes
puncturing the dark indicated Confederate strongpoints, and it was
toward these points that the remainder of the Third Iowa and the
Tenth Missouri as well as the Fourth Iowa were directed."

General Upton led the renewed attack himself. The men rallied
one another, "yelling 'Selma! Selma! Go for the bridge!'" Noble's 3rd
Iowa got into the forts and part of the 4th Iowa overlapped. The
inexperienced Confederate defenders panicked.

Meanwhile, Captain Hinricks had finally located Lieutenant Colonel
Benteen. "I was never so mad in my life," he fumed afterwards, "particularly as at that time the Col. (Benteen) passed & when I reported
the fact that several men were wounded and horses killed, he made
use of the expression, 'I'll give a god damn if the last god damn one
gets killed.' I think the Gentl(e)man don't know it all yet himself,
or he would not form 125 yards from a battery what had the range
as it had it, particularly when there is no need for it. My men all
wished him a speedy journey to hell."

Both men were excited. Hinricks' "several men" turned out to be
the two he had seen wounded. They were the only two 10th Missouri
men wounded at Columbus. The only man killed had been with
Captain McGlasson. Benteen had lost control of his men and, when
upbraided by Hinricks, lost control of his temper too.

While the two men were snapping at one another, a valiant company commander of the 4th Iowa (Captain Lot Abraham of D Company) had reached the footbridge. A Confederate tried to set it
afire, but one of the 4th Iowa men with Abraham shot down the
would-be arsonist. Abraham and his men rushed across the bridge
and assaulted the battery that Lieutenant Owen had been called
away from earlier. Captain Lot Abraham captured it.

Benteen got his men reorganized to lead them across the bridge in Abraham's wake. The rest of the brigade swarmed all over the Confederate strongpoints. The defenders who weren't shot down fled in all directions. "We were master of the city," Hinricks boasted. The defenders on the Columbus side, afflicted by the same panic, also folded up. By 11:00 p.m. Benteen's men had crossed the 400 yard covered bridge and fanned out into the town of Columbus. They were not opposed.

General Upton's casualties were amazingly light. He reported a total of five killed and 28 wounded in both Winslow's and Alexander's Brigades. Benteen's 10th Missouri had one killed and two wounded. The heaviest casualties were in Noble's 3rd Iowa: thirteen total. The fruits of victory were huge, but paled in comparison with the accomplishment at Selma. General Winslow, assigned to inventory the town, reported that his brigade had encountered a total of twelve artillery pieces in the fight and had captured them. General Upton said that the total of artillery pieces captured (not necessarily involved in the fight) was 24 and that 1500 prisoners had been taken. No accurate figure was ever established for the Confederate dead.

The citations were justly extravagant. The 4th Iowa headed the list. Five of their men eventually won Medals of Honor for their conduct that night. All five, as well as two men from the 3rd Iowa, were decorated within two months for captures of enemy colors under fire. These citations, coupled with similar ones for Mine Creek and Selma (as well as one awarded in the 1890s for an act of bravery at Pea Ridge in 1862), brought the total number of Medals of Honor in Winslow's Brigade to thirteen for the war, a record since unapproached.

In Benteen's 10th Missouri, Captain McGlasson and Lieutenant Owen were singled out by both Generals Upton and Winslow. General Wilson amended the official reports to include Lieutenant Colonel Benteen. "I would also request," he wrote on 7 June, "that Lieut. Col. F.W. Benteen, Tenth Missouri Cavalry, be brevetted brigadier-general for gallant and meritorious services, not only during the recent campaign in Georgia and Alabama, but for distinguished and conspicuous bravery in the pursuit of Price out of Missouri." General Wilson's request was ignored.

From this oversight has come the suggestion that Benteen was denied a deserved promotion because he was a Southerner and lacked political influence. There is no evidence to support this notion. Indeed, there is nothing in Benteen's own writings that suggest he believed this himself. At the time that General Wilson wrote the endorsement, Colonel John W. Noble had just been promoted to Brevet Brigadier General. In terms of seniority within Winslow's Brigade, Benteen was next in line. However, the war was over by then and Winslow's Brigade was in the process of being dismantled. As far as the Washington authorities were concerned, Benteen was a Missourian, a loyal Union man at that, *not* a Southerner. His promotion was denied simply because the war ended before his turn came. Had he been in another unit, or in another theater, things might have been different. On the other hand, he had advanced from a civilian sign painter to a lieutenant colonel of cavalry under circumstances that were not strictly related to proven ability. He was lucky, in one way, that he got as far as he did, what-might-have-been notwithstanding.

There is no question that by the end of his life he had come to resent this slight. Clearly, however, his being denied a general's star in 1865 was not the result of any anti-Benteen bias on anyone's part. He was highly regarded by his superiors.

The next day, 17 April 1865, in North Carolina, General Sherman and Johnston met and agreed to an armistice that effectively removed the last major Confederate army from the war. Benteen's men, seeing the sights in Columbus and assisting in the destruction of war-related goods, were unaware of the development. The following day, they were in the saddle once again as Wilson's cavalry pressed deeper into Georgia. Their next objective was Macon.

The Confederate defenders of Macon had learned of the armistice and did not oppose Wilson's advance into the city. Both sides remained under arms, edgy and waiting for confirmation of the armistice. Benteen's men rode into Macon without any feeling of hostility. They even fraternized with their erstwhile foes.

"Tell me nobody that a natural hatred exists among both parties that will last for generations," Captain Hinricks rationalized "Only a fool or a beer house soldier will ever advance that small talk. Soldiers of the field, who has fought each other on many a hot field are the ones that will fraternize first & I should not wonder at all to see those politicians as 'War to the Knife & Knife to the hilt' men at home get sound thrashings from both parties when the boys come home."

Benteen, as well as other commanders in the victorious Union Army, came face to face with a timeless problem confronting all winners of war. This problem ("Bring the Boys Home!") was aggravated in the American Civil War by the fact that the vast majority of troops under arms were volunteers, enlisted for the duration of the conflict. When the conflict finally ended, they naturally clamored for a discharge. Morale and discipline plummeted because of the certain knowledge that 'it' was all over. Having suffered and sacrificed throughout the conflict, they saw no further need for sacrifice or suffering. There immediately arose another problem that outweighed the clamoring of wives and relatives: the end of hostilities eliminated the justification for living off the land. In simple terms, this meant that Wilson's cavalry corps could no longer obtain food and forage from the populace and countryside by taking it. They were (for the first time since March) dependent on their own lines of supply. And, their bases of supply were hundreds of miles through war-devastated country in the rear. Instead of a feast, the end of the war brought a kind of famine.

On 26 April, Captain Hinricks learned (from a Southern newspaper) that President Lincoln had been assassinated, "It seems to be true," he commented. "Everybody is of the belief that the rebels don't make much by it." Two days later, Winslow's Brigade received orders to march to Chattanooga for mustering out. The orders were a trick.

The entire brigade was halted in an open field about six miles north of Macon and the officers were summoned. Hinricks reported that the officers were "marched to Genl. Winslow, Col. Benteen leading us. We found the Genl. surrounded by all the balance of the officers of our brigade. Every enlisted man was carefully kept away. The Genl. presented a letter from Major Genl. Wilson. (He) told us that it was of the most private character. It was an order to have every enlisted man searched of the whole command & everything taken away from the soldiers what did not belong to a soldiers outfit. . ."

The mass shakedown proceeded with officers searching companies not their own. "Some fellows had 5, 6 gold watches & jewelry enough to commence a store. Many of them tried to bury their spoils in the ground. Many tried to hide it effectually on their horses or persons. Some throwed things behind them. One fellow deposited two gold watches in a place — below his mare's tail, but the obstinate brute would not serve in that capacity & kicked up behind until the watches dropped, amidst the shouts of the boys." An ambulance wagon was pressed into service to hold the recovered booty and the troops, thus lightened, returned to their Macon encampment. "The boys made the best of it," Hinricks laughed. "They could by asking each other as they passed for the time of day."

Two days later they mustered for pay and official notification of the peace was given at the inevitable dress parade. The men cheered. They remained in Macon, impatient about mustering out, until 5 May, when they again received orders to march. Again, the orders were not to go home. They were to begin a scout of central Georgia to see if they could find a single fugitive: ex-Confederate President Jefferson Davis. The object of their search was rumored to have on his person millions of dollars in gold (an obvious impossibility) and a $100,000 reward on his head.

A patrol from Wilson's cavalry corps eventually did capture Davis outside Milledgeville, Georgia, but Benteen's 10th Missouri had no hand in it. Instead, they found themselves in a camp about fifteen miles from Atlanta without rations on 8 May 1865. There, about 9:00 in the morning, the troops went on strike, shouting "Hardtack! Hardtack!" over and over. By 1:00 o'clock the Army rations had arrived, meager portions of cornmeal and maggoty pork. Captain Hinricks in a high dudgeon sought out Lieutenant Colonel Benteen to register his complaint. "It didn't do any good," he recalled bitterly in the last entry of his diary. "The Gentl(eman) was busy reading a 20 cent novel & couldn't attende to the wants of they men what had made him a man."

Hinricks had a point. It was, as he put it, "a burning shame." The troops had gone without food before, but a war had been raging. They were understandably loathe to accept inadequate government rations as "the reward the soldier gets what has periled his life a hundred times for his country." On the other hand, there was nothing Benteen could do about it. He was at the mercy of the Union Army supply system and strictly forbidden to supplement its inadequacies by the traditional method of gathering what he lacked from the surrounding countryside.

Still, the running conflict with Hinricks illuminates a little of the character of the Civil War-era Benteen. He had been under the command of Major General James H. Wilson for a scant five months, but had already adopted the senior officer as a role model of sorts. Less than two years later, he would name his oldest son after General Wilson.

James Harrison Wilson had been born at Shawneetown, Illinois, to Harrison and Katherine (Schneyder) Wilson on 2 September 1837 and had graduated sixth in his class at West Point in 1860. His rise in the Army during the Civil War was meteoric. He served on the staffs of both Generals McClellan and Grant and was a brigadier general of volunteers by October 1863. As Chief of the Cavalry Bureau from January to April of 1864, he aroused the antipathy of Andrew Johnson, war-time governor of Tennessee, a fact that had repercussions after the war when Johnson suddenly became President. As Military Governor of Georgia, he became Benteen's mentor, encouraging the older man in his military ambitions and providing what assistance he could to further Benteen's career.

Wilson's biographer has described him at great length and some of the conclusions are pertinent here — in an attempt to understand Frederick William Benteen. Bear in mind that these are only conclusions of a 20th Century scholar about *Wilson* and whether or not they can be transferred to Benteen is highly debatable, but Benteen unquestionably patterned himself after Wilson.

According to Wilson's biographer, "he felt threatened not only by those trying to grasp rank or position which he himself coveted, but also by those whom he narrowly conceived to be trespassing upon his exclusive bailiwick. . . (He) displayed a curious double standard in his attitude toward authority and rank. . . He had displayed no awe toward those whom society regarded as his superiors."

"On the other hand," this modern analyst goes on,

(He) would not tolerate anyone who questioned his authority or suggested that his orders were, just possibly, ill-considered. This intolerance of criticism when exercising authority stemmed as much from his iron-handed attitude towards command as from his boundless self-esteem. . . He found it supremely difficult to forgive any wrong, tangible or imaginary. He was able to assume a neutral or casual relationship with few persons; he regarded most as either strong allies or bitter foes. . . His great virtue, as also his vexing limitation, was his firm belief that he could do things better than almost anyone else; and, for the most part, he may well have been correct.

Finally, "he was concerned about lending encouragement to his men and bolstering their morale. In the midst of battle he could be counted on to exercise a stabilizing influence by exemplifying coolness and clear thinking."

How much of Wilson's powerful personality rubbed off on Benteen may never be known. Nor is there any objective gauge of the effect of the Civil War (bloody combat, hard campaigning, prolonged absences from Kate, the feud with his father) on Benteen. One thing is morally certain, however: the proud cavalry colonel who marched his regiment into Atlanta, Georgia, on 9 May 1865 was the same character who served sixteen years as a captain in the fabled 7th Cavalry. Whatever influences had molded him were ineradicable.

9

The Atlanta Year

On 23 June 1865 Lieutenant Colonel Frederick W. Benteen was ordered to report to his new division commander in Macon: Brevet *Major* General Edward F. Winslow. Wilson's cavalry corps, the largest cavalry force ever assembled in the war, was being disbanded. Three days later, the men of the 10th Missouri were divided into two groups. Those whose enlistments were to expire before 1 October were to be mustered out at Nashville, Tennessee. Those whose enlistments were not due to expire before that date were assigned to the 2nd Missouri Cavalry (Merrill's Light Horse), commanded by Colonel Lewis Merrill. Major Williams was designated the commanding officer of the fraction who would remain in the Army a few months longer. Lieutenant Colonel Benteen was ordered to take the balance to Nashville.

Benteen's conference with Winslow brought about another change not reflected in the orders disbanding the 10th Missouri. Benteen was to be promoted to full colonel and given command of one of the newly created volunteer units. He was ordered to take the balance of the 10th Missouri to Nashville and while there find "suitable and competent officers to fill vacancies in his (new) Regiment."

Most of the Civil War soldiers wanted to go home. There *were* some who had liked their military experience well enough to want to remain in the Army. Benteen was one. The prospects of going from a lieutenant colonel in a dashing cavalry regiment to a St. Louis sign painter held no appeal for him. Actually, the prospects of the new regiment were not all that promising either, but Benteen realized that if he turned down the offer, "his chances for any future career (in the Army) would have been doomed." The regiment that he was given was created from the Negro followers of Wilson's Cavalry Corps in its march through Alabama and Georgia. They were designated the 138th USCT. (The initials stood for United States Colored Troops.) They were to garrison Atlanta.

Benteen was not exactly enamored with Negroes. While it would be a gross mistatement to assert that he despised them, he held them in pretty low esteem. His attitude, given the times and circumstances, was not at all unreasonable. Use of Negro troops was still largely experimental. Their combat record in the Civil War was spotty: excellent in some instances, marginal in many, and downright unacceptable in a few. "By the end of the war nearly 180,000 Negroes had served in the Union Army and taps had sounded over the bodies of 33,380 of them who had given their lives for freedom and Union. Despite the record there were many who still doubted that the Negro could be a first-rate combat soldier, and his future in the Army of the United States remained clouded in uncertainty."

Furthermore, Benteen was a Southerner by upbringing and had been associated with Negro slaves and servants since his infancy. He certainly did not regard them as equals. He had not considered the Civil War as a crusade to free slaves, but rather a struggle to preserve the Union and cause his "deluded Kinsmen (to) see the error of their ways." He felt that secession was a "sad infatuation" and even went so far as to assert: "Slavery wasn't the issue of the war. . . I never found one abolitionist in the northern army." While there certainly were abolitionists in the northern army, they were probably a minority — especially among the western troops with whom Benteen associated. Years later, Benteen commented that Negroes were a "race. . . that I could take no interest in — and this on account of their 'low-down' rascally character."

Nevertheless, the colonelcy of the 138th USCT was the only assignment he could hope for in the foreseeable future and he duly repaired to Nashville to recruit officers from the ranks of men in Winslow's old brigade who were mustering out. His second-in-command was George Curkendall, a former major of the 3rd Iowa who had been the Provost Marshal of Selma after its capture. His adjutant was Lieutenant John L. Walsh from the 10th Missouri. The rest of his officers he found from among the non-commissioned ranks of Winslow's men.

On 15 July 1865 at Nashville, Benteen mustered in to the new volunteer organization as a colonel. Four days later, he mustered out of the 10th Missouri. The actions were backdated so that his promotion took effect 1 July. He returned to Atlanta with enough officers to fill all but two of the ten companies authorized. (*Cavalry* regiments were authorized twelve companies and three majors; *infantry* regiments — which is what the 138th USCT became — were authorized only ten companies and one major. Both cavalry and infantry *companies* were authorized three officers each.) By 1 September, Benteen had recruited his full complement of officers and was busy drilling and training the ex-slaves who filled the ranks.

Naturally, Negro troops were not much appreciated in Atlanta. The officers who commanded them were regarded as little more than carpetbaggers. But, aside from the inevitable resentment, there were no ugly incidents and the 138th USCT's tour of duty in Atlanta was generally peaceful.

On 3 October Colonel Benteen was appointed commanding officer of the Atlanta garrison and held that position until the last day of November. On the last day of his command, he purchased 115 acres about 3½ miles south of the city that had hitherto been the Haydon Plantation. He liked Atlanta and had decided early in the fall of 1865 to make his new home there. His regiment remained in existence for only another month. On 6 January 1866, the 138th USCT was disbanded (along with most of the volunteer regiments at that time) and Benteen became a civilian once again. He went to work developing his property into a farm.

By the spring of 1866, conditions on Benteen's new property, which he later named Hermitage Heights, were sufficiently civilized to permit him to bring his wife from St. Louis to live with him. Benteen and his Negro servants were still living in tents, but he had constructed stables and corrals for his horses.

On Sunday night, 6 May, 1866, Benteen was attacked by a band of outlaws. About ten o'clock that night, Benteen was in his tent reading while Kate was busy writing letters to her friends. They heard a shot. Benteen seized up a pistol and rushed out to see what was going on. He saw three men approaching his tent, two coming directly towards him, a third angling in from the side.

"Who comes there?" he shouted. When no one answered (or stopped moving toward him), Benteen ditched his money and watch behind a bush and opened fire. The assailants, who turned out to be four in number, returned the fire and wounded Benteen in the right hip

and left calf "severely." The four men overpowered him and took his
weapon, a pocketknife, and an empty money belt. They demanded
his money, but though wounded, he refused to reveal where he had
thrown it. They then forced him to accompany them to the stables.
Benteen took them to the wrong stables at first, but upon the ruse
being discovered, was forced to accompany the robbers to the stables
where his four horses were kept. One of his Negro servants (perhaps
the only male employee) had been wounded slightly by the shot
that startled Benteen. With Benteen and his Negro looking on help-
lessly, the four men broke the door to the stables with an axe and
took the four horses, one of which had Benteen's "fine fair leather
military saddle." They fled south, accompanied by others of their
band hiding in the woods.

Benteen recovered from his wounds, as did his Negro servant, and
posted a $400 reward for his horses — to no avail. The miscreants
were obviously local men, for they knew about the horses. They might
have been ex-Confederate soldiers driven to desperation, *or* they
might have been just the usual riff-raff that plague the law-abiding
in all periods of history. They certainly provided Kate Benteen with
a memorable introduction to life on a Southern plantation.

Shortly after this incident (and perhaps as a direct result of it),
Benteen's father came to Atlanta. The elder Benteen had spent the
war years since the capture of the *Fair Play* as a prisoner of war.
He had been released by the war's end, aged and in ill health, as yet
unaware of the role his son had played in his imprisonment in the
summer of '62.

Fred Benteen "reconciled" with his father and made him the mana-
ger of the newly-purchased farm. Benteen himself was physically
unable to undertake the chores for a few weeks, but the reconciliation
was only incidently related to his need for a competent overseer or
even an obligation to his father's support. Benteen was looking to
the future.

The summer of 1866 found the U.S. Congress in the throes of passing a new act of legislation that would expand the Regular Army
and fill in its officer ranks with men who had served with distinction
during the Civil War. Benteen had exercised his option by accepting
the colonelcy of the 138th USCT. He was thinking seriously about
a career in the Regular Army.

The Army Act passed on 28 July 1866, creating thirty new regiments
of which four were cavalry. Two of the four were to be filled with

Negro recruits — the 9th and 10th Cavalry regiments. The other two, the 7th and 8th Cavalry regiments, were to be filled with white recruits. All four of the new cavalry regiments raised were to muster in out West and serve on the Plains against Indians.

In September of 1866, Benteen applied for a Regular Army commission in one of the new cavalry regiments. He provided the essential credentials: at least two years of service as an officer in the Civil War army and letters of recommendation from high-ranking officers and politicians who knew of his character. Among those recommending Benteen for a commission were Generals Curtis, Pleasonton, and Upton as well as the mayor of St. Louis and the governor of Missouri.

In 1891, Benteen told a correspondent that in 1866 he could have gone into the 10th (Colored) Cavalry as a major, but preferred a captaincy in the 7th Cavalry. From this off-hand remark has come the tale that Benteen turned down a major's commission in 1866. There is no documentation to support this. According to the correspondence still extant in Benteen's A.C.P. files in Washington, he was offered a commission as captain in the 7th Cavalry — and promptly accepted. What the paperwork does not indicate now (if it ever did) was whether or not Benteen might have been commissioned a major in the 10th Cavalry. The offer that he implied he had turned down was apparently never committed to paper, but this is certainly not proof that it never existed. His admission in 1891 was made ruefully and he did accept a majority in a colored regiment seventeen years later with minimal reluctance.

Benteen had no earthly reason for making up a tale that could: a) make himself look rather foolish, and b) be readily disproved. Apparently, there was an unofficial offer (perhaps verbal) in 1866. Exactly who made the offer, exactly what the offer was, and the attendant circumstances may never be known.

On 24 November 1866, Benteen wrote to Secretary of War Edwin M. Stanton accepting a captain's commission in the 7th Cavalry. He was ordered by the Adjutant General's office to report for duty with his new regiment — at Fort Riley, Kansas.

Benteen spent the next six weeks making preparations. His father would manage the farm. Kate, about six months pregnant, would remain in Atlanta until suitable quarters could be obtained for her out West. Benteen apparently assumed that it would be spring before he could have Kate brought to her new home on the Plains, which would give her the benefits of a civilized Atlanta at least until the baby was born and old enough to travel. There was never any question that she would eventually join him, in contrast to their prolonged separations during the Civil War.

In January 1867, Benteen boarded a train and departed for the 7th Cavalry headquarters at Fort Riley. He would remain with the 7th for the next sixteen years.

10

The 7th Cavalry in Kansas

Fort Riley, Kansas, located at the junction of the Republican and Smoky Hill rivers, was "a post consisting of six magnesium limestone two-story barracks built around a parade ground nearly 600 feet square" in January of 1867 when Frederick William Benteen stepped off a Union Pacific passenger car and saw it for the first time. Fort Riley had been established in the spring of 1853 and named in honor of a forgotten Army colonel. On 29 January, when Benteen arrived, its garrison consisted of one company from the 37th Infantry and six companies of the newly-organized 7th Cavalry.

Cavalry officers from other regiments had filled in while the officers assigned to the 7th made their individual appearances. The companies had filled up to almost overflowing. The long delay by Washington in filling the officer ranks meant that the enlisted men had to wait for months for their commanding officers to show up. Benteen was assigned command of H Company, which had 71 men the day he arrived. (M Company, the only company in the regiment with a larger complement of enlisted men, had 76.) H Company had been commanded by 1st Lieutenant Samuel Hildeburn of the 3rd Cavalry prior to Benteen's arrival and he remained with Benteen for over a month before rejoining his own regiment.

Benteen remarked that he arrived at the post "not quite an orphan and unknown." The commanding officer of the 7th Cavalry (and, indeed, of the entire District of the Upper Arkansas that extended west to New Mexico Territory) was Colonel Andrew Jackson Smith, a tough, 52-year-old former dragoon officer who had risen to the rank of major general during the Civil War. It was this same A.J. Smith who had commanded Benteen's 10th Missouri at the battle of Tupelo in July of 1864 and who had witnessed the pursuit of Price in Missouri that fall. The officer chosen to be Smith's aide-de-camp and who was filling in as the commanding officer of I Company of the 7th Cavalry was Captain Henry E. Noyes of the 2nd Cavalry. Captain Noyes had been Major General James H. Wilson's aide-de-camp on the raid through Alabama and Georgia in 1865. Both men knew Benteen personally and by reputation. The *post* commander at Fort Riley (and lieutenant colonel of the 7th Cavalry) was George Armstrong Custer. He had never seen or heard of Benteen. For that matter, Benteen had never seen Custer before, though he couldn't help but have heard of the Boy General.

George A. Custer had been born in Ohio in 1839, making him Benteen's junior by five years. He had graduated from West Point in the second class of 1861 and been commissioned a second lieutenant in the 5th Cavalry. Within a year, he was a staff captain assigned to General McClellan's Army of the Potomac headquarters. In June of 1863, Captain Custer was suddenly elevated to the rank of brigadier general of volunteers by the same Major General Pleasonton who had commanded Benteen and was given the justly-famed Michigan Cavalry Brigade. In this capacity, he rose to a prominence exceeded by few generals of the war. (He was *not* the youngest brigadier general of the war. At least two others vied for that distinction, Dodge and Pennypacker. But two years after his first dramatic promotion, Custer became the second youngest major general in American history.) Custer ended the war commanding a division of cavalry that blocked Lee's retreat at Appomattox and led directly to the famous surrender near there. After the war, Custer commanded the cavalry forces of the army that was rushed to Texas for occupation duty and to menace the French-backed government of Mexico. The end of the volunteer organization in 1866 that had taken away Benteen's colonelcy made Custer a mere captain in the 5th Cavalry. The Army Act creating the new regiments soon brought him rapid promotion, but by declining command of the 9th (Colored) Cavalry, he was only elevated to lieutenant colonel.

Custer was almost 27 years old when he joined his 7th Cavalry regiment at Fort Riley in November of 1866. He was a tall man with thinning blond hair worn long. He was possessed of a nervous energy that either grated on the nerves of those around him or else fascinated them endlessly. He was, by all accounts, a brave and competent officer, fully capable of leading a regiment of cavalry. Custer was a teetotaller, a rather homely-faced man who spoke with a noticeable stammer when excited. His wife of a couple of years, Elizabeth Bacon Custer, accompanied him and was present when Benteen arrived. "Libbie" Custer was a small, sweet-faced woman, less than 24 years of age, and one of the very few officers' wives who accompanied her husband wherever permitted, accommodations or none.

On 30 January 1867 at Custer's quarters in Fort Riley, Benteen paid the customary courtesy call and met for the first time the man who would become his nemesis. They didn't hit it off at all. Custer, as was his wont, monopolized the conversation. He trotted out his scrapbook to impress his new subordinate with his successes in the late war. Benteen was not favorably impressed. When Custer showed his valedictory order composed for his old 3rd Cavalry Division, Benteen thought that it "abounded in bluster, brag and gush." Benteen was especially offended by what he regarded as a slight of *his* former commanding general, James Harrison Wilson. What exactly Custer said at that meeting has never been recorded. He undoubtedly meant well. Unfortunately, Custer and Wilson had been rivals and Custer was noted for his sarcastic manner of speaking. It is almost certain that at some point in his monologue, he made a deprecatory comment about Wilson. Benteen, having fought what he justifiably felt was the greatest cavalry campaign of the war under Wilson, took offense.

Benteen offered to show the Custers General *Wilson's* valedictory order. Mrs. Custer, apparently more alive to the undercurrents than her husband, cut in quickly with a diplomatic remark to the effect that "Genl. Wilson wrote beautifully." "They must, after reading same," Benteen later observed, "have seen what was in my mind's eye."

The visit ended with some irreparable damage done. Benteen *never* completely overcame a sense of resentment. He did not seem to resent Custer's superior rank. The aspects of the visit that he recalled years later and that never stopped rankling were Custer's egotism and lack of regard for Benteen's hero, Wilson.

"Well," Benteen concluded, "the impression made on me at that interview was not a favorable one. I had been on intimate personal relations with many great generals and had heard of no such bragging as was stuffed into me that night." It wasn't the low point in the Custer-Benteen relationship by any means, but it was a bad beginning.

Not long afterwards, in late February, Benteen was invited back to the Custer residence for a more informal get-together. This time, there was no stilted conversation. The occasion was a poker game. Initially, the ante was a dime and the game progressed unremarkably with two of the five officers eventually dropping out. Mrs. Custer watched the proceedings with amusement as Custer proceeded to win. "Now, Autie," she told him, "you must give them their money back." Custer did no such thing, of course, and as soon as Libbie had retired for the evening he raised the ante to $2.50. Benteen, Custer, and 1st Lieutenant Thomas B. Weir, who had served under Custer in Texas, were the only hands left in the game. They both agreed to the raise in stakes. Benteen observed that as long as the game was dime ante, it was still a gentleman's game, but that when the ante went up so steeply, that "all friendship has got to cease, or one is apt to find himself pretty well begrimed and a long way from water quite early in the game." By reveille, Benteen had collected the pot and a $150 IOU from Lieutenant Weir besides. The loss didn't seem to bother Custer — or Weir (who Benteen asserted never paid his debt), but it gave Benteen a gloating revenge for the unsatisfactory interview of the previous visit. From that day forward, he regarded Custer as a rotten poker player.

The 7th Cavalry in February 1867 consisted of all twelve of its authorized companies, though only 25 of its 44 authorized officers had reported for duty. That month, two of the six companies stationed at Fort Riley departed for other posts in Kansas. By the end of February, the regiment could report that four companies were assigned to Riley (A, D, H, M), two were assigned to Fort Harker (F, G), one was at Fort Hays (E), one was at Fort Wallace (I), one was at Fort Dodge (K). The remaining three were assigned to posts in eastern Colorado: two at Fort Lyon (B, C) and one at Fort Morgan (L). *At no time* prior to the Little Big Horn campaign of 1876 were all twelve companies united in one location. This was a typical arrangement for frontier cavalry regiments.

The senior major of the regiment, Alfred Gibbs, commanded the post at Fort Harker. Major Gibbs, a pre-war Dragoon captain, was the officer who organized the regimental band (Another officer, believed by some to have been Captain Myles Keogh of I Company, introduced the Irish carousing song, *Garryowen,* as the regimental march.) The only other major then assigned to the regiment was Major Wickliffe Cooper, who had commanded the 4th Kentucky Cavalry regiment on Wilson"s Raid in 1865. A third major was in the process of being assigned. He was Joel H. Elliott, a 26-year-old

former school administrator who had served with distinction as a
company commander in the 7th Indiana Cavalry regiment during the
war. (The 7th Indiana had been part of Karge's Brigade in 1864
and a portion of that regiment was assigned to Winslow's for the
Price Raid. Benteen had commanded some of the 7th Indiana for a
few weeks, but Joel Elliott was not among them.) Elliott had applied
for a commission early in 1866 and expected to be made a lieutenant
or, at best, a captain. To his utter astonishment (not to mention the
puzzlement of future historians), he was offered the junior majority
in the 7th Cavalry. The explanation is simply that the War Department lost his paperwork until all the commissions below that rank
had been awarded and when confronted by Elliott's powerful sponsor,
Governor Oliver P. Morton of Indiana, had hastily "found" a vacancy
for Elliott. There is little evidence that the officers of the 7th, including Benteen, resented Custer's appointment to lieutenant colonel, even
though three (Thompson, Robeson, and West) had also been generals
in the Union Army. There *was* some initial resentment, understandably, at Elliott's elevation. One company commander went so far as
to accuse Elliott of "bad management" when engaged in a later campaign, but Eliott's personality was sufficiently winning to mute any
serious criticism. He became genuinely popular with the erstwhile
generals and colonels he commanded and became a fast friend of
Benteen's in particular.

With the departure of Lieutenant Hildeburn in March, Benteen
was the only officer in H Company and would remain the only one
until late in September. One of the other companies at Riley (M)
that would be closely associated with Benteen's H Company for many
years to come had two officers: 1st Lieutenant Owen Hale, a former
lieutenant in the 7th New York Cavalry, and 2nd Lieutenant William
W. Cooke, a former lieutenant in the 24th New York Cavalry. H & M
Companies, which would become sister companies in the regiment,
were the largest of the twelve.

Lieutenant Cooke, a tall, handsome officer sporting enormous dun-
dreary sidewhiskers, was acting as the post adjutant when Benteen
arrived. The *regimental* adjutant was 1st Lieutenant Myles Moylan,
the erstwhile sergeant-major of the regiment. Libbie Custer later
asserted that the other officers initially would have nothing to do with
Moylan,even refusing to eat with him. There is no question that many
(especially Benteen) had no great regard for the splendidly mus-
tachioed Moylan, who had been an enlisted man in the Regular Army

before the war. In fact, he had been the first sergeant/acting commander of the small dragoon company that had supported Major Sturgis at Wilson's Creek in 1861. Moylan had been promoted from the ranks to second lieutenant in the 5th Cavalry. He had advanced steadily to the rank of captain before being abruptly dismissed from the army in October of 1863 for visiting Washington, D.C., without authorization. Promptly re-enlisting as one "Charles Thomas" in the 4th Massachusetts Cavalry, he had regained his former rank and had been brevetted major. He turned up in Kansas in 1866 as a private in the newly-formed 7th. Custer, who had known Moylan well in the old 5th, promoted him to sergeant-major and championed his application for a commission. Moylan encountered some difficulty, not so much from his blemished record as from his inability to pass the required oral exam. Custer exerted influence and Moylan was allowed to take the examination over. He passed the second time and was commissioned a *first* lieutenant. Custer made him the regimental adjutant.

The explanations customarily given for Moylan's unpopularity are unsatisfactory. Benteen hinted in later years that Moylan was suspected of enriching himself from the proceeds of government property to the tune of "$30,000," but his information for this accusation came from Lieutenant Aspinwall in 1873. Benteen had no inkling of any alleged dishonesty in 1867. Some have suggested that Moylan's dismissal tainted him with an unvoiced charge of cowardice, but there is no evidence to support this. Benteen very plainly stated that prior to the battle of the Little Big Horn (1876), he had "accredited (Moylan) in my mind with having some nerve." (Furthermore, Moylan won a Medal of Honor ten years later.) Others have pointed to Moylan's close association with Custer as grounds for his ostracism, but that makes no sense. Custer himself was probably *not* intensely disliked by the majority of his officers at any time in his career and certainly not in 1867. In fact, most of the officers at Riley in '67 were very much pro-Custer and would remain so all their lives: Captain Hamilton of A Company, Lieutenant Weir of Custer's staff, Lieutenant Cooke also of Custer's staff, and Custer's own younger brother, Tom, of A Company and the acting regimental quartermaster. Of the three officers remaining who were stationed at Riley at the time, only Benteen was noted for his anti-Custer feelings. Clearly, Moylan's close association with Custer had nothing to do with his being ostracised by the others.

There is a slight possibility that Moylan was unpopular because of his role as the adjutant. Yet, while it is evident that Cooke (Moylan's eventual successor as regimental adjutant) suffered a loss in popularity because of his job, even Cooke remained one of the boys until his death. *His* successor, George D. Wallace, was downright popular.

Libbie's assertion that Moylan was discriminated against because he had been an enlisted man is rather disingenuous. *Most* of the officers at Fort Riley in 1867 had been enlisted men at one time or another. In fact, aside from Custer himself, only two (Benteen and Lieutenant Samuel M. Robbins of D Company) had *not* been enlisted men at one time. There is no record of *any* former enlisted man promoted to officer grade being shunned by other officers in the history of the 7th Cavalry while Benteen was assigned to it. And, there was a multitude of former enlisted men made officer during those years.

The answer to Moylan's unpopularity cannot be found in the existing records. The only suggestion that has any merit in logic or in fact is the possibility that Myles Moylan was in some unspecified way an obnoxious individual. Perhaps he had bad table manners or an unpleasant body odor or was guilty of any one of a number of trivial, but delicate, crimes against society. Whatever the reason, Moylan was not well-liked, though he seems (with Custer's help) to have overcome the social barrier and in time became an accepted member of the officer corps.

Moylan once borrowed a horse from Benteen, "a very prettily made black horse whose skin shone like satin" named Midnight. He thought it would look grand at parades to be seen astride such a fine looking horse. Benteen loaned him the use of Midnight readily enough, but neglected to point out that the horse "couldn't stand the clanking and beating" of a saber scabbard. The reason Benteen did not divulge this potentially important fact was only incidentally related to his dislike of Myles Moylan. "There is an unwritten law in the cavalry," he later explained, "that when an officer is thrown from his horse while on duty, champagne must be forthcoming for the whole outfit at his expense." Benteen and his friends, knowing that the horse would try to spill its rider, "watched the situation with great interest," but Moylan had the last laugh. Midway through a parade, realizing that something had not been told him about the horse, Moylan received permission to exchange horses and returned to the parade field on his old mount. "We 'got no wine' from him that day," Benteen recalled.

One of the other officers at Fort Riley when Benteen arrived, whose company changed station in February, was 1st Lieutenant David W. Wallingford, the same Wallingford who had been a lieutenant in Jennison's Jayhawkers at the battle of Westport. Wallingford, who had originally been dismissed from the Union Army for pillage, was also unpopular. In fact, *he* was never accepted and was eventually forced out of the 7th for consorting with prostitutes and for general drunken behavior not considered conducive with the standards set for army officers.

Historians have provided lists of reasons for the deployment of the 7th Cavalry in Kansas and eastern Colorado in the spring of 1867, but the sum of them all is one word: Cheyenne. There were other Indian tribes, to be sure, but none in the 7th Cavalry's area of operations were as challenging as the Southern Cheyenne, whose land prior to the Civil War had been western Kansas and eastern Colorado. They were an Algonquian tribe of American natives (mistakenly, but persistently, dubbed "Indians"). The Cheyenne had been forest-dwelling Indians with home ranges around the Great Lakes area until about the year 1700. Then, pressured by hereditary enemies who had acquired firearms from French traders, they migrated south and west onto the western plains. They acquired horses and became a nomadic band of hunters who thrived on the animals of the plains, especially the buffalo.

The homeland of the Southern Cheyenne and their allies, the Arapaho, was unfortunately located for their future happiness. The old Santa Fe trade trail ran right through it. Then, in 1858, gold was discovered in eastern Colorado, bringing hordes of white miners and settlers through Cheyenne land. The Cheyenne, in common with most Indian tribes in North America, thrived in a world that was ecologically stable. They strove to adapt to nature, moving their homes when the grass was in danger of being overgrazed and the water polluted or drained low. They were efficient in terms of ecology, wasting little and taking, for the most part, only what they needed to sustain themselves. The white newcomers were from an entirely different culture, one which thrived on the exploitation of nature and they customarily took more than they needed in hopes of selling the surplus for a profit. These two cultures inevitably came into conflict.

The Cheyenne (and other Indian tribes) claimed with justification that the white men were upsetting the delicate balance of nature, threatening the existence of the Indians. To make matters worse, the Plains Indians in particular had adopted a life style that placed great emphasis on raiding. They took great pride in stealing up on unsuspecting foes (or game) and taking their needs by surprise or stratagem. The whites, understandably, saw this as stealing, plundering and marauding. To the Indians, especially the Cheyenne, all was fair in war and raiding. The most objectionable aspect of the Plains Indian culture in the eyes of the white interlopers was their treatment of captive women and children. The children were carried off to be raised as replacements for young Indians killed by enemies or disease. The women were made slaves, kept alive as long as they were strong enough to work or as long as there was hope of securing a good price as a ransom for their release. The Plains Indians were rather unique in the respect that they customarily gang-raped women prisoners. This was perhaps the least defensible aspect of Indian "culture" in the eyes of the Victorian Age whites. To the Indians, it was probably little more than a mix of business and pleasure, an effective technique of establishing superiority early in the captivity and insuring the docility of the prisoner. To the whites, it was barbarism pure and simple.

The Civil War stemmed the westward expansion only marginally. The Cheyenne, though uneducated, were not stupid. They could see that the white culture with its plots of land, wagons bearing supplies, and herds of domesticated animals seriously upset the ecological balance and threatened the natural habitat of the buffalo. The last straw was the railroads. The iron rails in themselves did not prevent the buffalo from roaming north to south, but the moving trains and crowds of railroad builders they brought severely restricted the movements of the buffalo. The Cheyenne tried at first to stop the railroads from coming through their land. They were unsuccessful.

The Cheyenne could not understand white values. They reacted with a campaign of petty harrassment that focused on isolated ranches, stage stations and railroad construction crews. They did not confront the railroad directly. (Indeed, it is hard to see how they could, even had they decided on such a course of action.) But, the stolen cattle and horses, burned homes, captive women and children, and even the occasional dead body did *not* cause the whites to pause and count the cost. It only made them madder and more determined to prevail.

In the end, it was the need for security of the railroads and their construction crews that brought the Army to Kansas in large numbers. Despite all the brave talk at the time (and since) about defending white civilization and protecting the poor, defenseless settlers, it was the powerful railroad lobby that got government protection. The Union Pacific Railroad was being constructed west from Omaha along the Platte River in Nebraska. A separate branch called the Eastern Division of the Union Pacific was being constructed from Kansas City west to Denver. (In late 1868, this Eastern Division was reorganized as the Kansas Pacific, but by that time, its westward progress had taken it through Kansas and the end of the serious threat to its existence from Indians.)

The Army troops in Kansas, especially the long-range cavalry regiments, were concentrated in forts along the southern boundary of the railroad right of way. The infantry troops provided most of the actual security for the railroad crews. The cavalry regiments, primarily the 7th in Kansas, formed a strategic strike force for penetrating the Indian lands in pursuit of hostile raiders. For these reasons, the cavalry was split up in companies from east to west most of the time. When an expedition was planned, the scattered companies would concentrate. By early 1867, the southern and westernmost posts were nowhere near a railroad. Rather, they were outposts, intended to serve as supply points for whatever expedition happened to be operating in their neighborhood *or* observation posts for Indian activity.

The Cheyenne had been victims of a frontier sneak attack on one of their encampments near Fort Lyon, Colorado, in 1864. This incident, the Sand Creek Massacre, had made them wary of white men wearing blue uniforms. They made no distinction between state volunteer troops (who had perpetrated the Sand Creek Massacre) and Regular Army regiments, such as the 7th Cavalry, which took their orders from a more remote Washington. Soldiers were soldiers to the Cheyenne. They had their own "soldiers," too: a loose organization of young warriors called the *Hotamitanio* (Dog Soldier Society). The military prowess of the Cheyenne Dog Soldiers was proverbial. Benteen later categorized them as "good shots, good riders, and the best damn fighters the sun ever shone on."

Benteen's attitude toward his Indian opponents was typical of that of an Army officer who was compelled to deal with them on a regular basis. Warriors of any society often find mutual respect among their enemies. This phenomenon is nearly universal and was touched upon by Captain Hinricks of the 10th Missouri in his rationalization for fraternizing with Confederates. Benteen fought Indians skillfully, even relentlessly at times, but he had a higher regard for them as human beings than he had for many of his fellow whites, especially politicians.

"I cannot say that I have had much heart in warring on Indians," he said, "for I have always been impressed with the belief that they were more sinned against than sinning." He *did* believe in compelling them to adapt to the white man's culture. He was certainly not alone in his belief. He told a newspaper reporter: "I think if the management of the Indians was turned over to the Army there would be none of those disastrous wars with which we are afflicted under the present system. The redskins would be honestly dealt with, and in a couple of years would be as easily managed as the same number of white men. If they were treated more considerately and received what the government allows them, I think there is no doubt they would be perfectly peaceable and tractable." The idea that administration of Indian affairs should be the Army's province did not originate with Benteen, of course. He was merely parroting what had become the party line of the professional soldiers who saw the graft and corruption of Indian agents as the root of all the evil. But Benteen went beyond the superficial protestations that were typical of frontier Army officers. He frequently invited his Indian friends into his home and made an effort to learn their language. He did not hesitate to eat with them (in sharp contrast to the unfortunate Myles Moylan.) "I noticed, too, something which I must confess brought a tinge of shame to my cheeks," he recalled after one such occasion, "and that was before eating, the chiefs looked heavenwards and mumbled something indistinctly (which I had neglected, and which I habitually neglected). After the meals, when their pipes were lighted, the same ceremonies were repeated, only in a language without words, the first two or three puffs being sent upwards to the Great Spirit, and the stem of the pipe then solemnly downwards to the 'grass that grows and the water that runs.' But, still, to our *fin de siecle civilization*, these people are thought of as heathens."

"We should treat the Indian as if he possessed some natural feeling," Benteen concluded. But that thought was the product of a 25-year career in the West. "When I accepted a captaincy in the 7th Cavalry," he remembered, "I had no idea whatever of remaining permanently, but was taken to it from the fact that the Indians seemed to have things pretty nearly their own way, and I knew that cavalry, well handled, should more than 'stand them off," which wasn't then being done."

Even after pitched battles with Indians and seeing first hand their depredations on helpless settlers and families, Benteen could not bear a grudge. He would have heartily concurred with the sentiment expressed by his good friend, Captain Tom McDougall, years later. McDougall spoke of the men "who were at one time my most hated enemy," declaring: "Poor human fellows, they did what all of us would have done, so I long ago forgave them from the bottom of my heart." Benteen said simply: 'I am not an Indian hater by a good deal."

By March 1867, the military heirarchy had come to the conclusion that a show of force was in order to overawe the recalcitrant Indians and compel them to submit to reservation life and leave the railroads alone. Major General Winfield S. Hancock, the department commander, resolved to march on the Indian encampments with a large force of combined cavalry, infantry, and artillery and demonstrate to the Indians the wisdom of ending hostilities peacefully as well as the Army's determination (and the means) for ending them violently if peace was not attained.

In the meantime, the Senate had approved awards of brevets to officers of the Regular Army for gallant, meritorious, or otherwise faithful services in the Union Army during the late war. *Brevets* were a curiosity of 19th century America and frequently caused confusion to the uninitiated. Brevets were essentially decorations — in lieu of medals. They were "promotions" to higher ranks than those actually held by the recipient. They entitled the recipient to be addressed by a title higher than the rank he really held and, for a time, entitled him to actually wear the insignia of that higher rank. In certain instances (rarely), the officer was even entitled to draw pay based on his brevet rank. Benteen was awarded two brevets for his Civil War services: major for Mine Creek and lieutenant colonel for Columbus. Thus, from the spring of 1867 on, Benteen was known to his contemporaries as "Colonel" Benteen, even though he remained a captain until 1882.

Most officers who had served in the Civil War were also awarded brevets. Custer, for example, was made a Brevet Major General and it is for this reason that he is known to history as "General" Custer even though he died a lieutenant colonel. Brevet awards were not consistent and not entirely fair, which generated a good deal of resentment among officers who felt they had been slighted. There was absolutely no correlation between rank held in the Civil War and brevet rank, contrary to popular interpretation. Lieutenant Cooke, for example, was never anything higher than a lieutenant throughout his army career, both during and after the war. Yet, he was brevetted a lieutenant colonel for bravery in several actions in the Civil War and died as "Colonel" Cooke.

Brevet rank had absolutely no bearing on seniority. A brevet colonel did not necessarily outrank a brevet major. Nor did a lieutenant such as Cooke, who was a brevet lieutenant colonel, necessarily outrank a lieutenant who had no brevet rank at all. Seniority remained established by Army list: up to the grade of major, it was established within the regiment, usually by date of appointment. Majors and colonels had their own seniority list within the *branch* of service to which they belonged (cavalry, infantry, artillery, etc.). Generals were appointed and promoted by the President with the advice and consent of the Senate. The seniority lists were well established and known. Benteen is frequently characterized as the senior captain of the 7th Cavalry. He was *not* — until 1875. He was junior to several other captains in 1867 and could not hope to be promoted to major until he became one of the senior captains of cavalry. It took him sixteen years to reach eligibility for major, based on the seniority system. (As a matter of fact, shortly after the brevets were conferred and Benteen became Colonel Benteen, *Captain* Albert P. Morrow — who had no brevets at all — was promoted to major.)

The Hancock War

General Hancock led his expedition out of Fort Riley on 27 March 1867, headed for a rumored congregation of Cheyenne and Sioux in the neighborhood of Fort Larned. The four companies of the 7th Cavalry at Riley (A, D, H, M) went with him under the command of Lieutenant Colonel Custer.

That same day, Kate Benteen gave birth to their first son in Atlanta. The boy was named Frederick Wilson Benteen in honor of his father and his father's Civil War hero, General J.H. Wilson. As events proved, "Freddie" Benteen was the only one of five children to survive childhood. But, it would be eleven months before his proud father first laid eyes on him.

Hancock's force reached Fort Harker (near present-day Ellsworth) on 1 April. There, Hancock's six infantry companies, one artillery battery, and four cavalry companies were joined by two more 7th Cavalry companies: F & G. A week later, the enlarged force reached the Indian agency near Fort Larned (near present-day Larned). Companies E & K of the 7th joined them there.

At Fort Larned, General Hancock invited the chiefs (of what was believed to be 10,000 Indians) to a pow-wow. Few turned up, however, pleading that they were otherwise engaged. They insisted that they were for peace and promised to comply with General Hancock's instructions if given a little more time.

"I think the Indians promised obedience and all that," Benteen observed, "but as the rivers and creeks were very high, they did not believe that we could cross them and get to their village which was some forty or so miles away." The village in question was on the Pawnee Fork of the Arkansas River about forty miles due west of Fort Larned. It consisted of about 250 tepees.

General Hancock had a surprise for them. He had with his force a company of engineers who were capable of building pontoon bridges across the swollen rivers and streams. Not trusting the Indian spokesmen, Hancock led out with his show of force toward the camp.

Hancock's fifteen companies arrived within sight of the large Indian village on 14 April 1867. "The Cheyennes had not time to evacuate their village," Benteen remembered, "our approach being so unexpected and rapid, but they came out to meet us in full paraphernalia, gorgeous array, both themselves and war ponies being bedecked and painted the very finest." Apparently the Indians decided to meet a show of force with a show of force. "They had some idea that they could withstand us," Benteen said. But, as Hancock's men deployed in a counter-demonstration, a party of Indian chiefs approached the General. Benteen asserted that they wanted "to outwit us with 'talk'," that "they wanted to gain sufficient time to remove whatever was of most value to them" in the village. The Indians certainly were not parlaying in good faith. They were, as Benten observed, playing for time. But, their delaying tactics were not just a matter of treachery. They had seen a large concentration of blue-coated soldiers moving toward their village before. It had resulted in the Sand Creek Massacre. They were naturally suspicious — and afraid.

About 10 o'clock that night, Hancock ordered Custer to surround the village with the eight companies of the 7th Cavalry, as he suspected that the Indians were going to take advantage of the dark to dismantle the village and flee. The cavalrymen assembled quietly and began a stealthy surround of the encampment, which as it turned out, was really a clump of small camps 'upon a series of islands in the north fork of the Pawnee." A reconnaissance party crept forward and returned with the astonishing news that the camp was deserted. "Every Cheyenne had disappeared almost as if by magic," Benteen reported.

Actually, there were two people found amongst the 150-odd tepees: an old man and a young girl under ten years of age, who upon examination, was found to have been gang-raped. There was some controversy at the time as to who had done the raping. Indian apologists accused the soldiers. The little girl insisted otherwise. "The Indian men did me bad," she said. She was apparently a half-breed captive.

Hancock surveyed the captured village, which proved to contain just about everything of value to the Cheyenne and Sioux who had occupied it before his coming. In their haste to get away, they took very little. Baffled, Hancock sent Custer's 7th after the fugitives.

It should have been simple. Most of the men were veterans at chasing fleeing Confederates. Benteen's 10th Missouri had thrived on similar assignments during the Civil War. But, the cavalrymen didn't even get a glimpse of the plains-wise Indians. Custer reached Walnut Creek late at night on the 15th. The next morning an incident occurred that lowered Custer another notch in Benteen's estimation. Early in the morning, dark dots and dust clouds were seen about eight miles to the northeast of Walnut Creek. Custer sent the two companies on the extreme right flank in pursuit, with instructions to catch the fleeing hostiles (if they proved to be such) and engage them until the balance of the command could be brought up.

It was a scout, in other words, and to be conducted by Companies H & G — jointly commanded by Captain Benteen. The fleeing hostiles turned out to be elk, deer, buffalo and antelope, grazing unconcernedly. "Well," said Benteen, "we slaughtered some fine meat, cut it up. . . and then started our return march to the camp we had left thinking we had solved the rumor of Indians being near pretty thoroughly." As they neared the Walnut Creek encampment they spied a figure (Custer) who, upon their approach, fled. Benteen reported to Custer upon arriving and received a mild scolding for causing the command to waste a day. "But I really hadn't," Benteen observed, pointing out that Custer could have gone on and the rest would have had no trouble catching up. "Custer didn't like us to have seen him scamper," he concluded.

Custer's eight companies arrived at Fort Hays on 19 April, expecting to find sufficient forage stockpiled there to enable them to pursue the fugitives for another twenty days or more. They found *one* day's supply of forage. They found something else: the fleeing Indians had not been too busy running to practice their old trade of raiding. "When Custer reached the Smoky Hill Road he found it was a shambles — stage stations burned, stock run off, and citizens butchered." Scouts, one of whom was Wild Bill Hickock, were dispatched to neighboring posts with the information. One of the scouts got through to Hancock the same day that Custer was riding into Fort Hays. Hancock promptly put the abandoned village to the torch. This drastic action was done over the protests of the Indian agents and generated a controversy that endures to this day. It also generated a war.

There will always be debate about the cause-and-effect relationship of Hancock's village-burning and the Indian raiding that plagued the settlers well into the fall of 1867. Hancock's own thinking seems to have been that the village was burned because of the raids along the Smoky Hill River, while others have argued that the raids were in retaliation for the burning. The chronological sequence of events gives more support to General Hancock, but this must be tempered with an understanding of the Indians' frame of mind when they saw Hancock's army moving in on them. This, in turn, must be weighed against the reasons for Hancock's being in Cheyenne territory with an army in the first place — and on and on it goes. Benteen put the blame on the Cheyenne and their Sioux allies, softening his condemnation with the observation: "doubtless they thought that hate and defiance was about all that was left for them to show." Their hate and defiance was kept up at the expense of the Kansas settlements until the Indians had acquired enough through plunder and hunting to enable them to winter in something akin to the style in which they were accustomed.

On 2 May 1867, General Hancock's force joined Custer's cavalry at Fort Hays. Hancock's presence and the impossible situation got on Custer's nerves. Captain Albert Barnitz of G Company confided to his wife in a letter that "General Custer has become 'bilious' " and "appears to be mad about something" and "is really quite 'obstreperous'." A few days later, the situation got so bad that Barnitz was forced to complain: "Every time that a new Officer of the Day has been detailed of late, he has found it very convenient to become

sick. . . for 'tisn't pleasant, of late, to carry out all Genl. Custer's
caprices. . ." He specified the officers who shirked the onerous duty.
"Capt. Benteen, Wallingford, Nowlan, Jackson, and I don't know
how many others report sick! (in consequences of the general 'cussed-
ness' of things, I suppose!!)."

Benteen was spared any more tribulation on 12 May by being detailed to report to Fort Riley with five witnesses for a general court-
martial of some deserters in his own company. He remained on detached service at Riley until July, missing out on the famous (or
infamous) Custer expedition to Nebraska that resulted in a court-
martial and suspension from duty for the Boy General. He got away
just in time. Three days after Benteen left, Barnitz wrote these words
to his wife: "Things are becoming very unpleasant here. General
Custer is very injudicious in his administration, and spares no effort
to render himself generally obnoxious. I have utterly lost all the
little confidence I ever had in his ability as an officer — and all admiration for his character, as a man, and to speak the plain truth
I am thoroughly *disgusted* with him! He is the most complete example
of a petty tyrant I have ever seen."

On 1 June, the petty tyrant of whom Barnitz complained led out
from Fort Hays with six companies (A, D, E, H, K, M) on a reconnaissance into southwestern Nebraska to find the Indians. Five days
after Custer left, a flood washed away the cavalry camp there and
inundated the main post itself, forcing the Army to relocate Fort
Hays about 15 miles distant.

On 8 June in camp near Medicine Lake Creek, Nebraska, a shot
rang out in the tent of Major Wickliffe Cooper. The unfortunate
Cooper was found shot in the head and the general assessment has
been that he committed suicide because of *delirium tremens* and
despondency. Benteen (who was not there) asserted that Cooper
"shot himself — suicide — because the damned fool Dr. (Lippincott)
acting under orders from Custer, wouldn't give him even a drink of
whisky to 'straighten out' on." It took Cooper's widow (who had
been pregnant at the time) almost twenty years to get the "official"
verdict of suicide changed to death by hands of persons unknown.
Chroniclers of the event have usually attributed the Congressional
action of 1885 to sympathy for Mrs. Cooper, being the only way that
could clear her application for a pension. (As a widow of a suicide,
Sarah Cooper was not entitled to a pension.) Yet, on closer inspection, it seems pretty clear that the Congressmen were not so much

moved by sympathy for Sarah Cooper's plight as they were by certain discrepancies found upon investigation of the circumstances surrounding Cooper's death. An unknown party was seen fleeing from Cooper's tent just after the shot was heard. Cooper, who expected to visit his pregnant wife soon, had only about $20 on his person despite the fact that he had drawn two months of his major's pay a week before. His friend, Captain Edward Myers of E Company, reported that Cooper's life had been threatened by an unknown party. Finally, there were no powder burns on Cooper's face or head.

Benteen may have been right for all that. Cooper *was* a heavy drinker and a chronic gambler to boot. Still, whether murder or suicide, Cooper's death cast a pall over the 7th Cavalry officer corps. The immediate effect of Cooper's death was the elevation of Joel Elliott to second major of the regiment. Elliott's slot was filled by two men in rapid succession, neither of whom joined the regiment before they died. The third replacement did — in November. He was Major Joseph G. Tilford, the same man whose court-martial findings had been published with Major Thomas Hynes' in May of 1864.

The six companies wandered through northwestern Kansas and southwestern Nebraska hunting for Indians. On 24 June 1867, some Sioux found them. The Indians' attempt to run off the cavalry horses was foiled by an alert sentry, who was wounded in the fray. He was an H Company man, the first H Company casualty to Indians in the regiment's history. (H Company was commanded in Benteen's absence by A Company's first lieutenant, Tom Custer, younger brother of George A. Custer.)

On 7 July 1867 there occurred an incident that did much damage to Custer's reputation. Four men deserted from the command between the north fork of the Republican River and the south fork of the Platte River. Custer angrily ordered the men pursued and brought back. All four were wounded, one of them severely. Benteen claimed that they "were shot while begging for their lives." None were Benteen's men, though his company (in his absence) had the highest desertion rate in the regiment. "One of the deserters was brought in badly wounded," Benteen said later, "and in extreme agony from riding in wagon (over the Plains without a road), screamed in his anguish. Gen. Custer in passing by, rode up to the wagon, and, pistol in hand, told the soldier 'that if he didn't cease making such fuss he would shoot him to death!' How's that for high?"

Four days later, Custer's command found the bodies of a small patrol from the 2nd Cavalry that had been sent to find them. (This was the famous Kidder Massacre.) On 15 July, Custer reached Fort Wallace (the westernmost post in Kansas) and immediately set off with a 50-man patrol for Fort Hays. He was ostensibly seeking supplies and orders from his superiors, though events proved that the forced march east was prompted as much by a desire to see Libbie Custer as it was for military reasons. One day out of Wallace, Custer met Benteen, who was leading a small column of Negro infantrymen and some Gatling guns to Fort Wallace. The next day, two of Custer's men, unable to keep up, were killed by Indians harrassing the rear. Custer did not turn back, a fact which stirred much controversy and which was added to the list of charges against him. On 19 July, by order of General Hancock, Custer was arrested on a string of charges stemming from his conduct on the expedition to Nebraska.

Benteen pushed on to Wallace, arriving 17 July. On his arrival, he "received a great awakening." There, he learned that while at Fort Hays two men from his company had been shaved and "'spreadeagled' on the plain until they cried 'Peccavi'" for visiting the post without permission. There, he learned of similar instances of brutality on the expedition to Nebraska. "Men of the command were soused in the Platte River, a lariat having been tied to their legs, and this repeated till they were nearly drowned." There too, he learned of the harsh treatment of the deserters, especially the four who had been shot, including one who had died for lack of medical treatment. The men were mostly from Captain Robert M. West's K Company, which did not concern the commander of H Company directly. (Captain West was a professional soldier Benteen's own age who had been a brigadier general of cavalry during the Civil War. He also had a reputation for heavy drinking that marred his brilliant career. Benteen described him as "a distinguished man, but given at times to hellish periodical sprees.")

Benteen also learned of the callous abandonment of the men of Custer's party that were killed by Indians the day after Benteen's party had passed. Custer "hadn't the time," Benteen said, to go back for the men when they were reported missing. Benteen confined his official actions to taking down affidavits from parties concerned about the treatment of his own H Company men — and forwarding the same to General Hancock. West took similar action. Reviewing the charges, General Grant ordered Custer court-martialed on 27 August. The court-martial commenced at Fort Leavenworth on 17 September and concluded there on 11 October. Custer was found guilty of all the charges and specifications and, after some quibbling about the wording, was sentenced to be suspended from rank and duty for one year. "We were free of Custer," Benteen said.

Benteen remained at Fort Wallace, seeing no action, until 19 September. He accompanied the acting regimental commander, Major Elliott, as far as Fort Hays and remained there until the balance of Elliott's command (four companies) went to Medicine Lodge Creek in Kansas as escorts for the peace commission that signed a treaty with the hostile Indians there. The most important proviso of the controversial Medicine Lodge Treaty was that the Indians in Kansas were required to remain *south* of the Arkansas River, effectively clearing the country north of the river for white settlement and railroad construction. In return, among other things, the government promised to provide the Indians with supplies — especially rifles and ammunition to aid them in hunting game.

The treaty signed, Elliott's 7th Cavalry dispersed for the winter to various posts throughout Kansas and Colorado. Elliott himself was given command of Fort Harker on the Smoky Hill River near Ellsworth. He arrived there 4 November with M Company under Lieutenant Owen Hale. On 10 November, Benteen's H Company joined them and went into camp for the winter.

Fort Harker was Benteen's first permanent duty station in his Regular Army career. It had been established during the Civil War and named in honor of a general of Sherman's army who had been killed in Georgia. The original site had been moved away from Ellsworth in January 1867 and it was to the new Fort Harker that Benteen found himself assigned. The garrison that winter consisted of two companies of the 5th Infantry in addition to Major Elliott's two companies of the 7th Cavalry. Benteen's close association with his one-time junior, Major Elliott, began at Fort Harker.

Benteen's first subordinate in H Company joined him there: 1st Lieutenant William W. Cooke. Canadian-born William Cooke had joined the Army in New York state where he had gone to attend college during the Civil War. As a reward for his skill in recruiting, he was given a commission as second lieutenant in the 24th New York Cavalry in January of 1864. He fought with some distinction in Virginia, especially around Petersburg, Benteen's birthplace, being promoted to first lieutenant and wounded twice. After the war, he was given brevets to the rank of lieutenant colonel for his conduct on the battlefield. Cooke was a tall, well-built man of 21 years when Benteen met him. He affected an unusual growth of sidewhiskers called dundrearies in that day, which grew to enormous proportions. He was reportedly the fastest runner and best shot in the regiment.

(Actually, a feckless young lieutenant named Frank Y. Commagere had been assigned to H Company the previous month in a vain attempt to make a better officer out of him. The experiment proved a failure and Commagere returned to Fort Leavenworth where he eventually resigned his commission.)

The other cavalry company commander at Fort Harker that winter was 1st Lieutenant Owen Hale of M Company. "Holy" Owen, as he was called for his colorful profanity, was considered an excellent cavalry officer. He was 24 years old when he joined Benteen at Harker, a New Yorker who could trace his ancestry to the Revolutionary War hero, Nathan Hale. He had been an enlisted man and later an officer in the 7th New York Cavalry during the war and had been breveted captain for gallant and meritorious services. He and Benteen became fast friends.

Hale's second lieutenant was another Canadian: 19-year-old Donald McIntosh, a part-Indian who had served as a civilian clerk during the war. "Tosh," as he was called, was a slow-moving, amiable officer who would remain closely associated with Benteen until his own death at the Little Big Horn eight years later.

Elliott, Cooke, Hale, McIntosh, and Benteen formed five of what Benteen later referred to as the "mess of seven" — meaning, seven officers of the original 7th Cavalry who messed (ate) together. The identity of the other two is something of a mystery. Benteen asserted late in his life that Owen Hale (who died in 1877) was the last of the original seven to "bite the dust" (aside from Benteen himself). From the military records and duty stations of the balance of the 7th Cavalry officers in the fall of 1867, the names of two other "candidates" emerge: Captain Robert M. West of K Company and Captain Edward Myers of E Company. Both K and E Companies were with Benteen until reassigned in November.

Fort Harker was important to Benteen's life in one other respect: it was the first Army home of Kate Benteen and little Freddie. They joined Benteen at Harker in February of 1868. Benteen got to bounce 11-month-old Freddie on his knees for the first time at Harker. The Benteen quarters were on the east side of the parade ground, south of what had become the Kansas Pacific Railroad. The surrounding countryside, on both sides of the Smoky Hill River, was rolling prairie almost as far as the eye could see. It meant good hay for the cavalry horses and excellent observation in the event of Indian attack. Fort Harker, like most western posts, was *not* enclosed by a stockade or wall. Indians, naturally, avoided troop concentrations like Fort Harker and, aside from an occasional alarm caused by horse-stealing Indians or nervous settlers in the vicinity, the winter passed uneventfully.

In March 1868, General Hancock was replaced as department commander. The new commanding general of the Department of the Missouri was Major General Philip H. Sheridan. This officer is the same man for whom Benteen's company had provided an escort in 1862. Both had been captains then. By 1868, Sheridan was a major general while Benteen was still a captain.

The Scrap at Elk Horn

The coming of spring 1868 brought anxiety to Kansas. The Cheyenne, Arapaho, and other Indian tribes south of the Arkansas were coming out of their winter camps to resume their nomadic hunting. To make matters worse, the government was having second thoughts about supplying them with guns and ammunition. The agents were uneasy. The military responded by sending a force of cavalry under Major Elliott's command to the agency near Fort Larned in July 1868.

Elliott went into camp with four companies brought down from Fort Leavenworth. Benteen remained at Fort Harker where he had been commanding officer since 3 May. He had taken full advantage of his position and the depot there to remount his own company (and M Company) with horses intended for Colonel Benjamin H. Grierson's 10th Cavalry regiment. "I simply exchanged some horses for others I thought would suit us better," he recalled drolly. When his castoff horses showed up in the 10th Cavalry branded H and M "7 C," there were complaints. Eventually the horse-swapping incident came to the attention of General Sheridan, but in the meantime more serious matters had occupied everyone's attention.

While Major Elliott was providing security for the agents near Fort Larned, some of the young men from the Cheyenne and Arapaho camps got impatient and started off on a raid — ostensibly against their hereditary enemies, the Pawnee. From contemporary accounts, it is pretty clear that the younger, more hot-headed warriors had given up on the arms issue and had decided to capture what they needed in the traditional manner. Ironically, as they were about 80 miles to the north commencing a reign of terror through central Kansas, the government agents were issuing muzzle-loading Lancaster rifles to the more patient elders near Fort Larned.

Benteen rode into the pow-wow and annuity issue at Fort Larned with H & M Companies on 13 July. Three days later, the six companies under Elliott's command were joined by Captain Hamilton's A Company and, a week later, Lieutenant Wallingford brought B Company up from Fort Dodge to a chilly reception from the other officers.

On 5 August 1868, while the cavalrymen were amusing themselves visiting the Indian camps and making friends with their foes of the previous summer, an incident occurred that gave Benteen (and others) an anecdote to pass on. An enormous rabid wolf entered Fort Larned and commenced biting a number of the military people there. According to Barnitz (who was also there), the wolf "ran into the hospital and bit a man lying in bed — passed another tent, and pulled a man out of his bed, biting him severely — bit one man's finger nearly off — bit at some woman, and I believe one or two other persons in bed. . . pounced upon a large dog he found there and whipped him badly in a half a minute. . ." The wolf then bounded up on a porch and bit Lieutenant John P. Thompson of the 3rd Infantry "quite severely in a number of places" before coming to grief trying to do the same to a sentry guarding a haystack. The sentry shot the wolf. Thompson's clothes saved him, "but it scared Thompson 'pissless', as we say in the cavalry," Benteen recalled, "and well it might!"

Six days later, word of the Indian raids along the Saline River to the north reached Fort Larned. "Around ten o'clock on the morning of August 10, a Monday, the Indians appeared on Spellman's Creek about sixteen to eighteen miles above Ellsworth. They went first to the homestead of a man named Shaw, beat him badly, and drove him from the house. The Indians then raped Mrs. Shaw and her sister, and perhaps another woman, reportedly for some time, with thirty or forty Indians taking part and eventually leaving the women unconscious. The Indians then attacked other homesteads, being driven off from some, but overrunning others and raping other women, though the news accounts were not specific." Benteen's H Company and Hale's M Company were dispatched to Fort Harker.

Benteen took a small force on ahead as fast as he could push them, passing a small stone Army post called Fort Zarah (named in honor of the Zarah Curtis with whom Benteen had locked horns in 1862). He instructed Holy Owen Hale to bring the balance as fast as he

could follow without killing the horses in the process. Benteen reached
Harker (about eighty miles away) in two days. There, he dispatched
a sergeant and guide to the Saline River while gathering up a scratch
force of forty men from his own men and those who could be spared
from the post. The scouts returned that night "with the cock-and-bull
story that the Saline River was too high to ford." Benteen led out the
next day (13 August) with his forty men toward the river. Once
across the river, which was plainly not unfordable, Benteen's small
force went into camp for breakfast. They remained there for about
an hour or so and moved on, heading toward known settlements along
the river. They had not gone a mile when Benteen, topping a rise
with his scouts, found himself "confronting about fifty braves." He
hastily ordered his pack mules corraled and left them in charge of a
sergeant and ten men. The rest galloped over the rise in a column
of twos and "were into that gang of astounded reds before they were
aware of it." The fifty Indians that Benteen had almost literally
bumped into were part of a force that probably exceeded 200, as
Benteen's men quickly discovered. (The Indians were in the process
of raiding a small ranch and carrying off two young girls.) Benteen's sudden appearance startled them and forced them to flee.
Although he was chasing over 200 Indians with thirty cavalrymen,
Benteen did not have time to count the cost. He later guessed that
the column-of-twos approach over the hill gave the Indians the impression that his small force was much larger. By the time they
realized their mistake (if ever they did), Benteen's men were "almost
trampling on their 'gee-strings'."

At the top of a river bank, Benteen found the two girls, abandoned
by their would-be captors. He instructed them to keep moving downstream and kept up his pursuit. (The girls spent a scary night alone
on the prairie before being discovered by a rescue party.) Benteen
and his men kept up the pursuit for nearly twenty miles. "My men,
as well as myself," Benteen remembered, "were armed with Spencer
Repeating Carbines and Colt's Revolvers, and as the Indians in their
retreat kept well bunched, we would dismount, pump five shots from
the carbines into the mob, reload, and thus having given our chargers
a breathing spell, would mount and get as close to the gang again as
we dared, and repeated the same tactics. . ." Benteen later had second
thoughts about the efficacy of such a zealous pursuit, but at the time,
he kept it up with relish. He later learned the reason for the precipitant departure of the young Cheynne. "They were scared by us," he

said, "and having many wounded, and the getter-up of the raid — the Pipe Bearer — being killed, their medicine was of no further use. In fact, 'twas very, very bad, and so they ran away, to which I add, and for that same fact, the settlers on those three rivers, as well as my small squad of cavalry, had great cause to be truly thankful that the medicine was a trifle mouldy."

The running engagement near Elk Horn Creek lasted until dark. When Benteen decided it was useless to pursue after dark with tired horses, he halted, had huge bonfires built in the prairie, and sent back for his packs and their ten-man escort. He reported 3 Indians killed and 10 wounded, all of whom were apparently carried off by their fellow raiders. Benteen lost not a man. It was the first undisputed victory of the 7th Cavalry and made Benteen a hero to the settlers of central Kansas. He was brevetted to the rank of full colonel for his actions that day, one of the last brevets awarded before they were frozen until 1890. The next day, Benteen began a cautious scout of the Saline River to the west, looking for signs of further depredations and reassuring the settlers. He sent a dispatch to Fort Larned reporting the encounter and warning the agents to be on the lookout for the raiders who would "doubtless" be found at Fort Larned "engaged in howling for the issue of arms to them." Benteen was ordered to scout almost to the Colorado state line and go into bivouac near the forks of the Republican River.

A few days later, Benteen's H Company was joined by Captain West's K Company. Benteen declined the reinforcements but before West left, challenged K Company to a baseball game. Benteen and West captained their own teams. The game was played in the middle of the prairie after placing sentinels around the diamond to watch for marauding Indians or wandering herds of buffalo. It was the first recorded instance of Benteen's playing baseball, but not to be the last. He was a basball buff and became quite well known throughout the Army as an enthusiast of the game. His H Company would eventually form an organization called the Benteen Baseball Club and boast among its members a couple of professional caliber players. H Company "trounced" K Company that hot summer afternoon, according to Benteen.

After seeing no further action, Benteen was recalled to Fort Harker. There, he renewed his acquaintance with Phil Sheridan. Benteen commented about the "wonderful difference" in Sheridan's status as compared to their last meeting in 1862. "Benteen," Sheridan replied seriously, "I saw chances, in fact sought them, got the opportunities, and, well, I did the very best I could with them, and here I am. God bless you! Let's take a drink."

"Such an invitation needed no repetition to me," Benteen commented drily. Benteen was a drinker. There was never any question about it. Toward the end of his career, his drinking caused problems, but he was never a chronic alcoholic. His granddaughter later asserted that he customarily "went on a binge about once a year lasting several days."

Philip Henry Sheridan had indeed come a long way since March 1862. Benteen had known him at just about the lowest point in his career. Sheridan had been placed in arrest for a squabble with one of General Curtis' staff (similar to Benteen's difficulty with Zarah Curtis) and had been sent to St. Louis for trial. General Halleck had other plans for Sheridan and sent him to Corinth just as Grant was driving on Vicksburg and, as Benteen put it, "from that day on, why, he sailed like a comet!" He was a major general at the war's end, commanding all the cavalry forces in the Army of the Potomac. (One of his most competent subordinates was Custer.) The difference between Sheridan and Custer was basically that Sheridan, the *only* commander Grant brought with him from the West, was a major general in the *Regular Army*, while Custer had been a major general of volunteers and a mere captain in the Regular Army.

Sheridan was determined to end the Indian wars in Kansas once and for all. He seems to have come to the conclusion early in the summer that a winter campaign would be necessary to render the Cheyenne tractable. To this end, he began marshalling his forces, keeping them busy throughout the summer and fall scouring the northern and central parts of Kansas and keeping the Indians on the run. He intended to keep up the minor campaign until the snows came and he could concentrate his forces for a strike against a basically immobile Indian winter camp. One of the skirmishes Sheridan's policy brought on was what is known to history as the Battle of Beecher's Island. A group of fifty frontiersmen under Sheridan's aide, Major Sandy Forsyth, was jumped by Cheyenne just over the Colorado state line in September. They held out for several days until a relief column could get to them from Fort Wallace. There were two other minor skirmishes in the area just north of Benteen's baseball diamond, in the general area where Custer had come to grief the previous summer. The second of these inconclusive battles was fought by Negro cavalrymen escorting a new major of the 5th Cavalry to his duty station. That major was Eugene A. Carr, the same Carr who had fought at Wilson's Creek as a captain and at Pea Ridge as a colonel.

While these events were transpiring, H and M Companies of the 7th Cavalry, jointly commanded by Benteen, were appointed escorts to Major General Sheridan. Their first stop was Fort Larned. On the way, Sheridan was pleased with Benteen's command and commented: "Benteen, this is the best mounted squadron of cavalry I ever saw." After Fort Larned, the escort took Sheridan as far as Walnut Creek (the site of Custer's scampering the previous spring) where an infantry company was supposed to take up the escort. The infantry company could not be found and Sheridan asked Benteen if his horses could make it to Fort Hays. "General," Benteen replied, "do you suppose I got poorer horses for those I swapped off to that other regiment?" Sheridan said nothing, But Benteen knew by the twinkle in the general's eye that he "would hear no more of the horse swapping complaint." Benteen took over when the guide became lost and led Sheridan into Hays following Custer's route of the previous year.

While performing his escort duty for Sheridan, Benteen was approached by Lieutenant Colonel J. Schuyler Crosby, Sheridan's adjutant, and offered the field command of the entire 7th Cavalry. Crosby gave Benteen the impression that the offer had come from Sheridan. "I politely but firmly declined the compliment of being so selected," Benteen realled, recommending instead that Custer's sentence be remitted and that the Boy General be given the honor instead, thinking that Custer "would have, and exhibit, more sense and judgment than he had during his former short tour in command."

Whatever the reason, it is a fact of history that on 24 September Sheridan wired Custer and asked him to return to duty. "Generals Sherman, Sully, and myself, and nearly all of the officers of your regiment, have asked for you," Sheridan told Custer. "So Custer came," Benteen related.

But, he did not come back chastened, by any manner of means. He joined with Sheridan, Benteen and the escort at Fort Hays and pushed off at once for the command in the field led by Major Elliott and Lieutenant Colonel Alfred Sully of the 3rd Infantry, who were winding down an unsuccessful campaign against the Cheyenne in the sand hills of southern Kansas. Custer, Benteen, and the others reached the cavalry camp on the Arkansas River below Fort Dodge (called Camp Sandy Forsyth) on 10 October.

Lieutenant Colonel Custer, restored to favor, began a series of forced marches in pursuit of his elusive foe, much to the disgust of Captain Barnitz who saw the activity as pointless. According to Barnitz, Custer's strategy was to keep the Indian ponies on the move until they were so worn down the cavalry could strike. Custer planned the big strike for March 1869, but events and the proverbial Custer Luck pushed the planned date up considerably.

On 27 October, Custer "cast around for some officer to send to Fort Harker" after a shipment of fresh horses there and some new recruits. The officer selected to make the hazardous 180 mile round trip was Benteen. Before leaving, accompanied by a single orderly, Benteen was given a request by Custer. Would Benteen be so kind as to send Mrs. Custer (in Fort Leavenworth) $100 when he arrived at Harker? "I then began to see why I had been selected!" said Benteen. "It was known that I always had plenty of money in the regiment." Nevertheless, Benteen agreed and set off after dark with his single orderly for Fort Harker. (The identity of the orderly remains an intriguing mystery. There is a distinct possibility that his name was Joseph van Holt Nash, a boyhood companion of Benteen's from Petersburg who had been a major on the staff of Confederate General Fitzhugh Lee during the Civil War. Benteen merely commented that his orderly, a native of Petersburg and a former Confederate major, "was under an assumed name" in the 7th Cavalry. Nash was definitely a close friend of Benteen's in retirement.)

Benteen and his orderly reached Fort Harker without incident. On 4 November, Benteen, the orderly, 2nd Lieutenant William J. Volkmar of the 5th Cavalry, 2nd Lieutenant Chancellor Martin of the 3rd Infantry, Mrs. Martin, and 77 recruits left Fort Harker for Camp Sandy Forsyth. They arrived at Fort Larned and learned that a Mexican wagon train loaded with guns and ammunition had gone on ahead. Benteen hurried to overtake it and reached it near Big Coon Creek just as a party of about 100 Indians began an attack on the train.

Benteen lit into the attacking Indians with about a third of his command of recruits and drove them off before Lieutenant Volkmar, bringing up the balance, could arrive on the scene. They pursued the war party to the Arkansas River and then, with Benteen concluding "'twas worse than useless to pursue," went on to Camp Sandy Forsyth. No one was killed, apparently, though the lives of the wagon train members, especially the wagonmaster, had been saved by Benteen's charge.

Benteen reported to Custer on 10 November, poorer by $100, but richer by the experience. (As it happened, the trail of the Indians Benteen had driven off led the 7th Cavalry to a Cheyenne encampment on the Washita River two weeks later.) Upon his return, Benteen found that Custer had taken away his "fine mount of horses" in a little exercise called *coloring the horses*. The coloring of horses was a tradition of crack European cavalry regiments whereby the horses were arranged within the regiment by color and by company, each company having horses of the same color. Benteen was furious with Custer for doing so "at the beginnings of the severest campaign that ever cavalry underwent" and with his own first lieutenant, Cooke, for "looking on, permitting — or at least acquiescing in it." Captain Albert Barnitz amplified on the objections of the more conscientious company commanders. "I have bitterly opposed the scheme," he told his wife, "all my old horses were well trained, and the men were much attached to them." Benteen, who had gone to extraordinary lengths to obtain the best possible horses for his own company, was penalized in effect by the change. So was Albert Barnitz, who was still fuming two days later: "have felt very indignant and provoked all evening in consequence of General Custer's *foolish, unwarranted, unjustifiable* order with regard to the new horses. . . It is sufficient to say that I am thoroughly *disgusted* and *disheartened*."

Captain Louis M. Hamilton, a Custer loyalist, liked the new arrangement. "(Custer) has transferred the horses from squadron to squadron, so as to have them assorted by color," he told his mother. "I have got black horse(s). . . and he has given me the honor of arming my squadron with Colt's revolvers, making mine the light squadron." (Hamilton commanded A Company; the other companies were armed with Spencer repeaters in addition to pistols.)

The coloring of horses change turned Benteen's H Company into a company mounted on bay horses. There were several other bay horse companies, sorrels, and a black and gray horse company. M Company got "mixed" horses — the leftovers. "My $100 and horses went about the same time," Benten said disgustedly.

Captain West, acknowledged leader of the anti-Custer clique, went to Custer to make peace. "Custer tried to steer the conversation into a different channel but was ineffective. West continued: 'Well, General, I am sincere in what I say and to prove it to you I give you my hand on it.' With that he extended his hand. Custer quietly but firmly ignored it. West continued to hold out his hand and then repeated his request. Custer said: 'Colonel West, I do not intend that the past shall influence my official conduct toward you. I intend to deal justly by you but to do so I do not think it necessary to take your hand. I will not take it.' The interview was closed." Benteen arrived at the conclusion that West felt "Custer would catch and salt him away surely"; West made an effort to secure a post trader's license, even though it eventually meant resigning his commission.

Surrounded by these grim undercurrents (and mounted on unfamiliar horses), the 7th Cavalry broke camp and headed south into Indian Territory (now Oklahoma) to commence the winter campaign Sheridan had been planning.

12

The Battle of the Washita

Lieutenant Colonel George A. Custer led eleven companies of the 7th Cavalry south from Camp Forsyth toward a new camp in the Indian Territory on 12 November 1868. Lieutenant Colonel Alfred Sully of the 3rd Infantry was in overall command of the expedition (in the beginning) which included infantry companies, artillery, and some engineers besides Custer's 7th. (The only 7th Cavalry company not along for the expedition was L Company commanded by General Sheridan's younger brother, Mike. Captain Sheridan's men remained in Colorado.)

After six days of marching, scouting and fruitless patrolling, the expedition reached a satisfactory site: on the North Canadian River about 40 miles south of the Kansas state line. The new post, promptly dubbed Camp Supply, was staked out and the soldiers went to work: sawing logs, unloading prefabricated window sills, digging wells, and so forth. Within two days, the fort in the middle of the wilderness had begun to take shape. Eventually there would be a log stockade with blockhouses on two sides enclosing the critical supplies and officers' quarters. The cavalry camp (tents) was outside the stockade.

On 21 November, General Sheridan arrived, preceding an escort of Kansas volunteers. The knowledge of the imminent arrival of a regiment of Kansas volunteers had generated a small crisis. The colonel of the Kansas volunteers was the erstwhile governor of the state, Samuel J. Crawford. Mustering in as a full colonel, he outranked both Sully and Custer. Sully decided to assume command by virtue of his brevet rank (brigadier general). Custer got into the act, pointing out that his brevet rank was major general, thus he outranked

Sully and Crawford. When Sheridan arrived, he sustained Custer, much to Sully's chagrin.

There was a terrific snowstorm on the night of 22 November. The officers called on stocky, bullet-headed General Sheridan, who impressed them with his genial manner. He brought the go-ahead for a winter campaign against the Cheyenne. Several of the chiefs were that very moment hastening to Fort Cobb to enroll in the agency presided over by Colonel William B. Hazen. Hazen had been instructed not to accept Cheyenne and Arapaho and he was forced to tell his supplicants that they could only make peace with Sheridan. Sheridan was not really interested in any peace *until* the Army had won a victory. He believed firmly that the troubles in Kansas would not be resolved until the Indians, the Cheyenne in particular, were defeated. His instructions to Custer were explicit: "kill or hang all warriors and bring back all women and children."

Monday morning 23 November 1868, with over a foot of snow deposited by the blizzard the night before still covering the ground, Custer's column marched out, its band playing "The Girl I Left Behind Me." Forty selected sharpshooters had been culled from the ranks of all eleven companies and assigned to a special unit commanded by Benteen's lieutenant, Cooke. The column set off on a generally southwestern line of march, headed toward the Texas state line. The weather turned bitterly cold and the men, even clad in buffalo fur overcoats, were chilled to the bone. The sun was bright on the second day out, causing snow blindness from the glare on the newly fallen white powder that had frozen to a crust that crunched with every step the horses took.

The next day, 24 November, featured more of the same, though the skies were overcast providing some relief from the glare. Benteen and his company brought up the rear, providing escort for the wagon train. In the afternoon, the skies cleared and it warmed up a bit. The column plodded on all that day and the next, camping at dark and moving out again before first light. They reached the Canadian River on the evening of 25 November and encountered difficulty feeding the horses. They had to tramp out a patch of snow in front of the horses and lay the forage in front of the animals. Naturally, many of the men gave up precious hours of rest to hand-feed their mounts. (Cavalry without horses or even with starving horses is useless for all practical purposes.) The horses fed, the men tramped out patches of snow and tried to pitch their tents in the dark. Many gave it up

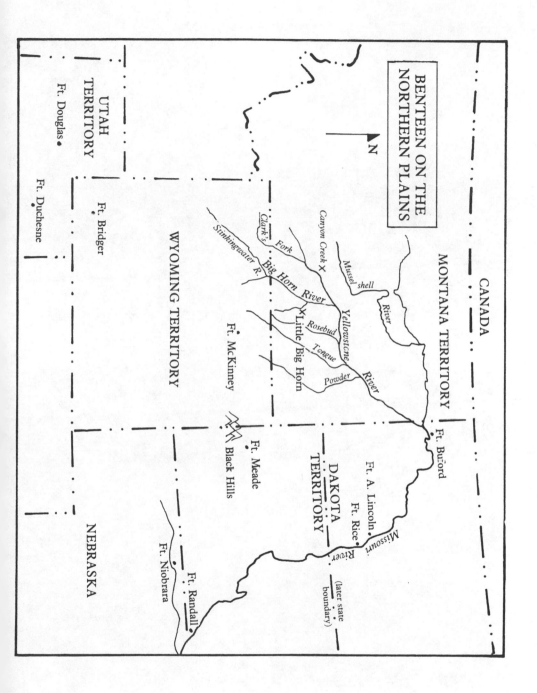

BENTEEN ON THE
NORTHERN PLAINS

N

CANADA

MONTANA TERRITORY

Ft. Buford

Mussel shell River

Canyon Creek ✕

Yellowstone River

Clark's Fork

Big Horn River

Stinkingwater R.

Rosebud

Tongue

Powder River

Little Big Horn

Ft. McKinney

WYOMING TERRITORY

Ft. Bridger

UTAH
TERRITORY

Ft. Douglas •

Ft. Duchesne •

Ft. A. Lincoln •
Ft. Rice •

DAKOTA
TERRITORY

Missouri River

(later state
boundary)

Ft. Meade •

Black Hills

Ft. Niobrara •

NEBRASKA

Ft. Randall •

William W. Cooke

Joel H. Elliott

Robert M. West

Owen Hale

as a lost cause and merely wrapped themselvs in blankets and buffalo overcoats and swigged down scalding coffee to keep warm.

Reveille sounded about two hours before the dawn on Thursday 26 November (Thanksgiving Day) 1868. The day began excessively cold and foggy. The 7th Cavalry marched as one column for about a mile until they came to a ford in the Canadian River. Here, Custer called a conference and instructed Major Joel Elliott to take three companies (G, H, M) and proceed upstream (west) looking for a trail. Custer took the balance across the river and headed generally south. Once across the river, Custer reorganized the wagon train. The regimental quartermaster, Lieutenant James M. Bell, broke out seven of the wagons and stocked them with the reserve ammunition. The balance (about 100 wagons) were left in the custody of the officer of the day, Captain Hamilton of A Company, whose job on the 26th was almost identical to the one Benteen had done on the 24th. The difference was that the seven wagons under Lieutenant Bell were intended to keep pace with the column in the event of a rapid pursuit.

Custer himself galloped ahead of his column and climbed a hill, surveying the surrounding countryside. He saw nothing and was about to return to his command when suddenly he saw a black speck moving toward his column. It was coming from the direction Elliott had taken less than an hour before. Custer galloped toward the figure.

Less than two miles from Custer's crossing, Captain Albert Barnitz, leading Elliott's battalion, had stumbled onto a trail in the snow. He halted and called Major Elliott forward. What had caught Barnitz's eye was the depth of the trail that had been snowed over. He knew that buffalo did not move in blizzards, hence their trails were deep — *under* the snow. The trail he spotted had been beaten on *top* of snow and then snowed over. Furthermore, it ran parallel to the river. He knew that buffalo invariably ran perpendicular to water courses — directly at them. Elliott urged Barnitz to follow the trail. A mile further on, they came across what had obviously been a camp. Ponies had been nibbling at the barks of the trees. After another mile, a trail was discovered that had not been snowed-in yet: a fresh trail "which had obviously been made in the afternoon of the previous day, by a war party of from one to two hundred Indians. It was known to be a war party from the fact that the Indians had no dogs with them, whereas hunting parties are always accompanied by dogs." Fred Benteen, on seeing the trail, was convinced that it was the trail of the same party he had encountered at Big Coon Creek two weeks before. Major Elliott sent the courier back to Custer. His three company command formed into a column of fours and weapons were readied.

Elliott's men crossed the river in pursuit, finding an abandoned pack mule on the south bank. They pressed south by west, leading their horses up steep inclines and riding them down the reverse slopes. They halted for an hour after noon for a meal and then pushed on. The courier returned from Custer on a fresh mount with instructions for them to press on until 8:00 p.m. if the main column had not caught up by then.

Custer cut across country with the main column and found Elliott's men about 9:00 p.m. — an amazing feat of navigation. (Custer, whatever his faults as a commander, was undeniably a crackerjack guide.) His main column had encountered more difficulty than Elliott in crossing the river, as the ice downstream was thick enough to cover the river but not thick enough to bear the weight of the cavalry horses — not to mention the wagons in the rear. The ice had to be broken and cleared before they could cross. On the south bank, once the news of Elliott's find was circulated, Captain Hamilton requested to be excused as Officer of the Day and be allowed to command his own company in the van. Custer refused at first, but Hamilton found a young lieutenant in I Company (Edward G. Mathey) who was suffering from snow-blindness and willing to trade places. Custer authorized the change and Hamilton took the lead. As the day wore on, the sun beamed bright and warm. The snow began to melt and Custer's men found themselves hampered somewhat by mud and slush. They linked with Elliott and took a one hour break.

By 10:00 p.m., they were in the saddle again, all eleven companies, minus Bell's seven wagons and single ambulance and Mathey's large wagon train far behind. The wagons, even Bell's lightened loads, were having trouble keeping up. Those under Mathey made no attempt to keep pace, nor were they expected to. Two hours later, Custer's reunited column struck the winding Washita River and began crossing and recrossing it in a seemingly aimless manner as they followed the trail before them. About an hour and a half later, the Osage Indian guides halted and informed Custer that the Indian camp was on the other side of a group of hills in front of them. The Osage could smell fire, they said. Custer dismounted and crept to the top of the ridge before him. He lay down along its crest and surveyed the river bed below.

Returning from his reconnaissance, he sent for the officers. One by one they crept to the top of the ridge, peering vainly in the dark for a glimpse of the village below. Custer, in a whisper, pointed out the features of the countryside surrounding the suspected Indian camp and led his officers back down the reverse slope of the hill. Here, they conferred. Custer organized the 7th Cavalry into four attack battalions. Major Elliott, taking G (Barnitz) and H & M (Benteen) was to swing wide to the north and come in on the suspected camp from the northeast. No one knew it at the time but there were other villages in the direction Elliott was to follow. The camp they were surrounding had a little over 50 tepees and probably not more than 150 warriors against Custer's 700 men of the 7th. The other villages, that Elliott would, in effect, have his back to, probably had a combined population of over 8000 and maybe 2000 warriors. Captain Myers, with E & I Companies, was to cross the river and attack the village from the opposite direction to the one taken by Elliott. Captain William Thompson, with B & F Companies, was to follow Myers, then swing wide to the east and come in from a third direction. Custer himself, taking the balance which included two companies under Captain Hamilton, two companies under Captain West, and the forty sharpshooters under Lieutenant Cooke, would come over the ridge directly into the camp below.

The attack was to begin at first light, the signal was to be the regimental band playing "Garryowen" from the top of the ridge they huddled behind. Custer calculated that they would have three or four hours to accomplish the surround. Major Elliott, having the longest and most difficult approach, was to lead out first.

Elliott was delayed getting started because Captain Benteen's H Company had been assigned to the rear of the column. Silence was imperative, so it took Benteen a while to get to his men and whisper instructions down the line. Major Elliott and Captain Barnitz moved out thinking that Benteen and Hale were right behind them. As they began to move, the dogs commenced barking. Custer ordered them silenced and the troopers dutifully lassoed the animals and cut their throats, including two of Custer's own stag hounds. Major Elliott had difficulty finding a way around the hills and, at one point, was forced to countermarch back down his own trail in the dark for a short distance until he could find a way around the hills that was passable and still not too close to the suspected Indian village. Then, when he and Barnitz reached what they thought was the jumping off place, they found to their horror that what they had assumed was Benteen's two companies in the rear was actually the regimental band. It took a precious hour to get the band back where it belonged with Custer and Benteen's men guided to the proper location.

(Benteen was suffering from snow-blindness to some extent, having lent his colored goggles to Dr. Lippincott. The condition steadily worsened over the years. Benteen's eyesight was never perfect after the Washita.)

Once together at last, Major Elliott's battalion was deployed. Benteen's H Company was on the extreme right flank, mounted. Hale's M Company (also under Benteen's command) was in the middle, almost straddling the river. Captain Barnitz's G Company was on the left flank (the village side) of the river, a skirmish line dismounted in front and a column of mounted men behind. They crept forward through the cottonwoods that lined the river bank. They flushed an Indian guard, but did not fire for fear of giving alarm before the other battalions were in position.

The other battalions were in position by that time — with the exception of Captain Thompson's B & F Companies who had been forced to halt far from their assembly point because the terrain was too open. When the attack was finally launched, Thompson's men were a few minutes late, leaving a critical gap in the ring around the village. Just before dawn, the fog that had settled in the valley of the Washita caused a brilliant morning star to glow in such an eerie manner that Custer thought it was a signal rocket from the village. (Only after reflecting on the improbability of the Indians having or using signal rockets did Custer's anxiety wane.) He later described the atmospheric phenomenon vividly: "Slowly and majestically it continued to rise above the crest of the hill, first appearing as a small brilliant flaming globe of bright golden hue. As it ascended still higher it seemed to increase in size, to move more slowly, while its colors rapidly changed from one to the other, exhibiting in turn the most beautiful combinations of prismatic tints." He started his battalion over the crest of the ridge and down its reverse slope toward the village. Cooke's sharpshooters were dismounted and sent forward to a clump of trees lining the river bank. Hamilton's and West's four companies remained mounted in column. The regimental band halted near the crest, waiting for the signal. Custer ordered the overcoats and haversacks jettisoned and left a small guard over them. He ordered Lieutenant Godfrey to take K Company straight through the village in order to corral the pony herd plainly visible beyond it. The men edged forward.

Custer has been taken to task by some historians (both contemporary and current) for not ascertaining that the village he so enthusiastically jumped that morning was indeed hostile. It *is* true that his reconnaissance was strictly tactical. However, as is usually the case in such controversies, the critics do not seem too specific on what exactly he *should* have done under the circumstances. Given that he was on a punitive expedition with specific orders to "kill or hang all warriors" and on the hot trail of a war party, it is hard to see what he could have done differently. When his experience with the village on Pawnee Fork the previous April is taken into account, Custer's anxiety to attack is understandable. He could not very well have announced his arrival in ringing terms and challenged those who wished to fight to separate themselves from those who did not.

On the other hand, the chief of the village had been to Fort Cobb and offered to enroll in the agency, apparently in good faith. His own people, especially his wife, had urged him to move away from the Washita, fearing a repetition of what had happened to them at Sand Creek four and a half years before. There *were* hostile warriors in that camp who had raided settlements in Kansas. The critics who charge that Custer did not *know* this when he gave the signal to attack ignore the sequence of events. He may *not* have known for a certainty, but he had very reasonable grounds to assume the village he was about to hit contained hostile warriors.

Upon reflection, the most remarkable aspect of what was to become the battle of the Washita was the relative ease with which the Indians were surprised. For all their Plains savvy and skill in guerrilla-type warfare, the Cheyenne that day (and others at different times) were taken unaware by what seems to be an astonishing carelessness (or at least lack of security) on their own part. The assertion that the Indians were surprised only by the treachery of the U.S. government will not stand up in the light of the chronological sequence of events.

Just before dawn, the first shot rang out. It was fired, as it turned out, by a blanket-clad Indian at some of Hale's men northeast of the village. The Indian had apparently ventured out of his warm tepee to check on barking dogs when he spied the cavalrymen. Simultaneously, other shots were fired. Other Indians were making similar discoveries. Custer signalled the band to strike up "Garryowen" and led the four companies under his immediate command across the river and into the village at a gallop. The band got through one chorus of the regimental marching song before the bitter cold caused their spittle to freeze. The blocked instruments tootled off into an embarrassing medley of squeaks and blares. West's and Hamilton's men thundered forward.

With the exception of B & F Companies under Captain Thompson, all the 7th Cavalry attack units were in position and closing in rapidly on the village. The first ones into the village were mounted, of course, but their fire was not very accurate. (It could not very well be, with the horses rearing and plunging.) The Indians put up a stout defense that was extremely valiant under the circumstances, but Cooke's sharpshooters and the dismounted skirmishers added accuracy to the volume of firepower. The cavalrymen were in among the tepees before the Indians could lay down a base of fire. Those Indians who sought refuge in the ravines and nearby woods were shot down by the dismounted cavalry in the village and by Cooke's sharpshooters on slightly higher ground across the small river. Many of the women, children and elderly noncombatants wisely remained inside the tepees, adding their keening wails of distress to the commotion outside. A young Cheyenne girl who survived remembered: "The air was full of smoke from gunfire, and it was almost impossible to flee, because bullets were flying everywhere." Yet, somehow, many did manage to flee, finding the gap caused by Thompson's tardiness.

Captain Benteen intercepted one of the fugitives, a teen-age boy who proved to be a nephew of the village chief. Benteen signed peace and gestured for the boy to surrender. For reply, Benteen got three pistol shots in rapid succession, one plucking at the sleeve of his overcoat and another wounding his horse in the neck. The horse toppled, but Benteen rolled clear and came up shooting. He killed the boy.

Custer later reported the incident both in his official report and in his book, *Life On the Plains*. While the official report was in no way derogatory, for some strange reason Custer referred repeatedly (eight times in two pages) to "Major" Benteen in the book version, even though Benteen was a brevet colonel. There is no satisfactory explanation for the demotion. Years later, Custer used the incident to "twit" Benteen about being a boy-killer, so perhaps the "Major" business was a sly dig as well. Custer made a number of assertions about the battle that cannot bear close scrutiny, but he was not alone in this. Benteen in later years claimed that his companies "captured fifty-five prisoners before a trooper of any of the other three columns could get into the village." Since there were only fifty-three prisoners taken from the village that day by the entire 7th Cavalry, this means that some of Benteen's prisoners were later killed or got away. This is entirely within the realm of possibility, given the circumstances, but Benteen's figure seems an exaggeration.

Captain Barnitz (on Benteen's left) was severely wounded in the abdomen pursuing three Indians fleeing through the gap caused by Thompson's late arrival. He dismounted in great agony and knelt in a snowdrift to minimize internal bleeding. A couple of his own men found him and carried him in a blanket to the small knoll south of the village where Custer had established a command post.

Major Elliott shouted to Lieutenant Owen Hale: "Here goes for a brevet or a coffin!" and followed another party through the same gap, accompanied by several men from Benteen's and Myers' battalions. Elliott's command pursued the fugitives for about four miles without catching them.

The 7th Cavalry had possession of the village within ten minutes. The Indian efforts to resist were less successful than their efforts to flee. One party of warriors, estimated at more than thirty, were systematically shot down in a ravine they had occupied by Cooke's sharpshooters across the river. The chief of the village was shot off his horse by one of Hale's men near the river. His wife, mounted in front of him, was shot down as well. The bodies fell into the freezing water. Inevitably, some of the cavalrymen were hit, too. Captain Hamilton died early in the fight, shot down in the village, perhaps by a stray shot from one of his own men. Only one other trooper (Cuddy of B Company) was killed in the village that day, though several were wounded. The Indians perished by the score.

Lieutenant Godfrey, in compliance with Custer's last-minute instructions, took his platoon from K Company straight through the village and through Benteen's men in search of Indian ponies. Godfrey's men crossed the river and galloped north. About two miles from the village, they corralled about three hundred horses, ponies and mules. Godfrey turned them over to Lieutenant Law's platoon, which was right behind, and pushed on. After another two miles, Godfrey topped a rise and noticed a large number of tepees along the river about a mile away. There were more, it seemed to Godfrey, than there had been at the encampment he had ridden through. His sergeants urged him to turn back and the young West Pointer wisely complied with their request. He realized that the village attacked was but one of a number of camps along the Washita River. He moved back toward the first village, noticing a large number of Indians beginning to appear on his flanks, out of range. When he got back near the point where he had turned over the captured ponies to Lieutenant Law, he heard heavy firing across the river on the other side of a large hill mass.

The heavy firing that Godfrey heard was Major Elliott and sixteen enlisted men fighting for their lives. Elliott had pursued well beyond sight and sound of the village and, noticing the sudden appearance of the other Indians that Godfrey had seen, turned and headed back. Their horses were winded and unable to outrun the Indians who were closing in on all sides. Elliott made a desperate dash for a dry creek bed about two miles from the village but was forced to pull up short when the Indian pursuers beat him to it. He dismounted his small command and formed a circle in some tall grass where the snow had melted. The men lay down and began shooting at the surrounding Indians.

Godfrey, on returning to the village, had another hundred or so ponies given to him by Benteen, who had captured them with the aid of M Company's first sergeant, a handful of enlisted men, and a colorful civilian scout called California Joe. Undoubtedly, Godfrey told Benteen of the fight he had heard two miles away as well as the intelligence he had gleaned about the other villages and Indian reinforcements. Within minutes, Godfrey's information was verified. Hundreds of armed Indians appeared on the skyline around the captured village, out of range. They completely surrounded the village, even driving Custer's coat-and-haversack guards across the river. Cooke's sharpshooters, having waded across the river and retrieved their mounts in the meantime, were able to stand off the new threat.

Meanwhile, Major Elliott's party was fighting a losing battle for survival. The Indians surrounding them crept closer and closer. First one, then another dashed up to the circle of dismounted cavalrymen and counted *coup*, a peculiarity of Plains Indians that involved the warrior striking the body of a living foe. The Indians later reported that the fight against Elliott was over "inside of two hours." He was outnumbered at least ten to one. Benteen commented: "Elliott, like myself, was 'pirating' on his own hook; allowed himself to be surrounded and died like a man."

In the village, where the fighting had petered out to a few scattered shots, the situation was beginning to look a little bleak. The overcoats and haversacks of Custer's four companies were lost and ammunition was running dangerously low. It was at this point that Lieutenant Bell, the quartermaster, arrived on the scene with his seven wagons and an ambulance loaded with blankets and ammunition. The surrounding Indians were plainly surprised to see him suddenly turn up and Lieutenant Bell gave them no time to react. He placed his small command into a column and dashed for the village — right through the astonished Indians. "Several of his mules were killed in the galloping fight, and his tar-soaked wagon wheels became so hot they were set ablaze. But he and his men reached the village amid cheers and shouts of their comrades, and the wagons were quickly jerked over by the troopers who then grabbed handfuls of ammunition." (Bell's dashing ride was greatly appreciated, arriving as he did in the nick of time, and it set a precedent that would later have a very important effect on Benteen's career seven and a half years later.)

Godfrey, on his return to the village proper, reported to Custer, who instructed him to begin an inventory of the tepees and place the captives behind the wagons Bell had just brought in. Custer wanted one of the tepees kept as a personal souvenir, but ordered the others burned, with all their contents. Godfrey went to work.

The rest of the companies, which included Thompson's men by then, were placed in a large circle around the village. Periodically, one or another company would charge the surrounding Indians, who always pulled back. They were careful not to get too carried away with their charges and always stayed within sight and supporting distance of the others. The exact number (or precise location) of these limited counterattacks is not known. Benteen implied that he had led at least one of them and that another, featuring Myers' E Company, came close to the spot where Elliott and his men had perished. One of Elliott's party, Sergeant Major Walter Kennedy, had been axed to death on the far slope of the high ground surrounding the village to the east. It is almost certain that at least one of the charges rode right past his body without seeing it. Custer later wrote that the charges "were soon able to force the line held by the Indians to yield at any point assailed. This being followed up promptly, the Indians were driven at every point and forced to abandon the field to us. Yet they would go no further than they were actually driven."

Sometime in the midst of all the charging, California Joe came to Custer and reported that he could bring in a large herd of ponies if he was given some help. Custer was unable to provide any help

at that time and was astonished minutes later when Joe brought in
the herd assisted by some captured squaws. Benteen was disgusted
when Custer later gave Joe credit for capturing *the* pony herd, saying: "as surely as there's a sun, I conceived, and we carried it out,
and Custer knew it." There were at least *three* separate pony herds
captured at the Washita. Godfrey, it seems, captured about 300 with
his platoon early in the fight. Benteen and 1st Sergeant Duane of
M Company added a smaller herd to that bunch shortly afterward.
Benteen may have corralled the third herd that California Joe brought
in, though this is not conclusive. However they were captured, Custer
could count 875 horses, ponies and mules by late afternoon. After
picking out some for his captives to ride back to Supply and a few
more for himself and some of his men, he ordered the balance killed.
Godfrey, having completed the inventory of the village and the burning of the spoils of war, was given the task. At first, Godfrey's men
tried to lasso the ponies and cut their throats as they had done with
the dogs the night before. But, the method proved too slow and
unsure as the ponies (naturally) fought it. Custer ordered Godfrey
to shoot them. Even this was not efficient enough, so other companies
were pressed into service and all engaged in an orgy of horse-shooting
that lasted until almost dark.

Benteen later expressed great disgust at Custer's method of dispatching the horses. He claimed that it endangered the men holding
the perimeter. Since at least 700 horses were killed in this manner,
that meant an incredible amount of lead was flying and Benteen had
a point. He implied that he remonstrated with Custer about it, but
received a sarcastic reply. While the shooting was going on, Elliott
was forgotten. This made Benteen very angry. Custer later asserted
that "parties were sent" looking for Elliott. He never specified who
or where and Benteen, to his dying day, insisted that there were no
search parties.

About eight o'clock that night, Custer formed his command and
led them north by east in the direction of the villages Godfrey had
reported. They formed into a column which included the captives,
Bell's wagons and the regimental band playing an old Negro spiritual
called "Ain't I Glad I've Got Out of the Wilderness!" (This tune, also
called "Jine the Cavalree," is nearly identical to "The Old Gray Mare"
and was very popular during the Civil War.) The 7th Cavalry with
captives, wounded, two of their dead, and Custer's souvenir tepee
marched boldly down the Washita.

Custer implied that they reached the site of the camps Godfrey had reported and countermarched back toward the destroyed village because the other Indians had fled. He stated explicitly that he was concerned about the hundred or so wagons left behind with Lieutenant Mathey's 80-man escort and was anxious to get back to them before the Indians found them. His critics (who do *not* include Benteen in this one instance) have generally pooh-poohed Custer's rationalization. They have pointed to the relative impregnability of large wagon trains to Indian attack and cite numerous examples from the Frontier Wars period. They have also argued the insanity of Indians searching for a wagon train in one-foot snow drifts while their women and children were still threatened by the force of 600 or more cavalrymen. Custer merely added fuel to the fire by admitting that he believed the wagon train could not get through to *him,* considering the terrain he had covered since he had left it.

As in most controversies in the study of Custer and his 7th Cavalry, this one can never be satisfactorily resolved. Benteen's objection to the withdrawal from the Washita was based on the lack of concern shown for Elliott's fate. There is no question that Custer and Elliott were not close. What Custer might have done had the missing men been commanded by Captain Hamilton, Lieutenant Weir, or even his own brother Tom, is an intriguing question, but unproductive. Custer moved back through the village and down his own back trail until 2:00 a.m. on 28 November.

Apparently convinced that the Indians had given up pursuit, Custer halted and ordered Captain West's K Company forward to link with Lieutenant Mathey and the wagon train while the others rested themselves and their horses and built huge bonfires in the snow to keep warm. They moved out before first light and found West, Mathey, and the rest of the wagons about 10:00 in the morning. Custer kept the reunited column moving until late afternoon.

When they finally halted on the other side of the Canadian River, Custer called his officers together. He told them that he would forgo the customary written reports from each subordinate, substituting a single report of his own writing based on oral reports from the others. Accordingly, the officers squatted around Custer's fire and began a group recital of the events. Casualties were the predominant topic.

"The Indians left on the ground and in our possession the bodies of 103 of their warriors," reported Custer. However, this figure (103) was *not* a body count as implied. It was a reconstruction based on the recollections of the officers at the conference. Right away, there were criticisms of Custer's figures. An officer stationed at Fort Cobb who wrote a report based on interviews with Indian survivors before Custer's report was published, said that there were about 75 warriors killed at the Washita and an equal number of women and children. Some have claimed that the number of warriors slain was as low as twenty. Given the facts that there were about fifty tepees, about 900 horses, and fifty-three women and children taken alive, the 103 figure seems a bit high for warriors alone. (To clarify, one warrior per tepee is a good rule of thumb, making allowances for those warriors whose full-grown sons still lived at home. In Cheyenne culture, if a man was a warrior, he had his own tepee, wife(s), horses, children, and so forth. It *is* conceivable that the village had only fifty tepees but over 100 warriors, especially as it was a winter camp and of a band that had seen some unfortunate times. However, 103 warriors with only 53 women and children — and the rest somehow getting away — is incredible. Some of those 103 "warriors" were women and children.)

Custer then proceeded with a laundry list of items seized in the village. Given his carelessness with figures, these must be taken with a grain of salt. However, Godfrey *did* inventory the take, so they are not entirely imaginary.

875 horses, ponies and mules,
241 saddles, some of very fine and costly workmanship;
573 buffalo robes,
390 buffalo skins for lodges,
160 untanned robes,
210 axes,
140 hatchets,
35 revolvers,
47 rifles,
535 pounds of powder,
1,050 pounds of lead,
4,000 arrows and arrow heads,
75 spears,
90 bullet molds,
35 bows and quivers,
12 shields,
300 pounds of bullets,
775 lariats,
940 buckskin saddle-bags,
470 blankets,
93 coats,
700 pounds of tobacco.

These quantities are consistent with what might be expected in a village having between 50 and 150 warriors. However, he was following war party his expert trailers believed to be *at least* one hundred warriors. Clearly, some of the Indians he was trailing lived elsewhere. (It is not conceivable that all the able-bodied males in the village — or even two thirds of them — were out on the same raid by coincidence. The village Custer hit was simply too small to support a war party as large as the one he trailed to the Washita.)

Custer went on to report that he had "secured two white children, held captive by the Indians." These two children must have evaporated on the way back to Camp Supply, for they never arrived there. In fact, aside from Custer's superiors repeating the assertion made, there is no further mention of them at all.

Custer reported his own casualties, stating that he had two officers and nineteen enlisted men killed. At the time he wrote those figures he had only two bodies. He assumed the remaining nineteen were dead. ((It turned out that there were only seventeen bodies abandoned, but two of the wounded died before reaching Camp Supply, making Custer a prophet if nothing else.) He said he had three officers and eleven men wounded with him, a total of fourteen wounded. (He had fifteen wounded, of whom two died.) In the light of his inability to get an accurate count from his officers of the men right under their noses, the Indian counts (based on bodies far removed from the conference) must be viewed with skepticism.

The only brevets awarded for the battle of the Washita went to Captain Hamilton, who was awarded posthumous promotion to major "early in the spring" of 1869 and Captain Barnitz, who was brevetted colonel at the same time. Only the dead and wounded officers were mentioned in Custer's report by name, except Benteen, who was reported as having "his horse shot under him." Custer stated only: "I cannot sufficiently commend the admirable conduct of the officers and men."

This half-hearted commendation (and not specifying officers by name) was more serious than it seems in retrospect. The post-Civil War army was rank-heavy. Many of the officers would remain lowly lieutenants for as long as twenty years. The brevets conferred based on Civil War performances were a sore point. Officers *expected* to be commended by name and recommended for brevets in 1868. Custer knew this. He later commended officers by name even after brevets had been frozen by Congress in March 1869. In view of the fact that the battle of the Washita was the first (and for many years the *only*) spectacular victory against Indians in post-war history, Custer's lack of recommendation jars. The day they arrived back at Camp Supply, Secretary of War *ad interim* John M. Schofield (the same Schofield Benteen had known in Missouri in 1861) wrote a letter to General Sherman. Schofield said in part: "Ask Sheridan to send forward the names of officers and men deserving of special mention." Custer's comment on this letter was that "it was impracticable to comply with the request" as "every officer and man" had "performed his full part" in the campaign.

Benteen observed that he and his men "received but faint praise" for their efforts "from the fact of Brevet Major General G.A. Custer not being very friendly disposed toward me." The authorities (Sheridan, Sherman, Schofield, *et al*) were prevented from correcting Custer's oversight in regards to commendations by virtue of the fact that Custer's was the only report submitted. The kindest explanation that has been offered for Custer's action is that he was in such a hurry to get a report in to General Sheridan at Supply that he did not take time to reflect on the battle and the actions of individuals there. In any case, he dispatched California Joe with the hastily written report and followed leisurely, arriving at Camp Supply amid great fanfare on 2 December.

The day after the 7th arrived, Custer called his officers together to compose a eulogy for Captain Louis M. Hamilton. Captain West took down the sentiments expressed and forwarded them to Hamilton's parents as a memorial. There was a similar eulogy composed for Major Elliott that said in part that he "fell in the attitude of defiant daring heroically rallying his men." Since at the time no one knew that he was dead, let alone how he died, this was clearly an exercise in poetic license.

Benteen, who had one man wounded from M Company and a total of ten men missing from H & M Companies who had disappeared with Elliott, never recorded his thoughts about the eulogies. He was busy preparing for a return to the area south of the Washita. General Sheridan, Custer's 7th Cavalry, and the Kansas volunteer cavalry left Camp Supply on 7 December, bound for Fort Cobb. Sheridan intended to negotiate with the Indian chiefs there and "demand of them the murderers of our people." He said that if his demands were complied with, the war would be considered over, but if they were not, "I will compel them, if I can."

The large column stopped briefly at the Washita battlefield on the afternoon of 11 December. They found Major Elliott's body — as well as the 16 men with him and Sergeant-Major Kennedy's. They were horribly mutilated.

Major Elliott: Two bullet holes in head, one in left cheek, right hand cut off, left foot almost cut off, penis cut off, deep gash in right groin, deep gashes in calves of both legs, little finger of left hand cut off, and throat cut.

Some of Benteen's men were similarly disfigured.

Corporal William Carrick: Bullet hole in right parietal bone, both feet cut off, throat cut, left arm broken, penis cut off.
Private Eugene Glover: Head cut off, arrow wound in right side, and both legs terribly mutilated.
Private William Milligan: Bullet hole in left side of head, deep gashes in right leg, penis cut off, left arm deeply gashed, head scalped and throat cut.

The rest of the bodies (privates from Companies E, H, I & M) were found in a tight circle with Elliott. Sergeant-Major Kennedy was found about a mile away. The mutilated remains were carefully buried with the exception of Elliott, whose body was placed in a wagon for shipment to a military cemetery. Benteen was appalled — and furious. "At the Washita," he wrote years later, "we lost Major Elliott, Sergt. Maj. Kennedy — a fine young soldier, and 16 enlisted men, and damn me if any search was made for them till a fortnight after. Now, as ever, I want to get at who was to blame for not finding out then!" As the burial party rejoined the column and the entire command set off for Cobb, Benteen had already decided "who was to blame": George Armstrong Custer.

The command reached Fort Cobb on 18 December. Benteen reported sick the next day and remained sick until 25 December. He had "chronic rheumatism" according to the medical records. He also had some bad news. His wife had given birth to a baby girl at Fort Harker. The infant's name was Kate Norman Benteen. She was born and died between the 13th and 19th of December. Captain Barnitz's wife, who was visiting Harker at the time, wrote: "Mrs. Benteen's baby died while I was at Harker. She was in very low spirits. Her own health was miserable & she was constantly anxious about her husband."

On 22 December, the sick Benteen sat down and wrote a letter. He addressed it to his old war comrade, William J. DeGress of St.

Louis. DeGress had been in the old pre-war Mounted Rifles regiment (by 1868 the 3rd Cavalry) and was very interested in hearing about the country, as he had traversed it himself as an enlisted man years before. Benteen took the occasion to write a critical account of Custer at the Washita. DeGress, possibly at Benteen's behest, sent the letter on to the Missouri *Democrat*, where it was published 8 February 1869. The New York *Times* reprinted it on 14 February. (Benteen denied that he intended it for publication, but its florid, melodramatic style is inconsistent with his claim that it was intended solely for DeGress's information. DeGress may have edited the letter — or had it edited — though.)

The letter from Fort Cobb was to have repercussions in the weeks ahead, but Benteen was probably unaware of the importance of it when he left Fort Cobb on 4 January 1869. The 7th Cavalry was going further west toward the Wichita Mountains to establish a military post more to General Sheridan's liking than Fort Cobb. On 8 January, they camped along Medicine Bluff Creek near what was to become Fort Sill. The captive Cheyenne women were still with them.

One of them was a young woman named Mo-nah-se-tah, who Custer described as: "an exceedingly comely squaw, possessing a bright, cheery face, a countenance beaming with intelligence, and a disposition more inclined to be merry than one usually finds among the Indians. She was probably rather under than over twenty years of age. Added to bright, laughing eyes, a set of pearly teeth, and a rich complexion, her well-shaped head was crowned with a luxuriant growth of the most beautiful silken tresses, rivalling in color the blackness of the raven and extending, when allowed to fall loosely over her shoulders, to below her waist. Her name was Mo-nah-se-tah, which, anglicized, means 'The young grass that shoots in the spring'." Benteen claimed that Custer "lived with her" and had been "seen many times in the very act of copulating with her!" Mo-nah-se-tah, as it turned out, was already pregnant. "Custer slept with her all the time," Benteen asserted, "though she was enciente and gave birth to a male child at Medicine Bluff Creek." To Benteen's sardonic amusement, the "issue" was "a simon-pure Cheyenne baby, the seed having been sown before we came down on their fold at Washita." The baby was called Tom by the cavalry officers and Yellow Bird by the Indians. "Mona," as Benteen called Custer's mistress, "had a hellish temper" and when her Cheyenne husband showed up, "gave him the marble heart in the finest of shapes." Benteen also claimed that Mona actually shot her

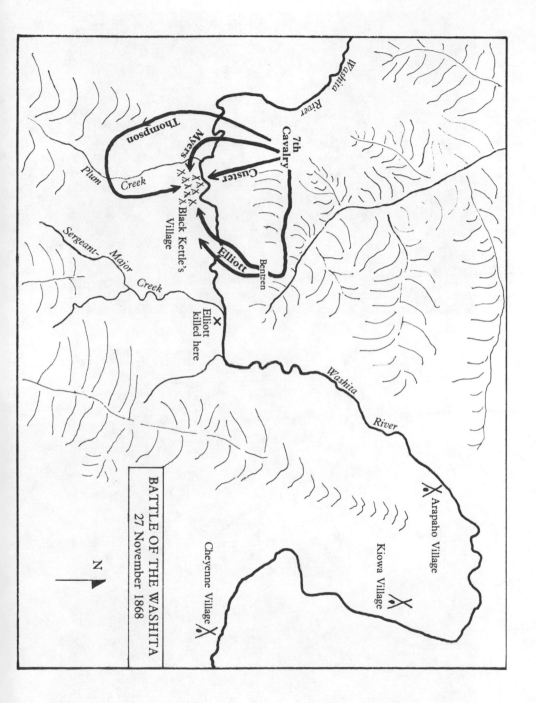

BATTLE OF THE WASHITA
27 November 1868

N

7th Cavalry

Washita River

Thompson

Myers

Custer

Black Kettle's Village

Plum Creek

Benteen

Elliott

Sergeant-Major Creek

Elliott killed here

Washita River

Cheyenne Village

Kiowa Village

Arapaho Village

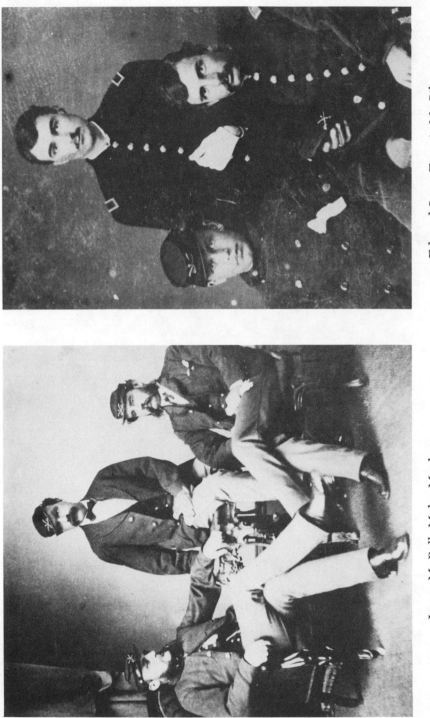

Edward Law, Francis M. Gibson,
Edward S. Godfrey

James M. Bell, Myles Moylan,
Henry J. Nowlan

husband and was heard at another time to exclaim, "Custer heap good!"

One day in late February, Benteen returned with a portion of the regiment on a routine patrol. Half-frozen, he stepped into the nearest tent to warm himself and had not been there but a few minutes when Lieutenants Tom Custer and William Cooke came bustling in. Tom had a copy of the Missouri *Democrat* of 8 February. He showed it to Benteen, saying: "Isn't that awful?"

"Why, Tom," Benteen replied, after having read a few lines of what he recognized as his letter to DeGress, "I wrote that myself."

Here is the letter that Benteen had written:

Fort Cobb, I.T. Dec. 22, 1868

My Dear Friend:

I wrote to you from Camp Supply, which place was left on the 7th, arriving at this post on the evening of the 18th. On the 11th we camped within a few miles of our "battle of the Washita", and Gens. Sheridan and Custer, with a detail of one hundred men, mounted, as escort, went out with the view of searching for the bodies of our nineteen missing comrades, including Maj. Elliott.

The bodies were found in a small circle, stripped as naked as when born, and frozen stiff. Their heads had been battered in, and some of them had had the Adam's apple cut out of their throats; some had their hands and feet cut off, and nearly all were mangled in a way delicacy forbids me to mention. They lay scarcely two miles from the scene of the fight, and all we know of the manner they were killed we have learned from Indian sources. It seems that Maj. Elliott's party was pursuing a well-mounted party of Cheyennes in the direction of the Grand Village, where nearly all the tribes were encamped, and were surrounded by the reinforcements coming to the rescue of the pursued, before the Major was aware of their position. They were out of sight and hearing of the Seventh Cavalry, which had remained at and around the captured village, about two miles away. As soon as Maj. Elliott found that he was surrounded he caused his men to dismount, and did some execution among the Indians, which added to the mortification they must have felt at the loss of the village and herds of their friends and allies, and enraged them so that they determined upon the destruction of the entire little band.

Who can describe the feeling of that brave band, as with anxious beating hearts, they strained their yearning eyes in the direction whence help should come? What must have been the despair that, when all hopes of succor died out, nerved their stout arms to do or die? Round and round rush the red fiends, smaller and smaller shrinks the circle, but the aim of that devoted, gallant knot of heroes is steadier than ever, and the death howl of the murderous redskin is more frequent. But on they come in masses grim, with glittering lance and one long, loud, exulting whoop, as if the gates of hell had opened and loosened the whole infernal host. A well-directed volley from their trusty carbines makes some of the miscreants reel and fall, but their death-rattles are drowned in the greater din. Soon every voice in that little band is still as death; but the hellish work of the savages is scarcely begun, and their ingenuities are taxed to invent barbarities to practice on the bodies of the fallen brave, the relation of which is scarcely necessary to the completion of this tale.

And now, to learn why the anxiously-looked-for succor did not come, let us view the scene in the captured village, scarce two short miles away. Light skirmishing is going on all around. Savages on flying steeds, with shields and feathers gay, are circling everywhere, riding like devils incarnate. The troops are on all sides of the village, looking on and seizing every opportunity of picking off those daring riders with their carbines. But does no one think of the welfare of Maj. Elliott and party? It seems not. But yes! a squadron of cavalry is in motion. They trot; they gallop. Now they charge! The cowardly redskins flee the coming shock and scatter here and there among the hills (to) scurry away. But it is the true line — will the cavalry keep it? No! no! They turn! Ah, 'tis only to intercept the wily foe. See! a gray troop goes on in the direction again. One more short mile and they will be saved. Oh, for a mother's prayers! Will not some good angel prompt them? They charge the mound — a few scattering shots, and the murderous pirates of the Plains go unhurt away. There is no hope for that brave little band, the death doom is theirs, for the cavalry halt and rest their panting steeds.

And now return with me to the village. Officers and soldiers are watching, resting, eating and sleeping. In an hour or so they will be refreshed, and then scour the hills and plains for their missing comrades. The commander occupies himself taking an inventory of the captured property which he had promised the officers shall be distributed among the enlisted men of the command if they falter or halt in the charge.

The day is drawing to a close and but little has been done save the work of the first hour. A great deal remains to be done. That which cannot be taken away must be destroyed. Eight hundred ponies are to be put to death. Our Chief exhibits his close sharp-shooting and terrifies the crowd of frightened, captured squaws and papooses by dropping the straggling ponies in death near them. Ah! he is a clever marksman. Not even do the poor dogs of the Indians escape his eye and aim as they drop or limp howling away. But are not those our men on guard on the other side of the creek? Will he not hit them? "My troop is on guard, General, just over there," says an officer. "Well, bullets will not go through and around hills, and you see there is a hill between us," was the reply, and the exhibition goes on. No one will come that way intentionally — certainly not. Now commences the slaughter of the ponies. Volley on volley is poured into them by too hasty men, and they, limping, get away only to meet death from a surer hand. The work progresses! The plunder having been culled over, is hastily piled; the wigwams are pulled down and thrown on it, and soon the whole of it is one blazing mass. Occasionally a startling report is heard and a steamlike volume of smoke ascends as the fire reaches a powder bag, and thus the glorious deeds of valor done in the morning are celebrated by the flaming bonfire of the afternoon. The last pony is killed. The huge fire dies out; our wounded and dead comrades — heroes of a bloody day — are carefully laid on ready ambulances, and as the brave band of the Seventh Cavalry strikes up the air, "Ain't I Glad I've Got Out of the Wilderness", we slowly pick our way across the creek over which we charged so gallantly in the early morn. Take care! do not trample on the dead bodies of that woman and child lying there! In a short time we shall be far from the scene of our daring dash, and night will have thrown her dark mantle over the scene. But surely some search will be made for our missing comrades. No, they are forgotten. Over them and the poor ponies the wolves will hold high carnival, and their howlings will be their only requiem. Slowly trudging, we return to our train some twenty miles away, and with bold, exulting hearts, learn from one another how many dead Indians have been seen.

Two weeks elapse — a larger force returns that way. A search is made and the bodies are found strewn round that little circle, frozen stiff and hard. Who shall write their eulogy?

This, my dear friend, is the story of the "battle of the Washita", poorly told.

That night, Custer assembled his officers in a Sibley tent and walked around in front of them whirling a rawhide riding crop in his hand. He told the officers that it had been brought to his attention that someone had been "belittling" his fight and that if he ever learned the identity of the author of an anonymous letter that had appeared in a certain newspaper, he would "cowhide" the culprit.

Benteen stepped outside the tent and ostentatiously checked the revolver he was wearing. He returned his gun to its holster and stepped back inside the tent. When Custer wound down his tirade, Benteen stepped forward.

"General Custer," he said, "while I cannot father all of the blame you have asserted, still, I guess I am the man you are after, and I am ready for the whipping promised."

Custer seemed genuinely astonished (suggesting that Tom Custer and Cooke had not deemed it proper to inform him of what they had learned). Custer was apparently quite taken aback upon learning that quiet, gentlemanly Benteen, who had never raised his voice, had written the offensive letter. He could plainly see the tall, husky man before him, a man who not only was toying with a revolver, but a man who was every bit as big as Custer. His face flamed and he stammered out: "Colonel Benteen, I'll see you again, sir!"

The crowd in the tent broke up in silence, seeing "no tears from whipping!" as Benteen recalled. Benteen went and collared DeBenneville Randolph Keim, a New York reporter who was in camp, and took him along when he had his inevitable interview with Custer. (Benteen had previously told Keim about the letter.) The two men entered Custer's tent. What exactly transpired has never been detailed. Benteen said simply that "Custer wilted like a whipped cur." Keim later passed the incident along to General Sheridan, whose guest he was. According to Benteen, "Sheridan gave Custer a piece of his mind about the matter", adding that he thought Sheridan "cared but little for" Custer after that. Benteen and Sheridan had a good relationship dating back to March 1862. (For that matter, it is a fact that Sheridan cooled toward his protege, Custer, by the early 1870s. However, many historians point to Sheridan's 1875 marriage to Irene Rucker as the turning point. Sheridan's new wife did not appreciate her husband's association with Libbie Custer.) In any case, as Benteen concluded, Custer "evidently knew whom to whip!"

Benteen told several people about the incident. Custer, it is apparent, never mentioned it again. It was the low point in the Custer-Benteen relationship and goes a long way towards explaining events that that occurred later. Despite the widening rift, Benteen never made an effort to get out of the regiment. Nor did Custer, when he had the opportunity a short time later, make any effort to get rid of Benteen. "I had far too much pride," Benteen said "to permit" Custer and his sychophants "driving me from" the regiment. There is also ample evidence that Custer did not reciprocate Benteen's loathing. Even Benteen recognized this. "I always surmised what I afterwards learned," he said after Custer was dead, "that he wanted me badly as a friend, but I could not be."

The 7th Cavalry remained at Medicine Bluff Creek camp for almost two months that winter. They spent the time escorting visiting officers to nearby Indian camps in the Wichita Mountains and constructing the new post. The camp was originally designated New Fort Cobb, but the name was unsatisfactory to all concerned. The 7th Cavalry officers, especially Benteen, wanted it named Fort Elliott in honor of their fallen comrade. Other regiments there, which included Colonel Benjamin H. Grierson's 10th Cavalry, had other ideas. General Sheridan intervened and named the post in honor of a former West Point classmate of his who had been killed in the Civil War. The new name, Fort Sill, endures to this day.

On 2 March 1869, the 7th Cavalry left Fort Sill in search of any one of a number of Indian bands who had not enrolled at the established reservations. Captain Myers was dispatched with his company and the wagon train to a camp near their old Washita battle site. The remaining ten companies, under Custer, scouted for Indians.

Two days later, Ulysses S. Grant was inaugurated President of the United States. The event marked the beginning of a controversial two-term administration. Its initial impact on Benteen's career was the advent of Grant's Peace Policy toward the Indians and a reduction in force of the Army. Two months later, the Union Pacific Railroad linked with the Central Pacific at Promontory Point, Utah Territory. The nation's first transcontinental railroad was complete. The Eastern Division (by then known as the Kansas Pacific) had not yet reached Fort Wallace in western Kansas and would not reach its destination, Denver, until the fall of 1870. The Indian tribes in and around Kansas were still considered threats to progress and the 7th Cavalry was to remain in Kansas until 1871.

In the meantime, they were busy completing Sheridan's work they had begun in November. Despite the fact that there was almost no forage to be obtained for their horses along the way, Custer's ten companies kept pushing across the western half of what is now Oklahoma. They encountered a small trail and, for lack of anything better to do, followed it. It was joined by another and then another and so on, until Custer was convinced that he was closing in on a Cheyenne concentration larger than the one he had hit at the Washita. On 15 March, they discovered a camp of about 200 tepees on Sweetwater Creek in the Texas Panhandle, just a little southwest of the Washita battlefield.

Custer went into the village for a parley, accompanied by Benteen's Lieutenant Cooke, and an Army doctor. He soon began to suspect that the Indians were stalling, preparatory to another vanishing act similar to the one they had pulled on Hancock at the Pawnee Fork almost two years before. Custer sent Lieutenant Cooke back to Benteen with instructions to bring the regiment to the village as fast as possible. Benteen tried to move the regiment at a trot but lost fifty horses almost from the start. On his own initiative, Benteen slowed the advance to a walk, fully aware that Custer was virtually alone in the hostile camp "undergoing their mummeries and medicine-making over him." The Cheyenne advanced boldly and started for the wagon train (the few wagons not left with Myers at the Washita). Benteen "signalled them that they must return to the village" with him and reported laconically, "they obeyed."

Benteen found Custer in the village surrounded by a group of chiefs while the squaws were sending up a series of wails. A large force of warriors circled Benteen's column menacingly, riding around them "in full paraphernalia of war bonnets, paint, etc., and whistling with their bone whistles." Benteen halted the column just short of the village and threw out a skirmish line. (In cavalry tactics, this involved one man in four holding the reins of the other three men in their designated ranks, thus freeing 75% of the mounted column to become dismounted skirmishers.) Custer told Cooke to bring two companies into the village and surround his would-be captors. At the same time, through an interpreter, he told the chiefs that they were his prisoners. "A cyclone couldn't have scattered the assembled Indians more thoroughly," Benteen related. In fact, their departure was so precipitant that Cooke's two company detail was only able to grab four Indians.

Custer, having learned of a larger village about fifteen miles away, sent one of the four prisoners to it with an invitation for its chief to meet and parley. The chief showed up on the afternoon of the 16th, having given the other village "ample time to shuffle out of harm's way." Custer told this chief that he had come to obtain the unconditional release of two white women who were known to be captives. He added that the three minor chiefs captured in the scuffle would remain as hostages until the women were released. The Indian promised to see what he could do and disappeared.

Custer mounted his command and set off in the direction of the second camp, carefully avoiding Hancock's mistake of burning the captured village. He did not want the responsibility for another season of Indian raiding to replenish the losses. When the 7th Cavalry arrived at the site of the second village, they found it had vanished. No one was especially surprised, least of all Benteen. " 'Tis scarcely necessary," he said drily, "to tell anyone having a knowledge of Indians that there were no Indians there to welcome us." Yet, some Indians began to arrive in small groups and listen to what Custer, through his interpreter and captives, had to say. Custer gave them an ultimatum: the white women before the sun went down or the three captives would hang. He even pointed out a cottonwood tree he had picked out for that purpose. The Indian captives, said Benteen, "exhorted their friends to be diligent." As it turned out, the women captives had to be purchased from the Indians who "owned" them by concerned friends and relatives of the Indian captives. This process would take some time, the delegates assured Custer.

Custer apparently just pointed to the tree, though given his loquacious nature, it is hard to believe he did not make some kind of a speech. In any case, "not much before the going down of the sun", according to Benteen, the two women appeared, dressed in flour sacks, decorated with Indian jewelry, and quite pregnant. Benteen later related that the Indians had ceased to maltreat the women after they had received news of the Washita. A brother of one of the women was with Custer. There was a joyous family reunion.

The Indians expected the three captives to be released. Custer had no such intention. Inevitably, another controversy arose. Custer insisted that he had not promised to release them, only to *spare* them, *if* the women were released. The Indians (and their supporters down to the present day) saw this as an example of the forked-tongue diplomacy frequently associated with the government. The answer, naturally, cannot be established. Custer liked to talk. He may have said anything. Benteen never regarded anything about the episode as an example of Custer's treachery. And he would have been among the first to point it out had he felt there was any validity to the charge at all.

On 22 March 1869, Custer's 7th Cavalry marched to the Washita battlefield to link with Myers and the rest of the wagons. Within five days, they were back at Camp Supply on the North Canadian, headed for summer posts in Kansas. On 4 April, they reached Fort Dodge on the Arkansas. Dodge had been garrisoned by B Company (Captain Thompson) almost since the 7th Cavalry was first formed. "He and his troop," said Benteen, "desired to remain there. I did not want it; this Custer knew." Custer also knew that Benteen's wife was seriously ill and that the infant Benteen girl had died during the winter. And, he had not forgotten that he "still owed" Benteen $100. "Custer paid me off for the letter in almost spot cash," Benteen concluded bitterly. Custer directed Benteen to remain behind the regiment and report himself for duty at Fort Dodge. Years later, Benteen could "still remember the fiendish gleam of delight that seemed to sparkle in the eyes of Adjt. Myles Moylan", who was the bearer of the order. Furthermore, Benteen's first lieutenant, Will Cooke, was taken away from him. Cooke knew in advance about the posting and arranged a transfer with Lieutenant Charles Brewster of I Company. He "never said good-bye even, nor did he ever ask the amt. of his mess bill!" Benteen complained many years later.

Benteen dutifully reported with his company to Major Henry Douglass of the 3rd Infantry at Fort Dodge. Major Douglass had been put on the Unassigned List and promptly signed over the post and property to Benteen on 9 April. (The reduction in force of the Army had begun, reducing 45 infantry regiments to 25; many of the excess officers found themselves temporarily unassigned.) Captain Benteen took advantage of his new position as commanding officer at Fort Dodge to approve an assignment for himself to Fort Harker on detached service until 15 May, commencing 19 April 1869. At Harker, he was engaged in seeing his sick wife and only surviving child (little Freddie) off to visit relatives in St. Louis for the summer as well as collecting H Company property still at the old post.

Upon his return, he was visited by Colonel William G. Mitchell, the inspector general for the department. Colonel Mitchell was surprised to see Benteen at Dodge and, in the course of business, asked him if he liked the assignment. "Not by a damned sight!" growled Benteen, insisting that Custer had banished him for writing the offensive letter. Benteen showed Mitchell the DeGress letter.

"Well," Colonel Mitchell said after reading it, "I'll fix this up for you the first thing I do on my return to Fort Leavenworth. You can be making preparations to join (the) regiment at Fort Hays."

Mitchell was as good as his word. Benteen's H Company departed Ft. Dodge forever on 2 June and marched into the cavalry camp outside Fort Hays on 8 June 1869. Enroute, they had encountered their erstwhile lieutenant, Cooke, who was escorting Colonel James A. Hardie (Inspector General, Division of the Missouri) to Camp Supply. Captain Benteen was beside the road butchering a buffalo cow. Cooke rode up to him and they exchanged their first words since Cooke's reassignment to I Company.

"At your old business, I see," Cooke quipped.

"Yes," Benteen replied evenly. "I can't keep out of blood."

Cooke then delivered what Benteen thought was good news. Colonel A.J. Smith had resigned his commission to accept the postmastership of St. Louis. The War Department promoted a senior officer, Lieutenant Colonel Samuel D. Sturgis of the 6th Cavalry, to be colonel commanding the 7th Cavalry. According to Cooke, Sturgis was the new commanding officer at Fort Hays. "I gave three hearty cheers!" Benteen recalled.

Colonel Samuel D. Sturgis of the 7th Cavalry was the same man Benteen had known at Wilson's Creek. He was the same man Benteen had heard reviled by the survivor's of Brice's Crossroads. Benteen had a low opinion of Sturgis that dated back to 1861, but felt on that spring morning that even Sturgis was preferable to Custer.

H Company remained in the cavalry camp outside Hays until 7 September 1869, when they were formally assigned to the fort itself for the winter.

13

Occupation Duty

The twenty-fourth day of August, 1869, brought Benteen to age thirty-five, a good deal heavier through the middle than he had been when he first accepted a commission, For some reason, perhaps hereditary, Benteen's dark brown hair had turned entirely gray by 1869.

A new officer joined H Company at Fort Hays, filling the second lieutenant vacancy created by the resignation of Lieutenant Oliver W. Longan, who had never gotten around to joining the company. The new officer, 2nd Lieutenant Charles C. DeRudio, was destined to remain with Benteen longer than any other associate in his military career. DeRudio's life to that point had been one of the most exciting imaginable, worthy of a full-length biography.

Carlo Camilio di Rudio was born 26 August 1832 in Belluno, Italy, of noble parents. He attended the Royal Austrian Military Academy in Milan, but ran away when the political troubles of 1848 brought the possibility of his having to fight Italian patriots in an Austrian army officer's uniform. He served with various bands fighting for Italian independence, including Mazzini's and Garibaldi's. He fled Italy and attempted to sail to America, but was shipwrecked off Spain and compelled to eke out an existence in Barcelona and later in Marseilles, France. From this period of his life came many tales, all thrilling but undocumented. He was supposed to have been a French army officer in Algeria, an exile in Switzerland, and a radical manning the barricades in Paris against Napoleon III's *coup d'etat*. He could conceivably have been all three — or none. In 1855, di Rudio turned up in England, working as a dock hand in East London. He apparently tried to supplement his income as a language teacher without much success. He allegedly went to Nottingham, but there is some doubt about this. (There is quite a bit of doubt about many of the details of di Rudio's early years. There are as many versions as there are writers on the subject. All the versions derive from di Rudio himself; he was notorious as a spinner of tall tales.)

On 9 December 1855, he married a 15-year-old illiterate named Eliza Booth, daughter of a frame work knitter. The wedding took place in Godalming, Surrey, the residence of Eliza and her family. (Eliza had been born and reared in Nottingham, which may account for *that* tale.) According to one account, di Rudio "seduced" young Eliza and was forced to marry her "to save her mother's shame." The newly-weds went to live in a tenement in East London, where their neighbors (who could hardly have been very affluent themselves) later declared that they "had never seen a family more wretched." Rumors persisted for years that di Rudio took in a little extra money by informing for the police. It is a fact that one day in April 1856, di Rudio was stabbed six times by a knife-wielding fanatic in a little restaurant that catered to Italian exiles. Three of the other victims that day were suspected police informers. While recuperating, di Rudio was approached by an agent of the fanatical Italian patriot, Felice Orsini.

Orsini had conceived a plot to assassinate the Emperor of France, Napoleon III. Eliza Booth di Rudio was given some money to tide her over and, on 7 January 1858, her impoverished husband left for France in the company of Orsini and at least two other conspirators. They arrived in Paris on 10 January 1858 and the next evening, di Rudio was shown the bombs that had been specially prepared for the assassination. An American Army officer who later saw one of the bombs described it as "about seven inches long by five in diameter and egg-shaped." They looked to di Rudio "like a clutch of monstrous bird's eggs, spiny and fantastic and yet hideously real." They were hollow, meant to be filled with gunpowder, and scored on the outside so as to fragment upon detonation. They were allegedly designed by a former Austrian army officer and manufactured in England as "gas fixtures." (Today they would be characterized as hand grenades.) There were probably six of them in all, in two different sizes. Only four were actually used.

In the late evening of 14 January 1858, Orsini, di Rudio and one other conspirator mingled among the crowd outside the Paris Opera waiting for Napoleon III and the Empress Eugenie to arrive. (A fourth conspirator had been detained by the police.) They concealed the filled and primed bombs in black handkerchiefs and waited as the Emperor's coach, escorted by a squadron of Lancers, pulled up outside the Opera. Fellow-conspirator Antonio Gomez threw the first bomb. Di Rudio followed it up with a second — a big one — and Orsini himself hurled at least one small one, perhaps two.

Miraculously, Napoleon III was only scratched. The Empress Eugenie received a small fragment in her eye that did no permanent damage, but 156 people, including many of the Lancer escort, were wounded. Eight of them later died. The total might have run higher, but Orsini "in his anxiety to obtain the maximum explosive force, had filled the bombs too full, and thus produced a fragmentation that was too minute." A little more than two hours later, a galvanized French police force arrested di Rudio in his hotel room. The others were captured that night.

Two of the Orsini conspirators went to the guillotine on 14 March 1858. One of the two spared, for reasons unknown, was di Rudio. He later claimed that he had been reprieved just as he was mounting the guillotine, though newspaper accounts of that day do not bear this out. He was indeed taken out of his cell that day, but instead of death was handed a commutation — life imprisonment. He apparently spent some time in French military prisons before being shipped to a penal colony in the French Guianas. He escaped "as by a miracle" under mysterious circumstances that suggest official connivance. There are three different versions of his escape, but he definitely arrived in the British Guianas on 15 December 1858. On 29 February 1860, he returned to his child bride in London.

The next few years of his life are a blank. He claimed that he had visited his old hero, Mazzini, gone on a lecture tour, and became interested in the struggle to preserve the Union in the United States. Whatever the truth is, he and his wife and children left London on a boat for America on 8 February 1864.

On 25 August 1864, in New York City, he enlisted in Company A of the 79th New York Volunteers as a paid substitute for a man named Ross. He gave his name as Charles C. DeRudio and his occupation as soldier. He did not relish his service as a private and wrote to a sponsor in New York: "I am in contact with some common and low fellows of this country and their company makes me disgusted with the service I am obliged to perform." He did not remain disgusted long. One of his sponsors was the editor of the New York *Tribune*,

Horace Greeley, who was exerting his not inconsiderable influence
in DeRudio's behalf. On 18 October 1864, outside the trenches at
Petersburg, DeRudio was handed a commission as second lieutenant
in the 2nd USCT regiment, then stationed on occupation duty in
Florida. DeRudio spent the remainder of the war with his Negro
infantrymen in Key West, mustering out 5 January 1866.

Another powerful sponsor, Senator Charles Sumner, succeeded in
obtaining a Regular Army commission for DeRudio after some initial
difficulty. DeRudio was made a second lieutenant in the 2nd Infantry
and was one of many officers who were put on the unassigned list
in the spring of 1869. But again, his sponsors came to his rescue and
DeRudio was transferred to the 7th Cavalry on 14 July 1869.

A little over a month later, he reported for duty as the second
lieutenant of Benteen's H Company, at Fort Hays. Despite his rather
checkered past, DeRudio was accepted by most of the officers of the
regiment uncritically. "Custer, in particular, was most impressed with
DeRudio's alleged title of Count." Benteen, naturally, was not so
uncritical, but befriended the suave Italian adventurer nonetheless.
He later asserted that he was DeRudio's only friend in the regiment,
and subsequent events tend to bear this out. "I treated him as a gentleman," Benteen said, "which he was not!" DeRudio had a reputation
for being quite a story-teller and as time wore on, the other officers
began to lose fascination with his "piercing black eyes, his witty
conversation, his deep bass chuckle" and even his enchanting English
wife. Benteen viewed DeRudio with a sort of affectionate bemusement.
"The 'Count' was always a fearful liar!" he said later, but seemed to
enjoy his company — and his wife's — as long as he and DeRudio
were together.

DeRudio was certainly qualified by his training to be an Army
officer and, as events proved, he was a fairly competent one. The
following year, while temporarily assigned to G Company, he escorted
a party of settlers into the Solomon River Valley and guaranteed
that he would protect them until they could get homes and defensive
structures built. The only real threat by then was small bands of
horse-stealing Indians from reservations further south. "That fall a
memorial signed by 115 settlers of Solomon Valley, Kansas, tendered
their thanks to 2nd Lieutenant DeRudio for standing off Indian attacks so effectively that only one settler was killed during that time."

In the winter of 1869-70, Benteen got his $100 back from Custer.
The regimental headquarters had moved from Hays to Fort Leaven-

worth before Benteen's arrival at Hays and there he heard by the grapevine that Custer had "made a haul at Jenison's faro bank." (The "Jenison" referred to was the notorious Jayhawker Jennison who had commanded a brigade of cavalry at the battle of Westport and in the pursuit of Price in 1864.) Benteen promptly dunned Custer for $91, allowing the remaining $9 as losses in poker games the two had engaged in since the loan. Custer replied that the amount was $92 and closed a check. Said Benteen: "I cooly returned on the same day a one dollar bill, thanking him for his promptitude in discharging his debt!" Benteen's handling of the year-old debt did not endear him to Custer. "After that," Benteen said, "you can imagine what dealings I had with the S.O.B. He had proved to my entire satisfaction that he was a cur of '1st water'."

At about the same time, Benteen became better acquainted with Custer's new immediate superior, Colonel Sturgis. From Sturgis he learned other things that lowered his already poor opinion of Custer. According to Sturgis, who had been Custer's subordinate in the volunteer organization right after the war, Custer had engaged in a "gouge game on the U.S." with respect to quartermaster and subsistence contracts in Texas in 1865. Sturgis, who succeeded Custer in that department in 1866, "came prepared with papers and affidavits" to prove the "rascalities" of Custer and his family, including his father, Emmanuel Custer. "Knowing the man," Benteen said, Sturgis "came prepared for war."

There is no factual evidence in existence that Colonel Sturgis had anything strong enough to bring formal charges against Custer. And, for all Benteen's talk of "war" between the two men, the only act recorded was Sturgis' relieving the 7th Cavalry quartermaster, Lieutenant A.E. Smith, a Custer man. Even Benteen admitted that Sturgis had relieved Smith "for lying to him." But the allegations did some damage. Benteen began to reflect on some strange things he had witnessed while with Custer. He kept them in the back of his mind and found what he considered proof of Custer's crooked dealings with post traders, but this did not come until after Custer's death.

On 18 March 1870, a new major reported for duty with the 7th Cavalry at Fort Hays: Marcus A. Reno. He and Benteen formed a relationship that was hardly different from the one Benteen had with Custer. They clashed almost at once.

Major Reno was born 15 November 1834 in Carrolltown, Illinois, and entered West Point 1 September 1851. It took Reno six years to complete a four year course at West Point, having been set back two successive years for disciplinary reasons that seem trivial today. In one case, he was court-martialed for "deficiency of conduct," a catch-all that merely meant that he had acquired more than the number of demerits allowed for such infractions as visiting a tavern that was off-limits, carving his initials on a tree, and failing to walk a sentry post "in a soldierly manner." The second setback was prompted by another court-martial for singing on sentry duty and "contemptuously" telling the arresting officer that he knew of no rule against singing on guard duty.

Reno finally graduated in June 1858, almost squarely in the middle of his class in academic standing. He was commissioned a second lieutenant in the 1st Dragoons, stationed on the Pacific Coast. The Civil War brought Reno rapid promotion to captain in the Regular Army. On 1 January 1865 he was appointed colonel commanding the 12th Pennsylvania Cavalry and later that year was breveted brigadier general of volunteers, an honor that had eluded Benteen. Reno served with distinction throughout the war, being wounded at the fight at Kelly's Ford in 1863 and serving on the staff of General Sheridan in the Shenandoah Valley in 1864. He had married a wealthy woman named Mary Hannah Ross at Harrisburg, Pennsylvania, during the war and the Renos had one small son.

The end of the war found Reno reduced to captain in the 1st Cavalry. He returned briefly as an instructor at West Point, then pushed on to occupation duty in New Orleans, before finally reporting to his regiment in Washington Territory. When Major Alfred Gibbs died in December 1868, Captain Reno was promoted to major, 7th Cavalry. He did not join the new regiment until 18 March 1870 and then, at Fort Hays, met Captain Benteen for the first time.

Sometime during the spring of 1870, as H Company was having their Spencer repeating carbines replaced by .52 caliber single-shot Sharps carbines, Benteen and Reno got into a brawl at the Post Trader's. (The exact date and attendant circumstances have never been detailed, but Fort Hays was the only post Benteen and Reno shared until after the battle of the Little Big Horn.) One night at the Post Trader's, "before a crowd of officers," Reno "attempted to bully" Benteen. In the scuffle, Benteen addressed his superior as a "dirty S.O.B." and slapped his face, offering Reno "satisfaction" if the insult were not sufficient. Reno declined further combat with Benteen. Reno from that point on was not "all dying with love for" Benteen

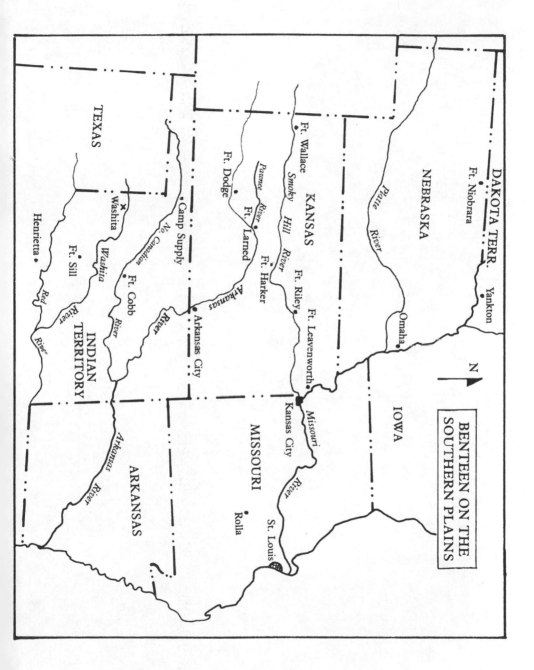

BENTEEN ON THE
SOUTHERN PLAINS

N

DAKOTA TERR.

Ft. Niobrara

Yankton

NEBRASKA

Platte River

Omaha

IOWA

Ft. Wallace

KANSAS

Ft. Dodge

Pawnee River

Smoky Hill River

Ft. Larned

Ft. Riley

Ft. Harker

Ft. Leavenworth

Kansas City

Missouri River

Missouri River

TEXAS

Washita
×

Camp Supply

No. Canadian

Arkansas River

Arkansas City

MISSOURI

Rolla

St. Louis

Henrietta

Ft. Sill

Washita River

Ft. Cobb

River

INDIAN
TERRITORY

Arkansas River

ARKANSAS

Red River

River

Edward G. Mathey

Charles H. Rea

Marcus A. Reno

Charles C. DeRudio
with one of his daughters

and the proud, silver-haired captain could never regard Reno as "a bosom crony." "My opinion of Reno," Benteen said drily, "was not an exalted one."

And yet, Reno seems to have come away from the incident with a respect for Benteen. Reno was known throughout the regiment for his sarcastic manner of speaking and for being somewhat abusive and difficult to deal with even when completely sober. There is no evidence prior to 1876 that Reno had any special problem with alcohol, though his subsequent career in the regiment was ruined by a series of incidents that stemmed from overindulgence in drink. The two men adopted a formal, superficial relationship related to duty and had little to do with one another until the battle of the Little Big Horn and its aftermath.

Benteen spent a month in the spring of 1870 visiting his wife's relatives in St. Louis. Upon his return, he found that Lieutenant Brewster had taken H Company to Colorado for a summer of patrolling under Major Tilford. Benteen himself was put on detached service and kept at Hays until 1 July. It was then that he became acquainted with 2nd Lieutenant Charles H. Rea, a 22-year-old West Pointer who had just come from Fort Leavenworth, where Custer was stationed.

Rea had graduated high in his class at West Point in 1869 and joined the 7th Cavalry the previous summer. He was, in Benteen's words, "the brightest man and in every way the best fitted for a cavalry soldier." Rea related a story that caused Benteen's ears to prick up. It was about Custer.

Rea had become smitten with a certain lady of easy virtue and had "paid her assiduous court — on C.O.D. order." One day, while riding with her outside Leavenworth, Rea was startled by a group of officers and some women, one of whom Rea named for Benteen. This woman was known to be another lady of easy virtue, though Rea was unaware of it at the time. Rea fled at their approach, leaving his prostitute behind. But, he lost his forage cap in getting away and Custer (who was in the approaching group) found the cap and "persisted in demanding the resignation" of Lieutenant Rea.

Benteen concluded from this story and others he had heard that Custer was "criminally connected" with the second prostitute and "criminally intimate with a married woman" at Fort Leavenworth. Benteen felt the persecution of Lieutenant Rea was a case of hypocrisy on the part of Custer. (Rea did resign under pressure that fall and became a merchant in St. Louis for a time before joining the police department of that city. He retired from the St. Louis Police Department in 1906.)

On 1 July 1870 Benteen left Fort Hays to join his company in the field. He remained in a camp on the Big Sandy River (near present-day Lamar) until that fall. He brought his H Company back to Hays, arriving 4 November. Two weeks later, his first lieutenant, Charles Brewster, resigned rather than face a Benzine Board.

Benzine Boards were the Army's answer to the reduction-in-force of 1869-70. Major General Winfield S. Hancock, the former Department of the Missouri commander, headed them up, giving them another nickname: Hancock Boards. The boards solicited unit and post commanders to submit names of officers under their command who were believed to be unworthy of retaining a commission. The boards met, heard the evidence, and occasionally dismissed an officer from the Army. Several officers in the 7th Cavalry were recommended for these boards, but Benteen was not among them. Despite his bad relations with his superiors, he was not then (or ever) considered an inefficient officer. The boards did an injustice to some officers, but the consensus of historians of the period is that they were effective in ridding the Army of many undesirable officers. Many, such as Brewster, resigned rather than face them.

Charles Brewster was a Custer man. He had served with the Boy General during the Civil War as a captain and commissary of subsistence. He had been assigned to the 7th as a first lieutenant in I Company until exchanging places with Lieutenant Cooke in April 1869. Colonel Sturgis recommended Brewster for a Benzine Board on the grounds that Brewster was "a very trifling character" who "brings neither energy [n]or industry into play in the execution of his duties and besides all this is unreliable and untrustworthy never hesitating to tell a lie when it suits his purpose." How much of Sturgis' opinion derived from Benteen's assessment can only be guessed at, but Benteen did write a letter (with other officers) in 1878 urging rejection of Brewster's appeal for return of his commission, stating in part that Brewster was "totally unfit, in every way, to be an army officer." He added that he could think of "nothing in Lt. Brewster's military career, in the 7th Cavalry, that would at all redound to his credit, but many things to the contrary."

Brewster's replacement was 1st Lieutenant Henry J. Nowlan, who had been the regimental commissary of subsistence for three years. Nowlan had an unusual background. He was British, an 1854 graduate of the Royal Military Academy at Sandhurst and a former British Army officer in the 41st Foot. He came to America in 1862 and secured a commission in the 14th New York Cavalry. The next year, he was captured by Confederates and spent the remainder of the war in Andersonville prison camp in Georgia. When the postwar Army was organized, Nowlan was one of the 7th Cavalry's original second lieutenants and one of its first promoted to first lieutenant. He was assigned to Benteen's H Company for a month before moving on to another vacancy in L Company, ultimately becoming the regimental quartermaster in 1872.

Nowlan's replacement never joined H Company. He was 1st Lieutenant Charles S. Ilsley. The reason Ilsley never joined was symptomatic of a problem that plagued the 7th Cavalry as long as Benteen was with it. Ilsley was an aide-de-camp to Brigadier General John Pope of Omaha. There were a number of 7th Cavalry officers similarly assigned only on paper, including three company commanders: Dayton (M), Sheridan (L), and Tourtellotte (G). These men spent most of their military careers in staff positions far removed from the regiment simply because Army policy at the time dictated that all general staff officers not assigned to a specific staff department be assigned to a line regiment. To further reduce the officer strength of the regiments, many officers spent long periods of time on detached service: sitting on various boards, recruiting, or filling largely ceremonial positions around the country.

Benteen got to know Ilsley later. He did not like the man, dubbing him "Captain Marmalade." Ilsley, a captain in a Maine infantry regiment during the Civil War, eventually left Pope's staff and became commanding officer of E Company — the "Gray Horse Troop" — when Captain Myers died. Benteen came to view Ilsley with "the most supreme contempt," for reasons unspecified.

In February 1871, M Company, H Company's "sister" in the regiment, got a new commanding officer. Its original commanding officer, Captain Dayton of General Sherman's staff was discharged at his own request. M Company's original first lieutenant (and *de facto* commander), Owen Hale, had previously been promoted to captain and given command of K Company. (Captain West, K Company's original commander, had decided to get away from Custer while the getting was good and, in the spring of 1869 following the Sweetwater Creek incident, had secured the post tradership of Fort Sill. He died of sunstroke that fall before he could open his store.) Captain Hale

replaced West in K Company and Tom Custer became the first lieutenant (and acting company commander) of M Company.

Tom Custer was superceded in February 1871 by yet another transfer from the unassigned list: Captain Thomas H. French. "Tucker"
French, a fat officer with a squeaky voice, became a close associate
of Benteen's. He was arguably one of the bravest officers in the regiment and one of the select few toward whom Benteen felt kindly
disposed. French had enlisted in the 10th Infantry (Regular Army)
during the Civil War and had been given a battlefield commission
for bravery in action around Petersburg. Remaining in the Regular
Army after the war, he had been steadily promoted, reaching the rank
of captain by 1868. French had an unfortunate weakness for heavy
drink that would eventually prove his undoing. He arrived at Fort
Hays just as the regiment was preparing to deploy to Kentucky.

The deployment of the 7th Cavalry to various posts in the South
came as no surprise to its officers and men. The new assignment had
been rumored for months. The reasons for stationing the 7th Cavalry
in the South in 1871 are quite involved, but they all boil down to two:
completion of the railroad through western Kansas, and the activities
of certain Southern organizations such as the Ku Klux and White
Leagues. The Indian troubles on the Plains were far from over, but
the occupation of the South was becoming a dangerous business for
some of the carpetbagger officials and the newly-enfranchised Negroes.
The rise of white-supremicist organizations like the Ku Klux is a
difficult phenomenon to explain briefly, but it is a fact that by the
early 1870s, officials in the South, especially federal marshals, were
in need of military protection. The government responded by sending cavalry units, the 7th Cavalry in particular, to posts scattered
throughout the South as mounted policemen.

To a man like Benteen, who regarded himself as a Southerner in
spirit, this task was "the most unsatisfactory work that a cavalryman
can be detailed for." To make matters more palatable for him, however, the reassignment gave him a chance to relax with his wife and
son in more civilized surroundings. He had just learned to his chagrin
that Kate Benteen had decided she liked Southern plantation living
after all. "If you liked the place down there so very well," Benteen
scolded her in a letter, referring to their farm outside Atlanta where
Kate had spent most of the winter, "and had told me so, long ago — I
doubtless could have enjoyed myself much better than I have done."
Kate had used the rumored redeployment as an excuse to drag her

feet about returning to western Kansas. Benteen complained bitterly about her prolonged absence and told her: "I would blow my damned brains out before I would live through another four months like it. So, for Christ's sake come home quickly."

Kate dutifully hurried to Fort Hays, possibly as much galvanized by her husband's threat to "sell or give away everything around the premises" if she did not "hurry and come back" as she was by his insistence that he missed her sorely. In May 1871, Captain and Mrs. Benteen and little Freddie boarded a train for Kentucky.

In Louisville, they were visited by Custer, his brother Tom, and Lieutenant Cooke, seeking Benteen's agreement to change his impending assignment to Nashville, Tennessee, with M Company. Custer claimed that H Company would not be allowed to remain in Nashville and that M Company (of which his brother Tom was first lieutenant) would gladly swap its assignment to South Carolina for Nashville even though only temporarily. Benteen insisted on taking the matter up with Colonel Sturgis. Custer told Kate that whenever he recommended anything to Benteen, he could be sure that Benteen would do just the opposite. Kate agreed with Custer and told her husband that he was "dead wrong."

When Benteen found Sturgis, he was told the truth of the matter. Custer, in Sturgis' words, was a "lying whelp" and just trying to get Tom Custer out of having to go to South Carolina. Benteen took great satisfaction in being able to refuse Custer's request. His H Company went to Nashville and remained there for almost the entire time the 7th Cavalry was in the South.

The garrison at Nashville consisted of just two companies of the 16th Infantry and that regiment's headquarters. It was also the headquarters for the Department of the South, which was responsible for Army troops in Tennessee, Georgia, Alabama, Florida, North Carolina, and South Carolina. The commanding general of the Department of the South was Brigadier General Alfred H. Terry, a former lawyer who had risen to high rank during the Civil War and who had remained in the post-war Army as its only non-West Point general for many years. The commanding officer of the garrison at Nashville was Colonel Galusha Pennypacker, who had been one of Terry's best subordinates during the war. (Pennypacker was promoted to brigadier general of volunteers at age 22, making him a younger brigadier general than Custer.)

Two days after his 37th birthday in 1871, Benteen was inducted into the International Order of Odd Fellows, a lodge organization in which he remained active until his death. Whenever H Company was deployed for brief periods of time into Alabama as escorts for federal marshals, Benteen managed to get himself assigned to detached service. Not that the work was strenuous; the company was usually broken up into small detachments commanded by sergeants or corporals and there was really no need for the company commander to supervise a corporal's guard.

The horses of the company were gradually exchanged for excellent thoroughbred horses that thrived in the South and Benteen found himself once again commanding a well-mounted company. Recruits poured in to bring the company up to strength, then authorized at sixty men. One of them was Charles Windolph, a young German immigrant who would eventually become H Company's first sergeant. Windolph remembered his first meeting with Benteen. "I thought he was about the finest-looking soldier I had ever seen. He had bright eyes and a ruddy face, and he had a great thatch of iron-gray hair. It made him look mighty handsome." After ten years service with Benteen, Windolph concluded that he was "just about the finest soldier and the greatest gentleman I ever knew."

Another future first sergeant joined H Company about this time: Joseph McCurry, a 23-year-old Pennsylvanian who was a baseball pitcher of professional caliber. McCurry was made first sergeant of the company within two years, perhaps one of the youngest first sergeants in the Army at the time, certainly the youngest in the 7th Cavalry. His baseball prowess may have had something to do with it, but McCurry also organized other sports activities in the company and even instituted a glee club. Benteen recognized the natural leadership qualities young McCurry possessed and promoted him steadily. On 1 March 1873, an organization of fifty-four enlisted men (virtually all of them) and the officers was officially named the Benteen Baseball Club at Nashville. Sergeant Patrick Connally was the president of the club and Joseph McCurry was the captain of the Benteen Nine.

On 2 April 1872, Kate Benteen had another baby, a girl named Fannie Gibson Benteen. Since 1st Lieutenant Francis M. Gibson was transferred to H Company from A Company three months later, there may have been a connection there. However, Benteen's superior at Fort Hays (whom he much admired) had been Major George Gibson of the 5th Infantry. Fannie Gibson Benteen may have been named after either one of the other — or both — but the most likely candidate is Major Gibson.

Benteen did not have a very high opinion of Lieutenant "Frank" Gibson, saying: "I don't think there was a poorer lieutenant in the Army." "Gib," as he was also known, had a reputation for being a practical joker and something of a lightweight as a cavalry officer. He was 25½ years old when he joined H Company in Nashville that summer, a former Army Pay Department clerk from Philadelphia who had been granted a direct commission from civilian life. He had previously been a second lieutenant in Moylan's A Company.

Benteen was also critical of Gibson's wife. Interestingly, Kate Garrett Gibson, who was the sister of Lieutenant Donald McIntosh's wife, left behind no negative evaluations of Benteen. Neither she nor her husband seemed to be aware of Benteen's low regard for them, a fact that argues eloquently for the atypical (but more accurate) image of Benteen as a soft-spoken, courtly gentleman who kept his personal feelings to himself. Frank Gibson later wrote to his wife that Benteen was in his opinion "one of the coolest and bravest men I have ever known." His wife in turn left behind papers and correspondence that her daughter later used to write a book about life in the 7th Cavalry that is thrilling if somewhat inaccurate.

Benteen, to the end of his life, had great respect for General Alfred H. Terry. Significantly, when Terry was reassigned in 1873 to the Department of Dakota (comprising most of the modern states of Minnesota, North and South Dakota, and Montana), he requested that the 7th Cavalry be given to his command. The only 7th Cavalrymen he had hitherto seen for any length of time were Benteen's H Company.

14

Dakota Territory

The situation in the Department of Dakota in the spring of 1873 was somewhat unique, but not entirely atypical of the U.S. government's problems with Indians on the Plains. At about the same time commissioners had arranged the Medicine Lodge Treaty with the tribes Benteen had faced in Kansas, another group of commissioners made a treaty with the more numerous Lakota Indians in the north. The Lakota, also known as Sioux, were given a reservation that essentially was the western half of what is now the state of South Dakota — west of the Missouri River. They were required to enroll in agencies that were originally located on the Missouri River (for ease of transportation of supplies to them). The southern-most agency was abandoned when some of the Sioux insisted on locations closer to their traditional homeland. It was duly replaced with two other agencies in northwestern Nebraska. The treaty promised the usual annuities and protection from white interlopers in the designated reservation. It also allowed the Sioux to roam and hunt in a vague area north of the Platte River and east of the Big Horn Mountains. But, the real bone of contention in 1873 was what came to be known as the "unceded lands," another deliberately vague territory around the Powder River in what is now eastern Wyoming and southeastern Montana. The government promised to keep white intruders out of these unceded lands and to allow the Sioux to wander through them, hunting buffalo and following their traditional life style.

The unceded lands did not include the Yellowstone River valley and unquestionably did not include the northern bank of that river. Yet, the Sioux were numerous, belligerent, and had defeated the

Army in 1867, forcing government abandonment of three forts in the general vicinity of the unceded lands. They considered (with some justification) that the land north of the Yellowstone River was also theirs by right of possession. It would have become an issue sooner or later, but a white enterprise, the Northern Pacific Railroad, made sure it was sooner.

The Northern Pacific Railroad was constructed with relative ease and speed across the Dakota prairie from Duluth, Minnesota, to what became Bismarck, North Dakota, by 1872. Survey parties, headed by a former Confederate general (and West Point classmate of Custer's) named Thomas Rosser, continued westward toward their ultimate destination in the Montana hinterland. In the fall of 1871, they had crossed the Missouri River west of Bismarck, surveying the rail route. They were escorted by six infantry companies and spent only a month working before hostile Indians and winter weather forced a postponement until the next spring. The following year, Colonel David S. Stanley of the 22nd Infantry escorted Rosser's surveyors even further west with 12 companies of infantry. The parties remained in the field from mid-July to mid-October, having several clashes with hostile Sioux. The following year, 1873, General Terry returned to the Department of Dakota and planned an even more extensive expedition for surveying along the north bank of the Yellowstone River. This expedition, once again commanded by Colonel Stanley, was escorted by no less than 19 infantry companies and 10 companies of the 7th Cavalry under Custer. It was known to history as the Yellowstone Expedition of 1873 or the Stanley Expedition.

In April 1873, the entire 7th Cavalry was transferred to Dakota Territory, garrisoning posts along the Missouri River and making preparations for the summer expedition. Two of the companies (D & I under Major Reno) were sent north to Fort Pembina to escort a party of international boundary surveyors. The other ten companies assembled in late June at Fort Rice.

On 20 June 1873, the Stanley Expedition left Fort Rice for the wilds of Montana. Predictably, Benteen and Custer clashed almost at once. The issue was a horse that belonged to H Company. Custer had taken it and given it to a civilian named Fred Calhoun to ride. (Fred Calhoun, who was angling for a commission in the 7th Cavalry, was the younger brother of Lieutenant James Calhoun of C Company and brother-in-law of Captain Myles Moylan of A Company. James Calhoun had married Custer's younger sister, Margaret, in 1872.)

Colonel Stanley's commissary of subsistence on the expedition, Lieutenant P. Henry Ray of the 8th Infantry, came to Benteen. He was riding a mule and asked the gray-haired captain if Benteen could "not do better for" him. Benteen pointed out the horse that Fred Calhoun was riding and told Ray the facts. Ray's subsequent complaint to Colonel Stanley "got Custer in arrest", but Stanley later got drunk and "the game was thrown into Custer's hand."

On 23 June, Lieutenant Fred Grant of the 4th Cavalry (son of the President) came to Custer and informed him that Stanley's men were going through the wagons with axes looking for whiskey to destroy. Custer transferred the alcoholic beverages from the wagons of the sutler (travelling trader) who accompanied the 7th Cavalry to the wagons of the 7th Cavalry, an uncharacteristic action on the part of the teetotalling Custer. (Benteen explained it later by insinuating that Custer had an arrangement with the sutler.) But, Custer was foiled. To Benteen's amusement, Stanley's keg-busting detail found the whiskey, but not before Benteen, Lieutenants Fred Grant, Frank Gibson, and John Weston "had procured a quart." According to Benteen, Colonel Stanley did the same thing and became "stupidly drunk," allowing Custer to evade charges for having appropriated a government horse for Fred Calhoun.

Custer was accompanied on the expedition by a cook, whom Benteen described as "one of the blackest, most monkeyish looking African woman ever turned out." Years later, relaying some gossip the source of which has never been pinpointed, Benteen stated that Custer was "notorious" for sleeping with his black cook during the Civil War and that "this mixing with Africans was carried out on his campaigns with [the] 7th Cav. in Dakota." Benteen was scandalized and quoted the Latin phrase meaning: "There is no accounting for taste."

The allegations have never been proved. They are probably unprovable. There is a distinct possibility that Benteen's source was Joseph van Holt Nash, a former Confederate officer who may or may not have been the orderly who accompanied him on the dangerous ride to Fort Harker in the fall of 1868. The trouble with the assertion that Custer had sex with his cook (aside from its unsupported nature) is that Custer had more than one cook. And, the one who accompanied him during the Civil War was *not* the same one he took along in the Dakotas. Benteen did not say that she was, however, and never claimed to have witnessed any of it. He was merely repeating, uncritically, what he had been told. Had Custer's alleged dalliance been as obvious in 1873 as Benteen made it sound in 1895, there would undoubtedly be some corroborating evidence in existence. None has been found.

On 31 July 1873, Benteen was detached from the main column to remain behind at what became known as Stanley's Stockade, a supply point about twenty miles upriver from the mouth of Glendive Creek on the Yellowstone River. Some infantry under Captain Edward P. Pearson were left in charge and C and H Companies of the 7th Cavalry under Benteen were left behind to support the infantry. The rest of the expedition ferried across the Yellowstone and continued on with their business. Custer had two sharp clashes with Sioux warriors, the first on 4 August opposite the Tongue River confluence and the second on 11 August near the mouth of the Big Horn River. Benteen remained behind, enjoying an almost idyllic vacation and not seeing any of the action. He yearned for the company of his wife.

Benteen described Stanley's Stockade to his wife: "The Infty. are about 440 yards from us and have a stockade of logs containing forage, stores, etc. while we are nearer the river in the shade — they being in the broiling sun. . . I am intrenched behind breastworks of logs — which are well ditched — and really formidable." He added drolly: "I know of breastworks that I would prefer being *before* tho'."

Fred Benteen enjoyed a very healthy, frank relationship with Kate. Fortunately, a large group of his letters to her have been preserved. At one point later in his career, Benteen drew a very realistic sketch of an erect penis in the corner of a letter to Kate. She obviously cherished the remarks and drawings, for she preserved them. At the time of the "breastworks" comment, Benteen was a rather portly, gray-haired man of almost forty years and the woman to whom it was addressed was well past her 38th birthday and, while not as hefty as her husband, had long since lost her youthful figure. They had been married almost ten years and the really racy letters date from after their fifteenth wedding anniversary.

Benteen appended a rather treacly poem about "The Wife" that he had clipped from a Yankton newspaper and added: "Very little else, with your presence & Fred's is needed to make life at this point perfectly charming. I only wish you could have been here." Frederick and Kate Benteen had a happy marriage.

Benteen was inclined to be stiff and somewhat dour, which must have aggravated his relations with the high-spirited Custer. In the camp near Stanley's Stockade, a young lieutenant named Henry Harrington sneaked up on Benteen, who was hunting grouse, and

"regaled" him "with a poor imitation of an Indian's war-whoop",say-
ing: "Now, had I been an Indian your scalp would have been hanging
at my belt." Benteen pointed out some vedettes (mounted pickets)
and assured Harrington that even without those vedettes, there would
have been no surprise but a young lieutenant with a bellyfull of buck-
shot and advised him "never to try that game again."

But he did have a sense of humor (or at least a sense of the ridicu-
lous), as an incident about the same time proved. Captain Pearson,
the infantry commander, asked to borrow a horse to go hunting wolves.
Benteen loaned Pearson a horse. Unfortunately, the horse stepped
in a prairie dog hole and the would-be wolfer "kept going over the
horse's head." The horse was not injured, but Pearson was. "I don't
know how many bones got broken," Benteen recalled, "but like Mer-
cutio's wound, 'enough'!"

On 10 September, Colonel Stanley, Lieutenant Colonel Custer, and
the rest of the expedition arrived opposite the Stanley Stockade and
Benteen spent a day or two ferrying channel catfish that he had caught
across the river to them. They had suffered some casualties in their
two clashes with Indians, but Custer had handled the cavalry well.
One of the wounded, Lieutenant Charles Braden of L Company, had
a shattered thigh that eventually forced his retirement from the Army.

The entire column, united once again, set off for Fort Rice. Custer
detailed Benteen to lead the surveyors on a detour back through the
bad lands. Benteen regarded the assignment as punishment "for the
grand time I had" while the others were marching across Montana.
Custer though, said Benteen, "hadn't sense enough to know that nothing was too difficult for me to do that took me away from his immediate proximity." On 22 September, Stanley's Expedition arrived at
Fort Rice and began dispersing to the posts that had been assigned
to them for the winter. Benteen's H Company as well as C, K, & M
Companies were assigned to Fort Rice under Captain Verling K.
Hart and later, Major Joseph G. Tilford.

Fort Rice had been built during the Civil War and named in honor
of Brigadier General James Clay Rice, who had been killed in that
war. It was located on the west bank of the Missouri River about
thirty miles south of Bismarck and Fort Abraham Lincoln. When
Benteen arrived in the fall of 1873, it still had three sides of a log
wall ten feet high around it. The north side of what had been a stockade approximately 800 by 500 feet had been removed, but the two
blockhouses still remained atop the northeast and southwest corners

of the wall. There were buildings enough for four companies, seven officers quarters, two storehouses, a library building, a bakery, hospital, guardhouse, and assorted buildings associated with a frontier Army post. They were arranged in a hollow square around a parade ground, but the corrals were outside the walls. There were no settlements in the immediate vicinity, a rarity among Army posts. There were, however, Indian agencies north and south of the fort.

The most remarkable aspect to Fort Rice, in common with all posts in what was then the Dakota Territory, was the weather. Summers were short and hot. Winters were long and bitterly cold, the mercury frequently dropping to fifty below. During the first winter Benteen spent in the Dakotas, his little baby girl, called "Fan," died. Benteen later asserted that all his children, save Freddie, died of spinal meningitis and there is reason to believe that Benteen himself was a carrier of tubercular meningitis. If so, he probably transmitted the disease to his infant children, rendering them especially vulnerable to an early death. He later admitted that he suffered from an unnamed spinal disease and revealed that information in such a way that indicates he connected his own problem with the death of his children. Lacking medical facts, it is impossible to confirm the connection, but Benteen himself felt there was a connection and undoubtedly was burdened by the knowledge, whether true or not.

Significantly, Fort Rice was thirty miles away from Fort Lincoln, the regimental headquarters and the home of George Armstrong Custer. There is no question that Custer sought to distribute the companies of the 7th Cavalry so as to concentrate in other posts those officers with whom he felt uncomfortable. M Company's first lieutenant, Tom Custer, was put on detached service and spent the winter at Fort Lincoln with his brother, while the balance of the company remained at Fort Rice with Benteen. Similarly, the first lieutenant of Hart's C Company, James Calhoun, was placed on detached service at Fort Lincoln, the remainder of the company following him there a month after the assignment of posts. That left Benteen in the company of Major Tilford, Captains Hale and French, and Lieutenants Godfrey, Mathey, and Aspinwall.

Jack Aspinwall, for whom Benteen had "the highest opinion of his honor and integrity," was made the post adjutant. In Colorado in 1870, according to Benteen, Aspinwall had been "skinned" of about $1600 by Custer and his card-playing cronies, whom Benteen characterized as "those damned cormorants." Benteen, as acting post commander at Rice, made Aspinwall the commissary of subsistence there, unwittingly "putting temptation in his way." But, as long as Benteen commanded the post, the large amounts of money in the post safe under Aspinwall's care were untouched. "On all the inspections," Benteen said, "this money was there, all correct." When Major Tilford returned, Aspinwall deserted, but left the money behind. Some time later, Benteen went to Fort Lincoln on business and was presented with a petition to recommend Fred Calhoun for the vacancy created by Aspinwall's disappearance. Benteen refused to sign it, pointing out that the statute of limitations in Aspinwall's case had not expired and that there was a "genteel sufficiency of that clique" (Custers and Calhouns) in the regiment already. Despite Benteen's opposition, Fred Calhoun did get a commission — in an *infantry* regiment. He did not retain it. "A something I look on as a kind of swindling of the government," Benteen groused.

Jack Aspinwall, a West Point graduate, was eventually dropped from the rolls as a deserter and turned up in Montreal working for a street car company. He was apparently murdered in 1881, according to Benteen, though the official verdict was that Aspinwall was drowned. Benteen pointed out that the drowning had been in "a small pool of water, 18 inches in depth" and that Aspinwall's gold watch was never found. The precise reason for Aspinwall's desertion has never been established, though Benteen believed that Aspinwall ran off because he could not get a leave of absence approved. In any case, he took no government property.

Edward S. Godfrey was Captain Owen Hale's first lieutenant in K Company at Fort Rice. Godfrey, an 1867 graduate of West Point, was a lean officer with acquiline features who grew a colossal mustache during his service with the 7th Cavalry. He was, by all accounts, an excellent cavalry officer after a rather shaky beginning under Captain Albert Barnitz in the old G Company. He was the officer Custer had detailed to round up the ponies at the Washita. Benteen had a very close relationship with "God" throughout their association and confided in him. Later, when Godfrey began to write for publication articles that were laudatory of Custer, Benteen turned scornful. But, during the years they were together, they got along very well.

Benteen felt differently about the other first lieutenant at Fort Rice that winter. He was a French-born ex-Civil War infantry major named Edward G. Mathey. Benteen detested Mathey, possibly because, as he put it, "I always knew he was one of the fellows that did Custer's dirty work." Mathey, a small-boned, average looking officer with a neat mustache, was dubbed "Bible-Thumper" by the other officers for his colorful profanity. "Of all the nonentities with which a troop of cavalry could be damned, as its head and front," Benteen later said, Mathey "fills the bill."

Benteen had no great regard for Major Tilford, the off-and-on post commander. However, he seemed to enjoy the company of the hard-drinking, obese West Pointer. Tilford had been court-martialed during the Civil War about the same time Benteen's enemy, Thomas Hynes, was dismissed. Benteen later came to resent Tilford's inability to endure the privations of the field, attributing it to Tilford's age (46) and poor health. He later declared that if he were permitted to decide, he "would have no regimental officer in the cavalry beyond the age of 45 years." Tilford was unsuccessful in using his age and infirmities to escape duty with Custer's Black Hills Expedition the following summer.

The Black Hills had been eyed enviously by non-Sioux for years. It was on the western edge of the reservation provided for the Sioux by the Laramie Treaty of 1868. It was well within the bounds of the vague unceded lands that the government had promised to preserve for Indian use only. Yet, in the summer of 1874, Lieutenant Colonel Custer led a twelve company expedition into the Black Hills in compliance with orders.

The stated reason for the expedition was to reconnoiter the region with a view toward establishing an Army fort somewhere in its vicinity. General Sheridan was dissatisfied with the Sioux reservation arrangement that featured military posts on its perimeter. He wanted a fort *inside* the vast reservation to take advantage of interior lines and speed up pursuit of hostiles when that became necessary. In effect, he wanted a military way station in the middle of the reservation to eliminate the need for slow and heavy supply trains that had hitherto accompanied all punitive expeditions.

Custer, with Sheridan's full knowledge and approval, took at least two miners into the Black Hills with him. Furthermore, they spent all their time looking specifically for gold. It was hardly a scientific outing. There is good reason to believe that General Sheridan, for one, *hoped* that the rumored gold would be found and that the resultant flow of white miners into the region would give him justification for breaking up the very large Sioux reservation into manageable size. The Sioux raids against other Indians and white settlers, especially

George A. Custer, Thomas C. Custer
and Elizabeth B. Custer

Samuel D. Sturgis with "Jack" and Nina

Thomas H. French

At Fort Rice, Dakota Territory, September 1874
C.C. DeRudio, Dr. John Williams, E.S. Godfrey, two ladies and
girl, V.K. Hart, Lewis Merrill, Mamie Merrill (in back), R.H.L.
Alexander, Owen Hale, F.M. Gibson, J.G. Tilford; Roma, Italia
and America DeRudio, Eliza Booth DeRudio, J.W. Scully, Freddie
Benteen, Kate Benteen (front), F.W. Benteen (center, right)

Joseph G. Tilford

Frederick W. Benteen in 1871

the attacks on the railroad surveying parties north of the Yellowstone, indicated a problem that needed a solution. To make matters worse, the undefeated Sioux were using the reservation and its agencies in particular to draw government rations and supplies while at the same time roaming through the unceded lands and all too frequently spilling over the designated boundaries to raid when they took a notion.

The 7th Cavalry began gathering at Fort Lincoln in late June 1874 for the Black Hills Expedition. In the end, ten cavalry companies went, bolstered by two infantry companies for camp and wagon security. (Companies D & I of the 7th remained on boundary survey escort duty under Major Reno.) Once again, Lieutenant Fred Grant, the President's son, went along as an acting aide. Besides the military people which included three doctors, there were three newspaper correspondents, four scientists, two miners, four guides, and a photographer. General Terry sent his chief engineer, Captain William Ludlow.

As they gathered at Fort Lincoln, the officers paid their customary courtesy calls. As usual, Custer made a special effort to avoid any display of personal animosity. Libbie, his wife, never acquired this trait.

"My husband urged that it would embarrass him if others found out that I had surmised anything regarding official affairs," she said. "He wished social relations to be kept distinct, and he could not endure to see me show dislike to anyone who did not like him. I argued in reply that I felt myself dishonest if I even spoke to one whom I hated."

One whom she hated was Fred Benteen. And, her manner conveyed her feelings. Benteen remembered her as "cold-blooded," "just about the most penurious of women," and "about as avaricious and parsimonious a woman as you can find in a day's walk."

"As everyone visited us," Mrs. Custer recalled, "there was escape for me, but I do not like to think now of having welcomed anyone from whom I inwardly recoiled." Custer kept an eye on her behavior and if he found it "not sufficiently cordial," he would afterward mock her efforts with "a burlesque imitation." Years later, she recalled his caricature of her "advancing coldly, extending the tips of her fingers, and bowing loftily to some imaginary guest." Libbie Custer was much amused by what her husband insisted was one of her shortcomings. Benteen was not.

After Custer's death, Libbie refused to receive Benteen. "I believe her principal objection to me," Benteen said, was that she had heard him quoted as having said: "Custer never killed anything but horses anyway!" Benteen denied ever having said any such thing, but admitted that he might have "had it ever occured to" him.

The Rice and Lincoln detachments united, Custer's expedition set off for the Black Hills on 2 July 1874. They were prepared for hostilities, but found that the outing was little more than an extended picnic. The two miners (and quite a few of the soldiers) panned for gold, finding traces in several places. From these discoveries came the report that there was "gold at the grass roots" in the Black Hills.

The most exciting action was provided by the Benteen Baseball Club. They joined with some men from C and K Companies and fielded a team called the Athletes. However, they met defeat at the hands of an all-star team from the Fort Lincoln companies called the Actives. The final score was eleven to six. With the fast pitching of Joseph McCurry and the heavy hitting of James Curley, they got a measure of revenge on a pickup club of teamsters from the wagon train. That score was twenty-five to eleven. Benteen was photographed after one of these games sitting in the tent of Major Tilford, celebrating with a champagne dinner. Custer, of course, was absent from camp when the bubbly flowed.

All was not fun and games. Benteen had to bury two of his own men in shallow graves covered with quicklime. One had died on the way to the Black Hills, apparently as much from medical malpractice as from disease. One died on the way back. A noncommissioned officer of H Company named Ewart left a diary graphically depicting (among other things) his gray-haired company commander standing bareheaded over the second grave solemnly reading the funeral service while the rest of the column hurried on. Custer could not spare the time for the second funeral. He was anxious to get back to Libbie and Fort Lincoln.

On the way back, they came across an abandoned camp site that all agreed was the largest concentration of Sioux ever before known. Luther North, one of the guides, remarked that Custer was lucky that he had not found the camp site still occupied. Custer replied brusquely that his 7th Cavalry could whip any concentration of Indians anywhere in America. Benteen did not record his opinion.

Captain Hart of C Company was notified by courier that his child was very ill at Fort Rice and he left the column one day before its arrival at Fort Lincoln. Custer, after approving the defection, placed a guard force around the expedition to prevent anyone else from following suit. His first-with-the-news status preserved, Custer marched the expedition into Fort Lincoln on 30 August 1874.

Almost at once two of the Fort Rice companies were dispatched to Louisiana. K Company went to Shreveport while Benteen's H Company was assigned to New Orleans. Benteen's men left Fort Rice 2 September, thus avoiding the Dakota winter that year. They remained in Louisiana until spring and did not return to Rice until the fall of 1875.

The reason for the deployment was political. The state elections of 1874 had been violent and those elected had good cause to fear for their safety. As with most Reconstruction governments, the Louisiana state officials elected in 1874 were not very representative of the electorate. It was left to the Federal government to play the role of the heavy and provide troops to legitimize a carpetbagger state government. As events proved, it was the last time Washington supported an unpopular state government with soldiers. The Civil War had been over ten years. The Reconstruction was in its death throes.

For Benteen, it was an opportunity to relax and enjoy the city of New Orleans. Once again, his cavalrymen were broken up into small patrols to escort local and federal law enforcement officers. Benteen himself had little to do with the execution of these duties. His was the only cavalry company in New Orleans, the balance of the garrison being fifteen companies commanded by Colonel Phillipe R. de Trobriand.

General Sheridan came to visit New Orleans and surprised everybody there but Benteen by the enthusiasm he showed in greeting the gray-haired cavalry captain. "He threw his arms around me and hugged me," Benteen remembered with pride, "telling me he was glad I was there, and I know he was." The two men often went to the race tracks together. "Custer," Benteen commented, "at the time was foaming at the mouth at Lincoln." (This was about the time Custer produced his *Life On the Plains* book in serial form for *Galaxy* magazine.)

In April 1875, about the same time that Benteen was teaching himself French and his company was being issued the new (1873) single-shot Springfield .45 caliber carbines, Kate Benteen had their fifth child: a boy named Theodore Norman Benteen. The Benteens also acquired a young Negro servant boy named Frank "Cuff" Jones, who would accompany them back to Dakota Territory and be involved two years later in a scandal that would cost one officer his commission. Benteen kept up on developments. He learned that over 800 miners had flooded into the Black Hills in defiance of the 1868 treaty. He also picked up a piece of regimental gossip that eventually would be the undoing of another officer.

Lieutenant James M. Bell had a high-spirited young wife named Emiline. Benteen heard that an infantry officer who had been transferred from New Orleans to the northern part of the state "got after" Mrs. Bell. He heard also that the popular young second lieutenant of B Company, Benny Hodgson, had fallen for her charms and was on the point of tendering his resignation over the affair. "She doubtless was a nymphomaniac," Benteen concluded. Later, the reputation of Mrs. Bell got Benteen involved as a witness in a court-martial of an officer who tried (without success) to test Benteen's conclusion.

On 5 May 1875, Benteen's H Company was reassigned to the Dakota Territory. They arrived at Fort Randall on the Missouri River on 1 June and spent the next six weeks preparing for a summer campaign in the Black Hills.

The Benteen Baseball Club was active at Fort Randall that summer. Three days after their arrival, they challenged Colonel Pinkney Lugenbeel's 1st Infantry garrison to a game and won by the whopping score of 54 to five. Lieutenant Tom McDougall's E Company tried their hand at the hapless Randalls, but lost 32 to nineteen, largely because Colonel Lugenbeel's men had borrowed the Benteen ace, Sergeant Joseph McCurry. The McDougall nine got an opportunity to revenge themselves on McCurry by taking on the Benteen Baseball Club, but lost 33 to six.

Sergeant Ewart, the chronicler of the Benteen Baseball Club, summed up the record shortly before his discharge in the spring of 1876. He said that the Benteens had played a total of seventeen games between their inception in 1873 at Nashville and the coming of the Dakota winter in the fall of 1875. They won twelve of these games, scoring an aggregate total of 464 runs to 230 runs of their varied oppositions. He concluded: "Taking into consideration the fact that constant movings, expeditions, fatigue and their military duties prevented practice games or anything like a gymnastic training, one cannot help but admire the grit and pluck that caused these 'ball tossers' to continue in the face of so many discouraging obstacles." Ewart left out battle casualties, but these were soon to come.

By 12 July 1875, Benteen was commanding a battalion consisting of his own H Company, Tom McDougall's E Company, and Captain Myles Moylan's A Company on an extended patrol into the Black Hills to evict miners. They were unsuccessful. By that fall, the number of miners had grown from the 800 of the previous year to over 15,000. In the process of rounding up miners, Benteen came face-to-face with another officer who would have a very important influence on his future career: Brigadier General George Crook.

George Crook was five years older than Benteen and a former classmate of General Sheridan's at West Point. He was a tall, hawk-faced professional soldier with a reputation as a superb Indian fighter. He had been a cavalry division commander during the Civil War under Sheridan and, like most of his contemporaries, had been considerably reduced in rank in 1866. Like Custer, Crook began his post-war career as a lieutenant colonel. However, largely as a result of his brilliant campaigning in Oregon and especially in his subsequent tour in Arizona Territory, he had been elevated to brigadier general. When Benteen met him, Crook was the commanding officer of the Department of the Platte, whose jurisdiction covered the area south and west of the Black Hills.

Crook wanted to know what Benteen was doing in the Black Hills. Benteen told him, not needing to point out that he was under orders from General Alfred H. Terry, commanding general of the area north and east of the Black Hills and the officer directly responsible for the large Sioux resrvation. To clarify, Crook was out of bounds. Still, he cross-examined Benteen in the brusque, taciturn manner for which he was noted. Benteen replied tartly that he had not yet reached the rank where he could issue his own orders. Crook did not seem to take offense, but he had failed to impress Benteen favorably — a situation that time and subsequent events did not alter.

Nevertheless, Benteen followed Crook's advice and desisted in the roundup of miners until they had met at Frenchman's Creek on 10 August. Thousands gathered to petition the U.S. government and to lay out Custer City. Benteen was given some corner lots in the city named after Custer, much to his chagrin. He never returned to claim them.

While at the meeting, Benteen took it upon himself to demonstrate to a visiting Sioux chief the small yields of placer mining. The Indians could not believe their eyes. They insisted that the thousands of trespassers had not come to get the little speck that Benteen had taken hours to turn up in his demonstration.

Benteen led a group of miners out of the Black Hills after the conference. He took them east across White Clay Creek and Wounded Knee (later to become places of destiny for the 7th Cavalry after Benteen's time). As he led the miners out toward Randall, Benteen looked back on the Black Hills and forward across the Great Plains and reflected on the plight of the Indian.

Years later, he wrote about his feelings for the Indians and their land. "My conscience was never wholly at ease while engaged in warring with them and routing them from their paradise," he said. "I have no great fondness for our *fin de siecle*, grand civilization as it is, for I think 'tis just a trifle overdone and I cannot but look back to the old times, when I first knew the bands of Northern and Southern Cheyennes, and saw with gladness how little was required to make a people supremely happy, but by some miscalculation our government never lost the gentle art of making enemies of them."

Benteen reached Randall on 25 August. The miners passed a resolution declaring (in part) their "heartfelt thanks and lasting gratitude" to Benteen and his men "for their unremitting kindness and courtesy" and vowed that "the gallant commander" (Benteen) and his men would "ever hold a high place in our esteem and a sacred spot in our affections." Benteen left Randall and headed for his winter post, Fort Rice, arriving 20 September 1875.

Benteen found himself the post commander at Fort Rice, as Major Tilford had taken an extended leave of absence. There were only three companies assigned to Fort Rice that winter: H and M Companies of the 7th Cavalry and D Company of the 17th Infantry under 1st Lieutenant James Humbert. The newest officer on the post was no stranger to Benteen or any of the others. He was the oldest son of the regimental commander and had just graduated from West Point. He was 2nd Lieutenant James G. "Jack" Sturgis. Benteen appointed young Sturgis post adjutant.

The Panic of 1873 had stalled the progress of the Northern Pacific Railroad at Bismarck. But, the discovery of gold in the Black Hills had generated an influx of white interlopers far more serious to the Indians than any railroad survey or construction crew. The government had not succeeded in persuading the Indians to either sell or lease the Black Hills. On 3 November 1875, President Grant chaired a secret meeting with several high officials including the Secretary of War, the Secretary of the Interior, and Generals Sherman and Sheridan. He apparently decided at that meeting that he would not attempt to enforce the provision of the treaty of 1868 requiring the government to evict intruders on the Sioux reservation. He would, in effect, wink at illegal settlements such as Custer City that were springing up on Sioux lands despite the Army's efforts to keep them out.

Six days later, the Indian Bureau submitted a report claiming that the Sioux Indians were completely out of hand and urged that roamers in the unceded lands be forced to remove themselves to the reservation proper and enroll in the agencies there. There was not necessarily a connection between the two events, though the timing was suspicious. The first word that comes to mind is: collusion. And, there may well have been a conspiracy to justify an attack on the roamers outside the reservation boundary. It looks even today like a classic case of intimidation. There *was* documentation supporting the Indian Bureau's uncharacteristic claim that they had lost control. How much the *de facto* seizure of the Black Hills in a time of economic depression had on the turnabout can only be guessed at. Even in retrospect, with the cool logic of noninvolvement, the sequence of events appears too pat to have been mere coincidence.

At any rate, on 6 December, the Bureau of Indian Affairs circulated an announcement to the effect that the roamers in the unceded lands had until 31 January 1876 to report to their respective agencies and that Sioux found outside the reservation after that date would be rounded up by the Army. The roamers generally ignored the ultimatum. Many claimed later that they had never been reservation Indians. To further complicate matters, the Indian agents along the Missouri River had acquired a reputation for chicanery that was repugnant in the extreme. According to their records, *all* of the Indians drew rations and other annuities. Because of their reputation for dishonesty, the Indian agents' claims have been pooh-poohed by historians down to the present day. However, there is no question that some of the annuities, especially weapons and ammunition, ended up in the hands of those same Indians who claimed they had never received anything from the government but maggoty pork, sandy flour, and threadbare blankets. The much-maligned Indian agents seem to have been correct in that most of the Sioux had indeed drawn rations and so forth. There was enough dishonesty to go around and certainly was not confined to the proponents of one side or the other. But, in the end, the Sioux War of 1876 was deliberately provoked by the U.S. government for various reasons, some of which did not (and still do not) reflect great credit on the honor of the American people.

The Sioux Indians were portrayed by many historians as arrogant, deceitful, intractable savages, perpetrators of unspeakable atrocities, who respected only force, and were stumbling blocks on the road to expansion and progress. In latter days, the image has turned almost 180 degrees. The Sioux have been depicted as unfortunate victims of a cynical government, a noble, almost innocent people maltreated without justification. The truth does not necessarily lie in the middle, even if it could be established. The only honest assertion that can be made is this: The Sioux were neither of the extremes; they were, if anything, a little of both. The same could be said of the government, its agents and politicians.

The Army was caught in the middle. Certain circles in recent times have made it fashionable to fault the Army's conduct of the Sioux War on moral grounds. Others have argued that the soldiers were only carrying out orders. Aside from almost hysterical charges of genocide, both sides of the issue have valid points. However, the moral question was effectively mooted long before the soldiers got within sight of an Indian tepee.

Benteen, a typical military man, never doubted that what he was doing was right. He, like so many others, did not relish the task. He was close enough to the Indians to understand them and feel sympathetic to their plight, but he was also aware that they were not entirely innocent or put-upon. He later regretted what he had done, but only to the extent that he regretted it was necessary. Speaking of one Indian chief in particular whom he had come to know well, he said sadly: "The times were just against him."

That winter, his youngest boy, little Theodore, died and was buried at Fort Rice. Benteen was 41 years old, his rendezvous with history just a season away.

15

The 1876 Campaign

On 5 May 1876, Benteen at the head of Companies H and M departed Fort Rice for Fort Lincoln, "leaving laundresses and heavy baggage behind." They arrived in camp outside Lincoln the next day and waited for the rest of the expedition to gather. With Benteen came Captain French, First Lieutenants Mathey and Gibson, and Second Lieutenant Jack Sturgis. Lieutenant DeRudio was already at Lincoln and had been since February.

In December of 1875, Captains Hart and Thompson had left the regiment. Hart went to the 5th Cavalry as a major and Thompson retired for age. Lieutenant Tom Custer had been promoted to captain and given command of Hart's C Company. Lieutenant Tom McDougall had been promoted to captain and given command of Thompson's B Company. DeRudio had been promoted to first lieutenant and assigned to E Company. He would have been its commanding officer, since Captain Ilsley was still on staff assignment, but General Terry decreed otherwise. He directed Major Reno, the acting regimental commander, to place DeRudio in A Company under Captain Myles Moylan and transfer A Company's first lieutenant, A.E. Smith (who had been Terry's aide during the Civil War), to command E Company.

When Benteen arrived at Lincoln, he found the forlorn Italian dandy had been barred from Moylan's mess (a strange turn of events) and "had to trudge 3 times daily to Fred Gerard's shack to get something to eat." (The Fred Gerard referred to was a squaw man who had been employed as Fort Lincoln's interpreter and who supplemented his income by selling eggs and butter to the military there.) Benteen promptly took DeRudio under his wing "and in a word, set him on his feet, straight up!" He found a horse for his former second lieutenant, scrounged some clothing and equipment for him to use, and invited him back into the old Fort Rice mess.

General Sheridan plotted the strategy for what was to become the Sioux War. He wanted to strike at known or suspected camps of roamers in winter, as he had done with much success in the Indian Territory in 1868-1869. One column, under Colonel John Gibbon, was to move south from posts in Montana Territory and block Sioux flight north of the Yellowstone River. A second column, under Custer, was to move west along the Yellowstone River until the camps had been located and then strike while Gibbon's men blocked any retreat to the north. A third column under General Crook was to strike from eastern Wyoming simultaneously, blocking any retreat to the south.

As it happened, Gibbon got to the Yellowstone without any difficulty, but a lack of supplies and bad weather prevented Custer's yet unassembled column from leaving before May. On 17 March, General Crook struck the first blow. Some of his cavalry found a Northern Cheyenne camp on the Powder River and attacked it. To Crook's chagrin, they were unable to hold the camp and even lost the horses they had captured in their attack. Because of the bitterly cold weather and uncertainty of resupply, Crook abandoned the field until spring. He returned to his forward base, Fort Fetterman, and commenced a court-martial of some of his cavalry officers involved in the Powder River fiasco.

General Terry took command of what was to have been Custer's column, bolstering it with some additional infantry units and waited for the snow to melt and the ice to thaw. Custer, in the meantime, had embroiled himself in a political squabble by his testimony before the Clymer Committee. President Grant was deeply offended by what he regarded as disloyalty on Custer's part. He believed that Custer had implicated his brother, Orville Grant, in the post trader scandal associated with W.W. Belknap's malfeasance. A lot has been written about Custer's appearance before the congressional hearing and Grant's reaction to it, but little of it pertains to the life of Frederick W. Benteen.

Benteen certainly felt that the post traders were crooked. There is no record of his having blamed Custer in any way for testifying as he did. But, the upshot of the scandal was that President Grant had Custer arrested in Chicago for absenting himself from Washington without authority. Grant's position is hard even today to defend and, as it was, proved untenable in 1876. Rather churlishly, he assented to General Terry's request to allow Custer to participate in the upcoming campaign with the proviso that Custer go *only* as commanding officer of his own regiment, the 7th Cavalry. General Terry was directed to command the expedition in person.

For a while, when Custer was under an official cloud, it appeared that Major Reno would command the 7th Cavalry. Reno himself thought so and even telegraphed a request to Terry in St. Paul that said in part: "Why not give me a chance as I feel I will do credit to the Army." Terry politely demurred.

Many stories have been told about the meeting between Custer and Terry in St. Paul that led to Terry's request that Custer be allowed to go along on the expedition. Custer allegedly got down on his knees and pleaded with Terry, tears in his eyes. Once the permission had been granted, Custer informed Terry's engineer officer, Captain William Ludlow, that he intended to "swing clear" of Terry at the first opportunity as he had done with Colonel Stanley three years before. The story about the tears and bended knee may be exageration, but the Ludlow tale seems to be the truth. General Sherman, commanding general of the Army, endorsed Terry's request, telling Terry to instruct Custer to refrain from taking newspaper correspondents on the expedition. Custer took one correspondent with him nonetheless. The kindest adjective that can be used to describe Custer's actions is: controversial.

When Custer and Terry arrived at Fort Lincoln in early May, they found that Major Reno had divided the 7th Cavalry into four battalions of three companies each. Custer promptly reorganized the regiment into two wings of six companies each. (For the first time in its history, all twelve companies of the 7th Cavalry were assembled in one place.) The right wing, commanded by Major Reno, consisted of Companies B, C, E, I, F, L. (Majors Tilford and Merrill were absent as were Colonel Sturgis and twelve other officers, including three company commanders.) The left wing, consisting of Companies A, D, G, H, K, M, was given to Captain Benteen, who since the departure of Hart and Thompson the previous December was the senior captain of the 7th Cavalry.

The next day, Benteen reported to Custer's tent and, in the presence of Mrs. Custer, was warmly greeted by his nemesis. Custer remarked that, during his adventures in the capital, he had been visited by a reporter named Lawrence A. Gobright. ("Larry" Gobright was one of the founders of the New York Associated Press during the Civil War and the only reporter in history who ever attended a Lincoln cabinet meeting. He was, in his day, considered the most influential newsman alive. He was also Fred Benteen's older cousin.) Benteen's suspicions were aroused when Custer dwelt on his meeting with Gobright, implying that Gobright had seemed very interested in how his young cousin was doing.

"Yes," said Benteen noncommittally, "we've been very dear friends always."

Custer, Benteen thought, feared that Gobright's influence could be used against him if Benteen sought to involve his cousin in his relations with Custer. Benteen was fully determined to "hold my own like a man" and refused to call on his cousin for "preferment" at any time. Custer, having just been badly bruised in a political squabble and much in need of "some such influence," made a special effort to get along with Benteen.

"I then began to scent out the cause of [the] wing distribution," Benteen remarked, adding that he was too proud to use his influential cousin for his own advancement. There is no question that Custer warmed a bit toward Benteen in early 1876. The Gobright connection may have played a big part in this about-face. However, Custer, being under something of a cloud, was anxious to restore himself in the good graces of his superiors and, incidentally, the public. He seems to have embarked on an uncharacteristic course of confiding in his subordinates and seeking their voluntary support. No doubt he realized that any hope of success he was to achieve in field operations would be enhanced by rooting out the dissension in the regiment.

Whatever the reason, Benteen was effectively commanding officer of half of the regiment as it set off to find the Sioux holdouts on 17 May 1876. DeRudio was detached from Moylan's company to be Benteen's adjutant. Moylan's second lieutenant, Charles Varnum, was put in command of the Arikara (Ree) Indian scouts. The Rees were traditional enemies of the Sioux and familiar with the area around the Little Missouri River where the Indians were believed to be encamped.

General Terry believed, based on reports passed to him by General Sheridan, that the hostiles had over 1000 tepees and about 5,000 warriors. Neither he nor Custer expected them to all be in one camp, but Custer at least was confident that the 7th Cavalry could handle that number even if all were encountered at once.

Captain Moylan commanded A Company in Benteen's wing. Captain Weir commanded D Company, assisted by a young West Pointer, 2nd Lieutenant Winfield S. Edgerly. G Company was commanded by 1st Lieutenant Donald McIntosh. *His* second lieutenant, George D. Wallace (a West Point room-mate of Varnum's), was detailed as the engineer officer for the wing, responsible for the itinerary, mileage, and rough mapping of the terrain traversed. 1st Lieutenant Frank Gibson commanded H Company. K Company, Holy Owen Hale's, was commanded by 1st Lieutenant Edward S. Godfrey, as Hale was detached to cavalry recruit training at Jefferson Barracks. Godfrey was assisted by a young West Pointer from Texas: 2nd Lieutenant Luther R. Hare. Captain French commanded M Company, assisted as usual by 1st Lieutenant Mathey. Their young second lieutenant, Jack Sturgis, had been detailed to E Company in Reno's wing.

Besides Benteen's six-company wing, there was Reno's wing of approximately the same size, three companies of infantry, a gatling gun detachment, more than forty Ree scouts under Varnum, over two hundrd wagons, and more than 150 civilian teamsters. The cavalry was informally organized into battalions, much like Reno's previous arrangement. On the march, one of the battalions rode in front of the wagon train, one rode behind, and one rode on each flank. Benteen's designated battalion commanders were Captains French and Weir.

The 7th Cavalry was authorized close to 800 men by Army regulation. As they marched from Fort Lincoln, they could account for almost 750 present for duty. None of the individual companies had the authorized 64 men, but some of them like French's M Company came pretty close. Benteen's H Company had 47 men. In short, there was no drastic shortage of enlisted men in the 7th Cavalry in May 1876. The officer strength was something else. The regiment was authorized 42 officers. Only 28 marched with the regiment. A 29th was borrowed from the 20th Infantry, though he was partially disabled. He was 2nd Lieutenant John J. Crittenden, son of Colonel Thomas L. Crittenden of the 17th Infantry, and blind in one eye as the result of an accidental explosion. Benteen had eleven officers in his wing, with Lieutenant Varnum attached to the scouts for the duration.

All the cavalry troopers were uniformly armed. They had single-shot Springfield carbines with the Allin trapdoor modification (making them breechloaders) and 1873 Colt six-shot revolvers. They carried sabers as far as the Powder River and at least one officer carried one after the rest had been boxed up and left behind. To all intents and purposes, the 7th Cavalry went into action without the *arm blanche*, as the saber was known.

At 5:00 o'clock in the morning on 17 May 1876, the so-called Dakota Column marched. They were serenaded by the splendid regimental band playing "The Girl I Left Behind Me." Wives from Fort Lincoln followed for a short distance as the column headed west toward the Little Heart River. Mrs. Custer and at least one other, it seems, went all the way to the first camp site, which was reached after a fourteen mile march at about 2:00 o'clock in the afternoon. There, the troopers were paid and the paymaster escorted the wives back to the post. The reason for paying off soldiers a day's march from the temptations of civilization is self-evident.

The weather had been an enemy before they left Fort Lincoln. It scarcely proved friendlier on the march. On the second day out, it hailed for about two hours. The wagons got stuck. The column was moving considerably slower than a cavalry column ordinarily marched. The wagons were only part of the reason. The terrain and weather varied with each day and had quite an effect on the rate of march. But, the most cogent reason for the uncharacteristically slow rate was the infantry. The "walk-a-heaps," as the Indians called them, could not keep up with the fast-moving mounted men and the rate of advance had to be geared to the lowest common denominator: the lowly doughboys of the 6th and 17th Infantry, who were along to provide added security for the wagon and camps. They averaged 12-15 miles per day.

Every little stream and river encountered caused delay. Troopers in the advance battalion for the day were designated pioneers and spent most of their duty day constructing log and earth bridges across the water courses. The bridges were not intended to be permanent, only strong enough to bear the weight of loaded wagons. Two weeks out of Lincoln, General Terry complained in his diary that Custer was "behind playing Wagon Master" and that he had "left the column early in the day without any authority whatsoever." Terry had not yet heard of Custer's boast to "swing clear."

The night that Terry penned his criticism of Custer, it snowed heavily. It snowed some more the next day and Terry, on the advice of his senior surgeon, Dr. J.W. Williams, kept the column in camp until 3 June.

The scouts were miles ahead of the column every day. They camped separately and rarely were seen by the main column. They ranged far ahead, looking for signs of hostile Sioux. On 4 June, they found the first such signs. The long-abandoned camp they found was obvious indication that the Indians were considerably further west than hitherto expected. Terry and his scouts knew — or firmly believed — that Indian camps would be found along a river bank, almost certainly a river flowing north into the Yellowstone. There were five such rivers in the area where the Sioux were believed to be roaming. The Dakota Column's tactics, therefore, might be considered analagous to a modern police cruiser moving along one road and searching down the length of each perpendicular street it crosses. Terry's men had crossed the first such "cross-street," the Little Missouri River, before the snowstorm. They found no evidence of recent Indian occupation.

On 7 June, they reached the next major river: the Powder River. Terry wanted to send a scouting party of six cavalry companies down the river valley to the south (actually *up*river) to determine whether or not there were any Indian camps along its winding banks, but first he wanted to make contact with the so-called Montana Column of Colonel John Gibbon's. Thus, on 8 June he took a company from each wing of the 7th Cavalry (D & I Companies) and went downriver (north) to the Yellowstone. There he found the sternwheel steamboat *Far West*, which would ferry him to meet Gibbon, the man who had been patrolling the north bank of the Yellowstone since February. Terry also found that a stockade had been erected at the mouth of the Powder River (as had been planned) by three companies of the 6th Infantry from Fort Buford.

He steamed a short distance up the Yellowstone (west) to confer with Colonel Gibbon, who had six companies of his own 7th Infantry and four companies of the 2nd Cavalry spread out along the north bank of the Yellowstone. Benteen, who was not along, knew Gibbon well by reputation. The hawklike infantry colonel had been a major general during the Civil War and at one point had commanded the famed Iron Brigade. In fact, Gibbon's successor to the command of the Iron Brigade had been another one of Benteen's influential cousins: Brigadier General Edward S. Bragg, by 1876 a state senator in Wisconsin. E.S. Bragg was at that time running for the U.S. Congress and would within a few years become one of the ranking Democrats on the House Military Affairs committee.

Terry decided to bring his Dakota Column to the stockade on the mouth of the Powder River and leave all his infantry and wagons there. At the same time, he decided that Major Reno's wing would be given the scouting assignment. Reno's six companies were to push south up the Powder River, cross over a couple of tributaries near its headwaters and move north along the next river to the west, the Tongue River. At the mouth of the Tongue, they would reunite with Benteen's wing and another strategy meeting would be held based on the intelligence Reno's men would have gleaned from the scout.

On 10 June, Reno and Companies B, C, E, F, I, L set off about 5:00 o'clock in the evening. The rest of the Dakota Column tried to find an easy route north to the Yellowstone. Apparently, Lieutenant Gibson of H Company let Terry down, for the General recorded in his diary: "Also sent Gibson to find pass to plateau. Gibson did nothing." In the end, it was Custer who played guide for the column and they reached the mouth of the Powder River on 12 June.

The next day Benteen began a long letter to his wife at Fort Rice. He complained about the weather — it had turned unseasonably warm after all the snow and rain. He depicted himself sitting in his tent wearing only underwear and slippers and feeling generally pessimisstic about the expedition. He told her of the arrangement he had made taking DeRudio away from Captain Moylan to be adjutant for the wing, adding: "No one likes to serve with Moylan." He repeated the rumor that his next station would be the mouth of the Tongue River to await Reno's return. "Thence we start, I suppose," he said, "on the active part of the expedition." His wing was waiting the return of General Terry from yet another conference with Colonel Gibbon. "Many of us are of the opinion," Benteen said, "that we shall have no opportunities of exhibiting our prowess on redskins — & I am one of these; 'But, you can't always tell'!" He apologized to Kate for not having more news, saying: "I don't run around much — as you know."

At 7:00 o'clock in the morning on 15 June, Custer and Benteen's wing started off for the mouth of the Tongue. They left behind the wagons, the infantry, the regimental band, and about 150 recruits. The reason for leaving the band and recruits behind was simply that so many horses had broken down on the march to that point that Custer and Terry had decided to dismount a portion of the regiment so as to insure that the balance of the command would be well mounted. Benteen's men carried sixty days worth of rations on mules, which had been cut out from the wagon train. There were about 200 of these mules, watched over by about twenty-five of the teamsters.

Benteen's wing reached the Tongue River encampment the next day and sat down to wait for Reno.

On 19 June, a dispatch rider arrived from Major Reno with the astounding news that Reno had scouted the *Rosebud* as well as the Powder River and had discovered a large abandoned Indian camp along its bed. He was at the mouth of the Rosebud and headed east toward the Tongue. Galvanized, Terry sent one of his staff officers (his own brother-in-law), Captain Robert P. Hughes, to intercept Reno and tell him to halt at the mouth of the Rosebud. When Hughes returned, Terry noted in his diary: "Reno gave him no reason for his disobedience of orders."

Reno's astonishing display of independence caused Terry to deviate from his original plan. The only river not yet scouted was the Big Horn River. But, Reno had found (on the Rosebud) an abandoned camp site and *a large trail headed south,* indicating to Terry that a large Indian camp could be found along the banks of the Big Horn River, but considerably further south than had been anticipated. Terry came to believe that an Indian camp might be along one of the Big Horn tributaries between it and the Rosebud — such as the Little Big Horn River.

The next day, Custer took Benteen's wing to the mouth of the Rosebud, reuniting it with Reno's six companies. The following afternoon, Custer, Reno, Gibbon and Terry had a three-hour conference on board the *Far West.* Reno had some explaining to do. From all accounts, he did not do a very good job. Terry was angry because Reno had disobeyed orders and scouted the Rosebud on his own initiative. Custer was angry because Reno had not followed the trail that had been discovered to determine a camp, its approximate strength, or likely location. When things calmed down, Terry had decided to send all twelve companies of the 7th under Custer on a scout up the Rosebud, to complete the job disobediently begun by Reno. Custer was instructed to scout all the way to the headwaters of the Rosebud, whether the trail proved to go further westward before that point was reached or not. Custer was then supposed to swing north, cross the divide between the Rosebud and the Big Horn, and move along the Little Big Horn until he joined forces with Terry, who would accompany Gibbon's command. Gibbon was to move to the mouth of the Big Horn and begin a sweep south. When the conference finally broke up, Terry promised to send Custer a written copy of his instructions the next day. The 7th Cavalry was to begin its move up the Rosebud on 22 June.

Unbeknownst to any of the men of both the Dakota and Montana Columns, General George Crook had made contact with the Indians they were seeking on 17 June, while Reno was illegally scouting the Rosebud and Benteen waiting at the Tongue River. Actually, the Indians had found Crook on the Rosebud River about forty miles south of where Reno was scouting. The Indians had attacked Crook's camp and fought a rousing battle that lasted almost eight hours. On more than one occasion they had come close to wiping out a portion of Crook's command, which consisted of *fifteen* cavalry companies, five infantry companies, and about 200 Indian scouts. (Crook's command was thus only slightly smaller than Terry's and Gibbon's combined.) In the end, it was the intrepid Indian scouts and the steadfast "walk-a-heaps" who saved Crook's cavalry from annihilation. The Indians who opposed Crook were an alliance of various Sioux bands, Northern Cheyennes, and some Arapaho. They probably numbered more than 700.

Crook decided that he had taken all he could. Without any attempt to inform anyone else of his experience, he retreated to his base camp near present-day Sheridan, Wyoming, to wait for reinforcements. Terry, Gibbon, and Custer, in their ignorance planned a campaign that put two columns in motion, out of supporting distance of one another, against a concentration of hostile Indians that had whipped Crook. Had they known what had happened to Crook, they probably would have made other plans.

Custer's scout, in particular, was vulnerable. He had less than fifty Indian scouts, only a half dozen of whom actually knew the terrain over which they were to traverse, and he had *no infantry* supports. Crook's experience on the Rosebud on 17 June had proved, if nothing else, the vital necessity of having sufficient numbers of reliable Indian scouts and infantry with long range rifles, tight defensive positions and concentrated firepower.

Custer, described by witnesses as strangely subdued, even depressed, called his officers together. He relayed the instructions from General Terry. He ordered that the mules be loaded with additional forage. When two of Benteen's officers, Moylan and Godfrey, protested that the mules were overloaded as it was, Custer uncharacteristically backed away from his order. He suggested that the officers find a way to take some salt (for preserving horse and mule meat).

He said, in a rather discouraged tone, that the troopers might have to eat dead mules before the scout was over.

There is no satisfactory explanation for the curious change of mood that had come over Custer. His political troubles were behind him. Aside from Reno's strange departure from his brief, there was no reported clash with any officers. General Terry had just given him what he had sought all along: an independent command with a very good chance of being in position to get in the first blow. He certainly was not daunted by the possibility of a fight with Indians. Yet, he was subdued, even melancholy.

That night, he and Benteen "engaged in some personalities and recriminations." Lieutenant Richard E. Thompson of Terry's staff witnessed it. He said later that the issue was the battle of the Washita. Apparently, Custer "twitted" Benteen about having killed a teenage boy at the Washita and Benteen replied angrily that he "hoped he would be better supported" in the upcoming fight than he had been at the Washita. The discussion "waxed rather warm," according to Thompson, who observed: "It was plain to be seen that Benteen hated Custer."

The twelve companies of the 7th Cavalry spent the morning of 22 June preparing to move out. Packs were loaded, horses inspected and saddled, and company assignments made. By noon, they were ready. They formed into a column of fours and marched past an impromptu reviewing party of Terry, Gibbon, and Major James S. Brisbin, the 2nd Cavalry commander present.

As they marched past Terry's reviewing party, the mail that the *Far West* had taken on near the Powder River was on its way to Forts Lincoln and Rice. One letter was from Fred Benteen to Kate and scrawled hastily across the bottom was a post script.

"Everything packed — ready to leave," it read, "God bless all of us."

16

Thursday, 22 June 1876

"Trumpets sounding, horses prancing, guidons waiving, proudly the twelve troops of the Seventh U.S. Cavalry passed in review before Brigadier General Alfred Terry, commanding the Department of Dakota, at noon on the 22d day of June 1876."

That is how Benteen described the beginning act of the event that would make him famous as a supporting player in an American history drama. Apparently, the paragraph quoted was written in the 1890s, after Benteen had retired from the Army. Cavalry companies were not officially known as *troops* until September of 1883, though the two terms, company and troop, had been used interchangeably since the Civil War on an informal basis.

Twenty-two June was the first day of summer, but in eastern Montana Territory on that day in 1876, it appeared more like the first day of spring. A very heavy, cold north wind pushed at the backs of the mounted men and the sun, though directly overhead, was obscured by dense, gray clouds from the north. The 7th Cavalry paraded before Terry one company at a time. Though never established, it seems that the companies marched in *wing* order, even though Custer had abolished the wing organizations since his talk with Terry on the previous night. Another educated guess is that *Reno's* old wing led the march, followed by the six companies that had been Benteen's responsibility for over a month. Their probable order of march was alphabetical: A, D, G, H, K, M Companies. Whatever the order, it is a fact that French's M Company was the last in the parade, for it was to M Company's first lieutenant, Edward G. "Gus" Mathey, whom Custer turned as the pack mules stumbled past the reviewing party. Mathey and a small detail were directed to take charge of the packs.

The entire regiment moved south up the Rosebud, crossing it about five times on the first day of march. They broke their column-of-fours formation as soon as they had marched past General Terry. The scouts trotted far to the front and were lost to sight. Under Lieutenant Varnum, they worked both sides of the river, while the main column stayed on the west bank of the river for the most part.

The 7th Cavalry went into camp about 4:30 in the afternoon after marching about twelve miles. They seemed to have moved away from the unseasonably cold weather of the Yellowstone. With each half mile, the sun had peeped out further from behind disintegrating clouds and the air was warmer. It was so much warmer that the men began to take off their blue tunics or brown buckskin jackets. They camped at the base of a steep bluff close to the Rosebud, which was only three or four feet wide and just inches deep at that point.

The men began the ritual. Saddle girths were loosened and sergeants (or corporals) inspected the horses' skins under the saddle blankets. If the horses' backs were still wet with perspiration, the troopers were instructed to leave the blankets on a little longer. If they were dry, off came the blankets. The saddles and bridles were wiped, the eyes of the horses were sponged, the heads and manes wisped, the hooves inspected and picked. Finally, the unsaddled horses were fed, watered, groomed, and lariated to fourteen-inch picket pins in the areas designated to each company for picketing horses.

Fires were built, canteens were filled, and the precious, though monotonous, hardtack and meat broken out. Coffee was boiled and those who did not choose to bathe in the trickle that was the Rosebud River at that point filled their pipes or chewed issue tobacco or just skylarked with comrades. The tents had been left behind at the Powder River, so the shelters were constructed go-as-you-please with blankets and canvas shelter-halves and the tree branches available. Inevitably some of the enlisted men got tapped for guard duty. Red-brassarded orderlies rode up and down the length of the camp summoning the officers to an Officers' Call at Custer's bivouac.

They assembled before Custer just about twilight: 28 officers, an Army surgeon and two civilian doctors under contract to the Army. (Lieutenant Nowlan, the quartermaster, had remained with General Terry.) Custer's instructions were so perfunctory that they were almost banal. "These directions," Benteen remembered, "were wholly rudimentary and as the regiment had been campaigning for the past nine years with nearly the same officers," it jarred their senses to have them repeated. "Custer had never before seen fit to counsel or direct us as to the ABC(s) of our profession," Benteen said. With a slight stammer and a change in tone, Custer moved on quickly to a topic not considered ordinary by those who knew him: loyalty. He professed to be willing to accept advice from any officer present, but wanted it distinctly understood that he would not tolerate grumbling. He mentioned that he had heard of certain officers who had griped to Terry's staff about Custer's actions on the march out. "It was then patent to us," Benteen said, "for what purpose the 'Call' had been sent forth, and as my relations with Lieut. Col. Custer were not of the warmest personal nature, I was anxious to learn the names of the officers whom he evidently distrusted."

Lieutenant Edgerly of D Company later recalled a comment by Custer that brought Benteen red-faced to his feet. Custer had alluded to a certain regiment that had been judged by a certain department commanding general as "being a good one if only he could get rid of the old captains and let the young lieutenants run the companies." (This was almost certainly General George Crook commenting on the 3rd Cavalry regiment.)

"It seems to me, General," Benteen rumbled to Custer, "that you are lashing the shoulders of all of us to get at some. Now, as we are all present, would it not do to specify the officers whom you accuse?"

According to Edgerly, Custer snapped back: "I want the saddle to go where it fits."

There must have been some more discussion, because Benteen recalled Custer eventually answering him almost wearily: "Colonel Benteen, I am not here to be catechised by you, but I will state publicly for your own information that none of my remarks have been directed at you."

The rather dour Officers' Call broke up after the Custer-Benteen clash, each officer returning to his own command and then mingling with other officers. Benteen's lieutenant, Frank Gibson, recalled a comment made by Lieutenant George D. "Nick" Wallace to Lieutenant Edward Godfrey.

"I believe General Custer is going to be killed," he blurted out.

Godfrey wanted to know why Wallace thought so.

"Because I have never heard him talk like that before," replied

Wallace seriously. Godfrey made no reply, but both he and Gibson recalled the incident vividly years later.

Benteen returned to a homemade pup tent in his own company area. He apparently was kept up most of the night by Lieutenant DeRudio, returned to A Company by the breakup of the wing organizations. DeRudio was an amusing story-teller. Benteen was designated Officer of the Day for the next morning, the 23d.

Even after more than a hundred years, Custer's strange talk on the night of the 22d has never been satisfactorily explained. It cast a pall over the regiment to some extent, but its negative effect was more apparent after the battle of the Little Big Horn than it was at the time. If Custer was trying to root out the dissension that existed in the regiment, his ill-advised comment about older captains and young lieutenants could not have sabotaged his attempt more effectively. It sparked a confrontation with his senior captain, the second in as many nights. If the crack was not aimed at Benteen specifically, it made no sense. Prior to the previous night's clash, Custer had gone out of his way to be accomodating to Benteen in particular. Whatever message Custer was trying to convey at the bizarre Officers' Call has been lost to history. More importantly, it was lost on the officers to whom it was addressed.

17

Friday, 23 June 1876

As usual in the field, the regiment was in the saddle and underway before the sun came up. They marched south as they had the day before with one exception: three of the companies were assigned to ride *behind* the 160-or-so pack mules. They were to provide security in the event Indians worked their way in behind the column and tried to run off the pack mules. Captain Benteen, as Officer of the Day, was responsible for the designated three companies.

As the morning wore on, the packs became more and more unmanageable. Colonel Nelson A. Miles of the 5th Infantry (who was not there but free with his comments nevertheless), later remarked that the mules of the 7th Cavalry that day were the most poorly packed Army mules he had ever heard of. They were *not* trained pack mules. Prior to the Powder River, they had been pulling wagons. The packs kept slipping off and the mules wandered all over the valley of the Rosebud. By midday, the pack animals alone were strung out for about two miles.

Benteen became increasingly alarmed as the day wore on. The scouts and the lead elements had begun to discover signs of the Indian camp and trail that Reno's men had spotted almost a week before. As the news of Indian sign filtered down the column, Benteen became more anxious. At length, on his own initiative, he deviated from the arrangement dictated by Custer. Without telling anyone but those under his immediate control, Benteen placed one company in *front* of the pack train and another split into platoons on either side of the column of mules. He remained behind at the head of the third company in token compliance with his orders.

The new arrangement did not mean faster progress. It meant tighter control and security all around. The main column was far ahead, out of sight. Benteen was especially worried by the increasing gap between the mules and the other nine companies. He reasoned "that the pack train had better be 'rounded up,' or I might have a knotty explanation to grind out should it be lost."

His unauthorized arrangement narrowed the gap somewhat and Indian would-be mule thieves would have had a considerably more difficult time swooping in to run off stock because Benteen's men were intermingled with the mules. Still, it was no solution to the inevitable delays caused by the stubborn, ill-packed mules as they crossed and re-crossed the narrow, winding Rosebud River interminably. Benteen sighed, "I don't begin to believe that Job ever had much to do with shaved tailed pack mules."

It was late afternoon when the column halted and went methodically into camp. Horses were unsaddled, rubbed, and securely picketed after rolling in the grass for fifteen minutes or so. Farriers checked hooves assiduously. The men not on duty lounged in the grass in small groups or betook themselves to the water as they had the night before.

The packs were almost two hours behind the rest. Benteen found the adjutant, Lieutenant William Cooke, waiting for him to point out the bivouac areas of the three companies under Benteen's command. There was the usual commotion as designated representatives from each company sought out the mules that had company gear. Benteen jocularly tried to persuade "Cookey" to advise Custer of the modified arrangement he had made with the mule escort. Cooke rather frostily refused, telling Benten to bring the matter up with Custer himself if he cared to.

Benteen shrugged off the rebuff and concentrated on trying for a fish dinner. He was an avid fisherman, but the Rosebud River near the campsite was not giving up any fish that evening. Benteen complained that his attempt at seining "resulted mostly in 'water hauls'" and that he had to settle for the "S.O.B. and trimmings" (hardtack, bacon and coffee). He was joined as the sun went down by Doctor George E. Lord, the Army surgeon, who was so weak and exhausted that he declined to eat.

18

Saturday, 24 June 1876

Benteen got a chance to advise Custer of the new pack train arrangement as the regimental commander made his customary tour of the camp just before the first light. To Benteen's surprise, Custer not only approved the change, but indicated that he would pass it on as an instruction to the new Officer of the Day, Captain George W. Yates of F Company.

Benteen had a much easier day on the 24th. He was once again responsible only for his own company; and H Company, ably led by Lieutenant Gibson and 1st Sergeant McCurry, needed little guidance from Benteen. The weather once again proved scorchingly hot. Benteen in 1876 wore a rather shapeless black 1872 campaign hat equipped with eyelets and hooks to be used for a "cocked-hat" arrangement suggestive of Napoleon's marshals. He wore a blue regulation tunic that he later asserted "Mother" (Mrs. Benteen) had sewn, indicating that it was modified in some way. Benteen (when not dining on hardtack) was inclined to "beefiness," so it is not hard to imagine what the modification was. His hair was completely gray (perhaps even white) by 1876. His face was round, red, and smooth. He never had a beard.

The column was on the trail by the first light that peeped over the jagged foothills to the east and illuminated the rugged mountains to the west. The 7th Cavalry moved briskly at a fast walk, but the horses tired sooner than on the previous days, and within hours, the pace had slowed considerably — good news for Captain Yates and his mule escort. Deerflies and almost microscopic buffalo gnats plagued the horses as well as the men. The insects seemed to be concentrated in the shade of the rather skimpy cottonwoods along the shallow river. They swarmed into eyes and ears without regard to rank or position.

By midday, the regiment had covered about twenty miles. Custer halted near the site of what had been a Sun Dance tepee and sent for the scout commander. When Lieutenant Varnum arrived, he was raked over the coals because Lieutenant Godfrey had discovered a trail that had split from the main trail the column was following. Custer's instructions to Varnum had been most explicit: he was to be especially watchful for trails breaking away eastward. Varnum argued that the trail Godfrey had seen probably had rejoined the main trail further on. Custer insisted that Varnum personally investigate and halted the command while Varnum did so. After discovering that the breakaway trail had been made by travois poles apparently bearing loads that the Indians sought to find a smoother crossing of the Rosebud for, Varnum returned.

"I went an extra twenty miles for nothing," he later reported.

Shortly after Varnum's return, the 7th went into camp. Benteen was somewhat surprised by a hearty greeting from Captain Myles Keogh of I Company who had taken it upon himself to find a bivouac area for the senior captain and his company. Benteen and Keogh rarely associated with one another, though they had been in the regiment together for almost ten years.

About 5:00 o'clock on the evening of the 24th, Custer summoned another Officers' Call. Apparently, it was just for informational purposes. The column had been strung out for miles and rumors had inevitably run up and down the length of it. Custer told the assembled officers that the trail they were following was believed to break away to the west and cross a pass in the mountains just a few miles to the south of the cavalry camp. He indicated that some Crow scouts (who had been borrowed from Colonel Gibbon because of their knowledge of the country) were sent ahead to ascertain the location and direction of the trail. Lieutenant Mathey was asked which company's mules were causing the most problems. Gus Mathey replied that he was reluctant to make comparisons as all were doing the best they could under the circumstances, but that the mules giving the most problems were those that had been packed by G Company (McIntosh) and H Company (Benteen). McIntosh took the implied criticism "good naturedly", Mathey recalled years later, "but it made Benteen angry."

The meeting broke up and Benteen returned to his homemade pup tent. He invited Keogh, the Irish soldier-of-fortune, to share dinner with him. The two were joined by Gibson, DeRudio and probably Benteen's closest friend, Captain Tom McDougall of B Company. The jolly McDougall, later described by Benteen as "a whole-souled fellow," had been close to the senior captain since the days of the Black Hills expedition. In 1875, his company, then E Company, was assigned to Benteen's command and the two men became fast friends. Their companies swapped baseball players so regularly that the scores of the "McDougalls" and the "Benteens" are unreliable indicators of which company was actually playing. Captain Mac, as he was known, later asserted that Benteen "was always my strong friend, through thick and thin." Born 31 years before, the son of an Army officer, McDougall attached himself to a Union Army general while still a teenager and served as a volunteer aide-de-camp. In the last year of the war, he was rewarded with a commission in one of the Negro volunteer regiments. When the war ended, McDougall was a captain commanding a company of ex-Confederate prisoners styled "Galvanized Yankees" in service on the Plains. Made a first lieutenant of infantry in the post-war Regular Army, he transferred to the 7th Cavalry in 1870 and had been promoted to captain in December of 1875. McDougall in 1876 was still rather lean, but was beginning to put on weight. (Twenty years later, he weighed 300 pounds.) He was a very sociable fellow, remarkable for his entertaining way of speaking and his usually comic demeanor. He had a serious side, though, and was considered one of the better company commanders in the 7th.

While Benteen and his friends talked and rested, Custer's scouts returned with the information that the trail had indeed broken away to the west and crossed the divide. Based on that intelligence, Custer made a decision that some future historians would find inexplicable. He decided to disregard Terry's instructions to continue the scout to the headwaters of the Rosebud and instead made plans to follow the trail that semed to lead to the valley of the Little Big Horn.

Benteen, who thought he knew Custer's mind, was not surprised He claimed later that he'd had a premonition that there would be a march out of the Rosebud valley that night. Outside his pup tent, "the crowd was listening to one of the Italian patriot's, DeRudio's, recitals of his hair breath 'scapes with Mazzini, or some such man, in some other country." Benteen "rudely interrupted", telling the others of his premonition and rather crankily advising them to get some sleep or, at the very least, allow him to do so.

Sure enough, the words were no sooner out of his mouth when

an orderly blundered into Benteen while searching for Lieutenant Godfrey. Another Officers' Call had been summoned. Benteen offered a bet to Keogh and DeRudio that the summons presaged a night march. The two men declined to take the bet.

Benteen was late arriving at the assembly. His exact movements have never been detailed, but knowing that he believed a night march was in the wind and that his own company had been criticized for laxity in packing mules, it is a safe bet that Benteen decided to have a few well-chosen words with his sergeants. Custer had ordered that *each* company assign one non-commissioned officer and not more than six enlisted men to the pack train beginning the following day. Benteen evidently decided to put the required detail to work beginning with the night march. When he did arrive at Custer's bivouac, the regimental commander was gone. Lieutenant Edgerly of D Company cheerfully reported that Benteen's premonition was correct. The 7th Cavalry was to begin a night march out of the Rosebud valley.

The night march was grim. Years later, the Little Big Horn survivors remembered it vividly. They moved out about 11:00 o'clock that night and followed an intermittent stream bed up the incline toward the pass, or divide, of the mountains before them. According to Lieutenant Wallace, the itinerarist, they went not more than six miles, halting frequently and losing control over company integrity. The mules wandered all over the place. Benteen remembered assisting Captain Keogh in coaxing some of the mules across a stream in the pitch black of the night. Since his own H Company was near the head of the column and the mules were in the rear, it seems that Benteen spent at least part of the night insuring that his H Company mules were properly packed and escorted. He guided, as did the others, on sounds. The lead and trail men of each company were given the task of identifying their positions in the column by pounding on their saddle horns with tin cups or frying pans. At about 2:00 in the morning, the column halted.

Some of the men managed to catch some sleep by wrapping the reins of their still-saddled horses around their own arms and lying down on the ground. The water at the halting place was so alkaline that many of the horses and mules refused to drink. Whether authorized or not, many of the companies built huge bonfires.

The fires were plainly visible from a high point some miles to the south called the Crow's Nest, where some of Custer's scouts under Varnum had been sent. The scouts arrived at the high point just about the same time the column halted for the balance of the hours of darkness. They, too, waited for the coming of light to spy out the land west of the pass.

The fires were apparently started to cook meals. Benteen found Major Reno and Lieutenant Hodgson of B Company and invited himself to share breakfast with them. From Reno he learned that Custer had indicated at the Officers' Call that he would rest the 7th all day on the 25th while cautiously working closer to the supposed Indian camp on the Little Big Horn River. Custer had stated that he was going to attack at dawn on the 26th, just as he had attacked on the Washita seven and a half years before. From Lieutenant Hodgson, Benteen learned that the popular young officer had almost resigned his commission over his unfortunate experience with Mrs. Bell the previous summer and that he felt by leaving Louisiana "the weight of a mountain" had been lifted from his shoulders.

There *was* an Indian camp on the Little Big Horn River about 15 miles to the west. Though its exact size will never be known for a certainty, there were probably at least 1000 tepees in it. The roamers had banded together on hearing that the government had dispatched troops to round them up. The process of banding together had taken some time. In fact, it was just in the process of being completed when Custer's Indian scouts spotted smoke rising from the hostile tepees and an immense pony herd grazing on the table land just to the west of the smoke. No one in Custer's command could actually see any tepees, but the Crow scouts were convinced that the camp was on the Little Big Horn River. Custer, summoned to the Crow's Nest by Lieutenant Varnum's note reporting the discovery, studied the smoke through a cheap telescope and concluded that he could see nothing. He expressed doubts about the village's location. He was especially skeptical of the predictions of his scouts that it was the largest camp they had ever seen. One scout, a half-breed named Mitch Bouyer, repeated what he had been saying for two days: that the village was too big, too strong for Custer's 7th Cavalry. Another scout, a Crow named White Swan, told Custer through an interpreter that the plan to attack was a bad plan. Custer rather curtly told him that the plan was what was going to be carried out.

"General," Mitch Bouyer cut in, "if you don't find more Indians in that valley than you ever saw together before, you can hang me!"

"It would do a damned sight of good to hang you, wouldn't it?" Custer replied in his sarcastic manner.

Lieutenant Varnum was discomfited somewhat by Custer's language, asserting: "This was [only] the second time I ever heard Custer use such an expression." Custer was noted for eschewing profanity, even to the extreme of substituting innocuous expressions for words such as "damn." As the scouts retraced their path from the top of the Crow's Nest, Bouyer almost apologetically repeated his contention that the camp was too big for Custer's command. Custer airily replied that Bouyer need not go in with them if he was afraid.

The half-breed scout purpled with indignation. "I am not afraid to go in with you anywhere," he said thickly, "but if we go into that valley, we will both wake up in hell!"

Custer's reply was never recorded.

While Custer was having words with his doleful scouts, another event was taking place that would have a decisive effect on the outcome. Sergeant William A. Curtiss of Yates' F Company had received permission to back trail and hunt for one of F Company's pack mules that was discovered missing. As he and two troopers with him rounded a small knoll about two miles behind the hasty encampment, he spotted an Indian squatting down over a box that had fallen off a pack mule. Sergeant Curtiss and his men charged, firing. The Indian escaped. The cavalrymen pursued fruitlessly for a short distance and returned to the abandoned box. It was a box of hardtack. One piece of the meal cracker that made up the mainstay of the Army's diet in the field was lying in the sand beside it. The piece had been nibbled.

Curtiss' report of the episode galvanized the command. They mounted and began moving toward the divide. Years later, no one could tell who had given the order to move in Custer's absence. The unauthorized movement not only startled Custer, it startled two other groups of Indians roaming in the foothills. By the time Custer had rejoined — and halted — the regiment, he was convinced that his command had been spotted by Indian scouts from the hostile camp. Accordingly, he called his officers together to announce a change in plans. The attack, scheduled for the 26th, was to begin as soon as the regiment could get to the Indian camp. (Ironically, Custer's men had *not* been spotted by hostile scouts. The identities of some of the Indians startled by the approach to the divide has never been established, but the Indians who found the box of hardtack were Cheyenne. They were not associated with the hostile camp at the time. In fact, they were on their way to find it when they blundered onto Custer's cavalry.)

Charles A. Varnum, Nelson Bronson, F.W. Benteen, Benjamin H. Hodgson

Thomas M. McDougall

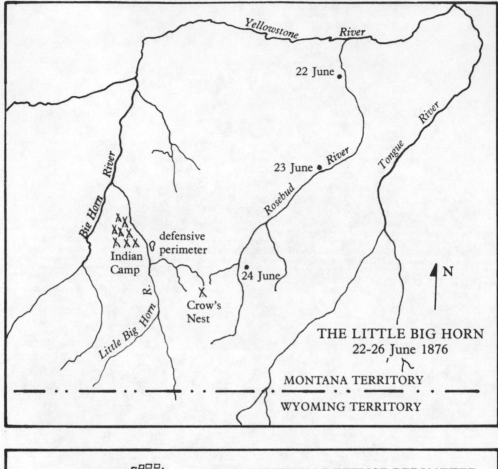

A △ A
A X X A
X A X X
X X X

Indian
Camp

defensive
perimeter

Crow's
Nest

Big Horn River

Little Big Horn R.

Yellowstone River

22 June

23 June *River*

24 June

Rosebud River

Tongue River

N

THE LITTLE BIG HORN
22-26 June 1876

MONTANA TERRITORY

WYOMING TERRITORY

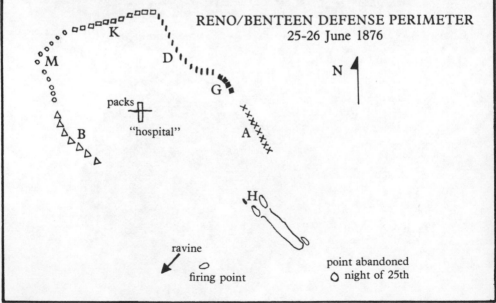

RENO/BENTEEN DEFENSE PERIMETER
25-26 June 1876

N

K

M

D

G

B

A

packs
"hospital"

H

ravine
firing point

point abandoned
night of 25th

19

Sunday, 25 June 1876

The Officers' Call gathered about 8:00 in the morning to hear Custer's revised plan. Custer explained the circumstances — what the scouts and Sergeant Curtiss had seen — and announced that he was going to charge the camp as soon as it could be reached. He repeated his instructions of the previous night concerning the details to be assigned to the packs. He also informed the assembled officers that the first company commander to report his company in compliance with those instructions would have the lead. According to Benteen, he also announced that the *last* commander to report would be responsible for the pack mules and their reinforced escort.

Benteen, who had already complied with Custer's instructions and whose company was closest at hand, stepped forward almost at once to claim the honor of leading the regiment. "I am really of the opinon," he later wrote, "that Gen. Custer neither expected nor desired that I should have the advance of the regiment." In any case, Custer had not much choice. He hesitated only fractionally and then stammered: "Very well, Colonel Benteen, you have the lead." Benteen's friend, Tom McDougall, was the last to report and was assigned the pack train escort.

Benteen led out, mounted on his bay charger, Dick. His horse was noted for its fast-walking gait and the column had not gone more than a mile when Custer caught up to Benteen and complained that the senior captain was setting too fast a pace. Custer then moved to the head of the column himself, accompanied by the chief trumpeter, sergeant-major, flag-bearing sergeants, and Lieutenant Cooke. Benteen observed Custer and Cooke in conference. The adjutant scribbled industriously in his notebook. The column moved over the divide and halted on its western slope. They dismounted.

Here, Custer divided the regiment into battalions. Benteen was directed to command not only his own H Company but Captain Weir's D Company and Lieutenant Godfrey's K Company as well. Major Reno, who had been without a command since the 21st, was given command of Companies A, G, M. Captain McDougall's B Company remained in the rear of the column escorting the pack train. The remaining five companies were assigned to Custer's personal command. (Some students of the campaign have asserted that Companies C, E, F, I, L were further divided into two battalions under Captains Yates and Keogh, but they remained under Custer in any case.)

Custer was obsessed, as were all the officers present, with the notion that the Indians they were seeking would flee upon their approach. They were ignorant of Crook's experience the week before, and every clash with Indians they had previously been engaged in — or even knew about — had featured an Indian flight when a village was approached by a large concentration of cavalry. Benteen later asserted that he was not so sure that the Indians would flee. Since Custer's modified plan meant that the cavalry would be riding hard for at least two hours to reach the site of the suspected camp, and since he firmly believed that his approach had been spotted by hostile scouts, he apparently concluded that he would have a running fight on his hands when he reached the proximity of the Indian camp. At noon, just after the division of the regiment into battalions, Custer decided to determine if possible which direction the Indians would flee. He could not have been worried that they might flee north; Terry was coming from that direction. If they fled south, on the other hand, he needed to do something to slow up their flight until the rest of the regiment could close in. Custer sent for Benteen.

The gray-haired senior captain reported for orders ahead of the long column of dismounted men (in fours) that was the 7th Cavalry. He was out of earshot of all but Custer and the small staff that customarily surrounded the regimental commander. All those present at the conference died a few hours later, except Benteen. He later claimed that his orders had been to mount the three companies assigned to him and strike out for a line of bluffs a couple of miles to the southwest of the position where Custer stood pointing. Benteen was specially instructed to send an officer and six enlisted men *ahead* of his three company battalion to do as much of the steep hill climbing as they could. The designated officer and men were to climb the precipitous bluffs and visually inspect the valley on the other side. If the Indians were spotted, Benteen was to "pitch in" to them and send word back to Custer immediately. If, on the other hand, Benteen saw no Indians fleeing, he was to return to the trail Custer and the rest would blaze down the west slope of the divide.

As it happened, one of Benteen's privates, ignorant about the cause of the delay, decided it would be a good time to seek out Captain Benteen and get his permission to be allowed to swap horses with another man. He edged forward and stumbled onto the Benteen-Custer conference. Private Charles Windolph backed away quickly when he realized he was intruding on an officers strategy meeting, but the words he overheard were burned indelibly in his mind and he was able to recall them seventy years later.

"Hadn't we better keep the regiment together, General?" Windolph heard Benteen ask Custer. "If this is as big a camp as they say, we'll need every man we have."

"You have your orders," Windolph heard Custer reply.

Benteen obediently led his battalion out of the column and started at a brisk walk toward the line of bluffs Custer had pointed out. Lieutenant Frank Gibson was sent galloping ahead with six enlisted men (and Benteen's French field glasses) to climb to the top of the bluffs and see what was in the valley beyond. Halfway to the bluffs in question Benteen was overtaken by a messenger from Custer. It was Sergeant Henry Voss, the chief trumpeter of the regiment. Voss relayed a message from Custer. Benteen was to go over or around the first line of bluffs whether or not his six man vedette party under Gibson saw any Indians in the valley beyond.

Benteen pushed on. Just as he reached the base of the bluffs that had been pointed out, a second messenger from Custer came galloping up. It was the regimental sergeant-major, William Sharrow. Sharrow told Benteen that Custer wanted the entire three-company scouting detail to go beyond the first line of bluffs into the valley beyond and to reconnoiter from the top of a second line of bluffs. If no Indians were seen from the top of the second line of bluffs, Benteen was to proceed into the second valley.

Benteen acknowledged the order and noticed as he watched Sharrow gallop away that the entire column of the 7th Cavalry was moving rapidly toward the Little Big Horn River. He saw what he thought was the Gray Horse Troop (E Company) galloping and concluded from his brief naked-eye observation that the command under Custer "had struck something." But, his orders were to push on to a second line of bluffs and he went, though he later characterized his orders from Custer as "senseless."

It is, of course, impossible to know what Custer was thinking based on second-hand accounts, but the obvious conclusion suggested by the two successive messengers is that Custer, in moving forward, realized that the terrain he had sent Benteen to scout was different than he had imagined when he issued the initial orders. Specifically, the "lines of bluffs" were further east of the Little Big Horn valley than they had appeared at the divide. Benteen, at the base of the first line of bluffs, could not be expected to realize this. Furthermore, Benteen was open in his opposition to Custer and the regimental commander could not help but realize that Benteen had misgivings about his assignment. Custer certainly did not want the Indians to escape to the south because Benteen had not scouted far enough in that direction.

But, the orders (for whatever reason they were given) had an unfortunate effect on Benteen. He concluded that Custer had sent him on an aimless mission, too hastily. When Gibson reported that the tops of the bluffs contained no Indians and that there was no valley to speak of on its other side, Benteen was even more convinced that Custer did not know what he was doing. He realized that he was beyond supporting distance of the rest of the regiment. In fact, his position, as his men finally worked their way into the badlands on the other side of the first line of bluffs, was almost identical to the position Major Elliott had found at the Washita. Straying too far from the balance of the regiment and with Custer preoccupied, Elliott had been surrounded and wiped out. "From being a participant in the battle of the Washita, Nov. 1868," Benteen said, "and from see-ing the manner the 7th Cavalry were handled there, by Custer, I formed an opinion that at some day, a big portion of his command would be 'scooped' if such faulty measures were persisted in."

Gibson had trouble keeping ahead of the column because of the roughness of the terrain and Benteen's men were forced to halt fre-quently to let their advance security take the lead. Gibson signalled from the top of the second line of bluffs — no Indians. When he came down and reported to Benteen that he could see no discernible valley on the other side and that what he could see for miles to the west looked unoccupied, Benteen decided to return to the main trail.

At the point Benteen turned back, Lieutenant Edgerly estimated the battalion had gone five or six miles. The terrain was so rough that the horses were having difficulty. Benteen concluded that Indians had better sense than to travel through such rough terrain, evidence to his mind that the Indians had not been there at all. The battalion had found no trails or abandoned Indian belongings. The last glimpse of the Custer column suggested that the others had found something. Benteen decided to find out.

Companies D, H, K reached Custer's trail ahead of McDougall's pack train and continued on until they came to a morass or "seepage of water" almost exactly halfway between the divide and the Little Big Horn River. Time estimates vary wildly and are highly controversial even today, but Benteen was away from the main trail at least two hours and maybe more than three. The fight had begun as Benteen and his men halted to water their horses and fill canteens. Benteen's charger, Dick, had a peculiarity. When the bit was removed from his mouth to allow him to drink, he would assume that he was free to roam and would bolt away after drinking if not lariated firmly beforehand. "I lariated old Dick to a stump of ironwood before removing the bit," Benteen recalled, "and after drinking he pulled taut on the stump, and looked as if to say: 'Well, I didn't much care to go off this time anyway'."

The men spent about twenty minutes watering horses and filling canteens. In the distance, to the west, they could hear the unmistakable reports of gunfire. Lieutenant Godfrey later remembered that Captain Weir "began to get uneasy" and came to Godfrey with a suggestion that the two company commanders form a delegation and urge Benteen to move on. Godfrey refused, telling Weir that he feared the senior captain would tell him to mind his own business. Weir manifestly impatient, mounted his company and, telling Godfrey: "I am going anyhow," set off on his own. Benteen mounted the other two companies and followed, As they pulled out, the pack train under McDougall was just beginning to arrive at the morass.

Benteen caught up with Weir and took the lead. He said nothing to Weir about the unauthorized movement. They had not gone a mile when they encountered a messenger on his way to the pack train. It was Sergeant Daniel Knipe of C Company with a message for the pack train commander to hurry to Custer's location. Benteen told Knipe that the packs were about a mile behind and pointed down his back trail. Sergeant Knipe remembered telling Benteen: "They want you there as quick as you can get there — they have struck a big Indian camp." He galloped away without any further enlightenment. What Knipe knew, but did not have time to explain, was that Custer had sent Major Reno and three companies across the Little Big Horn River to attack the camp and had himself swung north with five companies, paralleling the river. In short, Benteen was no longer following the trail of eight companies, he was following two different trails.

A short distance after Knipe left them, Benteen and his men found a burning tepee. Benteen dismounted and inspected the structure. It was a burial lodge. The fire had apparently been started by one of Custer's Indian scouts some time before. Benteen remounted and led his battalion down the trail. They had been moving quite slowly until reaching the morass. Once back on the main trail, the pace had picked up quite a bit. Godfrey later said that "between [the] water hole and [the] river Benteen and [his] men went at a gallop most of the time. The average speed was fast."

According to Benteen, the battalion was on a "stiff trot" when they came to a split in the trail about a mile past the Lone Tepee. Once again, they halted. Lieutenant Gibson, back in command of H Company, remembered that Benteen remarked: "Here we have the two horns of a dilemma." The trail split was disconcerting. The "they" who wanted Benteen to hurry had patently gone in two different directions. Captain Weir insisted that the trail to the left, leading to the river, was the one to follow. Apparently, he based his conclusion on the sound of gunfire coming from that general direction. (The old military maxim was: If in doubt, move toward the sound of the guns.) Lieutenant Gibson advised Benteen to stick to the right hand trail and Godfrey, apparently, seconded that motion. (There exists some confusion even today as to which trail they *did* follow. For a time, it seems, they tried to follow both.)

The dilemma was being resolved for them in the person of another messenger Benteen could see hurrying toward them on a limping horse. The messenger was one of Benteen's own men, a trumpeter from H Company who had been picked as regimental orderly that morning: Private John Martin. Martin was a young Italian immigrant who had considerable difficulty with English then and later. Benteen characterized him as "a thick headed, dull witted Italian, just about as much cut out for a cavalryman as he was for a King."

Martin had a message from Custer — a *written* message. He handed it to Benteen. It read:

Benteen
    Come on. Big
village. Be quick.
bring packs.
    W.W. Cooke
    P.S. bring pacs.

Benteen read it and handed it to Captain Weir who had joined him. Lieutenants Edgerly, Gibson and Godfrey hurried up.

"Where is Custer?" Benteen asked Martin.

The young trumpeter replied that Custer was "about three miles from here."

Benteen wanted to know if Custer was "being attacked or not." Martin replied that Custer was being attacked and was later positive that he said nothing more at that time.

"Well," Benteen burst out to the other officers rhetorically, "if he wants me to hurry to him, how does he expect that I can bring the packs? If I am going to be of service to him, I think I had better not wait for the packs."

There was no dissent recorded. "Well," Benteen remembered years later, "the packs were safe behind, I knew that better than anyone. I couldn't waste time going back, nor in halting where I was for them." Frank Gibson elaborated: "We didn't wait for the packs as we felt pretty sure no Indians had passed our rear."

Benteen asked Martin why the horse he rode was limping. Martin replied that the horse was just tired. Benteen pointed out an ugly wound on the horse's rump and blood splatters on the young mesenger's back.

"You're lucky it was the horse and not you," he said kindly.

Martin's message was far from clear. What he had *not* told Benteen was that he had left Custer's column advancing down a coulee and that as he looked back he could see Indians firing at the column. Some Indians had fired at Martin, causing the unnoticed wound to his horse. On his way back to find Benteen, he had glimpsed Reno's three companies in a dismounted skirmish line at the southern edge of an immense Indian village. Lieutenant Edgerly overheard Martin telling other enlisted men as he exchanged horses that *Reno* was attacking the village and scattering the Indians "right and left."

Benteen was confident that the Indians could not work in behind him and make off with the packs. He also knew that in waiting for them he could conceivably be sitting in one place for an hour or more. (There are some who contended later — and even now — that Custer's message through his adjutant was for Benteen to bring *only* the ammo packs — those mules who carried boxes of ammunition — and in a hurry. This supposition is far from conclusive. At the battle of the Washita, Lieutenant Bell had saved the day, in a sense, by bringing *all* the "packs" — wagons — in the nick of time. Sergeant Knipe's instructions had been to guide all the packs to Custer's location. The written message from Cooke did not specify ammunition packs only. It said merely "packs" — twice. Benteen plainly interpreted the message to be an order to bring *all* the packs. He could not see the sense of that order.)

Benteen's men began to trot toward the sound of the guns. Some, apparently Weir's company, went almost to the river. Gibson was positive years later that he and Godfrey and the other two companies followed the trail Martin had appeared on. Benteen, in front, was startled by the sudden appearance of about four Indians, who proved to be Crow scouts making off with some hostile ponies they had stolen. They informed Benteen rather emotionally that something big was happening on a bluff east of the river just behind them. They mimed the firing of many guns and kept repeating "Otoe Sioux. Otoe Sioux," which Benteen interpreted as meaning "Many Sioux. Or heaps of 'em." He trotted in the direction they indicated and was flabbergasted at the sight that greeted him.

Large numbers of mounted Indians were riding down a small number of cavalrymen in the valley of the Little Big Horn. Benteen could see the survivors of the rout headed for a high bluff less than a mile from his observation post. He gathered his three companies together in a single column, directed them to draw pistols, and charged toward the bluff at a gallop.

When he arrived, he swung his three companies into a line and dismounted skirmishers. The skirmishers trotted forward to the edge of the bluff to provide covering fire for the retreating cavalrymen. Some of Benteen's men rode to the edge of the bluff. One, a private named Jacob Adams, was called back sternly by Benteen. In the confusion, a hatless, hysterical officer ran up to Benteen. It was Major Reno.

"For God's sake, Benteen, halt your command and wait until I can organize my men!" he shouted.

Benteen, already in the process of saving Reno's refugees, noted that his arrival was in the nick of time. "A more delighted lot of folks you never saw," he remembered. He dismounted and handed the Cooke/Martin note to Major Reno.

"Where is Custer?" he asked.

Reno's reply was vague. He gestured toward the north and stated that he had last seen Custer an hour ago and that Custer had promised to support him. He went on at some length and with some emotion, even relating that Lieutenant Benny Hodgson had been killed.

"Well," said Benteen calmly, "we'll have to make a junction with him as soon as possible."

Reno got hold of himself and turned to the ragged line his survivors had formed on top the bluff.

"We have assistance now," he announced, "and we will go and avenge the loss of our comrades."

Benteen was appalled at the sight of the survivors. He noted that Captain Moylan of A Company was "blubbering like a whipped urchin." He noticed also that the Indians who had been enthusiastically riding down Reno's men were rapidly disappearing. He began to walk among the survivors to learn the situation.

Godfrey's second lieutenant, Luther Hare, who had been detached to help Varnum with the scouts that morning, greeted him. "We've had a big fight in the bottom," he reported, pumping his superior's hand, "got whipped like hell and I am damned glad to see you!"

Reno's three companies, it turned out, had been sent across the river to attack the village. They had advanced to within a few hundred yards of the tepees and then suddenly, unaccountably, Reno had halted them. He formed a skirmish line that engaged a large party of mounted Sioux without much effect for about fifteen minutes. Then, Reno had ordered the companies to take refuge in a wooded area in a bend in the river. They moved in, occupied the new position, and engaged the Indians at long range for maybe a half an hour. The Indians worked closer and closer and began to surround Reno's men. Reno concluded that Custer's promised support would not come in time and, without making his orders clear to his men, led a mounted retreat from their refuge to the bluffs where Benteen found them. At least half of one company — McIntosh's G — did not get the order. Those who did galloped toward the river with little organization. The Indians rode in close to them, hatcheting, shooting, whooping, and pulling men bodily off their horses. At the river, everybody bunched up in the attempt to get across and the Indians had a field day.

Some of the officers had attempted to stem the rout. Captain French had been more active than the other two company commanders. One of his men recalled that French, a fat man with a falsetto voice, had called out: "A — a — steady there men. Steady. Keep up a continual fire, you damned fools! Don't turn your back to the enemy. Steady, you damned fools!"

One of French's sergeants remembered: "The Captain waited until all his men got out of the timber then followed up in the rear. He drew his revolver and [was] firing at the Indians as they were riding alongside of him some twenty yards on either side of him. The Captain had barely chance to get to the ford and the Indians were so thick that you could hardly see what was going on until the Captain got on the other side of the river. He then dismounted from his horse, took his rifle and fired on the Indians while standing on the river bank."

Captain Tucker French, an undeniably brave man, was incensed by Major Reno's lack of leadership. He later claimed that he wished he had shot Reno before the retreat began. The company commander immediately behind him never made it to the river. Lieutenant Donald McIntosh, one of Benteen's original messmates, was cut down on the prairie on the west side of the river. Less than half of G Company made it to the bluffs alive in the retreat. Lieutenant DeRudio, Benteen's erstwhile adjutant, was missing, believed killed. Lieutenant Hodgson was definitely dead at the bottom of the bluff. So was one of the contract surgeons, Dr. DeWolf. The only remaining doctor, Henry R. Porter, was witness to a altercation between Major Reno and Lieutenant Varnum at the river.

Varnum, whose scouts had virtually vanished, had attempted to assert some control over the men from his own company, Moylan's A Company. Dr. Porter saw him gallop to the head of the column and call out: "For God's sake, men, don't run. There is a good many officers and men killed and wounded and we have got to go back and get them!"

Reno, according to Porter, practically bowled over the valiant Varnum, shouting angrily: "I am in command here, sir!"

M Company under Captain French got across the river more or less intact and, inspired by the example of their company commander and some of his cool, veteran sergeants, began to form a skirmish line. Company A, the object of Varnum's unheeded advice, was another story. They had failed to form any kind of a line once safely across.

Lieutenant Luther Hare, detached from K Company to assist Varnum with the scouts and temporarily without any command of his own, had "yelled out with a voice that could be heard over the field" at that point. "If we've got to die, let's die like men!" he was heard to shout at the A Company men. Then, after giving a wild rebel yell, had added: "I'm a fighting son of a bitch from Texas!"

One of French's men nearby witnessed the scene and heard Hare shout at Captain Moylan: "Don't run off like a pack of whipped curs!"

Major Reno, on reaching the safety of the top of the bluff, had heard Hare's yelling and ordered Moylan to form a skirmish line. Moylan was a little slow in complying and Reno had to repeat the order. Lieutenant Hare, observed French's man, "was game clear through" and "saved the command from a stampede then and there."

Dr. Porter found himself standing beside at hatless Major Reno at the top of the bluff as French's men and (belatedly) Moylan's men were providing covering fire for the pitiful handful of McIntosh's men under Lieutenant Wallace who were still running the gauntlet. As he watched, Wallace turned and covered the retreat of about ten men and, with their deliverance, the Indian attacks abated. Turning to Reno, Porter remarked quietly: "Major, the men were pretty demoralized by the rout, weren't they?"

Reno puffed up indignantly and snapped back: "No! That was a cavalry charge, sir."

Benteen walked among the survivors and heard the excited reports. French's M Company, one of the Fort Rice companies, had done well. Moylan's A Company had escaped more or less intact, though they had quite a few wounded. McIntosh's G Company had ceased to exist as a fighting unit for the time being.

As inevitably happens in an emergency situation, there was a noticeable lack of central leadership. Everyone in a position of responsibility, it seems, assumed that the first priority was additional ammunition. They had seen the large number of Indians. Benteen and Reno conferred again briefly. From this conference came the decision to appoint the gallant Lieutenant Hare as Reno's adjutant and send him back to the pack train as fast as he could go to bring some of the ammo packs up right away. Hare had a little difficulty finding a horse as his own had been gravely wounded, but was underway within ten minutes of Benteen's arrival.

Hare found the pack train about two miles from the bluff. He informed Captain McDougall of the situation and requested the ammo mules. McDougall quickly had two of the mules cut out of the train and sent them forward with Hare as fast as they could run. He divided his own B Company into two platoons, placing one in front of the pack mules and one behind, with instructions to maintain unit integrity and hurry forward.

Hare returned to the position atop the bluff less than a half hour later. As it turned out, the ammunition that everyone had assumed was so desperately needed was not needed so badly after all. Only one box was opened. Hare noticed that there was a terrific fire fight going on some miles to the north. Others, including Godfrey and Varnum, heard the shooting and commented on it. Captain Weir and Lieutenant Edgerly decided that it was caused by Custer's five companies engaging the Indians. Weir decided to move toward the sound of the guns and asked Edgerly if he were willing to go along. Edgerly quickly agreed and Weir set off in search of Major Reno to get permission for the move.

Weir did not get Reno's permission.

What exactly transpired between Reno and Weir has never been established. Benteen said later that he never knew what the conversation was about, merely observing that "Reno and Weir were never friendly, but the cause of this I never inquired (about) or knew." Others indicated that Reno and Weir "engaged in a hot exchange of uncomplimentary language in which threats were made on both sides." Weir stalked off, mounted his horse and trotted off in the direction Custer had gone. Lieutenant Edgerly, watching the exchange out of earshot, concluded that permission had been reluctantly granted and led D Company out on Custer's trail.

As Weir's men pulled out, Captain McDougall arrived at the head of the pack train. He heard the firing to the north and saw Weir's company moving out all alone. He "went up to where Reno and Benteen stood talking and expressed to them" his opinion that the whole command ought to be moving toward the sound of the guns. The conversation between Reno and Benteen that McDougall interrupted with his advice has never been recorded. Benteen later said that, upon seeing Weir's company move out, he went to Reno and "inquired as to the whereabouts" of Weir's men, who were his responsibility. Reno unquestionably told Benteen that the movement had not been authorized, for Benteen later commented that, in his opinion, Weir had gone off "in a fit of bravado" intended to "show his smartness." McDougall, his advice ignored, later complained that

"Reno did not appear to regard the seriousness of the situation." The situation on the bluff when he arrived was certainly serious. Moylan's A Company had at least a dozen casualties. French's M Company had almost as many. McIntosh's G Company was only able to muster about a half dozen men.

Some of the men Reno had abandoned in the timber were still alive. In fact, as Benteen, Reno, and McDougall stood talking, a young civilian guide named George Herendeen was in the process of leading about a dozen of them to safety. The Indians had inexplicably all but vanished and Herendeen's small band of dismounted stragglers could be plainly seen hurrying across the prairie toward the safety of the bluff. The packs were up and Weir had already started the movement toward Custer, but the rest of the men of Reno's and Benteen's combined command remained atop the bluff for almost another half hour.

In the years to follow, both Reno and Benteen were roundly criticised for this delay. Benteen was in no hurry to get back on Custer's trail. He later asserted that movement toward Custer at the time was impossible. His lieutenant, Frank Gibson, elaborated in a letter to his wife just after the battle. "It was impossible," Gibson said, "as we could neither abandon our wounded men, nor the packs of the command." Any movement in Custer's direction would have to be at a pace allowing the slow-moving mules and hand-carried wounded men to keep up. Moylan's A Company was particularly slow getting organized. Stragglers from the timber were still coming in. Reno decided to take time out to bury Lieutenant Hodgson's body, apparently to keep Indians from mutilating it. He did not finish the burial at that time.

The exact sequence of events during the half hour delay has never been satisfactorily detailed. After about a half hour, Reno apparently concluded that he was ready to move and sent Lieutenant Hare ahead with instructions for Captain Weir to inform Custer that the rest were coming as quickly as they could. Hare galloped to Weir, who was about a mile or so north of the bluff position, delivered the message and returned. Benteen pulled out.

Benteen's sally consisted of French's M Company, Godfrey's K Company, his own H Company, and some men from G Company under Wallace. They apparently did not move in a single column, but rather by individual companies in a sort of fit-and-start arrangement. Moylan, unable to keep up, requested help from Captain McDougall in transporting his wounded. The entire seven-company force, Reno's by virtue of his superior rank, was thus strung out for a couple of miles. The men in the rear, in fact, never left the bluff.

Benteen reached a high point about a mile from Reno's position on the bluff and stuck his own company's guidon "in a pile of stones which were on the high point, thinking perhaps the fluttering of same might attract attention from Custer's commands if any were in close proximity." The act of appearing on the skyline and planting the guidon attracted attention, sure enough. Within minutes, Weir's D Company, having begun a descent into the coulee Custer had dispatched Martin from, came galloping back, "myriads of howling red devils behind" them.

"We then showed our full force on the hills with guidons flying," Benteen related to his wife right after the battle, "that Custer might see us — but we could see nothing of him, couldn't hear much firing, but could see an immense body of Indians coming to attack us from both sides of the river." Some of the others present, Godfrey in particular, claimed that they could see Indians riding over a ridge about four miles to the north shooting into the ground. All agreed that the Indians were soon headed directly for their position on the high point. Benteen was impressed by the aggressiveness and size of the Indian force. He decided to retreat to a better position.

"The reason for this," he explained, "is that there were a great deal too many Indians, who were 'powerful' good shots, on the other side. We were at their hearths and homes — they had gotten the 'bulge' on Reno, their medicine was working well, and they were fighting for all the good God gives anyone to fight for." They had also gotten the "bulge" on Custer, wiping out his five company command to the last man, though Benteen and the men with him did not realize it at the time. Lieutenant Gibson expressed the majority view-point when he told his wife that they had "concluded that he (Custer) had gone to the timbers about six miles off and fortified himself." Others thought that Custer had ridden off to link with General Terry. In any case, the consensus was that Custer had abandoned Benteen and Reno as he had Elliott at the Washita. During the next two days, there was a lot of speculation and bitter comment about this.

Weir's men came galloping up out of the coulee and Benteen, determined "that there was no necessity of having a repetition" of Reno's rout, ordered Captain French's M Company to form a dismounted skirmish line at a right angle to the river, let Weir's company through, and "take position on the point." French dutifully formed the line and let Weir's men through, but then, unaccountably, remounted and followed in a panicky retreat virtually identical to the one that had characterized the flight from the village under Reno. Benteen directed Godfrey to dismount his company and do what French had been unable to do. "Well," Benteen related years later, "French 'weakened' (no doubt of it!) though he let Weir through; but ye Gods, how he came too! 'Twas then I ordered Godfrey to take position on the point."

Benteen hurried to Reno and insisted that the command fort up near where Reno had taken refuge from the valley fight. Reno agreed and Benteen went to work laying out positions for the cavalry troops rushing back. He placed Wallace's miniscule G Company on the east side of one hill and "gathered the procession in as it came, stringing it around an arc of a circle" from Wallace's position west. In the end, Reno and Benteen occupied two hills with a shallow depression between them — ideal for corralling the horses and pack mules. Benteen's own company was placed alone on the second hill, the highest of the two. The resultant position resembled a tadpole from the air, Benteen's men being the tail.

The men of Reno's command took their new positions not a moment too soon. Large numbers of Indians appeared on all sides and began sniping at long range while darting forward from time to time as if about to rush the cavalry position. "I don't know how many of the miscreants there were," Benteen said, "probably we shall never know, but there were enough." The most vulnerable position was that selected for the hospital and pack mules in the small depression between the two hills. Captain Moylan's A Company was placed in a line behind a breastwork of boxes and leather saddle packs. They protected the hospital/packs from the east. Captain McDougall's B Company and Captain Benteen's H Company provided security for attacks from the west by an interlocking field of fire.

Benteen had placed Moylan's men behind the barricade. To their right, he placed his own company in a hairpin-shaped defensive position on the military crest of the highest hill. (The *military crest* is an imaginary point just below the skyline on the *forward* slope of a hill that commands the terrain in front as far as the weapons employed have range.) Wallace's initial position was also sited by Benteen. They were in a hastily-dug pit between Moylan's barricade and the top of the second hill.

Curiously, the other companies — placed either by Reno or their own commanders — were, with only a few individual exceptions, on the *reverse* slope of the first hill. Even today this arrangement is baffling to the mind of anyone familiar with standard military small unit tactics. To clarify, standard military tactics are (and were then) to place defending troops on the *forward* slope of a high ground and rely on entrenchments and concentrated firepower to provide security. The reverse slope admittedly puts the hill between the defenders and attackers, but sacrifices observation to a false sense of security. It also wastes the range of the defending weapons, as the attackers cannot be fired on until they are virtually on top the defended position. The correct placement (Benteen's) entails more immediate risk of exposure, but gives the defender the opportunity to use firepower to its maximum potential to "stand off" the attacker.

Six of the other officers present were West Pointers. They knew better. *All* of the non-West Pointers present were combat veterans. They knew better, also. There has been no satisfactory explanation for the peculiar lapse in military judgment shown by Reno and other commanders. As it turned out, H Company, on higher ground, suffered heavier casualties than necessary because Indians were able to work their way to the top of the first hill and fire into the rear and right flank of Benteen's men on the second hill. They were permitted to do this because the other companies were poorly positioned. In fact, after the retreat to what was to become known as the Reno/Benteen defensive perimeter, H Company suffered as many casualties as the other companies *combined*. As one expert wrote: "the other companies laid down on the job, literally as well as figuratively, and depended on (Benteen's H Company) to save not only their honor but their scalps as well."

Another writer on the subject of casualties there pointed out that Benteen alone of all the company commanders did not entrench on the night of the 25th, suggesting that Benteen's lapse in this regard explains the higher casualties in H Company. It does not. The casualties in H Company (3 killed, 11 wounded) were, with two exceptions, inflicted from the right and rear — *not* from the front. Benteen's men, in the correct defensive posture, did not need protection from the front. Their carbines were their protection. Concentrated firepower is far more effective than passive barriers in forcing an enemy to keep his distance.

Nonetheless, Benteen's men did entrench the following day. Sig-

Thomas B. Weir and Nina Tilford

John Aspinwall

Luther R. Hare

Francis M. Gibson

nificantly, their casualties did *not* abate. They stopped receiving effective fire from the Indians only after they (and some of Reno's men) had made short, dismounted charges against Indian positions the next day. Most of the entrenching done on the night of 25 June was unnecessary and, while it may have imparted a sense of security to those who did the digging, it was, from the tactical point of view, counter-productive. Benteen, in later years, was especially scornful of the role played by several other officers, even going so far as to imply that some of them were cowards. Several writers on the battle of the Little Big Horn have attributed this to an unspecified character flaw of Benteen's that rendered him incapable of seeing merit in any other officer. Given the tactical arrangement previously detailed, it is hard to see how Benteen could *not* have been scornful of some of his fellow officers.

As it began to get dark, the Indian attacks slacked off considerably. The Sioux and their allies were reluctant to fight at night, But, they did not leave the battlefield. They kept Reno and his seven companies effectively pinned down and waited for the morning sun.

There were still four men left alive in the timber whom Reno had abandoned that afternoon: Lieutenant DeRudio, Fred Gerard, a G Company man, and a half-breed scout. They decided to use the darkness to cover their bid for escape. In the middle of the prairie they ran smack into a party of Sioux warriors and were sent fleeing in different directions. They hid out near the river and waited for the sun to come up.

Benteen, in his wanderings up and down the lines, discovered some mules still carrying ammo boxes headed for the river — and Indian positions. He brought them back and, to his ire, found the pack train commander, Lieutenant Gus Mathey, "gossiping away like an old lady over her tea" instead of looking after his charges. Benteen blew his stack — the first (and only) time recorded by the Little Big Horn participants. He gave Mathey a "cussing out" in "broad Saxon." He later told his wife: "I never felt more like damning anyone in my life." The mules safely in place and Mathey put in his, Benteen returned to walk the lines with Lieutenant Gibson, kicking his men into wakefulness. He fumed about Mathey. "That fellow," he wrote to his wife, "is about as fitted for a soldier as our Fred is." (The "Fred" referred to was Benteen's nine-year-old son.)

The heat of the day gave way to a rather sultry night. It rained a little off and on, just enough to make everyone — especially the wounded — thoroughly miserable. Captain Moylan placed a picket line of four men under an intrepid sergeant named Stanislaus Roy in the dark *before* his barricade to give early warning in the event the Indians attempted to creep up on his vulnerable position. Benteen's men above them could not see the valley below, partly because of the darkness and partly because Benteen's line had been shortened after dark by bringing in the southernmost positions. Sergeant Roy and his three brave volunteers remained on duty in the open all night.

With darkness as a cover, the officers roamed about the lines more freely. Captain Tom McDougall pulled Benteen aside. "Fred," he said quietly, "I think you'd better take charge and run the thing." Captain Mac expressed a lack of confidence in Major Reno's ability and a fear that "the thing" could easily become "another Fort Phil Kearny Massacre." (In December 1866, Captain W.J. Fetterman and eighty men had been wiped out to a man by the Sioux near Fort Phil Kearny in what is now Wyoming.)

Benteen conferred with Reno. The major proposed that they mount every man and ride for the Powder River camp, abandoning the position under cover of darkness and leaving superfluous equipment behind. Benteen wanted to know what Reno wanted to do about the wounded men, many of whom could not ride.

"Oh," Reno said, "we'll have to abandon those that can not ride."

"I won't do it," Benteen answered.

Captain Weir sought out Lieutenant Godfrey, thanking him for the way his skirmish line (at Benteen's order) had protected Weir's retreat to the position. He then asked Godfrey: "If there should be a conflict of judgment between Reno and Benteen as to what we should do, whose orders would you obey?"

"Benteen's" replied Godfrey.

20

Monday, 26 June 1876

Benteen got little, if any, sleep that night. At first light, Sergeant Roy's gallant pickets came scampering in, followed by a fusillade from hidden Indian marksmen, and the fight was renewed. The Indians remained, for the most part, hidden from view in the sagebrush clumps and high bunch grass of the Montana foothills. They had the seven companies of Reno's command completely surrounded. They were concentrated in the ravines between Reno's men and the river and had worked their way up to occupy the position H Company had abandoned during the night.

Benteen moved up and down his lines, directing the fire. He had the heel of his boot shot off in the presence of Trumpeter John Martin, who remembered that the gray-haired captain merely muttered, "Close call; try again," as he flung the shredded bootheel toward the Indians.

Private Glease of H Company remembered that "Benteen was on his feet all day" and that he went around "encouraging the men." One of the things Glease remembered Benteen saying was: "Men, this is a ground hog case; it's live or die with us. We must fight it out with them." When the enlisted men chided him for "drawing the fire," Benteen was heard to say casually, "Well, they fire about so often anyway." Lieutenant Varnum, who served as a sort of unofficial adjutant for Benteen, remembered that "Benteen was the only man he ever saw who did not dodge when the bullets [were] flying — [he] seemed to pay no heed to them whatsoever."

The Indians who had worked their way up into Benteen's old position on the extreme south end of the high hill posed a real threat. Benteen ordered Lieutenant Gibson to hold the modified position and went down among the packs to gather a "Falstaffian crowd" from the men assigned to the packs. He gathered about fifteen men and delivered them to Gibson while he organized the rest of his H Company to lead a counterattack to take back the lost position. He instructed Gibson that the reinforcements "must hold" the modified position "no matter what became of" his party. One of the reinforcements, the civilian guide George Herendeen, later marvelled: "I think in desperate fighting Benteen is one of the bravest men I ever saw."

There was some delay as Benteen coolly made his way up and down the line of H Company explaining what had to be done. Private McDermott scurried up with a message from Lieutenant Gibson that the Indians were about to overrun the reinforcements. Benteen wearily made his way to the extreme south end of his own company position. Enroute, he shot an Indian who had briefly exposed himself.

"Though I'm rather fond of Indians than otherwise," Benteen recalled of the shooting, it gave him a sense of satisfaction to hit the Indian and "plump him thro' his spinal." He remembered that he was "so confoundedly mad and sleepy." Gibson was indeed having a very difficult time on top of the high hill. The Indians were creeping up to within rock-throwing range and it looked like they were gathering for a final rush. The rock (and dirt clod) throwing angered Benteen even more. "I was so tired," he said, "and they wouldn't let me sleep."

At about 9:00 o'clock in the morning, Benteen walked in front of his own lines in full view of the sniping Indians and shouted to his men that he was "getting mad." He ordered them to jump up at his command and charge the Indians to "skip them out." H Company followed him on a wild, screaming charge toward the Indians closest to their lines. "Why of course we hustled them out," Benteen recalled, and "they somersaulted and vaulted as so many trained acrobats, having no order in getting down those ravines, but quickly getting; de'il take the hindmost!" Only one cavalryman was killed: Private Meador of H Company, who was shot just as the charge had been recalled.

The precipitant departure of the Indians enabled Benteen to reoccupy the position he had abandoned during the night. It also gave him an idea about securing water by sending men down one of the ravines that seemed to have been abandoned completely by the Indians in their haste to get away from his charge. With marksmen firmly entrenched on the extreme south of the hill once again, Benteen sent four men, volunteers, to occupy a position in the open at the base of the hill that overlooked the ravine. The four, Sergeant George Geiger, Privates Otto Voit, Henry W.B. Mecklin, and Charles Windolph, all H Company men, stood or knelt on the lip of the bluff overlooking the ravine and fired into the foliage while a dozen or so volunteers from other companies dashed down its length to gather water. Miraculously, none of the men in Benteen's first water party was hit, though they were subjected to enfilade fire from Indian positions to the north of the hill Reno occupied. They filled camp kettles, pans, pots, and canteens and dashed back up the ravine to safety. Benteen regarded that event as the turning point, thinking that in gathering the water at such risk under fire they "rather impressed the Indians *that we were there to stay."*

Lieutenant Hare of K Company came over to watch the water gathering party go down the ravine. He stood with Benteen on the hill and noticed that the Indians in Reno's front were shooting "a hail of bullets at them." He asked Benteen if it was wise of them to stand and seem to desire drawing the fire. "Benteen," he recalled, "smiled and said: 'If they are going to get you they will get you somewhere else if not here.' "

Benteen went to Major Reno and asked for a company of reinforcements to hold his extended position. Reno replied that he could take any company he wished. Benteen selected French's M Company, one of his old Fort Rice units, and went to move French's men into the new position.

Private William Morris of M Company said later: "Benteen was unquestionably the bravest man I ever met." His first sergeant, John M. Ryan (who had no reason to love Benteen, having once been reduced to the ranks by him for stringing a private up by the wrists), stated: "Too much cannot be said in favor of Captain Benteen. His prompt movements saved Reno from utter annihilation, and his gallantry cleared the ravines of Indians." Lieutenant Varnum, who accompanied Benteen part of the time, said: "Benteen was really the only officer looking out for the whole command and he handled things well and fought very gallantly."

There was some delay in getting M Company from their original position to a new one supporting Benteen. After the battle, Benteen refused to endorse an application for a Medal of Honor to 1st Sergeant Ryan on account of the delay. But M Company, despite some grumbling, eventually moved to a position between McDougall's B Company and Benteen's men on the hill. Their redeployment caused the Indians to renew the attack on Reno's position. The immediate result was that Benteen's exposed men on the hill began taking heavy casualties again. Benteen went to Reno and, telling him "this won't do," urged a charge by Reno's men much like the one he had led earlier. After some delay, Reno led a short charge that effectively drove away the Indians who were sniping at Benteen's exposed position. One enlisted man was shot in the head and killed, though he seems to have been one of a very few who did not stand up and charge. Lieutenant Varnum was wounded in both legs. He limped back to a shallow trench and began pulling off his boots to examine his wounds. The Indians led a brief charge and their fire caused Varnum to drop his boots. When the attack was driven off, he tried again. Some Indian snipers spotted him and fired close to a boot, causing the enlisted man he was sharing the trench with to laugh. Varnum rather crossly called the man "a damned chucklehead" and picked up his own carbine to return the fire. He did not get around to having his wounds examined until the next day.

That afternoon, other parties from the various companies made the dangerous sortie down the ravine to gather water, protected by the fire from Benteen's men. At least one was killed and two or three wounded, but they managed to get the precious water for the wounded men.

About 2:00 o'clock in the afternoon the Indians set fire to the grass on the prairie between their village and the cavalry position. The fighting had died down, limited to occasional sniping from both sides. The cavalrymen began to move around more freely and tend to the business of improving their defenses. Sergeant Roy, who led the first water party and who may have participated in others, said: "Benteen saved the command, according to my opinion. He was a very brave and nervy man." Benteen had been hit by a spent bullet in the right thumb, the only wound he received during the battle. He continued to walk the lines, sucking his wounded thumb and superintending the gathering of water.

Just before dark, the Indian village was dismantled. The combined Sioux, Cheyenne, and Arapaho began a long march south toward the Big Horn Mountains in full view of the surviving 7th Cavalry. The column they made was fully two miles long, only partially obscured by the smoke from the prairie fire. The cavalrymen stood and watched the procession with awe. Lieutenant Hare later reported that the pony herd alone consisted of about 20,000 head. The beleaguered survivors were mystified by the move, some concluding that it presaged an attempt to overrun them once the women and children were clear, others concluding that it meant the imminent arrival of Terry's men from the north.

Lieutenant Varnum approached Major Reno with an offer to ride north with a single sergeant as companion to bring word of their plight to General Terry. "He did not reply for some time," Varnum remembered, "and then said he could not afford to lose two good shots & that we would get killed anyway. I said we might as well get killed trying to get relief as to get killed where we were. He said, 'Varnum, you are a very uncomfortable companion.' I left him."

When darkness came and no attack with it, the men began to shift their positions. They used Benteen's company as an anchor and, under the direction of Captain McDougall, repositioned themselves further south and closer to the river to escape the stench of dead horses and mules. They cautiously led some of the surviving animals down to the river to get their first taste of water in two days. Benteen's charger, Dick, had been wounded twice, but survived.

Fred Gerard and the half-breed scout came into the new position after dark. Lieutenant DeRudio and McIntosh's cook followed them in about midnight. All four had been hiding in the trees along the river since the afternoon of the 25th. Benteen was scornfully amused by DeRudio's tale of adventure. He told his wife later: "He has a thrilling romantic story made out already embellished, you bet! The stories of O'Neill (the man who was with him) and DeRudio's of course, couldn't be expected to agree, but far more of the truth, I am inclined to think, will be found in the narrative of O'Neill; at any rate, it is not at all colored — as he is a cool, level-headed fellow — and tells it plainly *and the same way all the time* — which is a big thing towards convincing one of the truth of a story."

Reno had the dead men buried and personally looked to the burial of Lieutenant Benny Hodgson. Those who were not employed in burial parties or in improving the new position got some sleep. Benteen, who had gone without sleep for four nights, was on the verge of collapse. Though never explicitly stated by anyone, he almost certainly took advantage of the lull to catch up on rest. The Indians who had surrounded them were gone.

21

After the Battle. . .

Dust clouds appeared on the horizon in the direction of the Indian camp about 9:30 the morning of 27 June 1876. Major Reno sent a couple of Indian scouts followed by Lieutenants Godfrey and Wallace to investigate. The dust clouds became a column of mounted men and the mounted men proved to be General Terry's.

Godfrey made contact with Lieutenant James H. Bradley of Cibbon's 7th Infantry and was struck speechless by the infantry officer's answer to the question: "Where is Custer?"

"I don't know," replied Bradley, who was functioning as Terry's scout commander, "but I suppose he was killed. We counted a hundred and ninety-seven bodies. I don't suppose any escaped."

Until that moment, no one of Reno's command had any certain knowledge of Custer's fate. No one had guessed that Custer had been wiped out, or at least no one had voiced that opinion. Most felt that Custer had abandoned them for one reason or another.

Within an hour an ashen-faced General Terry rode with his staff to Reno's new positions. To the inevitable "Where is Custer?," the courtly general replied in a broken voice: "To the best of my knowledge and belief, he lies on a ridge about four miles below here — with all his command killed."

Benteen blurted out: "I can hardly believe it. I think he is somewhere down the Big Horn grazing his horses. At the battle of the Washita, he went off and left a part of his command and I think he would do it again."

"I think you are mistaken," Terry replied, "and you will take your command and go down where the dead are lying and investigate for yourself."

Benteen led the portion of the 7th Cavalry that went to identify the dead, determine if they could what had happened, and learn if there were any survivors. They followed what they believed was Custer's trail down a narrow coulee that opened at the Little Big Horn River about three miles from their defensive positions. They doubled back back up a northern fork of this coulee until they came to the battle ridge. Almost at once they began to find dead bodies. Those closest to the village had been savagely mutilated, not unlike the bodies of Elliott and his men at the Washita. The bodies further north were not mutilated much, some were not even scalped, though all had been stripped. The bodies had been lying in the sun almost two days and were covered with flies. Still, many were recognizable. A private of H Company named Jacob Adams found Custer's body at the north end of the battle ridge. He signalled for Captain Benteen, who came at a gallop. Adams indicated the body and said it was Custer.

"That surely is General Custer," Benteen said.

Benteen said very little in later life about the bodies, understandably. He was very broken up on discovering the body of Captain Yates of F Company, a man he had known since the Civil War. Less than a month later, he recorded a nightmare featuring Captain Keogh of I Company undressing, prompted no doubt by the horror of seeing Keogh's naked, battered body that afternoon.

Benteen's first conclusion about the fight was that "nearly — if not all of the five companies got into the village — but were driven out immediately — flying in great disorder." After the Indians had driven Custer's men from the village or ford site, Benteen believed, "it was a regular buffalo hunt for them and not a man escaped. We buried 203 of the bodies of Custer's command on the 2d day after the fight. The bodies were as recognizable as if they were in life."

Years later, Benteen changed his mind about Custer's having reached the village or even the ford site, but from first to last, was convinced that Custer's fight had been a poor one. "I am reckless as to whose feelings I hurt," he said twenty years later, "but it is my firm belief, and always has been, that Custer's command didn't do any '1st-class' fighting there, and if possible were worse handled even than Reno's batt[alio]n. 300 men well fought should have made a better showing."

The bodies of three officers, including Lieutenant Jack Sturgis from Fort Rice, were not found — or not recognized. "It was the most horrible sight my eyes ever rested on," Lieutenant Gibson told his wife.

Years later, Colonel Nelson A. Miles of the 5th Infantry quoted an unnamed officer who was there that day with Benteen when Custer's body was found. According to this anonymous officer (who must have been Lieutenant Bradley), Benteen stood over Custer's body and remarked: "There he is, God damn him, he will never fight any more."

The somber, shaken search party returned to their position. "We found them," reported Benteen, looking "pale" and "troubled," "but I did not expect that we would." There was a lot of wild-eyed talk that night about the battle. Many of the officers were vehement in their condemnation of Major Reno's conduct during the battle. This was exacerbated when Reno produced his official report of the engagement that commended only one officer for exceptional conduct. The one officer was Benteen.

"During my fight with the Indians," Reno wrote, "I had the heartiest support from officers and men; but the conspicuous services of Brevet Colonel F.W. Benteen I desire to call attention to especially, for if ever a soldier deserved recognition by his Government for distinguished services he certainly does."

Without exception, those officers who survived and commented on the battle echoed Reno's sentiments about Benteen. "If it hadn't been for Benteen," Lieutenant Gibson told his wife confidentially, "every one of us would have been massacred. Reno did not know which end he was standing on, and Benteen just took the management of affairs in his own hands, and it was very fortunate for us that he did. I think he is one of the coolest and bravest men I have ever known." The civilian guide, George Herendeen, said simply: "I think Captain Benteen saved the fight on the hill."

Years later, Benteen commented on the lack of endorsement for other officers from Reno, saying that it was not his business to advise Reno on what to write in the official report, but had he known Reno would single him out to the exclusion of all others, he would have counseled Reno not to mention any one officer by name. "Had I anything to say in the matter," he insisted, "I should have recommended brevets, first Hare, then Varnum, and lastly, Godfrey, yes, Wallace, too, before Hare, then I think I should have stopped."

The next day, 28 June 1876, the survivors began to move their belongings and wounded across the river to a new camp. Lieutenant

DeRudio presented himself to Benteen and handed him a pistol, remarking that it was the one Benteen had loaned him at Fort Rice in February and that he was returning it. Benteen, already burdened with several extra weapons, rather brusquely told DeRudio to throw it down with the others. Afterwards, he observed: "now that is a specimen of the character of Italians", adding that he "wasn't surprised at such conduct", having "a pretty thorough analysis of (De-Rudio's) character."

Major Reno led the survivors over to the battlefield to bury the bodies. The burials were indecent by any standards. The torn and hacked and bloated bodies were covered over hastily with a pitiful layer of dirt and rocks — and sometimes tree branches nearer the river. More time and effort was spent marking graves than making them. The bodies of those officers identified were tagged by writing their names on pieces of paper and sticking them inside empty cartridge cases which were inserted in the ground next to sticks that marked the head of the graves. The enlisted men were not identified.

Transportation of the wounded was a problem as the reunited Dakota and Montana Columns headed north toward the Yellowstone River. They were only able to make about four miles on the night of the 28th, when stumbling and fumbling with hastily-constructed stretchers combined with a moonless night to make further progress under those conditions insane.

The next morning, General Terry decided he needed a map of the Custer battlefield and dispatched his engineer officer, Lieutenant Edward Maguire, back to draw the map. One cavalry company was sent along as an escort — Benteen's Company H. The men spent most of the day going over the field yet again, Benteen explaining to Maguire what had been found and where. As they headed back toward the main column, Benteen turned to Maguire and said: "By the Lord Harry, old man, 'twas a ghastly sight, but what a winner the U.S. government would have been if only Custer and his gang could have been taken."

Benteen had become convinced from the moment he laid eyes on Custer's disaster that Custer was solely responsible. He never wavered in that conviction. "Custer disobeyed orders," he asserted, "from the fact of not wanting any other command — or body — to have a finger in the pie — and thereby lost his life." Time and again, he would repeat his beliefs. Custer had disobeyed Terry's order to scout all the way to the headwaters of the Rosebud whether the trail led that way or not. Custer had unwisely split the regiment before having made any reconnaissance of the village. Finally, he concluded, "Custer galloped away from his reinforcements and so lost himself."

Benteen, his company, and Maguire reached the main column in the evening. By 6:00 o'clock everyone was underway again. Lieutenant Doane of the 2nd Cavalry had worked wonders with the improvised stretchers and the progress was so good that Terry kept everyone moving all night. A scout came back with the astonishing news that the steamboat, *Far West,* had ascended the Big Horn River and was anchored just a few miles ahead near the mouth of the Little Big Horn. Encouraged, Terry's men pushed on and reached the boat by sunrise of 30 June.

The wounded were placed aboard and the remainder marched north along the river while the boat headed for the Yellowstone. The boat made it to the Yellowstone on 1 July, the rest of the column arriving the following day. Terry took the wounded off the boat to use it for ferrying everyone across the Yellowstone, where they went into camp 2 July.

Benteen sat down and wrote his first letter to Kate since leaving the Powder River two weeks before. The letter was brief but was followed in the ensuing days by several known today as the Installment Letters. They were of varying lengths and often repeated information, as Benteen feared that some would not reach Fort Rice.

General Terry replaced the wounded on board the steamer and sent it down the Yellowstone to Fort Buford and then down the Missouri to Fort Lincoln. Grant Marsh, the steamer's captain, made the 700 mile journey by 11:00 p.m. on 5 July — in a record 54 hours.

The survivors in camp on the north side of the Yellowstone began writing official reports and letters to their kin. They remained in camp for a week. On 9 July, they received word of Crook's fight on the Rosebud, three weeks too late. "Crook has known where Terry's command was — all the time," Benteen wrote angrily to his wife, "but has held aloof from it — he wanting all the pie for himself." He reported the reorganization of the 7th Cavalry, which consisted of the seven companies saved and an eighth made up of survivors from the other five who had remained with the packs. Lieutenants Mathey and Varnum were given command of the provisional company.

"Reno has assumed command," Benteen reported, "and Wallace is Adjutant. Edgerly, Q[uarter]M[aste]r. By the deaths of our captains, Nowlan, Bell and Jackson, 3 'coffee coolers' are made captains

and Godfrey is Senior 1st Lt. Mathey 2d. Gibson 3d. Quick promotion." He commented on some of the Fort Rice officers. "I am inclined to think that had McIntosh divested himself of that slow
poking way which was his peculiar characteristic, he might have
been left in the land of the living," he said, pointing out that there
was ample time for those trapped in the timber by Reno's retreat
to get away once he (Benteen) had arrived. DeRudio, he said,
"deserves no credit for being caught in the woods, and after being
left there — kept there." He relayed some criticism of his own lieutenant, Frank Gibson. "I am told that H Co. men are terribly down
on Gibson," he said. "The men say of G[ibson] that he does nothing
but curse them in garrison — and when he gets in the field — cannot
do anything." (Ironically, as he was writing his comments about
Gibson, the object of his criticism was writing to *his* wife praising
Benteen as the savior of the command.)

On 18 July, for reasons never made clear, General Terry ferried
the men of his column back across the Yellowstone and readied
them for a pursuit that never got underway. "The movement is too
late," Benteen complained, "our golden opportunity has been lost.
We should, after having put the wounded on the boat, which was
then at the mouth of the Little & Big Horn Rivers, have returned
directly to the trail of the Indians which led from the scene of the
fight. Now, two weeks and more have been lost." The command went
into camp and waited for infantry reinforcements which began arriving 1 August. Benteen kept up his Installment Letters to Kate (or,
as he sometimes called her, "My Frabbie Darling").

"Had Gen'l Terry left Gen'l Custer at Lincoln — I — for one, feel
confident that we should have no disaster to chronicle," he told her,
"but — instead — that we should have gained such a victory that
would have ended the campaign." Years later, he elaborated on this
idea. Custer, he claimed, patently had not wanted to share any of
the glory with Terry or anyone else, "all of which Terry should
have had sufficient foresight to have seen, and he would have done
so, could he in his gentle, manly breast have conceived that so vile
a wretch as Custer was ever born of woman." He later detailed
all the little things that he believed were responsible for the dissension in the regiment which had not made Custer's hasty attack
any easier to carry out. "The regiment was in terrible shape from
the very beginning," he concluded, "and Custer was the grand mar-
plot and cause of it all."

While the troops idled away the midsumer, they inevitably engaged in postmortems of the fight. Some of these became rather heated as accusations and insinuations flew. Benteen, suffering from chronic neuralgia, had come down with dysentery as well and was still slowly recuperating on 4 August when he and Captain Weir got involved in an argument that almost led to bloodshed. The fight apparently started when Weir complained once again about Reno's failure to mention him in the official report of the battle.

About the same time, Benteen had taken a bottle to his tent and was in a near stupor. He summoned Charles Windolph and instructed Windolph to present his (Benteen's) compliments to the other officers and to inform them that they were all a pack of cowards — Captain French excluded.

In this condition (and frame of mind), Benteen interrupted Weir's tirade in front of "a dozen or so officers" with the declaration that Weir was "a damned liar." Weir responded heatedly that Benteen's remark meant "blood."

"Well," Benteen said, "there are two pistols on (my) saddle; take your choice of them; they are both loaded, and we will spill the blood right here!"

Weir declined the 'duel' and the next time he encountered Benteen "shoved out his hand to shake," apparently as a token of peace. "Aha!" said Benteen, "I scarcely knew what to make of it, but at the same time had his accurate measure." Later Benteen observed: "Now, really, when a man quietly and serenely composed and all that, thinks of it, what could Reno have said of Weir, confining himself strictly to the truth, that would have been at all complimentary to him? If I had been forced to mention him, there would have been nothing special, other than he exhibited a very insubordinate spirit, which came very nearly bringing disaster on himself and (his) troop."

Benteen sold Captain Yates' horse (the one that had been left with the pack train) and told his wife to let Mrs. Yates know that he had done so in compliance with her request. "You must write to her at Monroe, Mich.," he told Kate, "also to Mrs. Custer, there, assuring them all of my love and remembrance in their deep affliction."

It was beginning to look by the early part of August 1876 that the troops would be in the field all that year attempting to round up the hostiles. They had begun to get replies from their initial letters after the battle. "Miss Goody Two Shoes," Benteen told his wife, "in answer to your question, I can't for the life of me tell how long

this campaign is going to last — but — shouldn't be the least bit
surprised if it resulted in a winter's work — indeed — I feel confident that we shall have to look after them this winter."

The Indians had split up and were believed to have crossed the
Big Horn Mountains and headed east — toward Dakota Territory.
General Terry began transporting his whole command, which had
been much reinforced by infantry under Colonel Miles, to a camp
on the Rosebud River not far from where Custer's ill-fated scout
had begun. General Crook, similarly reinforced by the 5th Cavalry
under Colonel Wesley Merritt, was slow about linking with General
Terry, who was his superior (by date of rank). "Crook is following
exactly Custer's game," Benteen commented scornfully.

Terry's men moved south along the Rosebud, virtually in the tracks
that had been made by Custer's scout over a month before. On 10
August, they had a brief scare. Dust clouds, indicating a large force
advancing, appeared to the south. The eight 7th Cavalry companies
threw out skirmishers to receive what seemed to be hundreds of
Indian warriors. The lead figure in the advancing force closed the
distance and introduced himself. He was William F. Cody, guide for
the 5th Cavalry and better known as "Buffalo Bill." The Indians in
the van were Crow and Shoshone scouts — friendly. The figures
behind were not Indians but soldiers from the 2nd, 3rd, and 5th
Cavalry and the 4th and 9th Infantry. The officers of the various units
mingled with one another and traded information. The lieutenant
colonel of Merritt's 5th Cavalry was Eugene A. Carr, the man Benteen
had known at Pea Ridge.

The next morning, 11 August, General Terry as senior officer took
command of the largest column of Army troops ever deployed against
Indians to that time. He sent Colonel Miles' infantry back down the
Rosebud to the Yellowstone with orders to patrol up and down river
on the steamboats (there were by then at least three in constant
motion) and to prevent (or at least be cognizant of) the Indians
crossing the Yellowstone. At the same time he headed the remainder
across the divide separating the Rosebud and Tongue valleys on the
trail of the Indians. Two days later, Terry's men came upon a fresh
Indian trail that was not more than three days old. They tried to
hurry the pursuit, but pouring rain for days on end reduced the
pursuit to what historians later dubbed the Mud March. Wet, dis-
pirited, and unsuccessful, Terry's men slogged into camp on the
Powder River on 18 August. After much discussion (and some re-

criminations), Crook decided to take up pursuit with what remained of his own command, while Terry's men went to work constructing garrisons for a winter line on the Yellowstone.

Crook's march on the trail of the hostiles took him into the Sioux reservation, but at a terrific cost. Historians termed that phase of the pursuit the Starvation March. In fact, the only contact Crook's men made was an accidental brush with a small Indian camp near Slim Buttes as a well-mounted column was hurrying ahead to the Black Hills to secure rations for the balance of Crook's command. Lieutenant Colonel Eugene A. Carr came up with reinforcements just in time to secure the tepees captured and stand off a large force of Indian reinforcements. Among the Indian possessions in the small village captured, Carr's men found property of the 7th Cavalry, including a guidon and Captain Keogh's gloves.

Benteen, in the meantime, had celebrated his 42nd birthday at the Powder River camp. The date — 24 August — coincided with Lieutenant Hare's birthday and preceded DeRudio's by just two days. The three men had one big party. Benteen was offered a chance to take a two year assignment as recruiting officer in New York and wrote to his wife in a quandary. He wanted to wait another two years before accepting the assignment, but told Kate that he had not made up his mind and would not until he had seen or heard from her. "This campaign is 'played,'" he told her disgustedly as he griped about the unceasing rain. He was increasingly disillusioned with General Crook. "All the officers of Genl. Crook's command unite in saying that his fight on the Rosebud and June 17th amounted to nothing at all," he told "Frabbie," "and that if it had been managed by a subordinate — that a Genl. Court Martial would be the consequence."

Events moved faster than Benteen. He was placed on the recruiting assignment in September and sent east. He was in St. Paul (Terry's headquarters) when the rest of the 7th Cavalry marched into Fort Lincoln on 26 September. He had just gone to Colonel Sturgis and secured a release from the detail when the rest of the officers gathered in the Fort Lincoln Officers' Club for a blow-out.

They got roaring drunk. Major Reno, target of rumors and whispers since the day of the battle, lost control of himself and engaged in a brawl. He attempted to bodily eject one of the infantry officers and was wrestled to the ground by Lieutenant Varnum. Reno called for pistols, threatening to kill the valiant young officer who had made him "uncomfortable" for so long. One of the newly-assigned officers of the 7th, Lieutenant William W. Robinson, intervened and Reno pushed him away, shouting contemptuously, "Who the hell are you?"

In St. Paul Benteen was informed that his replacement would be Captain Weir. He was ordered to proceed as far as Philadelphia with assurances that Weir would be along to relieve him shortly. He went by way of Chicago (to visit some cousins of his named Zimmerman) and St. Louis (to see old friends and especially Kate's mother, Elizabeth L. Norman). He arrived at Philadelphia on 6 October at the height of the Centennial Exposition. There, he saw the sights while awaiting Weir's arrival.

The news of the Custer disaster at the Little Big Horn was very much the center of public attention and Benteen found himself beset by the curious, much to his embarrassment. He stayed at Major Lewis Merrill's home and tried to avoid strangers as much as possible. "I could receive lots and lots of attention everywhere I have been," he complained to Kate, who was still at Fort Rice, "but I have fought shy of everybody — and declined the many kind offers that have been made to me." He spent his days wandering through the Exposition (which did not impress him) and visiting old friends. He called on Verling K. Hart's wife and on the father of Benny Hodgson. He ran into ex-Lieutenant Edward Law, who had resigned from K Company to practice law in Pennsylvania and into Captain Tom Mc-Dougall, who was on leave of absence. He was visited by a young man named Robert Newton Price, who had been a West Point classmate of Benny Hodgson's. (Robert N. Price had briefly been an officer in the 10th Cavalry in 1869, but had been arrested for killing two privates in a quarrel and had been allowed to resign from the Army.)

He visited places dear to himself and Kate, places they had visited when first acquainted before the Civil War, and concluded: "I only wish I was snugly at Rice with you tonight." He expressed distaste for shopping for the wives of Fort Rice, but reported that he was dutifully rounding up requested items. "Had I lots of money," he confided to his sorely-missed wife, "for your sake I could endure civilization — or rather — cities — but really, were my tastes consulted — cities and I would be life long strangers." At one point, he revealed that he was "too much of a matter of fact fellow." He was irritated by the delay in Weir's appearance, concluding gruffly: "I want to get back, bad!"

Weir eventually showed up and Benteen hurried back to Fort Rice, arriving 28 October 1876.

While Benteen and his "darling Frabbie" were enjoying their reunion, events in two places, widely separated, were occurring that would result in another officer's disgrace. In New York, in the fall of '76, Captain Weir was approached by one Frederick Whittaker, a former officer of Custer's during the Civil War, who was putting together a biography of George Armstrong Custer. Weir gave vent to his frustrations, but refused to sign an affidavit that Whittaker pressed upon him. Weir, understandably, was very harsh in his criticism of Major Reno's conduct. Weir also had little love for Captain Benteen. Armed with information from Weir, Whittaker hurriedly wrote his laudatory biography and had it published in the winter of 1876. He accused Reno of cowardice and Benteen of what amounted to indifference and implied that had it not been for the actions of these two officers, Custer would not have been killed.

Weir took suddenly ill in early December. He had begun a correspondence with Libbie Custer and had confided that there was something he could tell her in private that he could not set down on paper. His illness was never accurately diagnosed. Thomas B. Weir died on 9 December 1876 of unknown causes, prompting rumors that he had been poisoned because of something he knew. His death has been attributed to "congestion of the brain" and "melancholia." He had gone to bed shortly before he died and refused to eat anything. Weir may simply have died of a stroke; the notion that he was murdered because he was in on some dark secret is absolutely preposterous.

Edward S. Godfrey was made captain by Weir's death. Whittaker also gained from it; he was able to use the dead Weir to great advantage as an "anonymous" source who could not be ferretted out and brought into open court. At the same time that Whittaker was damning Reno in print, the object of his attacks was in Fort Abercrombie (on the Dakota-Minnesota border) embroiling himself in another controversy.

Major Marcus A. Reno had heard gossip in the regiment about Mrs. James M. Bell some time before the winter of 1876 and at Fort Abercrombie that Christmas season, in the temporary absence of Captain Bell, he attempted to see for himself if the rumors were well-founded. He was eventually court-martialed (in March 1877) for seven specific incidents of "taking liberties with" Mrs. Bell. He put his arm around her on one occasion, took her hand on another, and when rebuffed, annoyed her with petty restrictions in his role as post commander, telling those who interceded for her about her bad reputation. Captain Bell, on his return to Abercrombie, was outraged. Benteen, commenting many years later, opined that Mrs. Bell had seen fit to "pose as an innocent."

While the seeds of controversy were being sown, Colonel Nelson A. Miles was rounding up most of the hostile Indians who were still roaming in the unceded lands. His winter campaign, featuring infantry mounted on captured Indian ponies, was one of the most remarkable of its kind in American history. The military authorities had known for some time that a spring campaign would be necessary in 1877 to finish the job botched by Crook, Terry, and Custer in 1876. Miles' campaign was insuring that there would be no *large* hostile villages.

Colonel Sturgis took the companies from Forts Lincoln and Rice into the Sioux reservation to dismount and disarm the Sioux there. He was largely successful, essentially impoverishing the Indians and making them totally dependent on the agencies for survival. The large Sioux bands remained a potential threat for the duration of Benteen's service with the 7th Cavalry, but there were to be no more pitched battles.

Fort Rice received a number of new officers. Major Tilford returned from another of his interminable detached service postings as the fort's commanding officer. Besides the sister companies of H and M, there were two other 7th Cavalry companies at Fort Rice that winter: A and D Companies.

Captain Moylan of A Company was on leave until February 1877 and his first lieutenant, Andrew Nave, was on detached service, so the company was commanded by a transfer to the 7th Cavalry: 2nd Lieutenant Ezra B. Fuller. There were a number of lieutenants transferred to the regiment as a result of the Custer debacle. Ezra B. Fuller was a West Pointer who had served briefly in an Illinois cavalry regiment during the closing days of the Civil War while he was still a teenager. He had graduated from the U.S. Military Academy in 1873 and been assigned to the 8th Cavalry until the fall of 1876. He brought three years experience with him to his new station and, as it happened, became one of the select few for whom Benteen had unbounded admiration.

D Company was commanded by Captain Godfrey, who was assisted by a first lieutenant named Eddy Eckerson, an officer who had served three years in Arizona Territory with the 5th Cavalry before being abruptly dismissed in the summer of 1875. He managed to have himself reinstated in early 1876 and was reassigned to the 7th Cavalry. His career in the 7th Cavalry was far from glorious, but Benteen was uncharacteristically charitable in assessing Eckerson's performance. The second lieutenant of D Company that winter was another officer Benteen took a liking to: Edwin P. Brewer. Enrolling at West Point at age 17 in 1871, Brewer resigned after a few months, but upon hearing of the vacancies in the cavalry caused by the Custer disaster, applied for one and received it in the fall of 1876. Brewer, who was carefully broken in by Benteen, went on to become a full colonel before retiring thirty-five years later.

H Company got a new second lieutenant. Actually, Lieutenant Ernest A. Garlington had been assigned to H before they departed on the spring campaign that resulted in Custer's death, but Garlington was still on graduation leave from West Point and did not join the regiment until fall. By then, he was a *first* lieutenant (thanks to the numerous vacancies created by the battle of the Little Big Horn), and assigned to G Company. His replacement was 2nd Lieutenant Albert J. Russell, a '76 West Point graduate who had been destined for the 10th Cavalry until the news of the Custer battle. Russell, about whom Benteen had mixed feelings, remained with H Company until after Benteen left.

French's M Company had a new second lieutenant also. He was John C. Gresham, a Virginian, classmate of Russell's and a brilliant young officer for whom Benteen recorded only warm feelings until the end of his own life. Gresham, like Fuller, put in a full career in the cavalry, rising to the rank of full colonel, and eventually winning a Medal of Honor at Wounded Knee.

The old stand-bys were also at Rice: French, Mathey, and Gibson. In addition, Captain James W. Scully was still post quartermaster. Scully would eventually retire in Atlanta and remain an associate of Benteen's until the latter's death. The post surgeon was Dr. Blair D. Taylor, a Virginian who with his wife became very close to the Benteens throughout his Army career. Taylor, in fact, was a pallbearer at Benteen's funeral and eventually retired (and died) in Atlanta.

The winter of 1876-1877 was perhaps the happiest of Benteen's military career. "Benteen was the hero of all America, credited with saving the remnant of the Seventh Cavalry," observed one young

officer who met him that winter. Military men, in particular, held
Benteen in high esteem. One of the 7th's new lieutenants, a canny
young West Pointer named Hugh L. Scott, expressed the sentiments
shared by many young Army officers at the time. Forty years later,
as a retired chief of staff of the U.S. Army, Scott wrote this of
Benteen:

> I found my model early in Captain Benteen, the idol of the
> Seventh Cavalry on the upper Missouri in 1877, who governed
> mainly by suggestion; in all the years I knew him I never once
> heard him raise his voice to enforce his purpose. He would sit
> by the open fire at night, his bright pleasant face framed by his
> snowy-white hair, beaming with kindness and humor, and often
> I watched his every movement to find out the secret of his quiet
> steady government, that I might go and govern likewise. For
> example, if he intended to stay a few days in one camp he
> would say to his adjutant, "Brewer, don't you think we had
> better take up our regular guard mount while in this camp?"
> and Brewer always thought it 'better' and so did everybody else.
> If he found that his kindly manner were misunderstood, then
> his iron hand would close down quickly, but that was seldom
> necessary, and then only with new-comers and never twice with
> the same person.
> Benteen's policy, which I adopted in 1877, has paid me large
> dividends.

In March of 1877, Benteen was put on detached service to go to
St. Paul to testify as a witness in the court-martial of Major Reno.
Benteen was questioned about an allegation that he had urged Reno
to remove Mrs. Bell from the regiment. He denied it, and was retained
as a witness for the defense. He wrote to his wife expressing the
opinion that Reno's prosecutors had not proved a case, but admitted
that as a witness he was not permitted to sit in on the deliberations.
On 16 March he was dismissed from the court-martial, as all but
the closing arguments had been heard. He boarded a train for Bismarck.

That next day, Fort Rice received a new post commander: Lieutenant Colonel Elmer Otis, an 1853 West Point graduate who had
spent the last twenty years in the 1st Cavalry. Otis was Custer's replacement, but Colonel Samuel D. Sturgis had been released from
the latest in a series of detached service postings away from the regiment and had returned to Fort Lincoln to command the regiment
in person for the first time since 1872.

Despite Benteen's impressions, the court-martial convicted Reno of all but one of the seven specifications involving his conduct with Mrs. Bell. In part, Reno's defense had been that putting his arm around her waist was to prevent her from falling and that the holding of her hand was an attempt to teach her "a Masonic grip." Not surprisingly, the court-martial board rejected his defense.

However, enough testimony had worked its way into the record about Emiline Bell's alleged conduct in Louisiana that the board members agreed with Benteen's conclusion that she was not "a true wife." The penalty by statute for conduct unbecoming an officer and gentleman was dismissal from the service, but the testimony about Mrs. Bell's dalliances elsewhere prompted the reviewing authorities in May 1877 to mitigate the sentence to two years suspension from rank, duty, and pay. Reno repaired to Harrisburg, Pennsylvania.

22

The 1877 Campaign

Lieutenant Colonel Elmer Otis marched the four-company Fort Rice battalion on 19 April 1877. On 22 April, they went into camp, as before, just outside Fort Lincoln and awaited the rest of the regiment. While in camp, Benteen was visited by Colonel Sturgis.

The burly, tobacco-chewing cavalry colonel informed Benteen that he had been "begged by Mrs. Sturgis" to give Benteen command of a battalion, but that under the circumstances, he could not do it. Lieutenant Colonel Otis and Major Lewis Merrill were present, he said, and had to be given commands commensurate with their ranks. Otis, in particular, was to have six companies and Sturgis could not justify giving Merrill the same three companies he would have to give to Benteen. (Sturgis's arithmetic was further frustated by the detachment of C Company under Captain Jackson to guard the mail route from Bismarck to Deadwood in the Black Hills. Hence, the 7th Cavalry was reduced before the summer campaign began to eleven companies.)

Benteen replied, "General, do not bother yourself about any command for me, as I know it will come when the opportunity presents itself, and I am really more interested in my own troop than in the whole balance of the regiment."

The question of command decided, the eleven companies of the 7th Cavalry under Colonel Sturgis left Fort Lincoln on 2 May 1877, bound for the Yellowstone River. They did not follow the route of previous expeditions straight west across the Bad Lands, but crossed the Missouri River and marched north along the *east* side of the river instead. They reached Fort Buford, near where the Yellowstone ran into the Missouri, without incident on 16 May 1877. Their purpose that summer was to patrol the Yellowstone River, rounding up stray bands of hostiles in the region and preventing a large band that had escaped to Canada the previous winter from slipping back across the border.

The day after his arrival at Fort Buford, Benteen wrote a letter to his wife. "I saw Reno's sentence in 9th Bismarck paper," he said. "He can congratulate himself in getting off thus easily, and can now visit Turkey where the 'scrouging' of women is not attended with as fatal consequences." He enclosed a "slip" (since lost) that apparently was an erotic sketch.

On 23 May, the 7th Cavalry was ferried across the Yellowstone and commenced patrolling its north bank. They went into camp near Cedar Creek on 29 May and were ordered to remain there by Colonel Miles. (Colonel Nelson A. Miles, as a result of his brilliant winter campaign, had been given an independent command called the District of the Yellowstone and, by virtue of being district commander *and* Colonel Sturgis' superior on the Army List, gave the orders that summer.)

Several of Benteen's letters to "My Frabbie Darling" still exist that were written from this camp. He mentioned that Robert Newton Price was working on the steamboats on the river that summer and that the two of them had visited "for a day or so." He repeated a rumor that Colonel Mackenzie of the 4th Cavalry and 86 men had been massacred at one of the Sioux agencies. (The rumor proved false.)

Lieutenant George D. Wallace was replaced as the adjutant by Lieutenant Ernest A. Garlington and given command of G Company. Lieutenant Edgerly had resigned his position as quartermaster the previous fall rather than serve under Colonel Sturgis and had been replaced by Lieutenant Varnum.

The 7th Cavalry at Cedar Creek spent most of their time sending out small patrols, usually commanded by the second lieutenants. All proved fruitless, including the one on 5 June in which H Company was dispatched to investigate rumors of hostile Indians nearby. Captain French's trumpeter observed, "Captain Benteen started out, delighted with the order. He is not the man to run away from an opportunity to have a little fun with the reds."

It was at this point that Benteen began a running comment about sprigs of "wild thyme" that he was to allude to in almost every letter from that period of his life. The tangible proof is long gone now, but it is almost certain that Fred and Kate were exchanging pubic hairs through the mail. Both seemed to have enjoyed the game.

Captain McDougall's B Company was detached on 29 May, assigned to patrol the south bank of the Yellowstone under the direct control of Colonel Miles, whose adjutant, 1Lt. Frank D. Baldwin, was sent to Fort Peck (near the international border) to learn what he could about the Sioux living in Canada. Said Benteen: "now, all this amounts to nothing in my opinion. No one can tell much about what is going to be done by the Indians. I think there are more of them south than there are north of [the] Yellowstone, that none of them will fight if they can help it, to which only getting on their village will push them. Of course, this is all guesswork, but I think pretty nearly correct."

Benteen was right — and wrong. The Sioux, both in Canada and on the reservation, did not fight. But, the day before he wrote those lines, the Nez Perce Indians in Oregon were commencing an awesome trek that would take them almost to the Canadian line — and two fateful encounters with the 7th Cavalry. The Nez Perce outbreak, of which Benteen was blissfully unaware, was an indirect result of the battle of the Little Big Horn. The majority of the Nez Perces were enrolled at the Fort Lapwai Reservation in Washington Territory. A number of small bands whose elders had refused to sign an 1863 treaty establishing the reservation declined to live near Fort Lapwai, preferring their ancestral haunts such as the Wallowa Valley in Oregon and similar non-reservation camp sites in Idaho Territory. The U.S. government, adopting a get-tough policy with non-reservation Indians, ordered the nontreaty Nez Perces onto Fort Lapwai by the end of June 1877. The Nez Perces were on their way toward a grumbling compliance when several of the younger warriors killed some white men in a dispute unrelated to the enforced removal. The tribal leaders met and decided to flee the inevitable reprisals. (They intended, apparently, to link with their Montana "cousins," the Crows.) They packed up their belongings on pony-dragged travois and, taking women and children, struck out for Montana Territory. Brigadier General Oliver O. Howard, in whose Department of the Columbia the Nez Perce lived, set out in pursuit. Because of the Columbia Horn fiasco the year before, the Army (and especially the public) were in no mood to humor Indians regarded as renegade. The Nez Perces were pursued with more enthusiasm than success.

The 7th Cavalry moved twice more in the month of June, movements dictated by rumors of Sioux slipping over the Canadian border and by Colonel Miles's obsession with capturing Sitting Bull. Miles was kept on a short leash by his superiors, who felt that he might, in his zeal to capture Sitting Bull, invade Canada and provoke an international incident. The 7th Cavalry spent most of the time until mid-August in camp. Mail couriers were occasionally intercepted and killed — or chased — by small groups of hostile holdouts, but nothing happened of a serious enough nature to warrant dispatching an entire regiment of cavalry. Benteen renewed his acquaintance with Robert Newton Price of Philadelphia, who got "drunk and perfectly stupid" on more than one occasion. Price was not the only one. Captain French began showing evidence of a losing battle with alcohol at that time. "I believe French expects to marry in the autumn," Beteen commented on one occasion. "He was in arrest for being drunk on duty a few days ago. He won't do to bet a cent on anyway." On another occasion, Benteen commented sadly, "He'll get dropped the 1st thing he knows."

He showed less charity for a sober (but absent) Gus Mathey, French's first lieutenant whom Benteen had never forgiven for his conduct during the Little Big Horn campaign. "Mathey isn't out here getting some of the scouting business," he railed. "The damned sneak knew when he went on leave that he wouldn't get back in time! He isn't at all missed or mourned for tho', but all knowing his sneaking way would like to see him beaten."

Benteen had also decided to get rid of his Negro servant "Cuff" Jones, on the grounds that Cuff was "very prejudicial to Fred's morale and conduct." (Benteen did in fact discharge Cuff upon his return to Fort Rice, but the youngster remained at Fort Rice to play an important role in the downfall of Captain French the next year.)

Lieutenant DeRudio, finally in command of the E Company he had been assigned to in December of 1875, managed to get an assignment to the Crow agency, much to the envy of the other officers. The detail was regarded as a plush assignment, a relief from the monotony of sow belly and hardtack and endless patrolling. After he had volunteered his company for the assignment to go with Lieutenant Doane of the 2nd Cavalry to Crow Agency, DeRudio tried to withdraw his request. He had learned that it was to last at least a couple of months and maybe as many as six. Since the cavalry expected to be home before October, DeRudio realized that he had talked himself into an assignment that was not so desirable after all. Benteen was amused. "So much for seeking a detail," he said. "Doane, to keep from being talked to death, should be well corked."

Benteen kept up his amorous (sometimes erotic) private talks with his wife. "Glad to know you are feeling so foxy," he said at one point, "shall endeavor to keep you busy at the game." All was not sweetness and innuendo, however. Kate back at Fort Rice was having difficulty with a female servant and was reluctant to let her go. She apparently ignored her husband's advice in the matter, but kept complaining about the situation. Finally, he exploded, "If you don't exercise some judgment and authority about those matters — don't complain to me," he wrote angrily. "For Christ's sake — or anybody else's sake! Let's hear the last of that matter. Bundle her off. Strangle her — Do anything you please with her, but let up on me about her. I am sick of the sing-song story — and if she worries you, why 'tis the easiest thing in the world to pay her, and send her off. If any more letters come about that matter, I will not answer them."

By the middle of August, the incredible progress of the Nez Perce was bringing them closer to Montana. They defeated every attempt to surround them and, on 9 August, badly defeated Colonel John Gibbon at Big Hole in western Montana, *after* Gibbon and his men had attacked their camp. It was the closest their pursuers had ever come to capturing the Nez Perce to that point. The valiant, dead-shot Nez Perce made Gibbon's men pay a terrible price. They killed 29 and wounded 41, hardly on the Little Big Horn scale, but too close for comfort. Among the soldiers killed was Lieutenant James H. Bradley, who had discovered Custer's companies on the battle ridge over a year before. Further east in Montana, Benteen and the rest of the 7th were made aware of the Nez Perce progress.

Colonel Miles ordered Colonel Sturgis to ready six companies of the 7th Cavalry to move toward Yellowstone Park to cut off the Nez Perce. "It is feared should 'Joseph' join the Crows," Benteen wrote after receiving the warning order, "that the Crow Nation might shake off their clouts, don their war-paint & skip on the 'war-path.' I — for one — don't fear anything of the kind, believing them to be too fond of sugar, coffee & flour — too little [fond] of the whistling of the merry bullet."

The sudden Nez Perce scare shed a different light on DeRudio's plush assignment. Benteen was highly amused. "I suppose DeRudio's Co. is now with the Crows — and — should they by any possibility unite [i.e., the Nez Perce and Crow Indians] DeRudio — were it not that Doane is a 'No. 1' officer — might, at least, get pretty badly scared — and maybe left hairless. Doane will manage affairs as well as they can be. DeRudio will blox everything."

The 7th Cavalry was ordered to go to the Judith Gap, a strategic pass through which it was believed the Nez Perce would go. Benteen was philosophical. "Chases after Indians," he said, "in so vast a country where we must go with a limited quantity of supplies is but a chance in a thousand to hit the mark you are aiming at. 'Tis terribly hard on horses and men — and but poor satisfaction at best should you gain the end." Benteen was not just trying to ease his wife's fears; he firmly believed that the 7th would not see any other fight like the Little Big Horn. "Have just returned from General Sturgis," he added at the end of his last letter before the march. "He thinks there are fair hopes of catching 'Joseph.' I don't."

Nonetheless, he straightened Kate out on his financial affairs and cleared up a life insurance problem. In a way, he was relieved to be sent against the Nez Perces, believing that the campaign would wear down the cavalry horses to the point that they would have to return to their respective posts. He was worried that Colonel Miles intended to keep them in his district all winter to settle a score with the hostiles in Canada. Firmly believing that the Sioux did not want to fight, Benteen could see no point in a winter campaign just to add to the laurels of Nelson A. Miles.

On 12 August, Colonel Sturgis led Companies F, G, H, L, & M west up the Yellowstone to Pompey's Pillar, then north toward the Musselshell River and the Judith Gap. Lieutenant Colonel Otis had been sent back to Fort Rice, suffering from diarrhea. Sturgis divided the six companies among Major Merrill and Benteen. (Companies B, C, & E had been scattered in detached service roles and Colonel Miles had kept Companies A, D, & K under Captain Owen Hale.) Merrill commanded Companies F, I, & L; Benteen, Companies G, H, & M. Lieutenant Gibson remained at Tongue River in charge of a supply depot. Benteen's own company marched under the leadership of Lieutenant A.J. Russell, but before contact was made with the Nez Perces, Sturgis assigned Company A's veteran second lieutenant, Ezra B. Fuller, to act as commander of H Company.

On 21 August, Colonel Sturgis received dispatches at his camp in the Judith Gap reporting that the Nez Perce were headed toward the Crow agency. He mounted his six company command and set out for the agency. Reaching it, he remained there until 31 August. The next day he set out to block the strategic pass at Clark's Fork Canyon.

On 1 September, Sturgis' six companies went into camp about 35 miles north of Clark's Fork Canyon. "Tomorrow," Benteen wrote, "we move to the mouth of the Canyon of the Clarke's Fork, thro' which — or the Stinking River Canyon they must come if they intend coming our way." Sturgis' move had placed the cavalry across the main route into Montana Territory from Wyoming Territory at that point — Clark's Fork Canyon. Clark's Fork was a branch of the Yellowstone River, where it came rushing down out of the mountains. "All my spare time had been put in trout fishing," Benteen informed his wife. ("He loved to fish," Private Jacob Horner of K Company remembered seventy years later, "and took every opportunity that presented itself. I saw him wade over his boot tops many times into the cold water to get mountain trout.") Benteen described Clark's Fork River: "We are in a small valley just at the foot of a high mountain, the top of which is covered with snow. The water which rushes down the creek comes like a train of cars down grade with brakes up — and the water is as clear as crystal — and cold as ice."

"If the Nez Perces come our way," Benteen predicted on 5 September, "or we can find them, there will be a big row." Based on their scanty knowledge of the terrain then, and the inadequacy of guides with certain local knowledge, the cavalry officers (Colonel Sturgis in particular) decided that the Nez Perce had to come by one of two routes: either straight down Clark's Fork Canyon or by a more circuitous route down the Stinkingwater River Canyon. The Stinkingwater (so called because of the reeking odor of sulphur and now called the Shoshone River) came down out of Yellowstone Park roughly parallel to Clark's Fork of the Yellowstone River but continued east to empty into the Big Horn River while Clark's Fork turned sharply north. The precipitous mountain country separating the two rivers was largely unexplored.

On 7 September, Colonel Sturgis made his move. He marched his six companies to Heart Mountain, the high ground commanding both potential outlets. Encountering a band of miners enroute, he dispatched at least two of them back up the Stinkingwater with instructions to locate the Nez Perces. The miners did not return. Somewhat alarmed, Sturgis sent out two scouting parties on 8 September. Lieutenant Luther R. Hare of I Company took twenty men on the trail of the miners up Stinkingwater River. Lieutenant "P" Fuller took a second party of twenty almost straight west toward the Clark's Fork defile.

Both scouting details returned to the camp near Heart Mountain late in the afternoon of 8 September with discoveries. Hare found the body of one miner and the wounded partner of the dead man about sixteen miles southwest of the Heart Mountain campsite. Fuller came in just after Hare and reported having seen a large Indian pony herd being driven toward the headwaters of the Stinkingwater. Fuller and a couple of veteran sergeants had observed what appeared to be the Nez Perce camp on the move from a high ridge about midway between Clark's Fork Canyon and where Hare had discovered the miners. The Nez Perce had vanished behind a ridge while Fuller was watching them, but they seemed to be moving leisurely south. Sturgis concluded from the two reports that the Nez Perces were attempting to slip around his left flank. He put his command in motion following the trail blazed by the unlucky miners and Lieutenant Hare. "We may corral the Nez P's," Benteen wrote, "but I think not." The further the 7th marched into the mountains in the black night, the less easy Benteen became. He "pumped" Hare and Fuller and became convinced that the cavalry was moving in the wrong direction. He went to Sturgis and "told him that he was deliberately going away from the Indians."

"No," Sturgis replied, "there is only one pass through which they can get; we will go up to the Stinkingwater and cut them off."

"General," Benteen argued, "when you know where Indians are, that is the best place to find them, otherwise you may not find them at all."

The route chosen by Sturgis over Benteen's protest was a difficult one. The cavalrymen found it necessary to dismount to climb the precipitous heights. "Some of the more weary grasped the tails of their horses and clung to them as they slowly ascended the heights." The officers put a stop to that practice and the cavalry pushed on.

On the morning of 9 September, there was a conference. Colonel Sturgis and Major Merrill were convinced that the 7th was "going to have a hell of a fight pretty soon."

"No," Benteen told them, "you'll find an abandoned camp, and the Indians gone through the gap left by us."

Benteen was proved right. The 7th marched all day for the next two days, gradually drifting north and operating in the proximity of

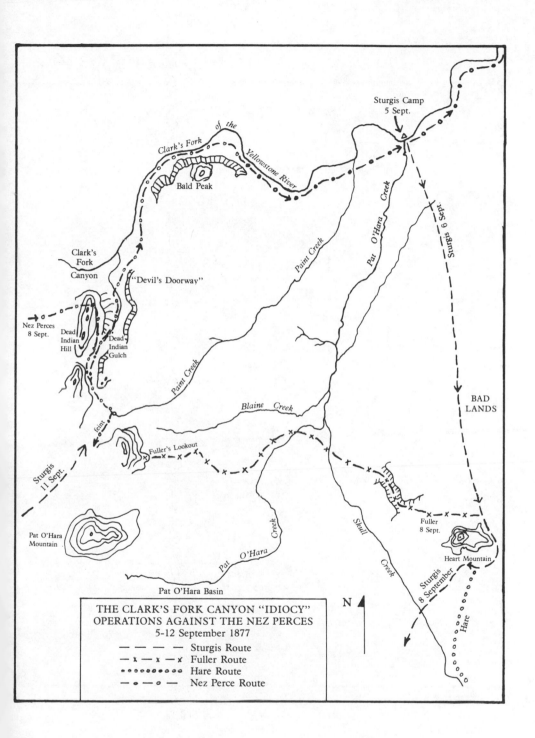

Clark's Fork *of the*

Clark's Fork

Sturgis Camp
5 Sept.

Bald Peak

Yellowstone River

Clark's
Fork
Canyon

"Devil's Doorway"

Paint Creek

Pat O'Hara Creek

Sturgis 6 Sept.

Nez Perces
8 Sept.

Dead
Indian
Hill

Dead
Indian
Gulch

Paint Creek

Blaine Creek

BAD
LANDS

Fuller's Lookout

Sturgis
11 Sept.

feint

Creek

Skull

Fuller
8 Sept.

Pat O'Hara
Mountain

Pat O'Hara

Creek

Heart Mountain

Sturgis
8 September

Hare

Pat O'Hara Basin

N

THE CLARK'S FORK CANYON "IDIOCY"
OPERATIONS AGAINST THE NEZ PERCES
5-12 September 1877

— — — — Sturgis Route
— x — x —x Fuller Route
•••••••••• Hare Route
— • — o — Nez Perce Route

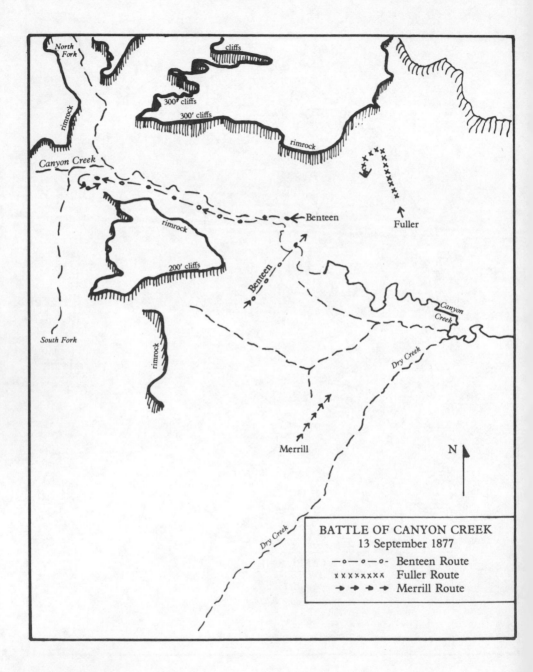

North
Fork

cliffs

300' cliffs

300' cliffs

rimrock

rimrock

Canyon Creek

rimrock

Benteen

Fuller

200' cliffs

Benteen

rimrock

South Fork

Canyon
Creek

Dry Creek

Merrill

N

Dry Creek

BATTLE OF CANYON CREEK
13 September 1877

–o—o—o– Benteen Route

x x x x x x x x Fuller Route

➡ ➡ ➡ ➡ Merrill Route

Fuller's sighting. On 11 September, they descended Dead Indian Gulch and a narrow pass they dubbed the Devil's Doorway down to the floor of Clark's Fork Canyon. That evening, they blundered into the camp of Brigadier General O.O. Howard. Sturgis had been neatly jockeyed out of his blocking position by the Nez Perces, as Benteen had predicted. The Indians had gone straight down Clark's Fork and gained two days march on the 7th Cavalry.

"The ignorance of the guides," reported Lieutenant Hare, "and their confusion in this respect misled the commanding officer as to the position of the two streams, when, had he been correctly informed, it would have been very easy to move to a position on the crest which would have commanded both outlets."

Sturgis was very embarrassed when he rode into General Howard's camp. "I fear you will be greatly disappointed," he wrote his superior, Colonel Miles, "when you learn that the hostiles have, by a sudden and unexpected turn, crossed this river (the Yellowstone) "and thrown us hopelessly, I fear, in their rear."

Benteen and his field adjutant, Arthur W. DuBray (Varnum's quartermaster clerk who was aspiring for a direct commission), placed the three-company battalion (Companies G, H, & M) into camp. Benteen went fishing. When he returned to camp, DuBray informed him that Sturgis had sent for him and that a "council of war" was in progress. "Mine was Cambronne's word repeated, through a Saxon phrase," Benteen remembered. (General Pierre Cambronne was the commander of Napoleon's Imperial Guard at the battle of Waterloo who, when called upon to surrender, had replied, "*Merde!*" which was bowdlerized into: "the Old Guard dies but never surrenders!" Benteen's expletive was, of course, "Shit!")

He went to see Sturgis and learned that a forced march was planned to begin before daylight on the following day, 12 September, to see if the 7th could overtake the Nez Perces. Benteen pointed out that it was drizzling rain and that the start would have to be delayed until light (to give the packers an opportunity to see the knots they would have to tie). The delay was authorized and, at first light, the 7th was underway. Near midday, the officers got together for another conference.

"Why in the name of all that's good," Benteen asked Sturgis crankily, "when we knew where the Indians were, did we not go to them?"

Sturgis's face, Benteen recalled, "got as red as a turkey cock's wattle" and the old colonel replied: "Colonel Benteen, that is not a fit question for you to ask; there will be too many people asking that same" [question].

Major Merrill contributed: "Well, they are gone now, and we can't catch them."

"Oh yes we can," Benteen said.

Sturgis wanted to know how. Benteen replied that by marching forty miles that day and fifty the next "if necessary."

Major Merrill took Benteen aside and confided that Sturgis had suggested something along those lines at the council of war and that he (Merrill) was to have rushed forward with his three companies (F, I, L), but that Sturgis had been dissuaded from separating the two battalions. Benteen tried to convince Merrill to talk Sturgis into sending Companies G, H, M, saying: "I'll guarantee that it will check them, and hold them, too, and we will not suffer any unneccesary loss." Merrill demurred. Benteen went to Lieutenant Hare and Lieutenant Garlington (Sturgis' new adjutant) and tried to get them to convince the regimental commander, to no avail.

Almost twenty years later, Benteen was still disgusted. "Sam D. Sturgis should have been tried by G[eneral] C[ourt] M[artial] for the Clark's Fork Canyon idiocy," he declared.

Nevertheless, Colonel Sturgis was sufficiently embarrassed by the fiasco that he pushed the 7th Cavalry until their horses were almost run into the ground. The command covered 48 miles on 12 September. They forded the Yellowstone near where Clark's Fork emptied into it and pushed on north.

About 10:00 in the morning of 13 September, Colonel Sturgis decided that further pursuit would only result in crippled horses and called a halt. He resisted Benteen's urgings to send one battalion on ahead without the packs. Despite Benteen's scorn, he had good reason for this caution. They were aware of the disaster that had befallen Colonel Gibbon at Big Hole. They were very much aware of the Custer disaster the year before, which had been attributed to a portion of a command outrunning its supports. Colonel Sturgis had lost his oldest son at the Little Big Horn and was understandably loathe to divide the command.

Just as the cavalrymen were going into camp, the civilian scouts came galloping in with the electrifying news that the Nez Perces were just a few miles ahead, making for Canyon Creek's gap in the rimrock. Major Merrill's three companies were mounted first and sent in pursuit, while Benteen's men had to wait for the pack mules to be re-loaded. Sturgis tried vainly to slow both battalions down, fearing that one or the other would be isolated by the Indians.

Canyon Creek was formed by the junction of at least three mountain streams and was still partially dry even after two days of drizzling rain on 13 September. The course of Canyon Creek had through eons worn a narrow slot (actually three different slots) in the yellowish-gray sandstone that formed the northern flank of the Yellowstone valley. The main slot, called Canyon Creek, was essentially a narrow pass surrounded by cliffs 200 feet high — and more. Lieutenant Hare remembered Canyon Creek as "deep cut with precipitous sides of about 160 feet in height." As Sturgis's men were soon to learn, the cliffs were about 100 feet higher on the north wall of the slot formed by Canyon Creek.

Major Merrill's battalion came upon the Nez Perces about six miles north of the spot where Sturgis had ordered a camp. Merrill "shook out" a skirmish line over the vocal protests of many of his men, including Lieutenant Hare from Sturgis's staff, who came galloping up loudly offering to command a mounted charge. The Nez Perces were about five miles from Merrill's skirmish line, moving laterally across the 7th Cavalry's front from right (east) to left (west) as they hurried up Canyon Creek to the "corner" in the rimrock. Merrill had concluded in his assessment of the situation that a mounted charge would not work because of the snipers posted in the washes and gullies parallel (and perpendicular) to Canyon Creek. Those snipers had engaged his lead company (Wilkinson's L Company) at long range and had convinced Merrill that a headlong charge would be suicidal.

It was after two o'clock in the afternoon before Sturgis and Benteen arrived behind Merrill's led horses. By then, Merrill's men had advanced slowly on foot less than a mile. The Nez Perces were tantalizingly close and the foot charge of Merrill's was obviously not going to head them off in time.

The wind was "blowing a gale" and the ground was still wet from the rain of the previous days. The troopers were not able to adjust their fire by marking the strike of their bullets churning up dust and, thus, fired too high. Sturgis stood in the rear of Merrill's led horses, squirting tobacco juice indiscriminately. ("The other officers moved away to avoid him," Private Jacob Horner remembered.) Sturgis, through a mounted courier, ordered Merrill to call up his led horses, mount his battalion, and support a charge by Benteen's men once Benteen had safely passed his flank.

Leaving Lieutenant Fuller and H Company as security for the pack mules, Benteen led G & M Companies across the open plateau toward the escaping Nez Perces. Dutifully, Major Merrill called up his led horses as soon as Benteen's men thundered around his left. The horses did not come. There was, as Merrill put it, "some unfortunate blunder" that led to the oft-repeated order being "misapprehended." To make matters worse, a force of mounted Indians suddenly appeared in the rear, causing panic and consternation until they were identified as Crow sight-seers. Merrill, seeing Benteen advance unsupported, elected to continue his advance toward Canyon Creek *on foot.*

The net result was that Benteen's charge was not supported and, though some of Wallace's G Company men got in among the Nez Perce horse herd that was bringing up the rear of the Indian column, the main body got through the pass ahead of Benteen and posted snipers atop the cliffs on both sides of the canyon. Benteen's mounted men, virtually unscathed by the snipers in the low washes, came under a very accurate, galling rifle fire. The charge disintegrated as Benteen, wisely, deployed his men on foot, seeking the shelter of the washes and gullies that the Nez Perce rearguard was rapidly abandoning.

When Merrill's men finally linked with Benteen's men, it was past 4:00 in the afternoon. Lieutenant Fuller's H Company, the only fresh troops on the field, were sent against the Nez Perce snipers lining the rimrock to the north. Fuller's men were pinned down. Major Merrill sent fifteen men from I Company under Sergeant William Costello to make an assault similar to Fuller's against the snipers on the southernmost cliffs. Using Fuller and Costello as "anchors," Colonel Sturgis re-deployed the 7th, pivoting the line ninety degrees. Benteen's two companies were sent forward on a second charge.

Though Benteen's second charge carried two companies to the point where the three mountain streams combined to form Canyon Creek, they were pinned down by accurate rifle fire from the clifftops to the north. Merrill's men, following Benteen's, got nearly to the same spot before darkness set in. Colonel Sturgis then pulled all his companies off the cliff faces and down Canyon Creek to the spot where Benteen had formed for his second charge. The Indians had escaped, it was dark, and the horses of the 7th had been pushed to their limit. Sturgis went into camp. He had lost three men killed and eleven wounded. The Nez Perce casualties, never ascertained, were almost certainly lower. They may not have lost anything but a few horses, as no bodies were ever found.

Benteen was disgusted by the timidity exhibited by Colonel Sturgis and by what he perceived as Merrill's incompetence. He had known both men in Missouri since 1861 and had heard complaints about them before. "They never lost a Reb or an Indian!" he concluded years later. "I can recall no more thoroughly disgusting campaign."

Sturgis's command spent the next morning in camp while the Crow sight-seers explored the canyon the Nez Perces had held. By midday, the 7th was underway in a cautious pursuit. They passed the Judith Gap they had been sent to hold and did not reach the Musselshell River until 19 September. There, they waited for Lieutenant Varnum's supply train from the Crow Agency and General Howard's slow-moving command.

"Sturgis was never very warm with me after the Canyon Creek affair," Benteen said years later. "Why? Because he knew I thought he was a coward." There was another reason for Sturgis's coolness toward the senior captain after Canyon Creek. Sturgis wanted what Benteen later referred to as "a hullabaloo of a report" from his battalion commanders. Major Merrill responded with a thirteen-paragraph report that is still thrilling reading today. Benteen's report was a curt four paragraph list of casualties, including the horses "abandoned in pursuit" for each of his three companies. Two weeks later, under pressure from Sturgis, he appended a report of similar length complimenting six officers, eleven enlisted men, and A.W. DuBray by name.

One of the officers mentioned for "conspicuous gallantry" by Benteen was Lieutenant Ezra Fuller, who had commanded H Company during the fight. Years later, Fuller was to say of Benteen: "I do not believe a more gallant man ever lived and he was the coolest man under fire that I ever saw." Private Horner, who had acted as Colonel Sturgis's orderly that day, remembered: "Benteen was one of the bravest officers I ever met."

On 22 September, General Howard caught up with them and all began a slow pursuit of the Nez Perce. Colonel Miles, who had been on the Yellowstone while Sturgis was being bested by the Nez Perce, grabbed every available man and set off cross-country to intercept

the Indians. Three of the companies he took with him were from
the 7th Cavalry: K (Captain Hale), D (Captain Godfrey), and A
(Captain Moylan). On 30 September, Miles' scratch force finally
cornered the Nez Perce in the Bear Paw Mountains. Captain Hale
and one of his lieutenants were killed; Moylan and Godfrey were
wounded.

Benteen received word of the Bear Paw fight on 2 October. Miles
reported that he had surprised the Nez Perce camp, a claim Benteen
viewed with skepticism. "You may possibly surprise those fellows,"
he told his wife in a letter, "but I guess he has learned that they
don't stay surprised worth a cent." Miles reported that he had thirty
wounded, which Benteen believed. The dispatch bearers insisted that
all of the 7th Cavalry officers with Miles had been killed. Benteen
did not want to believe it, though admitted that Miles "has got his
hands full."

The next day a scout came in who reported that "Miles had been
licked like hell." He also gave descriptions of the officers of the 7th
who had been killed. Benteen concluded that his old messmate Captain Owen Hale had been killed (he had) and that his long-time
first lieutenant Frank Gibson had been wounded (he had not). "I
am quite well," he reassured his anxious wife, "and like everyone
else heartily tired of this campaign." He was especially upset by the
rumor that Frank Gibson had been wounded, cautioning Kate to
say nothing to Mrs. Gibson "as I don't credit it" and as "it will doubtless upset her."

Howard's and Sturgis' combined commands hurried toward the
Bear Paws, but the 7th Cavalry turned back on 7 October when they
received word that the Nez Perce had surrendered to Miles. The next
day, Colonel Sturgis got permission to return to Fort Lincoln. Major
Merrill was left in command of the 7th Cavalry who remained on
the Missouri River below the surrender point, waiting for word to
return to their stations for the winter. The word did not come.

Major Merrill got permission from Colonel Miles to accompany
the wounded back to Dakota Territory, leaving Benteen in command
of what amounted to nine companies. Miles had notions about another winter campaign and Benteen, thoroughly fed up with the
campaign, wanted to get back to Fort Rice. He sent messages to
General Terry, who was engaged in a truce talk with the Sioux who
had fled to Canada, but the messages apparently did not get through.
Benteen later accused Miles of intercepting them. Miles wanted Ben-

teen to place the 7th Cavalry into winter camp near Fort Peck, but Benteen took advantage of the sudden appearance of General Terry to get the orders changed to a return home via Fort Buford.

Benteen marched the regiment to Fort Buford on 28 October and, upon his arrival, found that Colonel Miles was there. To Benteen's chagrin, Miles had succeeded in getting five of the 7th Cavalry companies detailed to escort Cheyenne prisoners to the rail head at Bismarck. He was forced to wait at the bitterly cold Fort Buford and console himself with letters to his wife. Captain French took the balance of the regiment — and all the married officers except Benteen — to Bismarck.

The letters to Kate Benteen from this period are highly amorous, the product of enforced separation and a concomitant longing for her company. Two of them that survive were decorated with drawings of an erect penis and all made frequent references to the "wild thyme" exchange the two had been carrying on. Aside from being titillated reading yet today, the letters from Fort Buford in November and December of 1877 are important as they reflected Benteen's first recorded misgivings about continuing his military career. The disappointing and frustrating 1877 campaign, coupled with the rise of Custer worship spawned by Whittaker's biography, deeply disgusted Benteen. The years ahead would only add doubts.

He grieved for his old comrade, Captain Owen Hale, who had been shot in the neck by a Nez Perce marksman. He recalled the "excessively buoyant" spirits of his old mess mate when they had parted in August. Hale had been made a battalion commender of Companies A, D, K. "What a lot of vanity & conceit the poor fellow cherished," Benteen said sadly. Hale's body remained in a "blockhouse on the hill" and the visit of a brother to Fort Buford disgusted Benteen profoundly. "His brother, who came out for his effects, scraped up all his effects that he could get his hands on, started off, leaving the body to be sent on, *when called for*. An epitome on the human race."

Kate reported from Fort Rice that Captain Thomas French had arrived and was apparently winning his battle with alcohol. Benteen was unimpressed. "Yes, French has conquered his desire for whisky just like I have mine for fucking," he said baldly, "no more — no less."

He admitted that he was avoiding the company of some of the more notorious drinkers at Fort Buford, denying that he himself was "a steady drinker." He told Kate: "That, you know, I am not." He conceded, however, that his drinking was "like the lava's flood," which coincides with the opinions of others who knew him. According to Lieutenant Garlington, Benteen was sober most of the time, but about once a year or so went off on a bender that lasted a few days. Under the influence, Benteen waxed sarcastic and hateful, saying things that Garlington insisted he would never have said while sober.

His comments to Kate contained some gems of self-analysis. "When I like anyone, I do it wholly," he told her, "and the liking comes gradually. I am a much closer observer than one who didn't know me would give me credit for." She expressed surprise that he had revealed something to her unasked. "A word to you 'en passant'," he replied, "when you wish to find out anything from me — or from anyone — don't go about it in a sneaking, Jesuitical way, but 'come to Limerick!' at once with the question."

Benteen kept Kate entertained with a steady stream of sly references to sex, alluding constantly to the sprigs of "wild thyme", her bedroom — "the Goose's Roost," "mink skins" (contraceptives), and enclosed on one occasion a picture of a woman he had found on a cigar box — a picture considered pornographic in 1877. He added a drawing of an erect penis behind it and called it to her attention. "Should the vignette cause you any peculiar sensation," he said, "a cure all can be found when Johnny comes marching home. A rude representation of the *rod* of correction can be found in the background."

Kate brought up the subject of leaving the Army. Benteen replied that by waiting until his twenty years was up, he could increase his monthly pay from $42.50 to over $175.00, higher if he could make major in the meantime. He was pessimistic about promotion, with good reason. He estimated that it would take him ten years. (As it turned out, it took him five.) "I think," he concluded, "after going on the recruiting detail next two years, then one can tell more about what is best to be done. I am getting heartily tired of this mode of life — and, the probabilities are that as long as I continue in the regiment I shall have a large portion of the active work shouldered off on me. This campaign has shown something of it."

He made no mention of the firestorm of criticism that was raging around his conduct at the Little Big Horn. He had not yet encountered it. The Army officers with whom he associated generally attributed the Custer debacle to disobedience of orders and an unwise (under the circumstances) division of the regiment. Benteen mentioned that some of the infantry officers under Miles at the Tongue River Cantonment (later Fort Keogh) were cool to officers of the 7th, but, at the time, he did not associate the reception with the Little Big Horn experience. (He had no reason to. Miles' men had spent the entire winter of 1876-77 on the Yellowstone essentially mopping up the mess Terry, Crook, and Custer had made that summer. Their lack of cordiality would have been based not on the mess, but on their having to clean it up, while the 7th Cavalry, safe and snug in established posts, got all the newspaper publicity.)

The Buford Letters also revealed Benteen's ribald sense of humor. "What did you dream of me that was so queer?" he asked Kate at one point. "That I had *two* cocks — or anything of that kind? A plurality of those things would be useless — worse, indeed — as a man in a hurry might piss all over himself. One for the purpose alluded to is all a cavalryman ought to have. It certainly is about all the use mine has been for nearly 8 months now."

In later years, he sardonically consoled himself with Sturgis' speech the previous May about commanding the reserve, concluding that the six companies who remained at Buford were that reserve. At the time, he commented bitterly — and repeatedly — about the fact that the field officers of the 7th Cavalry were not in the field. "No soldiers among the lot," he said, condemning Sturgis, Otis, Merrill, Tilford, and even the absent Reno in one short phrase. The passing years did not assuage his anger. Twenty years later, he asked a correspondent rhetorically: "Could a finely-tooth comb, well dragged, have pulled out the whole army a sorrier set?" To his dying day, he remembered "what a crowd of chumps the 7th Cavalry had among its field officers in 1877."

Benteen, who had hoped to be home for Christmas, did not get his marching orders until 19 December. He spent the holidays leading what remained of six companies of the 7th Cavalry through snow drifts on the way to Bismarck. He took H Company into Fort Rice 2 January 1878.

Lieutenant Colonel Elmer Otis was commanding officer at Rice that winter. The garrison had Captain John S. Poland's A Company, 6th Infantry and three companies of the 7th Cavalry — coincidently the same three companies Benteen had commanded on his controversial scout to the left at the Little Big Horn: D, H, K.

D Company was commanded by Captain Godfrey. H Company had

only one officer besides Benteen, as Lieutenant Gibson was detailed as Colonel Otis' adjutant and Lieutenant Russell was on detached service conducting insane prisoners to Washington, D.C. The new officer in H Company was a West Pointer named Wallis O. Clark, who was waiting for a change of assignment to the 6th Cavalry at Camp Lowell, Arizona Territory.

K Company was commanded by the newest captain in the regiment: E.G. Mathey. His first lieutenant, Charles Braden, was awaiting orders from a retirement board (because of the thigh wound he had received four years earlier) and was not present for duty. Mathey's second lieutenant that winter was a brand-new West Pointer named Heber M. Creel.

The 7th Cavalry spent the summer of 1878 patrolling the vast Sioux reservation without incident. The cavalry companies at Fort Rice were transferred to Fort Lincoln on 26 June 1878. The Benteens said farewell to their old garrison friends and left forever the little post on the Missouri River that had been their home for almost five years.

23

Fallout from the Little Big Horn

Fort Lincoln, the headquarters for the 7th Cavalry since 1873, was located on the west bank of the Missouri River about thirty miles north of Fort Rice. It had originally been founded in 1872 as Fort McKean (after a Pennsylvania volunteer colonel killed at Cold Harbor in 1864), but within a few months was re-named in honor of the murdered 14th President. The original post, built on a bluff overlooking the river, had quarters for three infantry companies. By 1878, the infantry garrison had been expanded to five companies. The cavalry post, built at the base of the bluff, originally had quarters for six cavalry companies. By 1878, the establishment of Fort Yates at the Standing Rock Agency sixty miles to the south, had eliminated the need for Fort Rice. Fort Lincoln's cavalry post was expanded to accommodate nine cavalry companies. The bustling frontier town of Bismarck, western terminus of the stalled Northern Pacific Railroad for four years, was across the river to the east.

In August of 1878, the Army was in the process of building a large fort in the Black Hills, designated as the new headquarters of the 7th Cavalry. The new post was laid out near the base of Bear Butte about fifteen miles north of Deadwood and designated Camp Ruhlen (after the regimental quartermaster of the 17th Infantry). Troops to assist in the building were escorted across the Sioux reservation all summer from posts along the Missouri River. It was during this process that Captain Thomas H. French of M Company got himself in serious trouble, as Benteen had predicted.

On 29 August, French moved a patrol from a temporary camp named after his former second lieutenant, Jack Sturgis, to Ruhlen.

He complained of dizziness which he asserted was caused by a combination of sunstroke and the effects of a head wound incurred when
falling from his horse the day before. He rode on ahead of his unit
and sat down under the shade of a tree to await their arrival. The
commanding officer, Major Henry M. Lazelle of the 1st Infantry,
later charged French with being drunk at the time.

French returned to Fort Lincoln and went on a short leave. He
returned in mid-October. In the meantime, Captain Benteen had
been sent from Fort Lincoln back down to Fort Rice to secure company equipment. Benteen was gone two months, returning 20 November 1878. (Fort Rice was declared abandoned 25 November.)

While Benteen was on detached service at Fort Rice, Captain
French led a wagon train from Fort Lincoln to Camp Ruhlen. On
the march, he exhibited signs of bizarre behavior, patently caused
by excessive drinking. On the evening of 19 October, he directed his
men to erect a wall tent for two laundresses and was rewarded by
a cup of something alcoholic. He quarreled loudly with one of the
laundresses, a Mrs. Egan, who was herself obviously drunk. The next
day, he turned over command of the column to Lieutenant Spillman
and rode off alone on his horse. He reappeared three days later on
the Deadwood stage, minus his horse. The next day, he rode in an
ambulance, the same ambulance occupied by "the said Mrs. Egan"
and the other laundress. One of the members of the group being transferred to Camp Ruhlen was Mrs. Eliza DeRudio. She reported French's
behavior to Major Lazelle and offered as a witness her new servant,
Frank "Cuff" Jones, who had been discharged from the Benteen household for being a bad influence on little Freddie.

On 7 November 1878, Captain French was too intoxicated to perform his duties as officer of the day at Camp Ruhlen. Major Lazelle
sent for him on the pretext of discussing a quartermaster order and,
after dismissing the other officers and clerks, asked French quietly:
"Have you not been drinking?" French denied it and Lazelle gave
him a stern lecture, then added kindly: "Don't you see that you are
ruining yourself and your reputation?" French broke down and cried,
allegedly saying: "For God's sake, give me a chance," that his "in-
firmity" had "mastered" him and in the past he had been able to
overcome it by going into seclusion and abstaining. He added that
he "was afraid" of himself.

Major Lazelle observed: "Maybe you don't try hard enough." French
responded by requesting a seven day leave of absence to cure his

illness. There must have been some more discussion never recorded, for French ended up pleading for four days grace. Major Lazelle abruptly relieved French of duty and ordered him to his tent. French wanted to know if he was under arrest. Lazelle replied: "No. Take your four days. It'll help you." At the end of the four days, French reported for duty. The adjutant informed him that he was under arrest. (Mrs. DeRudio had been busy in the interim and Major Lazelle felt compelled to charge French for his derelictions on the march in October as well as the almost-forgotten episode in August.)

On 11 November 1878, French, while under close arrest, visited the Post Trader's. He told the Post Trader, a Mr. Fanshawe, that if anyone inquired as to the reason for the visit, Fanshawe was to tell them that it was to get something to eat. French wanted to know if Fanshawe had any objections. The Post Trader said that he had none. Major Lazelle, on hearing of the exchange, tacked two additional charges onto French's account and requested a court-martial.

The court-martial met on 13 January 1879. Benteen missed it. So did most of the other officers of the 7th Cavalry, including Lieutenant DeRudio. They were in Chicago that day at another court — a court of inquiry to investigate allegations about Major Reno's conduct at the battle of the Little Big Horn. Frederick Whittaker, author of the first Custer biography, had also been busy. Apart from the sensation caused by his book, Whittaker had taken it upon himself to accuse both Major Reno and Captain Benteen of (in effect) abandoning Custer to his fate. On 13 June 1878, Whittaker had written an open letter to a Congressional delegate from Wyoming Territory suggesting that a Congressional inquiry be made into Reno's conduct. (Whittaker had apparently concluded by then that his charges against Benteen would not be supported by any surviving witnesses.) Congress went into recess before acting on the suggestion. Major Reno, still under suspension for taking liberties with Mrs. Bell, requested an Army court of inquiry. The court convened at the Palmer House in Chicago on 13 January 1879.

The purpose of a court of inquiry is to establish facts and possible basis for a court-martial. There is no question of guilt or innocence. In a sense, the court of inquiry process is analogous to the work of an investigating officer: swearing witnesses, obtaining statments under oath, presenting the statements thus obtained and the conclusions of the court to the convening authority. (In Reno's case, the convening authority was Lieutenant General Philip H. Sheridan.)

Since it is primarily an investigative process, a court of inquiry is not normally a public hearing. But, by early 1879, there was so much publicity surrounding the battle of the Little Big Horn, Custer, Reno, Benteen, and so forth that it was impossible to keep the public at bay without risking charges of cover-up. General Sheridan, confident that there was nothing to hide, allowed the public to attend.

Three officers were assigned to the board: Colonel John H. King of the 9th Infantry, Colonel Wesley Merritt of the 5th Cavalry, and Lieutenant Colonel William B. Royall of the 3rd Cavalry. Colonel King, by virtue of seniority, was the presiding officer and his own adjutant, 1st Lieutenant Jesse M. Lee of the 9th Infantry, was appointed Recorder.

Contrary to popular belief even today, the role of the Recorder in a court of inquiry is *not* analogous to a prosecuting attorney. The Recorder is charged with *recording* the proceedings, swearing the witnesses, determining in which order they are to appear, framing the questions to be asked, and elucidating to the satisfaction of the board the replies given. The recorder has no *case* to prove.

Lieutenant Lee was assigned a stenographer for the purpose of taking down the proceedings verbatim. Colonel King tried unsuccessfully to prohibit the press (the Chicago *Times* in particular) from taking notes verbatim, but when the paper took to publishing recollections of its reporters present, he relented and permitted the paper to obtain a stenographic account.

The Reno Court of Inquiry was a farce.

One story is that when the officers of the 7th Cavalry were on their way from Bismarck to Chicago, Benteen waved a copy of the Chicago *Times* in front of them that headlined the upcoming trial and said: "Gentlemen, we have got to defend the regiment." Another story is that Reno's lawyer, Lyman Gilbert, screened all potential witnesses for anti-Reno bias. Those who had evidence to give that was critical of Reno were reminded of "some things in the pigeon holes that could be used" against them. Fred Gerard, the Fort Lincoln interpreter, asserted that "any officer who made himself obnoxious to the defense would incur the wrath of certain officers in pretty high authority." (From the rest of the context, Gerard was plainly referring to General Sheridan.) In any case, the testimony taken in evidence was rather bland compared to the campfire discussions that had taken place immediately after the battle of the Little Big Horn.

Reno had few detractors under oath. Fred Gerard probably gave the most damaging account of Reno's fight in the valley. Mr. Lyman Gilbert cross-examined Gerard ferociously. Gerard (once fired from his post as Lakota interpreter and poultry peddler by Major Reno for allegedly stealing government property) could see no good in Reno. Two civilian packers testified that Reno had been drunk on the night of the 25th. Others, including Benteen, denied it. (There is a story that Benteen in later years told little Freddie flatly that Reno was drunk on the 25th of June, but it comes from a highly suspect source.) Captains Godfrey and Mathey came the closest of any of the officers present to giving damaging testimony against Reno, but they balked at describing Reno's conduct as cowardice.

Benteen himself took the stand. Because his testimony was patently hostile to Custer and rather obfuscatory, he found himself under attack almost at once. The tradition of attacking Benteen's testimony at the Reno Court of Inquiry has been upheld enthusiastically even in recent times. His figures, distances, and sequences are still dissected and contradicted. The most unpalatable assertion he made, in the opinions of the pro-Custerites, was that his return to the main trail was a violation of Custer's order. Since his orders were to return to the main trail after completing his scout, the issue is really: was his scout completed? His testimony at Reno's Court of Inquiry made clear his beliefs that he had not complied with the letter of Custer's orders, especially with regards to the "second valley."

Benteen was very careful to say nothing derogatory about Reno. The proposal by Reno to abandon the wounded never came out in the testimony. Fifteen years later, Benteen told a correspondent why. "As to queries before the Court of Inquiry," he said, "these I would answer now as I did then, and shield Reno quite as much as I then did; and this simply from the fact that there were a lot of harpies after him — Godfrey not the smallest of the lot."

Benteen was uncomfortable in Chicago, though his feeling had little to do with the court. "I have nothing but my uniform," he complained in a letter to Kate at Fort Lincoln, "and you can imagine how extremely disagreeable 'tis to be stared at on the streets as I am. I rarely ever go out of the hotel if I can avoid it." He was further discomfitted by a shopping list Kate had sent him. "If there is anything I hate, 'tis to run around shopping from the fact that I always take the 1st article offered, at the price asked." He dutifully rounded up the requested items, but warned Kate: "If you know of anyone that wants commissions executed, don't send them to me. I am decidedly not on it."

Reno's Court of Inquiry, intended to be a fact-finding forum, had degenerated into a public trial of Major Reno. Inevitably, it wound down with a rather faint-hearted conclusion. "The conduct of the officers throughout was excellent," the three colonels decided, "and while subordinates, in some instances, did more for the safety of the command by brilliant displays of courage than did Major Reno, there was nothing in his conduct which requires animadversion from this Court." Colonel Merritt, when questioned about the finding, allegedly said: "Well, the officers wouldn't tell us anything and we could do nothing more than damn Reno with faint praise."

The public furor generated by Frederick Whittaker and his ilk did not abate. It rages (on a more modest scale) even today. Benteen was thoroughly disgusted by the transformation of the human Custer into a folk legend. "I am not ready to subscribe to any effort of the public's opinion to convince me that Custer was a great man or great warrior," he wrote years later, "*au contraire,* he was quite ordinary."

Benteen's only regret about his testimony at the Court of Inquiry was that he "was not allowed to turn loose on Custer." There were those who disagreed that Benteen had not "turned loose" on Custer. Their principal spokesman was Frederick Whittaker. In a letter to the New York *Sun,* Whittaker assailed the Court as "a complete and scientific whitewash." He ridiculed Benteen as "a hero and a martyr," as "a wonderful Indian fighter and lady-killer" and concluded that "he gave his evidence like a little man." Whittaker went on to say that Colonel Merritt had done "most of the work of the decision" after having been "closeted with the Recorder alone for several hours." He implied that Merritt, "Custer's old rival," had done so because he felt "it" (unspecified) would "hurt the army badly."

Upon his return to Fort Lincoln, Benteen found a couple of letters from an old acquaintance: Robert Newton Price of Philadelphia, who had been a friend of Lieutenant Benny Hodgson's. Price wanted the famous Cooke/Martin note. Benteen sent it to him with a reference to Whittaker's latest sensational letter. "Can't you go for that Heathen Chinee?" he asked Price. "Rasp up your bolt of sarcasm which is so well hurled and give him a shake up for me."

Price responded with a letter to the Philadelphia *Times,* asserting in part that Whittaker had planned to present Reno's Court with an affidavit allegedly signed by the late Captain Weir, but had refused to produce it when confronted with Lieutenant Charles Braden. The

Albert J. Russell

Ernest A. Garlington

John C. Gresham

Lewis Merrill

Hugh L. Scott

Ezra B. Fuller

William H. Baldwin

Robert Newton Price

crippled Braden, in the process of obtaining a medical discharge, was prepared to swear that Whittaker had been "constantly pestering" Weir to sign a document and that Weir had refused "in the strongest language and most emphatic eloquence of a trooper." Price hurled his bolt of sarcasm well enough at Whittaker. He derided the biographer (whom Benteen later described as "an impecunious quill-driver") as "the inventor and sole proprietor of one of the most novel and stupendous advertising schemes of this or any other age."

The public glare on Reno's tribulations largely obscured the demise of Captain French. On 26 March 1879, his court-martial board published their findings. He was adjudged guilty of drunkeness on duty in the 29 August incident, the 24 October incident in which he rode in the ambulance, and the 7 November incident when Major Lazelle had to relieve him of duty. The riding with the laundresses in the ambulance (although French was not necessarily aware of their presence, being beside the driver in a stupor) brought another guilty verdict on a charge of "conduct unbecoming an officer and gentleman." French had handled his defense as well as it could have been conducted, effectively disposing of another drunk-on-duty charge stemming from the fateful march, a charge of misappropriating government property by losing his horse (apparently the beast showed up, for the charge was withdrawn), two specifications of a charge of breach of arrest stemming from the incident with Fanshawe (the Post Trader), and two of the specifications of conduct-unbecoming-an-officer-and-gentleman stemming from the march and the visit to Fanshawe's. Still, his trial was repeatedly delayed because French was too sick to attend. A doctor, called to explain his illness, testified that French was suffering from *delirium tremens*. Such conduct did not help his case and French was sentenced to be dismissed from the service. However, President Hayes mitigated the sentence to one of suspension of rank and duty for a year at half pay.

French was unable to return to duty, being too far advanced in alcoholism by the time his sentence was up. He was dropped involuntarily from the Army List on 2 February 1880 and his rank was given to Frank Gibson. French died a derelict at the Planter's House Hotel in Leavenworth, Kansas, on 27 March 1882, a tragic end for the man his own first sergeant later referred to "as brave an officer as ever served in the Seventh Cavalry." (There is strong evidence that French's drinking was caused by pain from a crippling Civil War wound, exacerbated by his horrific experience at the Little Big Horn and

failure of his marriage plans. There being no effective treatment for
his problems, physical or psychological, in the 19th Century, French
fell by the wayside.)

Benteen had no more than seen the result of Robert Newton Price's
sarcasm when he was placed on detached service. With Lieutenants
Gresham and Russell, he was assigned to testify at the court-martial
of Captain Charles Bendire, 1st Cavalry. (Bendire had made unflat-
tering remarks about Lieutenant Colonel Elmer Otis in their presence
during the Nez Perce pursuit.) Otis used the court-martial at Fort
Vancouver, Washington Territory to extract a fulsome apology from
Bendire. For the 44-year-old senior captain of the 7th Cavalry, the
trial was a vacation.

He saw Colonel Alfred Sully, whom he had known during the
Kansas years; saw General Howard, whom he had met during the
Nez Perce campaign two years before; saw Captain Sullivan, who
had been a staff officer in New Orleans in 1875; and visited a West
Point classmate of Luther Hare's — Lieutenant Charles E.S. Wood,
who was General Howard's aide-de-camp. He missed the mosquitos
of Fort Lincoln. He especially missed his wife. He wrote: "The grand
old Mount Hood peering at me thro' its white, white coverlids adds
to instead of detracting from the sense of loneliness." The abortive
court-martial lasted from 24-28 April. The next day, Benteen, Gresham
and Russell set out for San Francisco on a steamboat. They left Otis
in Portland.

While waiting in San Francisco to square accounts with the Army
paymaster there, Benteen confided his impressions of his travelling
companions to Kate. Russell, he complained, "cares only for himself,"
but Gresham was "a nice fellow; I like him more and more." One
reason for his favorable opinion of Gresham was that the young officer
had presented Benteen with a gift: a manzanita cane with a silver
head engraved F.W.B. "Now," he told Kate, "I wouldn't give the
damned thing hover-room. In fact, the only use I have for a cane is
to have it varnished, and that one I have. But it showed a good feeling — and brotherhood, which I tell you the other fellow hasn't got."
(In the 1890s, Gresham, by then a captain, was the only 7th Cavalry
officer who wrote to Benteen congratulating him on a brevet promotion to brigadier general.)

Benteen left Gresham and Russell in San Francisco to see the sights
while he struck out on his own for Sacramento. Theo Benteen, an
architect, lived there with his wife and three children. Theo was

Benteen's younger brother. The two brothers, who had not seen each other (or apparently written) since before the Civil War, had a pleasant meal together. Benteen was especially impressed by his seven-year-old nephew, William Henry Benteen, whom he described as "quite a broth of a boy" who could "read such books as Aesop's fables right off."

Benteen declined an invitation to visit his old Civil War comrade Daniel W. Ballou near Santa Barbara, California, on the grounds that he was homesick for "Frabbie." He did not enjoy the big city of San Francisco any more than he had Philadelphia or Chicago. "This is too rapid a town," he said, "and I am of the opinion that business of all kinds is finding its level. Extortions of all kinds are practiced on the unwary or verdant traveler. No baggage is touched for less than 50 cents. There are no such things as nickles out here." He complained that bootblacks, for instance, charged "a bit" and when given a quarter would return a dime, though "a bit" was otherwise 10 cents. "And so the damned town and country goes," he commented, "all trying to outswindle each other." He returned to Lincoln, grumbling about the exorbitant cost of travelling, on 18 May 1879.

Camp Ruhlen, re-named Fort Meade, had been built up enough to justify moving the headquarters of the 7th Cavalry. Benteen led H Company out of Fort Lincoln on 10 July to this new post. Colonel Sturgis brought the command into Meade on 17 July, assuming command from Major Reno, who had been restored to duty in May.

Reno was not destined to remain long. The animosity towards him had not abated. To make matters worse, he began to drink heavily, or at least, to comport himself in a manner that suggested frequent, uncontrollable use of alcohol. On 3 August, he was drunk at the Post Trader's house. On 5 August, he got into another brawl, this time with Lieutenant Nicholson, and belted the young officer over the head with a billiard cue. (There was evidence that Nicholson, a rather large man, had provoked the fight.) Finally, on 25 August, he was drunk again, smashing out a window with a chair and knocking money out of the hands of a saloon keeper.

Reno was placed under open arrest and charged with conduct unbecoming an officer and gentleman on 28 September 1879. (Ironically, though his court-martial board found him guilty of all three offenses, they did not find him guilty of conduct unbecoming an officer and gentleman. Instead, they found him guilty of the offense of conduct prejudicial to the good order and discipline of the service

— a technical flaw that opened the way for a review of his court-martial almost ninety years later.)

While confined to post in open arrest, Reno got embroiled in another controversy that effectively ruined his career. The drunk charges were not so serious that they need have caused a dismissal from the service even if proven. As Reno himself later testified, though: "it has been my misfortune to have attained a widespread notoriety through the country by means of the press, open to any enemy who know not why they are so, but like the village cur, bark when their fellows do, and a greater attention will be called to what I do than other officers not so widely advertised."

Reno was his own worst enemy. On the evening of 10 November 1879, he peeped into the window of Colonel Sturgis's house, specifically staring at Ella Sturgis, the Colonel's lovely, 21-year-old daughter. Ella, later described by Benteen as "a schemer from the head of the creek," called to her mother. She later testified that, while she recognized the peeper as Major Reno, she "was so frightened" because Reno's face "was very pale and he looked as if it was that of anger, as if to threaten." She claimed that her first impression was that she "would be shot" if she moved, knowing that Reno "must have feelings against my father." Buckskin Sam Sturgis came thundering down the stairs dressed in a night shirt and swinging a cane. He rushed outside, but the window peeper was gone. He returned, learned the facts from his hysterical wife and daughter, dressed, and made his way to the quarters of the regimental adjutant, Lieutenant Garlington. Sturgis later swore that he surmised the identity of the peeper from a conversation with Garlington, who had allegedly seen Reno in the vicinity of the Sturgis quarters earlier.

(There is evidence that Ernest A. Garlington was an unsuccessful suitor of Ella's. In fact, Benteen later observed to Edward Godfrey that he had "deplored" the way Garlington had allowed Ella "to twist him around so.")

Colonel Sturgis placed Reno under close arrest and preferred an additional charge. The trial, which began 24 November, was a sensational one. Reno had apparently failed to make a deal with the judge advocate to plead guilty to the second charge in return for a promise that Ella Sturgis be spared the embarrassment of having to testify. Reno had written a note to Mrs. Sturgis apologizing for the incident two days after the fact. He called on Captain Benteen to read the note. Benteen's comments were unrecorded and Reno sent the note, which said in part: "It would be a matter of deep regret to my dying day should you and she think me capable of an untruth, of being a spy or doing anything with a mean motive. This is the truth as I expect to answer for it before my God, and I sincerely ask your pardon for all that does not seem to you as innocent."

Benteen's role in the court-martial was to appear as a witness for the defense. Reno had stubbornly refused to cross-examine Ella Sturgis or even refer to her by name. Benteen was selected to convey Reno's feelings. Asked if he thought the note conveyed Reno's true feelings, he replied that it did not. The judge advocate pressed him on the point, asking him what he meant by that remark. Said Benteen drily: "I mean by this that he did not express all that he meant and felt, that he was dead in love with the young lady was my belief."

Not surprisingly, this kind of a defense was rejected by the court-martial board. They found Reno guilty of the window-peeping offense and guilty of the drunk charges. They sentenced the controversial Major Reno to be dismissed from the Army. However, their substitution of the charge in the drunkeness case was highly irregular, perhaps even illegal. General Terry, reviewing the findings, commented on it. "It should have been *not guilty* to the charge," he insisted, but passed the sentence up the ladder on the grounds that if he disapproved the findings, Reno would receive no punishment whatsoever.

The reviewing authorities struggled with the board's recommendation for "merciful consideration" signed by all but two of its members, as well as with their declaration that they had "performed the painful duty of awarding punishment in strict conformity to an Article of War which deprived it [the board] of all discretionary power." Even General Terry found the sentence "manifestly excessive." The Judge Advocate in Washington brought up the subject of Reno's past offenses, asserting that Reno could not "claim any great extent of lenity" in view of his previous conviction. The last military reviewer, General William T. Sherman, "respectfully recommended" to the ultmate reviewer, President Rutherford B. Hayes, that the sentence be "modified" to one year's suspension, confinement to post, and reduction of "five files in the list of Majors of Cavalry." For reasons never fully explained, President Hayes confirmed the sentence of dismissal on 16 March 1880. Benteen later implied that the President's wife, Lucy, had figured in the decision. Mrs. Hayes was apparently scandalized by Reno's problem, which indicated that he was, as one reviewer put it, "deficient in that respect to the female sex which is so essential."

Marcus A. Reno ceased to be an officer of the Army on 1 April 1880. His rank was given to Captain Edward Ball of the 2nd Cavalry. Two modern day biographers of Reno claimed that during his last days at Fort Meade, Major Reno was ostracised by the other officers. "Every officer of the post," they said, "with a single exception, made certain that he was seen in the act of turning his back on the disgraced man."

"The exception was Fred Benteen."

Though the story is unverifiable, it is in keeping with Benteen's character and in tune with his attitude toward Reno. He held no especial brief for Reno, but felt that "Sturgis treated Reno like a dog." He certainly felt that Reno was vastly preferable to any of the other field grade officers of the 7th Cavalry in 1880. "Poor a soldier as Reno was," he said, "he was a long way ahead of Merrill." Benteen dismissed Reno's offenses as "the most frivolous of charges" and asserted that Reno "was a far better soldier than Sturgis, and that isn't much praise."

The disgraced Reno moved to Washington and began a fruitless struggle to reclaim his rank. No less than nine bills were introduced in Congress for his reinstatement but none of them got out of the House Military Affairs Committee. Reno died in a Washington hospital 30 March 1889 of cancer. Later, there were rumors that he had committed suicide. Benteen scotched them. "I am as confident as I can be of anything I didn't see," he told the enquirer, "that Reno *did not* commit suicide, as I do not think that by any possibility he could summon up sufficient nerve to commit so cowardly a crime."

Life went on at Fort Meade. On 9 April 1880, Gibson, who had been promoted to captain commanding French's old company, was replaced in H Company by Lieutenant Charles A. Varnum, one of the select officers for whom Benteen had nothing but praise. Once the post was established, the 7th Cavalry spent summers patrolling the Sioux reservation and what had been the unceded lands. A large number of hostile Sioux remained over the border in Canada and, as long as they remained there, the war begun in 1876 could not be considered over. Colonel Miles was frustrated in his efforts to obtain a separate command even though General Sherman was his wife's uncle. Sherman appeared to be very reluctant to give the ambitious Miles more troops than he needed to man the forts along the Yellowstone for fear that Miles would invade Canada in his zeal to capture the Sioux who had escaped him in 1877. But, renewed construction of the Northern Pacific Railroad and its concomitant influx of settlers into what had been Sioux land decimated the buffalo herds and caused a small, but steady, trickle of hostile holdouts in Canada to slip over the border and surrender.

In the spring of 1881, Benteen took to the field again. The perennial threat posed by hostile holdouts in Canada was diminishing with each spring season. By the time Benteen had gone into camp near the headwaters of the Little Missouri River (called Camp Donald McIntosh), the Sioux Indians north of the border were a pitiful few.

That winter Benteen had encountered a man he had known in the Indian Territory in the late 60s. The man, whom Benteen later referred to only as "Tom Thumb," was a bank cashier in nearby Deadwood. He had been a clerk for the Post Trader[s] at Camp Supply in 1869: Tappan and Weichelbaum. Thumb told Benteen about an incident that had occured just before the 7th Cavalry was re-deployed into Kansas for the summer. Lieutenant David W. Wallingford had approached Samuel Tappan offering a bill of sale for a military ambulance and some horses in exchange for Tappan's giving George A. Custer $3500. Wallingford had stated that if the deal did not go through, Custer would march the regiment north without paying them, depriving Camp Supply (and Tappan in particular) of the revenue from a regiment of newly-paid cavalrymen. Thumb told Benteen in 1880 that Tappan had refused to be blackmailed.

Benteen remembered that the regiment had not been paid off at Camp Supply. He also remembered meeting Lieutenants Cooke and Tom Custer on the road to Fort Hays shortly after the incident Thumb had related to him. The two men had been escorting the Inspector General back to Camp Supply. "Tom Custer and Cooke were sent along to see that that proposal didn't crop out!" he concluded, convinced that Custer had been up to his ears in skullduggery. He also remembered that Lieutenant DeRudio had told him in 1873 that Custer had an $1100 investment with the sutler on the Stanley Yellowstone Expedition, the same sutler in whose wagons Custer had fruitlessly sought to hide the kegs of whiskey. The Tom Thumb revelation was different than the rumors Benteen had been hearing. It was, in Benteen's view, proof positive of Custer' rascality. Had he known at the time, Benteen believed, he "might have prevented [Custer's] being killed at the Little Big Horn," presumably by having charges brought against him that would have led to his dismissal.

By May 1881, Benteen had more immediate concerns than alleged conspiracies of the past. He had decided to accept a posting to New York, first on an Army Board evaluating magazine guns and then as a recruiting officer for the cavalry branch. He wrote to Kate at Fort Meade attempting to settle the matter of transporation east. The Benteens had solicited railroad passes through acquaintances past and present such as: Captain McDougall, Lieutenant Russell, Captain Gibson, and the new regimental quartermaster who had replaced Varnum — Lieutenant William Baldwin. Benteen had written previously to his old Civil War commanders, Edward Winslow and James H. Wilson, asking for passes. In 1881, the men were president and vice-president respectively of a New York railroad company.

Kate Benteen was anxious to visit relatives in St. Louis, so her husband arranged to go directly to New York alone. One of Kate's sisters was in New York: Anita Norman Dice, who had been a "flame" of Benteen's father before the Civil War. Mrs. Dice had apparently been converted to Catholicism and had changed her name to Diaz, much to Benteen's amusement.

On 28 June 1881, Captain Benteen left Fort Meade never to return. He left H Company in the capable hands of Lieutenant Varnum and made his way to the Army Building on he corner of Houston and Green streets in New York City. He spent the summer in the city during the week and repaired to the beaches on weekends.

On one of the pleasant summer evenings, he entertained Captain Godfrey and his family. The women and children went off and the two captains of the 7th Cavalry were left alone. Godfrey reminded Benteen that just before burying the dead on Custer Hill 28 June 1876 they had engaged in a brief conversation that had been interrupted. Benteen had told Godfrey then: "I could tell [you] things that would make your hair stand on end." Godfrey wanted Benteen to keep his promise to reveal those things.

"Don't you think it is just as well to let bygones be bygones?" Benteen asked.

Godfrey, an instructor at West Point by then, insisted that Benteen keep the promise long ago given to reveal the secret. Benteen then reluctantly told the story of Reno's proposal to abandon the wounded on the night of 25 June 1876. He had previously told other officers, including Varnum, Moylan, and Nicholson. As a result of the revelation, Godfrey became increasingly pro-Custer, much to Benteen's disgust. The two men continued to exchange confidences in correspondence for many years, but on the subject of Custer-Reno, they came to a parting of the ways.

Benteen spent October 1881 to January 1882 at the Springfield

(Massachusetts) Arsenal testing repeating rifles and carbines for possible Army adoption. The U.S. Army still used the Springfield single-shot shoulder weapon that had been designed before the Civil War and modified on at least two occasions: in 1866 and 1873. In other parts of the world, more modern weapons were appearing, some with a new cartridge featuring the so-called smokeless powder. Two of the weapons the Board On Magazine Guns tested and rejected for Army use were the Hotchkiss 1880, a tubular magazine gun that was subsequently made into a sporting weapon called the Winchester 1883, and a novel design by a man named James Lee that featured a *box* magazine and a *bolt-action*. The Army did not approve of Lee's design even though his prototype tested well. (In the early 90s, another Board On Magazine Guns adopted a bolt-action, box magazine weapon called the Krag-Jorgenson.)

In the summer of 1882, Theo Benteen fell to his death from a scaffolding in Sacramento, California. He left a widow and three children. Nellie, Theo's widow, asked Fred Benteen to take her son, William Henry (called Harry), and raise him. At about the same time, Henrietta Fairbanks asked him to take her daughter Leila. "I am sorry," Benteen told his older sister, "but I cannot afford to." He told her of Nellie's request and added: "I should like to." He told "En" that he had been plagued by financial worries, including two operations on Freddie's leg. (Freddie had contracted a bone disease, possibly osteomylitis.) To make matters worse, Anita Diaz had shown up "in a 1st class state of destitution," he related, "as is usual." Benteen complained that she was "hanging about" and had followed Kate and Freddie to a seaside hotel, but revealed that he "had the proprietor of [the] house send her away." (Benteen definitely had a penchant for the indirect.) "Something or other," he concluded to his sistser, "is always turning up to keep me in a financial tightness."

He was more accomodating with his wife's relatives. Kate's niece, Violet Norman was "adopted" by the Benteens later and remained in their household until her marriage in 1888. After his financial squeeze in New York had eased, Benteen was able to provide for his brother's children to some extent. His nephew, Harry, went to college and eventually became a surgeon.

On 4 October 1882, Benteen finished his service on the Board on Magazine Guns and on 21 October replaced Captain Edward J. Spaulding (2nd Cavalry) as Mounted Recruiting Officer at the New

York Rendezvous. There, on 23 January 1883, he was notified of his promotion to Major, effective 17 December 1882. Major Albert P. Morrow of the 9th Cavalry (the same man who had commanded the original E Company, 7th Cavalry in 1867) had been promoted to lieutenant colonel. Benteen, by December 1882 the senior captain in the cavalry service, was assigned to the vacant major's slot in the 9th Cavalry. On 19 March 1883, he was granted four months' leave of absence to finish a course in veterinary science. Detained briefly on official business at Fort Leavenworth, Benteen did not join his new regiment for active service until 20 July 1883 — at Fort Riley, Kansas (coincidently, his first duty station with the 7th Cavalry in 1867).

Back at Fort Meade, Charles C. DeRudio, made captain by Benteen's promotion, succeeded to the command of H Troop, 7th Cavalry.

24

The 9th (Colored) Cavalry Regiment

The regiment that Benteen joined in July 1883 had been formed in the fall of 1866 and had spent twenty-five years in Texas and New Mexico fighting various Indians, notably Apaches. The 9th was one of the two Negro cavalry regiments. Its officers were white and its enlisted men were originally recruited from the ranks of former slaves. They had quite a reputation by 1883. There were fewer desertions, fewer incidents of drunkeness, fewer reports of stolen property in Negro regiments than in white regiments. There were also more re-enlistments,, primarily because Army service was considered quite an opportunity and privilege to the black men of the 19th century, while their white counterparts in general scorned soldiers as shirkers and ne'er-do-wells.

In the beginning, they had been a rather sorry lot; few had any military experience, few could ride a horse, and almost none could read or write. To make matters worse, the Army had some difficulty in the beginning getting officers to accept commissions in Negro regiments. Custer and Benteen were but two of many who declined in 1866. In fact, in early 1867, there were a series of mutinies in the newly-formed 9th Cavalry in Texas that authorities, upon investigation, blamed on a lack of officers. Being assigned to serve in Texas was no help. There were incidents of racial conflict that kept cropping up well into the 20th century.

By the early 1870s, however, the 9th Cavalry had been thoroughly shaken down. The officers who had remained were excellent, for the most part, and the enlisted men who had remained were statistically superior to their white counterparts in the other cavalry regiments — with one exception: the sergeants were of little help in company administration. Army chaplains were assigned to Negro regiments to teach reading and writing and while there was some success in improving the literacy rate, the burden of company and regimental paperwork fell on the officers. In the field, however, against Comanches and Apaches, literacy counted for little and the Negro "buffalo soldiers" thrived.

Yet, the old prejudices lingered. Slavery in 1883 was still a living memory. The mutinies of the early years were considered proof of black inferiority by those who chose to believe that blacks could not be good soldiers. In Texas and New Mexico, in the course of serving the government, black soldiers were required to suppress civil disorders among whites. This did not enhance their reputation with the public. Their Indian opponents often thought higher of them than their white counterparts. It was the Indians who gave them the "buffalo soldiers" appelation, derived from the similarity of buffalo hair to the kinky, short black hair common to most Negro males.

Colonel Edward Hatch had commanded the 9th Cavalry since its formation. Benteen had known Hatch by reputation since the Civil War. Hatch was best known for his role in the famous Grierson's Raid through central Mississippi in the spring of 1863. He had gone on to become a brigadier general commanding a division of cavalry in Wilson's Cavalry Corps in 1865, a division that did not participate in Wilson's Raid. Hatch was a tall, blue-eyed New Englander, a year and a half older than Benteen. He had been a lumberjack and sailor before the war and had attended college in Vermont. When the Civil War broke out, Hatch had been a lumber yard owner in Davenport, Iowa. He had raised a company of the 2nd Iowa Cavalry and risen from captain to colonel commanding the regiment by June 1862.

There were whispers in the early 1880s (persisting to this day) that Hatch was involved in some skullduggery involving post traders, much like the allegations that surrounded Custer's dealings with Tappan in the late 1860s. Hatch's most vocal accuser was his own lieutenant colonel, Nathan A.M. Dudley, a rather controversial character himself. Like Custer, Hatch had aroused the ire of President Grant — in his case because of a dispute with a trader named John Dent, who just happened to be Mrs. Grant's brother. The allegations, never proved, seem to have been unfounded. Benteen heard the rumors about Hatch in 1883, but the preponderance of the evidence is that he got along very well with his new superior in the beginning.

After twenty-five years of some of the most thankless campaigning a regiment could ask for, the 9th Cavalry was re-assigned to Kansas and the Indian Territory in November of 1881. The move was intended to give them a well-deserved rest but did not work out that way. Aside from the always touchy (and dangerous) task of providing security for the Indian agents and generally keeping a benevolent eye on Cheyenne, Kiowa, Comanche, and other redoubtable former foes on the reservations, Hatch's men were employed to keep white settlers out of Indian Territory.

White intruders, styled Boomers in their day, had been making persistent efforts to settle unclaimed land in the Indian Territory since the end of hostilities on the Southern Plains in the early 1870s. It fell to Hatch and the 9th Cavalry to evict them. In August 1883, a man named William L. Couch led a group of settlers into what is now Oklahoma. Hatch's patrols from Fort Riley chased Couch out no less than three times. Benteen remained behind, commanding the post at Fort Riley in Colonel Hatch's absence.

On 7 September 1883, Benteen fell and injured his back. He was laid up for a week before being returned to duty. Two weeks after returning, he was still complaining about his "aches from falling" in a letter to Kate, who with Freddie was visiting friends in Philadelphia before joining her husband at his new station. She joined him in October.

In the spring of 1884, William Couch returned to Indian Territory with one thousand Boomers, settling in four camps along the North Canadian near what is now Oklahoma City. The 9th Cavalry took to the field yet again and coaxed the stubborn squatters to return to Kansas. On 16 May 1884, Major Benteen was assigned to command the post at Fort Sill.

Fort Sill, which had not existed as a permanent post when Benteen camped there in 1868-1869, was located in the middle of the reservation for the Kiowas and Comanches. It was garrisoned by two troops of the 9th Cavalry and four companies of the 24th Infantry (also a "Colored" regiment). One of the infantry companies at Fort Sill was commanded by a Captain Custer. Benteen must surely have been amused by Captain Custer's name, as the officer was known by his initials: "B.M." Bethel Moore Custer was no relative of Benteen's former nemesis. He had served as an enlisted man with a regiment from his own state, Pennsylvania, during the Civil War. Like Benteen, Captain B.M. Custer had accepted a commission in a USCT organization and, when the post-war Army was organized in 1866, had accepted a lieutenancy in a Negro infantry regiment.

The commanding officer at Fort Sill (and the reason for Benteen's being sent there) was Captain Charles D. Beyer of C Troop, 9th Cavalry. Beyer had been an enlisted man in the Regular Army throughout most of the Civil War, accepting a commission in a USCT organization as it ended. Made a captain in one of the short-lived infantry organizations of the post-war Army, Beyer transferred to the 9th Cavalry in 1871. By 1884, Colonel Hatch was convinced that Beyer was pocketing some of his troop's funds and sent Benteen down to Fort Sill to take charge of the situation. In the fall of 1884, Beyer was court-martialed for conduct unbecoming an officer and gentleman, a charge that specified seven separate instances of misappropriating government funds and lying to his superiors about it. The court-martial board, presided over by Colonel Joseph H. Potter of the 24th Infantry, found Beyer guilty of all seven specifications, which included: selling his own shotgun to the troop at an excessive price, purchasing sporting equipment that was disallowed and covering it up with a false report of having spent the money on apples, accepting kickbacks from personal servants, using government rations intended for his troop for his own benefit, and so forth. On 22 November 1884, Beyer was dismissed from the service; his place at Fort Sill commanding C Troop was taken by the senior lieutenant of the 9th Cavalry at the time, Gustavus Valois, who was promoted to captain.

Valois was born in Prussia, but immigrated to the United States as a boy. His real name was Gustavus Haenel, but he ran away from home during the Civil War and enlisted in the 4th Maryland Volunteers as Gustavus Valois, apparently to throw his parents off his track. After the war, Valois enlisted in the 5th Cavalry, becoming first sergeant of I Company within a year. When the 9th Cavalry was short of officers in the early years, the Army had taken to commissioning outstanding non-commissioned officers who were willing to serve in Negro regiments. Valois accepted a second lieutenancy (a direct commission) in the 9th in the summer of 1868 and had served with distinction.

The other 9th Cavalry troop commander at Fort Sill under Benteen was Captain Patrick Cusack of G Troop. Cusask was an Irish-born former enlisted man who had risen to the rank of sergeant-major of the 6th Cavalry during the Civil War. After the war, Cusack had accepted a captaincy in one of the USCT organizations and, in 1866, had been appointed second lieutenant in the 9th Cavalry. Though suffering from rheumatism by the middle 1880s, Patrick Cusack had quite a reputation for ability on the battlefield and had been steadily promoted, in addition earning two brevets for heroism in Texas and New Mexico Territory.

The senior lieutenant of the cavalry at Fort Sill was Ballard S. Humphrey, a Virginian who had been commissioned a lieutenant in the 4th Artillery during the Civil War, after having served as a battery first sergeant before the war. As a first lieutenant of artillery, he was pressured out of the Army in 1871 during one of the reductions in force and, after trying civilian life for two years, tried to regain his position. Instead, he was made a second lieutenant in the 9th Cavalry in late 1872 and it took him six and a half years to make first lieutenant again.

The other three cavalry officers at Fort Sill were West Point graduates: Lieutenants Emmet, Hutcheson, and Powell. By the early 1880s, the stigma associated with service in a Negro regiment had been largely erased and the younger officers were, with very few exceptions, graduates of the Military Academy. So were the junior officers of the 24th Infantry, whom Benteen appointed to the important positions such as adjutant, ordnance officer, signal officer, and post treasurer.

The post surgeon was also a Virginian: Dr. Jefferson R. Kean. Benteen, by this time in his life, had decided that he too was a Virginian and seemed to enjoy the company of Dr. Kean. For that matter, he had invariably gotten along well with all the Army doctors he had known and was especially fond of those who hailed from Virginia.

There was at least one person at Fort Sill who was not a stranger to Benteen: the chief of the Kiowa, Stumbling Bear. Benteen had known the old chief back in the days when the Kiowa were still raiding into Texas and their chiefs still locked in bitter rivalry for acknowledged tribal leadership. Kicking Bird, the pre-eminent peace chief, had been murdered. White Bear and Lone Tree, leaders of the hostile faction, had been imprisoned. And, the outwardly genial Stumbling Bear had endured to become the acknowledged chief of the Kiowa.

"The first thing which attracted my attention at the post was the huge form of old Stumbling Bear passing in front of my quarters,"

Benteen remembered. He called out to his old friend and, though the old chief was nearly blind, was recognized and warmly greeted as "Ole-Tanke, Ole-Tanke!" (Ole-Tanke meant, in Kiowa, Grayhead, Benteen's name among the Indians.) Stumbling Bear had once told Benteen that the cavalry officer was himself a Kiowa "in the long ago." Years later, Benteen fondly remembered his reunion with his Indian friend. "Here was this three hundred-fifty pound Kiowa chief blubbering in my arms for pure joy at having me back among them," he said.

Benteen recalled rather ruefully the time he'd had his mess cook prepare a big meal of roast turkey and invited the pre-eminent Kiowa chiefs to partake of it. White Bear, the somewhat notorious war-chief who subsequently committed suicide in a Texas prison in 1879, had refused to eat turkey, claiming it "would make a coward of him, and perhaps he would run away in a fight." He held out for "Wo-haugh," the Kiowa name for beef derived from the cowboy's cry of "Whoa".

Stumbling Bear, the last of the great chiefs, was a frequent guest of the Benteens at Fort Sill. Benteen remembered that the old man was highly intelligent and perceptive and seemed much amused by one of Benteen's nicknames for Kate: Pinkie. He was a great friend of young Freddie's as well, once making a set of bow and arrows out of Osage Orange for him. Benteen made a special effort to learn the Kiowa language and even produced a Kiowa dictionary of sorts.

Kate's mother, Elizabeth L. Norman, died 12 March 1884 at St. Louis. Her death left homeless a 21-year-old granddaughter, Violet Norman, and the Benteens promptly took her in. They had wanted to adopt Violet as early as 1877, but Violet had stayed with her grandmother until the death of Mrs. Norman made it essential that she find a home. Both Fred and Kate Benteen were very fond of Violet, their daughters having died in infancy. In fact, their oldest daughter, Caroline, would have been Violet's age had she lived. They were also anxious to find a prospective bridegroom for Violet among the many bachelor officers under Benteen's command.

In June 1884, a man named David Payne led another 1500 Boomers into the Territory. Payne, who died in November, had been an officer in the Kansas volunteer regiment that had participated in the Washita campaign from Camp Supply in 1868. The much-reviled 9th Cavalry had to take to the field, surround the illegal camps and persuade the would-be settlers that the U.S. government would not relent, even though the history of such settlements had provided nothing but

Freddie, Captain and Mrs. Benteen
in New York, 1882

Eugene F. Ladd

At the Custer Battlefield, June 1886 – D.F. Barry photo

1– Corporal Edward Hall
2– Sergeant George Horn
3– Captain Thomas M. McDougall
4– Mrs. James D. Mann
5– Major Frederick W. Benteen
6– Captain Edward S. Godfrey

7– Mrs. F.W. (Kate) Benteen
8– Dr. Henry R. Porter
9– Mrs. Frank D. Garretty
10– Captain Winfield S. Edgerly
11– Trumpeter George B. Penwell
12– White Swan

encouragement for the squatters. Benteen had been forced to abandon his police activities in the Black Hills after the government had backed down on that issue. He knew that it was just a matter of time before the government relented on the Oklahoma lands question. It was onerous duty, as the interlopers were not miners, but dirt-poor families trying to stake claims without the benefit of legal sanction.

In December 1884, Payne's right-hand man, William Couch, reappeared with three hundred Boomers. Colonel Hatch responded with what came to be called the Siege of Stillwater Creek. He surrounded the illegal settlement there and starved them out. The process took five days before Couch left the Territory, vowing to return.

The Indians were upset by the migration and, since the Indian Wars were considered over in that part of the country at least, were being regularly supplied with weapons and ammunition for hunting. The situation got so bad in February 1885 that Colonel Hatch sent for Benteen to command a squadron (the new official name for a cavalry battalion) along the Kansas/Indian Territory border near Caldwell, Kansas.

Benteen reported to his regimental commander for duty at Arkansas City, Kansas, on 4 March 1885. Hatch insisted that he had not requested the Department to order Benteen specifically. Benteen, having a copy of a letter Hatch had written saying just the opposite, was infuriated by Hatch's duplicity. The letter, still in existence, has Benteen's angry comment written on the back of it. In part, it characterizes Hatch as "a more thorough lying scoundrel than even Geo. A. Custer — if such were possible."

While patrolling the border, Benteen received word that his father had died in Atlanta on 9 March 1885. "After getting the 'Boomers' in a fair way of listening to reason," Benteen applied for a leave of absence to return to his home and settle his personal affairs. He left 16 March 1885.

Freddie remained in college until summer vacation and Benteen returned to Fort Sill with his wife and Violet only to learn that the 9th Cavalry was being re-deployed to Wyoming Territory. They packed their household belongings in wagons and set out with three other families (probably the Valoises, Cusacks, and Humphreys) for the rail head at Henrietta, Texas — sixty-five miles away. They expected to be on the trail three days, but, as Benteen put it, "every creek was a river and every river a lake" as a result of exceptionally heavy spring rains. Unable to ford the water courses, the group was forced to live off the land until the water levels receded enough to ford with loaded wagons. The men hunted game and the women cooked it in what became an extended picnic. Violet and at least one other young lady were thrilled with the adventure. According to Benteen, they "shrieked with delight" and talked excitedly of the "boss time" they were enjoying, never having roughed it before. The trip took twenty-three days.

They boarded a train at Henrietta that took them to Fort Riley, where the men, joined by Freddie on vacation from college, took command of their respective units and the 9th Cavalry marched overland to their new homes. Major Benteen commanded the 2nd Squadron on the march, leaving 12 June 1885. The 2nd Squadron, consisting of Troops B, D, E, H, L, arrived at Fort McKinney on 1 August.

Fort McKinney had been established near Buffalo, Wyoming in late 1876 as a forward supply base for troops rounding up the hostile Sioux roamers after the Little Big Horn fiasco. The 2nd Squadron garrisoned the post along with two infantry companies from the 9th and 21st Infantry regiments. McKinney was also the regimental headquarters of Hatch's 9th Cavalry, though seven of its troops were parceled out to other posts. Lieutenant Colonel Dudley had been promoted to colonel commanding the 1st Cavalry and was reassigned to Fort Custer, near the junction of the Big Horn and Little Big Horn Rivers (in Montana Territory). His replacement was an old acquaintance of Benteen's from the '76 campaign: James S. Brisbin, formerly major in the 2nd Cavalry.

Benteen was sick for a few days after arriving, but recuperated quickly. The abrupt change in climate and the questionable sanitary conditions in the field brought on a mild case of malaria. Kate and Violet joined him in September and all settled back into the routine of frontier garrison life. Benteen, still the junior major of the regiment, applied for an exchange of regiments with Major Lewis Merrill (of the 7th). Incredibly, the deal was approved all the way up the chain of command, including General Sheridan (the Commanding General), but a sharp-eyed lawyer-type in the Adjutant General's Office pointed out that the exchange was not in accordance with Army regulations. In accepting the exchange, Merrill would have become the *junior* major of the 9th, while Benteen became the *senior* major of the 7th. The deal was disapproved in January 1886.

Benteen was assigned duties as post range officer at McKinney and performed his assigned task despite chronic ill health. To his profound disgust, he learned that Colonel Hatch, citing the post surgeon, caused Benteen to be carried on the regimental and post returns as "sick in quarters" between 17 March and 23 June 1886. Hatch and Benteen were, by that time, barely on speaking terms and Benteen was surprised to learn later that he had officially ceased to be post range officer as of 1 May. Probably because of the friction with Hatch as well as his worsening health, Benteen began to seriously consider retirement. He had reached the rank of major and had passed the twenty-year milestone. He was eligible for a more comfortable retirement than what had faced him as a senior captain back in 1877 when he had first discussed retiring. Moreover, his property in Atlanta was no longer being watched by his dependable father.

On 23 June 1886, Benteen was placed on detached service to go to Fort Custer and attend the 10th Anniversary of the battle of the Little Big Horn. The occasion was organized by one of the 7th Cavalry's young lieutenants who had not been present when the battle was fought, but who had joined in the fall of 1876: Herbert J. Slocum. Fort Custer's new commanding officer, Colonel N.A.M. "Gold Lace" Dudley, detailed K Company of the 5th Infantry to escort guests to the battlefield encampment. This infantry escort was commanded by Captain Frank D. Baldwin, formerly Nelson Miles' adjutant-in-the-field. The second lieutenant was James E. Wilson, who as a sergeant had helped Lieutenant Maguire map the battlefield in 1876. K Company's first lieutenant that summer was a man named William H.C. Bowen, whom Benteen would come to know quite well in the years ahead.

The battlefield looked considerably different ten years after the battle. The hasty burials of 28 June 1876 had not endured natural erosion and the work of scavengers, primarily wolves. A year after the battle, Company I under Captain Henry J. Nowlan had returned to the battlefield and reburied human and horse bones, attempting to mark where each man had fallen with a wooden stake. They dug up Custer's bones and shipped them to West Point, where they were reinterred amid much hoopla on 10 October 1877. Benteen was philosophical. In 1879 he told Robert Newton Price: "Cadets for ages to come will bow in humility at the Custer shrine at West Point, and — if it makes better soldiers and men of them, why the necessity of knocking the paste eye out of their idol?" That same year, a log memorial had been erected for the fallen 7th Cavalry men at the battlefield. In 1881, it was replaced with a granite monument that endures to this day. "It is about as well — or perhaps better," Benteen said, "that the world should look back upon Custer as a martyr, [rather] than the full fledged, braying donkey that he was."

Lieutenant Slocum, organizer of the event, remembered years later that those in attendance "camped there a week and had a royal time." Captain Tom McDougall was one of them. He and Benteen celebrated their reunion with some heavy drinking. Captains Godfrey and Edgerly were there also. So were Dr. Porter and White Swan, the Crow scout who had argued with Custer the night before the ill-fated attack. The old veterans toured the battlefield and posed for pictures taken by the famed frontier photographer, D.F. Barry.

"Tell me, please," Benteen asked rhetorically years later

> was there any generalship displayed in so scattering the regiment that only the merest of chance, intervention of Providence — or what you will — saved the whole 12 troops from being 'wiped out'? That is all that I blame Custer for — the scattering, as it were, (two portions of his command, anyway) to the — well, four winds, before he knew anything about the exact or approximate position of the Indian village or the Indians.

Major Benteen returned to Fort McKinney on 30 June 1886. He had just one month to enjoy the amenities of an established post. In Utah Territory, the Ute Indians on the Uintah reservation east of Salt Lake City were becoming restless because of alleged inequities at the agency and smoldering resentment over their forced removal from Colorado six years before. In the fall of 1879 many of the same Utes had rebelled against an officious reservation agent and turned in fury on a cavalry column he had called in to help him. Further bloodshed (and an all-out-war) had been averted only by the intervention of a chief named Ouray. In 1886, Ouray was dead.

On 5 July 1886, the second major of the 9th Cavalry, Thomas B. DeWees, died. DeWees had been a captain in the 2nd Cavalry with Crook at the battle of the Rosebud ten years before. Benteen moved up one notch on the regimental roster and his former slot was filled by Captain James F. Randlett of the 8th Cavalry.

On 2 August 1886, Benteen was instructed to ready two troops of the 9th Cavalry (B & E) for a forced march.

25

Fort "DuShame"

Major Frederick W. Benteen dutifully packed his household belongings, supervised a hasty packing of the equipment of B and E Troops of the 9th Cavalry, and was on his way south. The column, with wives and children, made slow progress down the length of Wyoming Territory in the first two weeks of August. They reached the Union Pacific Railroad near Rock Creek, expecting to be allowed to go into camp there and sort out their equipment. Instead, they found orders directing them to board a specially provided train and hurry to Fort Bridger in the southwest part of the Territory. Brigadier General George Crook, the commanding general of the Department of the Platte (which covered the modern-day states of Nebraska, Iowa, Wyoming, and Utah), was waiting impatiently.

Until April of 1886, General Crook had been the commanding officer of the Department of Arizona. But, after a long quarrel with General Sheridan about the conduct of his campaign against Geronimo there, Crook had asked to be relieved from Arizona. Sheridan had promptly granted Crook's request and replaced him with Nelson A. Miles. Crook, still smoldering over the Geronimo debacle, was gratuitously insulted by recurring rumors about his conduct when last commanding the Department of the Platte ten years before. He had acquired the nickname "Rosebud George," a reference to his controversial fight on 17 June 1876 with the Indians who had wiped out Custer a week later. When Crook returned to Omaha, the headquarters of the Department of the Platte, he was more than usually sensitive to criticism.

On 7 August 1886, a young officer named Kennon overheard a

conversation between Crook and Colonel William B. Royall that he recorded in his diary. Royall had been the commanding officer of Crook's cavalry at the Rosebud. (He had also been one of the board members at Reno's Court of Inquiry in 1879.) According to Kennon, Crook rather heatedly told Royall:

> For ten years I have suffered silently the obloquy of having made a bad fight at [the] Rosebud when the fault was in yourself and Nickerson. [Major Azor H. Nickerson had been Crook's adjutant in 1876.] There was a good chance to make a charge, but it couldn't be done because of the condition of the Cavalry. I sent word to you to 'come in' and waited two hours — nearer three — before you obeyed. I sent Nickerson three times at least. Couriers passed constantly between the points where we were respectively. I had the choice of assuming responsibility myself for the failure of my plans or court-martialling you and Nickerson. I chose to bear the responsibility myself. The failure of my plan was due to your conduct.

It was a sore Crook who awaited the coming of Benteen's two troop squadron at Fort Bridger. He had already dispatched three companies of the 21st Infantry south into Utah Territory to the Ute reservation there. Crook was anxious to meet potential Indian trouble with an impressive show of force and to build a post on the reservation to be known as Fort DuChesne.

Major Benteen's men were crammed into three box cars and hurried west. Troop property was hopelessly mixed up. When they arrived at Bridger, they found that the impatient Crook had gone ahead with the infantry companies, leaving instuctions for Benteen to follow with the cavalry troops at once. There was not sufficient transport for most of the property that had been brought from Fort McKinney, so it was left behind with assurances that it would be sent along as soon as transportation could be obtained. The journey south was agony for Benteen. His back hurt, his eyes smarted, and he ached all over from neuralgia. He had developed a bladder problem that made even fifteen minutes in the saddle his limit. He stopped three or four times an hour to urinate. General Crook sent a courier back with instructions for Benteen to overtake the infantry companies which had a three day head start. Benteen did not make satisfactory progress, so Crook ordered him to split his squadron into two troops and send one ahead as fast as their horses could be pushed. Crook and the infantry arrived at a point about three miles above the junction of the DuChesne and Uintah rivers on 20 August. The next day, Crook designated the location as the site for the new post. Benteen staggered in with the trailing cavalry troop and wagon train on 22 August. Crook departed, making Major Benteen the commanding officer of the unbuilt Fort DuChesne.

On 23 August 1886, Major Benteen formally assumed command of the cluster of tents that was Fort DuChesne. His first priority was to calm potential Indian unrest. This he did without incident in the first days, assigning an infantry detachment under Lieutenant Henry D. Styer to guard the agency headquarters. He then turned his attention to building the post.

The building process was a fiasco. Much-needed supplies were delayed and the troops remained in tents until almost January 1887. Forage, food, and other essential supplies were slow in coming and were at exorbitant cost when they did come. Benteen found himself in the same position he had been in on the march from Macon in May of 1865 when his troops had started to mutiny over poor supply problems. The difference was that the dependable Negro troops of the 9th Cavalry were not expecting any discharge and did not revolt. They grumbled, naturally, and the 52-year-old post commander found himself once again frustrated by the seeming incompetence of military supply systems.

On 13 September, a Mr. George Jewett was appointed Post Trader and departed from Omaha for the new fort to set up his store. Jewett was especially close to General Crook's paymaster, Major Thaddeus H. Stanton. (He would in the days ahead become a bitter enemy of Major Benteen's.)

On Saturday, 25 September 1886, a wagon train, carrying some of the supplies left behind at Bridger a month before, finally arrived at DuChesne. Benteen, advised that the commanding officer of the wagon train was Lieutenant Harry L. Bailey of the 21st Infantry who had also brought his wife and a new officer for one of the cavalry troops, ordered Lieutenant John S. Parke to put a gun crew to work erecting a tent for the Baileys. Lieutenant and Mrs. Bailey arrived after Retreat (about 4:00 p.m.) and were warmly greeted by Benteen and the rest of the garrison. Benteen joshed the new cavalry lieutenant, Harry G. Trout, a recent West Point graduate, about his appearance. He remarked "in a good-natured way" that Trout "had the look of a cavalryman." One of the cavalry troop commanders, Captain J.A. Olmsted, who was also present, remembered that Benteen had also joked with Mrs. Bailey. Benteen told Mrs.

Bailey: "Your husband must have a hell of a time with you." Mrs. Bailey laughed and asked what he meant by that remark. Benteen replied that any woman with her eyes "would make it lively for any man." Violet Norman, who was also present during the exchange, remembered that her aunt's husband had said to Mrs. Bailey that any woman "having eyes such as yours must be a holy terror." Violet was certain that all present thought it was a very witty remark, especially Mrs. Bailey.

Captain Olmsted, who had known some difficulty with Benteen earlier in the day, regarded the exchange as insulting. He remembered something else. Benteen, he said, "then stepped around the corner of the wall tent, not going more than ten feet away from where the ladies were sitting, and urinated on the tent, so that we all heard it." Olmsted, mortally offended, "got up and left, not knowing what might happen next."

Two days later, Major Benteen aroused the ire of Lieutenant Lawrence J. Hearn by relieving him of duty as the post quartermaster and appointing Lieutenant Charles M. Truitt in his place. Hearn went to Benteen and demanded an apology for what he had heard Benteen had said about him in connection with the change in duty assignment. Benteen denied having said anything derogatory about Hearn or his performance and insisted that the change of assignment was made simply because Lieutenant Truitt had more experience as a quartermaster. Hearn accepted the explanation. In fact, Benteen had also replaced the post adjutant, Lieutenant Joseph W. Duncan, with Lieutenant Willis Wittich that same day.

Jewett's Post Trader's store was a popular place for the officers of Fort DuChesne. Major Benteen allegedly spent an inordinate amount of time there, drinking. Prior to 10 October, nobody could recall of a specific incidence of drunkeness on Benteen's part, except for the controversial episode with Mrs. Bailey at the tent, which Captain Olmsted attributed to intoxication on Benteen's part. Some officers felt that Benteen was drunk at the time; others did not, but admitted he had "been drinking."

On Sunday night, 10 October 1886, an incident occurred at Jewett's store that convinced those who witnessed it and heard about it that Benteen was "found drunk." Based on testimony given several weeks later, there can be little doubt that Benteen had been drinking rather heavily that night. About 11:00 o'clock that night, one of Jewett's employees came to the tent of Lieutenant Styer (who had been

replaced by then at the Ute Agency) and reported that Major Benteen and Lieutenant George R. Burnett of the 9th Cavalry were
drunk at the Post Trader's. According to Jewett's man who ran the
store, a Mr. John W. Vanderhoef, Benteen and Burnett had been
drinking steadily most of the afternoon and Benteen, in particular,
had been abusive to citizens who came in to trade, telling them that
the store was closed and to "hit the breeze" or "move your freight."
One of them ran and hid behind a stove, peeking around it at Benteen. The man was apparently playing. Benteen was not. "Boys," he
said angrily, pointing his finger at the peeking man, "there stands
the Mormon son of a bitch behind the stove! give me a revolver and
I'll make that Mormon son of a bitch pull his freight."

At the urging of Vanderhoef's son, Benteen and Burnett agreed
to leave the store about 9:00 p.m. They took the younger Vanderhoef
with them as they made a burlesque inspection of the guards. The
corporal of the guard had to be called out twice when Benteen insisted on ignoring the challenges of an infantry sentry. "You see the
difference, Ned," Benteen told Vanderhoef's son, "between the cavalrymen and the infantry." He and Burnett decided to return to the
store for some more drinking. It was then that Ned Vanderhoef sent
a runner to Lieutenant Styer to ask for assistance in getting Benteen
and Burnett to go home.

George R. Burnett was an 1880 graduate of West Point who had
distinguished himself in action in New Mexico Territory in 1881. In
fact, he was awarded the Medal of Honor for galloping to the assistance of a dismounted man under heavy fire and escorting that man
to a place of safety. He was especially close to Benteen and a frequent
drinking companion.

Later, John W. Vanderhoef recalled an incident with Major Benteen in the store that had occurred around the same time. Vanderhoef
did not remember the date, except that it had *not* occurred on 10
October. Though there is no proof, the incident Vanderhoef later
recalled must have happened the day before: Saturday, 9 October.
Benteen had been drinking in the store when Violet Norman and
Kate Benteen suddenly turned up. (From the way the story was told,
it seems highly probable that the two ladies had been summoned
much as Styer was the following night.) Benteen invited the ladies
to sit down and drink some ginger ale with him. According to Vanderhoef, "they objected to sitting, but wanted him to go home with them
right away." Benteen insisted on a token drink and the ladies obliged.

They then allowed him to escort them home. Once at home (a tent at that time), he remained.

Styer, a young West Point graduate who neither drank nor smoked, lacked the finesse that the ladies had demonstrated. Summoning the post surgeon, Dr. Robert Benham, Styer plunged in and tried to physically carry the obviously-inebriated post commander home. Benham and the younger Vanderhoef manhandled Lieutenant Burnett to his tent without difficulty. They returned to see how Styer was faring and found him standing over Benteen (who was lying in the mud) unable to budge him. Both Benham and Styer tried unsuccessfully to drag Benteen home. At length, Benteen stood and said: "Styer, I thank you for your guardianship." He then walked to his own tent unassisted.

On Thursday, 11 November 1886, Major Benteen sat in the Post Trader's with Lieutenant Burnett and a civilian doctor named Julius Robertson drinking ginger ale. The store was filled up with customers, mostly local men engaged in various businesses who, for one reason or another, had been given contracts for essential supplies. One of them, a man named Lycurgus Johnson, walked in and invited himself to join Benteen and Burnett. Benteen rounded on him viciously, calling him among other things a "Mormon son of a bitch." Johnson laughed it off and tried to buy a round of drinks for those present. Benteen pushed the money back and told Johnson to put it in his pocket, that he would not drink with anyone but officers of the Army. Johnson and a man named Sterling Cotton (sheriff of the county nearby) left the Post Trader's, as did most of the other civilians. Not enough of the despised civilian tradesmen had left to please Benteen. He instructed John Vanderhoef to prepare one of the back rooms that he and Burnett and Dr. Robertson might eat the noonday meal in privacy.

Vanderhoef did so and, in the process of serving the meal, exchanged words with Benteen. Dr. Robertson later said that Benteen made a remark "which evidently irritated Mr. Vanderhoef." The substance was a discussion of a questionable deal Vanderhoef's boss, George H. Jewett, had made with another businessman named Lorenzo Hatch. Vanderhoef, understandably, declined to comment on it and Benteen became angry and abusive, saying: "You are a regular old fart. You don't amount to anything anyway."

Vanderhoef accused Benteen of not being a gentleman. "I am a gentleman," Benteen snapped back. "I was born a gentleman. I was raised a gentleman, and I am a gentleman still." The two men engaged in an argument in which Benteen claimed that Jewett had been forced to borrow money from him "to run this little one-horse store of his." Vanderhoef, not caring to argue any more, left.

Lieutenant Burnett reproved Benteen for his language and conduct, asserting that Vanderhoef was only a loyal employee and that, furthermore, had gone out of his way to fix a meal and place of privacy for the officers. Benteen, apparently feeling contrite, sent a clerk after Sheriff Sterling Cotton. When Cotton arrived, Benteen apologized for his previous treatment of the merchant Johnson and (by implication) Cotton himself an hour before.

Cotton later claimed that Major Benteen was drunk and that at the end of the apology began to talk in a rambling manner about Mormons, asking Cotton if he was a Mormon. Cotton replied that he was not especially devout. Benteen then called Cotton and Johnson (not present) "God damned Mormons." Cotton, who was admittedly drunk himself, stood up and shouted: "You are a God damned liar, and you ain't no gentleman, or you would not talk to me that way."

Benteen jumped up, threw off his uniform jacket, let his suspenders slide over his shoulders, and rolled up his shirt sleeves. "Come on," he told Cotton, "and I'll let you know whether I am a gentleman or not."

Lieutenant Burnett intervened and told Cotton: "For my sake, desist." The sheriff agreed to leave and claimed as he did so that Benteen stood in the middle of the small room, suspenders slipped off, sleeves rolled up, shouting that Mormons were "a set of God damned sons of bitches" and that he was going to show Cotton "that I can whip you." Cotton staggered away. The next day, he claimed, Benteen asked him how he felt. Cotton replied: "I feel pretty damned rough." Said Benteen: "You must not notice it, it was just wine talk."

Cotton, Johnson, and Vanderhoef all united in saying that Benteen had been drunk. Doctor Robertson said that Benteen was not drunk, but that he (Robertson) was drunk. Lieutenant Truitt, the quartermaster, claimed that he had seen Benteen drunk one day about the time of the Post Trader incident, but could not recall which day it was. Lieutenant Wittich, the adjutant, claimed that he had done the routine business with Major Benteen every day and had not noticed him drunk on 11 November.

None of the other officers assigned to the post, when questioned about the incident under oath, could remember anything that had transpired that day. Only Lieutenant Truitt believed that Benteen had been drunk, but was not certain which day he had found Benteen drunk. He could not recall any particulars about a brawl in the Post Trader's.

The next day, 12 November, Benteen relieved Lieutenant Willis Wittich as adjutant and replaced him with Lieutenant Harry Bailey. He later said that the reason for this was that Department of the Platte headquarters had sent him instructions to the effect that the post adjutant and post commissary of subsistence could not be the same officer when there were sufficient officers to warrant having two different men occupy those positions. Benteen decided that Fort DuChesne had a sufficiency of officers and left Wittich as commissary of subsistence only. He also claimed that he felt Wittich was a "spy" for George Jewett and that he did not wish a man of questionable loyalty to continue as his adjutant.

The exact nature of George Jewett's activities at Fort DuChesne were never established. Benteen was positive that Jewett was engaged in some kind of skullduggery. He attempted to draw out some evidence of Jewett's machinations at his own court-martial, but his questions were consistently dismissed as irrelevant. His granddaughter later passed on her belief that there were some "inequities" at Fort DuChesne that Benteen had attempted to expose, but admitted that she knew nothing about the details. She said that the Benteen family always referred to the Utah Territory post as "Fort DuShame." Others called it "Fort Damn Shame." In view of the fact that the post was still largely a tent city by late December, the obvious conclusion is that *something* was wrong. Jewett had by some means managed to obtain contracts to build wooden houses and public buildings, but the buildings did not go up until after Benteen had been relieved of command. The arrangement featuring a post trader as a building contractor was not that unusual for 19th century frontier posts, but was an exception to the rule. Benteen implied that Jewett had used inside information gleaned from young officers, who were either friendly with him or in his debt, to outbid his rivals. Benteen never proved such activity and his one attempt to do so was struck down by senior officers.

But, the shame of a military post in late 1886 still in tents four months after having been designated a permanent post cried out for an explanation. General Crook, in Omaha, feeling some pressure from the Commanding General of the U.S. Army in Washington (by 1866 General Philip H. Sheridan), decided to find out what was the matter at DuChesne. He sent his inspector general, Major Robert H. Hall of the 22nd Infantry, to DuChesne to investigate and report.

Hall arrived at the post late at night on 29 November. Curiously, he did not pay a courtesy call on the post commander, Major Benteen. In fact, the only inkling Benteen had of his presence was a telegram sent the night before, which said simply: "I am here under special instructions from the Department Commander. I am very tired this evening, but shall do myself the honor of reporting to you tomorrow on arriving." The next day, without the promised reporting, Hall proceeded with the regularly scheduled inspection of the post, a process which consumed the entire morning. Benteen, anxious to know about the "special instructions" was kept in the dark. Hall merely told Benteen before leaving "that he did not see how any more could be done towards building" the fort than Benteen had done.

Major Hall's official report to General Crook was something else. According to Benteen, it was "simply infamous." It said, in part: "Probably the principal cause of delay has been the conduct of Major F.W. Benteen, 9th Cavalry, the officer in command. I was informed that he is frequently unfitted for duty through the excessive use of intoxicating liquors, and this for periods of two or three days at a time. During these attacks he is said to be obstinate and unreasonable, and so abusive to those about him as to make it impossible to transact any business with him. These attacks it is said have increased in frequency during the last two months, so that now he is very often thus disabled."

Major Hall's "infamous" report was dated 7 December 1886. On 18 December, Benteen's regimental commander, Colonel Edward Hatch, showed up at DuChesne and relieved Benteen of command. He then proceeded with an investigation of affairs at Fort DuChesne, looking specifically for evidence to support Hall's conclusion about Benteen's chronic drunkeness. Questioning the officers and civilians present, he drew up a list of six specifications, a list which included the 25 September incident with Mrs. Bailey at the tent, the 10 October incident at the Post Trader's, and the 11 November "brawl" with Sheriff Cotton. The other three occasions specified were never supported by any sworn testimony.

Benteen was especially mortified that Hatch was the investigating officer, characterizing his superior as "an avowed and bitter enemy of mine." Hatch sent the list of specifications to the charge of being found drunk on six occasions to General Crook. In the meantime, under circumstances never clearly set forth, Benteen was offered a six months leave of absence. He implied that the offer was semi-official in nature and that it had emanated from General Crook through the paymaster, Major Stanton.

On 3 January 1887, an article appeared in the Kansas City *Times* purporting to come from an unnamed enlisted man at Fort Leavenworth. The article, an important document in the Army career of Frederick William Benteen, said this:

FORT LEAVENWORTH

The recent assignment of Colonel Edward Hatch, 9th Cavalry, to the command at Fort DuChesne, Utah, has been the cause of more or less gossip among the officers and men at this post. All kinds of rumors have been in circulation as to this mismanagement in the location of the post and the administration of its affairs by those in authority. It was also reported that the supply departments of the Department of the Platte were the cause of much suffering among the troops stationed thereat. Matters kept going from bad to worse until it was finally determined to send an inspector to the post, investigate the conditions of affairs and report results. This culminated in directing Colonel Hatch to report to General Crook for instructions and his departure for DuChesne where he is now in command.

A few days ago a member of the 9th Cavalry belonging to one of the troops stationed at DuChesne arrived here, having been discharged from the service by expiration of term. While in conversation with him, the *Times* correspondent, who noticed that he was quite an intelligent man, proceeded to ask him for such information about affairs at DuChesne as he was able to give. The result below proves that he is either well posted or able to tell a pretty good story. If what he avers is true the matter should certainly be thoroughly investigated by the proper authorities and the blame placed where it properly belongs.

"The United States government," said this discharged soldier, "is noted for the bungling manner in which its agents transact the business placed in their charge, but I honestly believe that in the establishment of that post the army has outdone itself in that respect. From the time the orders were received at Forts McKinney and Sidney, up to the time of my departure from DuChesne, red tape has ruled supreme and with an iron hand, while the indifference of department headquarters and the incompetency of the department staff has exceeded anything heretofore heard of."

"When did you start for the point where the post is situated?"

"August 2 the order was received at McKinney and we were obliged to pack up and be on the road by August 4. The packing of all the property was poorly done, causing the loss of hundreds of dollars' worth of public and private property. The troops had not time to weigh a single package and couldn't properly mark any of them as we didn't know where we were going. But we got off on time, and after a pleasant march reached Rock Creek where we expected to halt a day for a breathing spell and get into a little better shape."

"Did you?"

"No, sir. We there found an order awaiting us to come on at once to Fort Bridger. An agent of the quartermaster's department was at Rock Creek to load the command. He put us aboard the cars in such a way, mixing up the companies and headquarters, that we wasn't straightened when I left there two weeks ago. The transportation furnished us by the Union Pacific railroad was the worst I have seen in the service, and I have been in it a good many years. For two large companies of cavalry, its officers and their wives, this road furnished three small, dingy and filthy emigrant cars. Old, and so dirty we had to clean them out before we could enter them at all. But this railroad is noted for being the meanest road to everybody in the United States, and this meanness seems to have permeated the whole corps of officials.

"On reaching Curtis Station we were rushed off that same night eleven miles to Fort Bridger where we expected to have a chance to rest. But no! Here we met the department commander who started us out for DuChesne before we could supply ourselves with the necessaries. We did draw rations, but were short of everything else, even forage, not having sufficient wagons. The companies of the 21st Infantry from Fort Sidney had started three days ahead of us, and we were told we must overtake them, and this over a mountain trail where infantry can make better time than cavalry. One day orders were received from the department commander to divide the cavalry and send one company ahead faster, as trouble was expected. Had there been trouble with the Indians, there would not have been a man left to tell the story. The department commander pushed ahead so rapidly in his ambulance, overtaking the infantry and making them march fifty miles the last day into DuChesne, thirty-two of it without water. These troops were so exhausted when camp was reached that had there been an attack the Indians would have killed every man of them without firing a shot. One day behind the infantry came one cavalry company and still a day behind this came Major Benteen and one company of cavalry and this over a mountain road and through canyons where these small detachments could have been literally eaten up by the Indians had they so chosen. Indians and citizens laughed at such a march and asked us if we had lost our senses.

"The department commander reached the site of the present post one afternoon, raised his hand and said, 'Here's Fort DuChesne,' and by sunrise next morning was well on his way back to Fort Bridger, obeying in this thorough [?] manner his orders to locate a new post. It evidently mattered not to him how uncomfortable the site might be. He well knew he would not have to be stationed there. So, like most army posts, we found ourselves located in the most dreary spot in the whole section of that desert country. Had the post been established fourteen miles up the river to the foot of the mountains, a beautiful site would have been obtained. The post, as now located, is on the Uintah River, a large stream of water so warm in summer that fish are not found in it during that season. The formation of the country is such that the camp gets the benefit of all the wind when it blows, which it does constantly in the fall, picking up the alkali dust, as fine as flour, covering everything with it. The sand is so fine that it sifts through the tent canvas so that the troops get it not only thoroughly ground into their skin, but have to eat no small amount of it with their meals. From the rosy promises made us at Fort Bridger by the department commander and his staff, we supposed that when we reached the spot where the post is now located, supplies would be promptly shipped us so we could begin making ourselves comfortable. The march from Fort McKinney had been so hurried that we left that post as light as possible — one suit of clothes and a blanket to a man, and barely tentage sufficient to cover the command, and a portion of this had to be left at Bridger for want of transportation. But we tried to be happy, thinking that thirty days at the outside would see us supplied. Day after day went by, and nothing came. We were evidently forgotten. The officers made the necessary requisitions at Bridger again as soon after getting to Fort DuChesne as possible. Pleading, begging and sharp letters were written by the post commander, demanding that his troops be supplied, but to no purpose. The days were long and hot, thermometers reaching ninety-six in the shade, while the nights were so cool that ice formed in our tents in the water buckets, making a change of sixty degrees in twenty-four hours. Men suffered for want of sufficient bedding, while the hard work we were compelled to perform soon wore out the one suit of clothes and we looked more like ragamuffins than soldiers of such a government as ours, and even up to the time when I left — less than two weeks, with snow on the ground — the company property was not all received, nor had the quartermaster's department clothing sufficient to issue to the troops.

At Fort DuChesne, Utah Territory, 1886
Seated: Violet Norman, Kate Benteen, Capt. Stephen P. Jocelyn
Standing: Lieut. Willis Wittich, Lieut. Charles M. Truitt,
Lieut. Henry D. Styer, Major Frederick W. Benteen

George R. Burnett

The "Pipe Photo"
of Frederick Benteen

Frederick W. Benteen in 1888

"But if the garrison couldn't be supplied, we had something to laugh at. The first teams that arrived had on shelter tent poles, an article that is never used. The next teams brought street lamps. Then came a train loaded with doors and window frames, but not a nail, a pick or axes or helve, and we were compelled to wait for these things for months. Good mules were sent us, but not a shoe has the post quartermaster been able to get for them. He has done the best he could, but had to work them night and day till the feet of some of them were worn to the quick and liable to die from that cause alone. When I left the blacksmiths were at work cutting up wagon tires and iron bunks to get iron to make shoes and save the mules. Their horses are barefoot and unable to take to the field at all. Not a veterinary instrument or pound of medicine has been received at the post.

"After months of delay, contracts were let. All the stoves at the post are coal burners, so the only fuel contracted for is wood, and rotten cottonwood at that to save $2 a cord, when the extra $2 would have purchased cedar. There is no earthly reason why the quartermaster's department should not have contracted for coal, there being plenty of it in that section. Even the post office department has gone back on the garrison and has no mail route that can be depended on; the government being too poor to pay what it is worth to bring it in from Price's Station, their nearest railroad station. It is left to the Union Pacific railroad to send it in from Green River, 200 miles over a bad road and by an unreliable courier who makes the trip or not, just as he pleases. There is plenty of fine timber about forty miles from there, but the only sawmills the government has sent them [are] old and wornout ones, not worth the price of getting them into that country. One of them has already blown up, killing one man and injuring two others. The other is at a standstill, it too having broken down. The troops are still in tents. Had the quartermaster's department done its duty the men would have been in quarters by the end of October.

"As you may know, such a state of affairs could not last long without complaints being made by some one. A scapegoat for all this had to be found. Major Hall, 22d Infantry, the acting inspector general of the department, was sent out to inspect [?] and investigate [?]. He came there and stayed a few days, made no investigation whatever, that is he did not ask a single question of an officer or man, as far as the garrison has been able to find out. He returned to Omaha and, it is said, made a most disgraceful report against the commanding officer. He may have obtained his information from Mormon citizens on the road back, and anyone who has anything to do with Mormons knows them to be the biggest liars in the country, and to have their ill will is really a recommendation for an honest man.

"Were I in Major Benteen's place I would not rest until the

whole matter was thoroughly investigated, not by any whitewashing board but by an officer who is not dependent upon favors from department headquarters.

"What I have related," concluded the soldier, "covers the whole matter and if it will be the cause of stirring up a hornet's nest I feel that a duty has been performed toward my suffering comrades at Fort DuChesne."

Naturally, General George Crook the "department commander" alluded to, was furious. He appended a second charge to Benteen's account: "conduct unbecoming an officer and gentleman" and listed as its specification the alleged brawl at the Post Trader's on 11 November. On 7 January 1887, just four days after the article appeared, Crook promulgated Special Orders #2, appointing a court-martial at Fort DuChesne to meet 7 February and try Major Frederick W. Benteen, 9th Cavalry, on two charges: being "found drunk" on six specific occasions and "conduct unbecoming an officer and gentleman" on one occasion. The semi-official offer of a six month leave of absence, never committed to writing, was withdrawn. On 16 January 1887, Colonel Hatch placed Major Benteen under arrest and read the charges to him.

Coincidently, in mid-January, Major Thaddeus Stanton confided to a young lieutenant in the 9th Cavalry named Eugene F. Ladd that George Jewett would not remain at Fort DuChesne so long as Benteen was commanding officer. This remarkable announcement was relayed to Benteen by Ladd at once. (On 30 May 1888, Ladd married Violet Norman, which might account for the rapidity with which the Stanton disclosure got to Benteen's ear.)

On 7 February 1887, ten officers sat on a board at Fort DuChesne to hear the evidence in Benteen's case. The senior officer present (thus, *president* of the board) was Colonel August V. Kautz of the 8th Infantry, a West Point classmate of General Crook's. (Kautz had commanded a cavalry division during the Civil War that included among its officers two men who served with Benteen in the 7th Cavalry: Albert Barnitz and Robert West.) The other full colonel on the board was John Gibbon's replacement as commanding officer of the 7th Infantry: Colonel Henry C. Merriam. There were three lieutenant colonels and five majors. A sixth major, Alfred T. Smith of the 7th Infantry, had been assigned but never showed up, being sick at Fort Douglas. The Judge Advocate (equivalent of prosecutor) was a trained lawyer: Captain Allan H. Jackson of the 7th Infantry.

Benteen's defense counsel was his own adjutant, Lieutenant Harry L. Bailey.

The court met briefly the first day and retired without commencing the trial due to fatigue of some of the members after an arduous trip to the post. The next day, 8 February 1887, the challenging for cause began. (Both Judge Advocate and defense counsel were permitted unlimited challenges to the seating of board members on grounds of demonstrated prejudice or similar unfitness to hear a case objectively.) Benteen challenged all of the members *en masse*, submitting a curious document called the "Challenge to the Array" in which he laid out his version of the events leading up to his court-martial. He introduced the Kansas City *Times* article in evidence, swearing: "By all that is holy! that I know or knew no more about this publication, or of the author of the same, than you do — or General Crook."

Benteen's wording of the disavowal was odd. Some have pointed to the statement as a denial of having had anything to do with the article that angered Crook. Benteen, very carefully, did not say that. On the contrary, there was (and still is) every reason to believe that Benteen was the guiding hand in the appearance of the article. The internal evidence (idocyncracies of phraseology and opinions colorfully expressed) suggest very strongly that Benteen had something to do with (at least) a draft of the information contained in the article. Furthermore, his own granddaughter (Anita Mitchell) admitted many years later that Benteen had written a letter to someone and that as a result of his having written this letter, he was court-martialed. She was "not sure how" the alleged letter related to the court-martial, but was positive that he had written one. Benteen had a history of tackling problems in an indirect manner and blowing off steam in a way that would cause his fulminations to embarrass the object of his scorn. The Kansas City *Times* article, like the Missouri *Democrat* letter that DeGress had published in 1869, apparently caused Benteen little personal embarrassment, but left a despised superior an object of public ridicule.

There is no absolute proof, naturally, but given the statements and the fact situation in 1886, the probable explanation of the article's publication is this: sometime after his relief by Colonel Hatch, amidst the rumors and post gossip about his fate, Benteen sent a letter to someone at or near Fort Leavenworth. This second party showed or gave the letter to a third party (possibly a newspaper reporter

Benteen did not know). The third party then wrote the article, taking large chunks of Benteen's comments and quoting them almost verbatim. (The most likely candidate for Benteen's conduit at Leavenworth is Captain Francis Moore of L Troop, 9th Cavalry, an associate of Benteen's at New York in 1882-1883, at Fort Riley in 1883, and Fort McKinney in 1885-1886. Moore, a Scottish-born former enlisted man, was certainly not the only person at Leavenworth who could have passed on Benteen's remarks, as Benteen had been at Fort Leavenworth himself as recently as 1883 and knew many of the officers, active and retired, who lived there.)

Benteen got the article introduced into the record of proceedings. The reviewers of the court-martial (the outcome of which was a forgone conclusion) would have what Benteen jocularly called a "Phat item" to inspect. General Sheridan would be one of the reviewers. Benteen was careful not to deny any complicity in the article. On the other hand, once he had introduced the article and his recitation of the events resulting from it as evidence of Crook's duplicity, he could not very well sabotage his own case by admitting any hand in authorship.

The court-martial board recorded no comment about the article, comments not being required of them. They did not attempt to prove or disprove Benteen's disavowal (such as it was) as the article was, strictly speaking, irrelevant to the issue of Benteen's alleged transgressions. They did reject the "Challenge to the Array," however, and proceeded with the court-martial. Benteen then challenged most of the board members individually. The board sustained his objection to the presence of Lieutenant Colonel Joshua S. Fletcher of the 2nd Infantry on grounds of prejudice, apparently accepting Benteen's contention that "some time ago I had a disagreement with him." The nature of the disagreement, stemming from an 1872 Nashville incident, was never specified, but the board excused Colonel Fletcher from hearing the case. They rejected all of Benteen's other challenges and proceeded to hear the charges. There were two: "drunk on duty, in violation of the 38th Article of War" and "conduct unbecoming an officer and gentleman." The acts of drunkeness specified were: 25 September, 27 September, 10 October, 10 November, 11 November, and 12 November. Benteen pleaded not guilty to all six specifications. The specification for the "conduct unbecoming an officer and gentleman" was this: "[Benteen] did, when in command of the Post of Fort DuChesne, Utah, conduct himself in a scandalous manner, in the post trader's store — using obscene and profane language; taking off his clothes, to quarrel with citizens, and exposing his person. This, to the dishonor and disrepute of the military service at Fort DuChesne, Utah, on or about the eleventh day of November, 1886." Benteen pleaded not guilty.

Captain Jackson, the Judge Advocate, introduced eleven witnesses for the prosecution in nine days. Lieutenant Bailey, for the defense, called ten witnesses in five days. On the 12th day (19 February 1887), Benteen suddenly introduced an enlisted man who had overheard one of the board members discussing the case with a witness for the prosecution, saying that he would "do all I could" in response to a question from the witness. Benteen wanted the board member, Major Andrew S. Burt of the 8th Infantry, thrown off the board for demonstrated prejudice. Major Burt took the witness stand and made a rather impassioned denial of any prejudicial remarks, insisting that he bore Benteen no ill will and that the remark overheard was not related to Benteen or his case at all. The court-martial board met in private and decided to disallow Benteen's mid-trial challenge. Major Burt remained on the board.

The record of proceedings, a public document today, showed that Benteen was "found drunk" in the opinion of three other officers on two of the occasions specified. The officers were noticeably reluctant to testify against Benteen and limited their remarks to assertions that he was, in their opinion, drunk on 25 September and 10 October 1886. Captain Olmsted's tale of the tent-pissing episode was drawn out on *cross* examination by Benteen himself. Even Olmsted insisted (rather forcefully) that he was Benteen's "warm personal friend." He went on to assure the court that he had "had the remark sneeringly made" of him that he was "a Benteen man" and that he had come "very nearly getting into serious trouble with an officer of this regiment because I took his part" in an unrelated episode.

Benteen attempted unsuccessfully to impeach Captain Olmsted. He was equally unsuccessful in impeaching the civilian witnesses against him, though his questions (consistently objected to by Captain Jackson and disallowed by the court) raised serious questions about the validity of the testimony given against him by the civilians.

Benteen took over his own defense on several occasions and earned objections not only from the Judge Advocate but also from members of the court for his flamboyant conduct. The cross examination of Dr. Benham, the post surgeon, was especially acrimonious. Benteen's somewhat caustic questions were objected to no less than eight times in the course of one afternoon. He was sustained, however, when he objected to Captain Jackson's questioning of John Vanderhoef on the grounds that Vanderhoef was testifying about allegations of drunkeness at times not specified in the charges. Benteen's strategy, though not exactly clear, seems to have been to impeach the testimony of as many of the witnesses against him as he could by bringing to the court's attention evidence of George Jewett's interest in the prosecution of the case. For the most part, Colonel Kautz and the other members of the board rejected testimony about Jewett and his alleged conversations with witnesses as irrelevant.

Benteen brought in three civilian witnesses, two of whom testified that Lycurgus Johnson and Sheriff Sterling Cotton (who had given the most damning evidence about the 11 November episode) were notoriously dishonest. Pressed for specifics, they related events that had happened in the past or that they had heard of. Captain Jackson objected to further testimony of this nature on grounds that it was hearsay. His objection was sustained by the court. Benteen then brought Lieutenant Ladd in to try and impeach Captain Olmsted's and Dr. Benham's testimony. Captain Jackson objected strenuously — six times in all — and Ladd's testimony was confined to what he had seen or heard on the six dates specified.

Perhaps Benteen's strongest potential witness was Lieutenant Burnett, his drinking buddy. Burnett was never called. On the 16th day of the trial (24 February 1887), Benteen abruptly folded. He introduced in evidence an order he had written when allegedly drunk and remarked casually: "Lieut. Burnett came to me just as I was coming to the Court, but I have told him that as I had already summed up my defense, I should not call him." He then proceeded to read his summation, a remarkable document called "Exhibit H," which is perhaps the closest thing to an autobiography Benteen ever wrote.

The first fourth of the document was Benteen's summation of the facts of the case and a brief on what the evidence presented had shown. The remainder of the forty or more pages was devoted to a recitation of his military career from 1861 through the battle of Canyon Creek in 1877. He included virtually every citation and mention in official reports he had earned over the years. (The object of this particular maneuver was not for the benefit of future historians; it was to place matters into the record that might persuade reviewers to mitigate any sentence recommended by the court.) Benteen dwelt at great length on his Civil War career and stressed the fact that his service in the Union Army had alienated him from his own father and had effectively split the Benteen household. His conclusion about the Civil War and its effect on his family was especially poignant. "Though the side for which I spilt my blood was victorious," he wrote in Exhibit H, "there was nothing left for my immediate family, but a harvest of barren regrets."

His theme was that his troubles at Fort DuChesne were caused not by drunkeness but by virtue of the fact that he was, as he put it, "too deucedly sober" in guarding the public interest against the schemes of George Jewett and his ilk. He concluded with a flourish. "I am free to confess," he said,

> that the building of a Post without lumber, nails or other materials, was just a trifle too much for me. I am not up to the trick! Nor am I up to the trick of being subservient to Paymasters and Sutlers, notwithstanding whose faithful friends they may be. A quarter of a century's service in glorious war, and this [is] the first time that any fault has been found with me, or charges have been preferred against me; during those 25 years I have striven to write my life in letters of light, with my sabre's point, on the scroll of my country's history, where my forefathers had inscribed the history of their lives, with the same kind of Graver. And now, at the age of 53 years, with my locks snowy white, gotten in the service of my country, it is just a little severe to be court-martialed for not falling into line with a Post Trader & Contractor.

Captain Jackson, the Judge Advocate, was taken aback by the sudden collapse of Benteen's defense and requested an adjournment until the following day to be given time to prepare his own summation. On Friday, 25 February 1887, Captain Jackson read a short brief to the court outlining the testimony given that, in his view, proved the government's case. He depicted the testimony relevant to the controversial brawl on 11 November as "of an overwhelming character and virtually opposed by nothing beyond an effort to invalidate the testimony" of the three civilian witnesses. Dealing with the charge of "conduct unbecoming an officer and gentleman", Jackson concluded: "It is for the Court to determine how far this remarkable details of conduct, abusive and sometimes obscene language, of the accused, are inconsistent with conduct that should characterize an officer and gentleman." He conceded that Benteen had presented "a brilliant history in the past replete with flowing records of soldierly achievement," but insisted that it only served to "dull the perception of other qualities which mar an example otherwise well worthy of imitation."

Colonel Kautz and the board members cleared the court and deliberated. They returned a verdict that same day. Benteen was found guilty on three of the six specifications of drunkeness: 25 September, 10 October, and 11 November. The other three specifications were rejected. The board also found Benteen guilty of conduct unbecoming an officer on 11 November, apparently accepting the testimony of the civilian witnesses. They did modify the specification somewhat. They struck out the words "and exposing his person," as the testimony had not borne out any evidence that Benteen had exposed himself. They passed sentence in accordance with the law. "The Court does therefore sentence him, Major Frederick W. Benteen, 9th U.S. Cavalry, to be dismissed from the United States Service." They adjourned at 2:00 p.m. 25 February 1887.

On 9 March 1887, Benteen journeyed to Fort Douglas (Salt Lake City) to await the inevitable review process as a guest of an old associate from the Ft. Lincoln days, Captain Stephen Baker of the 6th Infantry. Kate and Vi remained at DuChesne, where Colonel Hatch was in the throes of turning over command to Benteen's successor, Major James F. Randlett. The commanding officer at Ft. Douglas (and Benteen's "jailor") was Lieutenant Colonel Nathan Osborne, a member of the court-martial board. Benteen found others at Douglas who agreed with his assessment of Osborne as "a conceited kind of a pup — and a numbskull to boot."

On 11 March, General Crook endorsed the court-martial findings and forwarded them up the chain of command. He recommended that if clemency was to be extended to Major Benteen on account of his past record that "he receive some discipline for his insubordination and disrespectful language, and his unsoldierlike conduct, as shown in these proceedings, indicating, as they do, that he is sadly in need of such discipline."

On 9 April, General Sheridan endorsed the findings, merely recommending "remission of the sentence" for "reasons given in the record of his services."

On 20 April, President Grover Cleveland approved the findings, but mitigated the sentence of dismissal to one of suspension from rank and duty for one year at half pay, "in view of his long and honorable service and the reputation he has earned for bravery and soldierly qualities."

On 27 May, Major Benteen was notified of the modified sentence. The next day, he re-joined Kate and Vi at DuChesne. As early as 11 May he had written to Kate and talked of using a vacant set of officers quarters as a "base of operations for summer tours." The trio spent the summer "visiting" Fort DuChesne while Benteen applied for permission to spend the balance of his sentence outside the Department of the Platte, specifically at home in Atlanta, Georgia. On 16 September 1887, Benteen left DuChesne for the last time to undergo his year-at-½-pay in Atlanta. The enforced vacation gave him some time to look his property over carefully and take stock. He concluded that "it cost $10,000 more than my pay came to" through neglect of his property over the years. (He made it clear later that he did not regard the farm as being nearly as valuable as the land itself — "city blocks in prospective," he called it.) His son, Freddie, was inclined to follow in his footsteps as an Army officer. Kate expressed a desire to see Freddie appointed an officer. Major Benteen rejected the idea, but kept the issue alive for ten years — until it was too late (by Army regulations) to commission Freddie.

In April 1888, George Crook was promoted to major general and assigned to the Division of the Missouri headquarters in Chicago. His replacement was Brigadier General John R. Brooke, who had not joined when Benteen reported to Omaha on 17 April 1888. He spent the first three days undergoing a medical examination and complained to his wife that the examining doctor had "been testing my urine, shoving his fingers up my rectum, testing my eyes, and working about all of the pranks on me that he knew of."

He was informed that he was "booked" for Fort Robinson, Nebraska, where Colonel Hatch was commanding. He fought the assignment bitterly — and succeeded in getting assigned to Fort Niobrara instead. He told Captain Godfrey a few years later that "rather than stay with the crowd Hatch of 9th Cav. kept around him, I would have resigned outright." He told his wife upon receipt of the good news: "In getting away from Hatch all thought I had achieved a victory and my friends in Omaha were pleased at my having effected it."

Benteen arrived at Valentine, Nebraska 26 April 1888. Fort Niobrara, four miles east of Valentine, had been established in 1880 to keep an eye on the Sioux Indians at the Rosebud Agency just north of the fort. The commanding officer was Colonel August V. "Dutch" Kautz, the same man who had been president of Benteen's court-martial board. When Benteen arrived at the post, he found that Kautz

was absent, but that he knew many of the officers assigned there anyway. Two troops of the 9th Cavalry were assigned there — A and G
Troops, commanded by Captains Michael Cooney and Patrick Cusack
respectively. There were also six companies of Kautz's 8th Infantry
on the post. One of the post surgeons, Dr. Julian Cabell, was a Virginian and an old acquaintance of Dr. J.R. Kean's.

The weather in northern Nebraska that spring was particularly
bad. It rained or sleeted for the first week of Benteen's stay. He reported that he has met "with an unusually warm reception" and
assured Kate that he would have no difficulty getting along with the
officers at Niobrara. His physical condition had not improved. He
reported sick on 30 April and remained on the post returns as "sick
in quarters" during his stay there. He feared for a time that he had
Bright's disease, but the doctors, while mystified as to the cause of
his ailment, assured him that there was nothing wrong with his kid-
neys. He underwent frequent medical examinations, trying to determine the cause of an aching back and frequent urination.

By May 1888, he was convinced that he would be permitted to
appear before a medical retirement board at Fort Leavenworth, a
board of which Brigadier General Wesley Merritt was president. He
reassured Kate that there was no danger that he would take "the
step alluded to" (probably outright resignation).

In one of his letters to his wife at this point in his life, he brought
up the subject of Freddie's future. He hinted that he was interested
in setting Freddie up in the hardware business. He rejected Kate's
idea that his son become an Army officer. "I couldn't afford to let his
mother have her way and fix him up for the army," he explained
to Captain Godfrey, "as the army wouldn't have been any the gainer
to speak of; and the loss would have been Fred's." He admitted that
Freddie's own desires were for a military career, but, as he told
another correspondent, "he will be very well off in this world's goods
at no very remote date" and wondered "why should his life be wasted
in Army cliques?"

He regretted that the delay in obtaining a medical discharge would
prevent him from attending Violet Norman's 30 May wedding to Lieutenant Eugene F. Ladd. Both he and Kate regarded Violet as a daughter and were anxious that she "feel less dependent" on them. "The poor
girl, I fear," Benteen confided to his wife, "will not stand the strains
of wedded life very well."

On 3 June 1888, he received his orders to report to Fort Leavenworth to appear before a Medical Retiring Board. He arrived at Leavenworth on 10 June and began another round of examinations. On 27 June 1888, the board reported its findings. Major Frederick W. Benteen was: "incapacitated for active service because of defective vision, frequent micturition caused by either spinal lesion and inflamation of the prostate gland and neuralgia; all of which are incident to the service."

The paperwork for a medical discharge took almost a month. On 7 July 1888, Frederick William Benteen ceased to be an active officer of the U.S. Army.

26

The Final Atlanta Years

The Benteens spent the first four years of their retirement on the farm just outside Atlanta. In the summer of 1892, they took up residence in a town house they had purchased at 39 Pavilion Street overlooking Grant Park. Major Benteen, who was known as "Colonel" Benteen locally (because of his brevet rank) frequently spent the weekends alone on his farm while Kate enjoyed the amenities of civilized (and progressive) Atlanta of the 1890s.

It was during the retirement years that Benteen commenced correspondence with many old acquaintances. Two groups of letters survive to this day. Between the fall of 1891 and the summer of 1896, he kept a faithful correspondence with a former enlisted man named Theodore W. Goldin of Janesville, Wisconsin. There are some gaps in the letters to Goldin, but most have been preserved. Goldin, a lawyer, politician, and general gadabout, had briefly been a private in G Company in 1876 and 1877. His parents had secured his discharge on a complaint that he was underage and he returned to his native Wisconsin where he eventually became the Chairman of the (State) Republican Central Committee and a colonel in the Wisconsin National Guard. Goldin, who had apparently deceived Benteen into believing that he had served five years in the cavalry, was engaged in writing articles dealing with the history of the 7th Cavalry. Benteen generously supplied him with tidbits from his own recollections that make fascinating reading today.

For ten years, Benteen kept up a sporadic correspondence with D.F. Barry, the noted frontier photographer. Barry frequently donated pictures to Benteen, apparently in an effort to drum up business. The letters to Barry were not as informative as the letters to Goldin, but are just as fascinating to read. (Both the Goldin and Barry letters have been published in fairly recent times.)

Benteen found time to write some recollections of cavalry service and apparently intended these writings for publication. His closest friend in retirement was Joseph van Holt Nash, after 1894 the president of the American Book Company in Atlanta. With one possible exception, none of Benteen's writings were published during his lifetime. (They have since been incorporated into a book edited by John M. Carroll entitled *Cavalry Scraps.*)

The Benteens were not considered socially prominent. In fact, the husband of one of his granddaughters asserted that Benteen himself was regarded by many of the old families as little more than a carpetbagger. He was, however, welcomed into the homes of many prominent people. He became acquainted with the author Joel Chandler Harris and was a friend of the Candler brothers who founded the Coca-Cola Bottling Company in 1892. In fact, Judge John S. Candler was young Freddie's superior in the Georgia militia. Benteen was well acquainted with the mayor of Atlanta, the governor of Georgia, and prominent men such as Lowndes Calhoun, Joseph Jacobs, Sam Wilkes, and Charles S. Arnall.

On 27 February 1890 the Senate approved awards of brevets for gallantry in action against Indians, awards that had been frozen since March of 1869. The Army submitted 144 names, one of which was Benteen's. In April of 1892, Benteen was informed that he had been nominated for a brevet as Brigadier General USA for gallant and meritorious services at the Little Big Horn and Canyon Creek. (He was the only officer ever brevetted for the Little Big Horn.) On 28 May 1894, he wrote his letter of acceptance. He was not especially overjoyed, telling Goldin: "after 19 years of waiting, the U.S. had showered upon me, drenched me with the Bvt. of Brig. Gen'l for the Little Big Horn and Canyon Creek. *Same to Col. Merrill.*" Nevertheless, he posed for pictures in a general's uniform and signed his name as "Bvt. Brig. Gen'l. Benteen.

Freddie was his pre-eminent concern. The younger Fred Benteen had occasional illnesses and accidents, apparently no more than the average young man, but Benteen made note of each accident. On one occasion, commenting on Freddie's bout with the flu, he observed: "his mother is perhaps unduly excited as regards his condition. . . Women, as a rule arriving at facts intuitively or instinctively that we men have to get at through slow logic. . . As the mother has lost four children in touring around the continent, following the music of the cavalry trumpet, she of course clings the more tenaciously to this lone chick of ours — and he is a good son, and a good cavalryman, too."

In the fall of 1894, Freddie had an accident with a mowing machine and was months recovering from it. His father tried to sound nonchalant, but his anxiety is clear to even the casual reader of his comments on the accident. In the spring of 1895, a woman carriage driver slammed into a milk wagon driven by Freddie. The woman sued for $10,000. Benteen stalled her in court for three years, eventually settling out of court for $100, against the advice of his attorney. He claimed that he did not want to trouble Freddie about the matter any longer and, as he put it, "threw the $100 to the dog."

He commented freely in private correspondence about many of the officers with whom he had been associated in his twenty-six year Army career, especially Custer. But, though he wrote several small articles intended for publication, he kept his censurious comments out of them. He refused to talk to reporters about the battle of the Little Big Horn and fought shy of them as a general rule. From the perspective of retirement, he saw his cavalry service in softer lights. "Those were pretty rollicking gay days," he said on one occasion, "I don't regret a day I spent in the saddle."

One day in March 1896 he was entertained by a battalion of the 5th Infantry marching past his town house. The adjutant of the battalion hurried to 39 Pavilion Street to tell the 61-year-old Major Benteen that the soldiers had been instructed to give him a marching salute as they passed by. Benteen stepped outside, took the salute, and doffed his hat. "It does rather brace one up to see again a lot of jaunty, well-set-up soldiers," he said.

About a week later, William H.C. Bowen approached Benteen and asked for some particulars on the battle of the Little Big Horn that he might incorporate into an object lesson for officers and men of the 5th Infantry stationed at nearby Fort McPherson. Bowen was a captain in the 5th Infantry and had known Benteen for years. (He was the same Bowen whose company provided an escort to the guests at the 10th Anniversary ceremonies in 1886 near Fort Custer.) Benteen gave Bowen some pointers, but when invited to hear the lecture, refused, claiming that he had promised to take Kate and some family friends to see the famous actor Roland Reed in "The Woman Hater."

Captain Bowen then repeated the lecture in a church, offering the Benteens a reserved box. Benteen could hardly refuse. He went, placed three ladies in the box reserved for him, and, leaving his wife behind as chaperone, hid among the pillars in the rear of the auditorium. (Though never stated, he seems to have been in dread of being pointed out in the crowd by the speaker.) His review of the lecture was devastating. Bowen, he growled, could "not command good English"; the lecture, "pretty twaddy and uninteresting"; the slide show that accompanied the lecture, "pretty near the ludicrous." Benteen got riled up about the lecture. He told three of Captain Bowen's friends to discourage Bowen "from making a further damned fool of himself." He was incensed that Bowen had collected $100 for the church talk and was planning a third lecture at the Grand Theater. "I think the dummy is spieling for a position on the staff of General Miles," he said. (Nelson A. Miles, in 1895, had succeeded John M. Schofield as commanding general of the Army. Schofield had replaced Sheridan in the fall of 1888. Benteen knew all three generals well.) He was so angry at Captain Bowen that he was spurred into writing the only defense of Custer that can be found in his handwriting. "The lecture abounded in compliments to me," he explained to Theo Goldin, "but really, Colonel, I'm out of that whirlpool now; 'tis a dead, dead issue — stale, flat & c., and I do not want a doughboy to speak in any but respectful manner of a dead cavalryman." He accused Bowen of persisting with the lectures merely to make money or finagle a plush staff assignment. Since Bowen never saw Custer or Reno, Benteen insisted, he had no right to berate them. Furthermore, in Benteen's opinion, Bowen "in a measure of brain" was "incompetent to judge the worth of either of them."

But the passage of time did not mellow his feelings toward Custer. If anything, time merely intensified his feelings. He mentioned George Crook only once in his writings after retirement. He refused to alter his opinion of Nelson Miles even after Miles had become the highest ranking general in the Army. "Gen. Miles would have been a grand, strong friend of mine if I'd let him be," he said, "this I know absolutely from intimates of [Miles]," whom Benteen epitomized as "too much circus, too little brain!"

Benteen had long been noted for his mocking, picturesque manner of speaking. In cold print, without the benefit of his round red face beaming, his eyes twinkling, and his lips pursed in an ironic smile, the words seem harsh and vindictive. Many of his remarks were made tongue-in-cheek to an extent; some were not. He did not seem to mind that he was considered abrasive. "I've been a loser in a way, all my life," he said once, "by rubbing a bit against the angles — or hair — of folks, instead of going with their whims; but I couldn't go otherwise — 'twould be against the grain of myself."

Benteen's old first lieutenant, Frank Gibson, had retired from the 7th Cavalry as a captain in 1891 for medical reasons. Gibson got a job in the New York City Street Cleaning Department supervising the stables. Gibson's boss was George E. Waring, the same man who had commanded the 4th Missouri Cavalry during the Civil War and who had commanded Benteen on the scout from Batesville in 1862. Benteen pointed this out to D.F. Barry, attempting to help the younger man establish himself in New York as a photographer. He also gave Barry the names of other old associates who might help him drum up business.

Occasionally, the newspapers would pick up a story related to the 7th Cavalry history. Benteen commented on most that were brought to his attention. He kept in contact with several of his old associates and regularly kept abreast of the activities of the 7th. Even after an absence of more than ten years from the regiment, he still decorated his signature with crossed sabers and the numeral "7." He kept up a steady correspondence with the adjutant of the 7th in the 1890s: Lieutenant J. Franklin Bell. When he was awarded the brevet of brigadier general, he observed rather sourly that only John Gresham had bothered to write him congratulations. Once, the New York papers published a colorful account of a Sioux warrior named Rain-In-the-Face, who had been quoted as saying that he had killed Captain Tom Custer, cut out his heart, and eaten it. Benteen was solicited for an expert opinion. He began by asserting that few white men could speak Lakota well enough to translate accurately and allowed that if the translation in Rain-In-the-Face's case was correct, the Indian "must have been on his 'high horse' — and, lying like a Sioux!" Otherwise, he refused to comment on the accounts of the Little Big Horn that kept cropping up, "the game not being worth the candle," in his words.

He did not comment publicly on Edward Godfrey's famous 1892 account of the battle, though privately he was at his acrimonious best. Godfrey, he said, had "showed the white feather" along with three other officers at the Little Big Horn. "Godfrey," he asserted, "now that pretty near all of the old fellows have dropped out, intends to sound his horn a bit for the benefit of the bunch." He was especially disgusted that Godfrey had taken full credit for forming the skirmish line that had saved Weir, French, and their men on the retreat from the high point. "I sent word to Godfrey to hold his vantage point," he wrote in a private letter, "Godfrey can't remember the fact, though, now!"

On 24 May 1897, Benteen was visited by a reporter from the Atlanta *Journal*. He was very chary about talking to the man and gave little information. What he did give appeared in that evening's paper as "Brave Old Benteen: A Southern Federal." "There is nothing he dislikes more than publicity," the reporter wrote, "and if it were left to him none of his valorous deeds would be handed down to posterity." Still, according to the reporter, "General Benteen is very popular with newspaper men, though not for the stories he tells them. He doesn't talk about his experiences on the battlefield for publication." "The newspapers killed Custer," Benteen asserted in the course of an interview, "they puffed him up, and boosted him, and sang his praises to the skies until it ruined him."

Benteen got excited in the spring of 1898 as America went to war with Spain. He appeared to be anxious to have Spain taught a lesson and even went so far as to regale D.F. Barry with what he would have done "could I only have been President for a few days." He did an about-face on the subject of Freddie taking up a military career and seemed to be encouraging his son to go to war, or at least resigning himself to the notion that "there was no log-chain strong enough to hold him from it!" (Freddie *did* join the Army — after his father died. He was appointed a second lieutenant, though technically overage, by President McKinley who jocularly made Freddie swear he was twenty-seven — he was, in fact, thirty-two — and then seriously told him: "I'm going to give you a commission on the basis of your father's record." Freddie rose to the rank of lieutenant colonel, not retiring until the 1920s.)

Benteen himself never knew the outcome of the Spanish-American War. On Sunday, 17 June 1898, he came down with an especially virulent case of malarial fever that forced him into bed. The family doctor, Hunter P. Cooper, was summoned and concluded that the illness, though serious, was not life-threatening. Dr. Blair D. Taylor, then a major stationed at Fort McPherson, later asserted that Benteen did indeed recover from the fever. However, on 21 June, Benteen suffered a stroke that paralyzed one side and Dr. Cooper's prognosis was more grim. "Chances of his recovery were extremely slim," the newspapers later reported.

On Wednesday, 22 June 1898, shortly before 1:00 in the afternoon, Frederick William Benteen died.

In the last ten years of his life, he had ample time and opportunity to philosophize on life in general and on his own in particular. The seeds of fratricidal conflict sown in the Civil War, nourished by blood and hatred, had reaped a "harvest of barren regrets" for Benteen and his immediate family. "I fought for Old Glory and would do it again," he once said, "but I fought my own people." His post-war Army career was only slightly happier, marred by controversy he helped engender. Benteen was unquestionably disappointed, even embittered to an extent, but philosophical. Speaking of a researcher he had frustrated in a quest for information about the Little Big Horn, Benteen observed: "Where he hoped for pearls, got husks. Perhaps 'tis often so in everyone's life."

His funeral at St. Philip's Church on 25 June 1898 was well attended. The Reverend Albion W. Knight conducted the services which commenced at 4:00 o'clock. Kate and Freddie insisted that the military pallbearers, selected from officers serving at nearby Fort McPherson, relinquish their honor to several prominent men from the community until the procession reached Westview Cemetery. The honorary pallbearers included Georgia Governor William Y. Atkinson, Atlanta Mayor Charles P. Collier, Captain Charles S. Arnall, Judge John S. Candler, Dr. Amos Fox, Judge Lowndes Calhoun, Donald M. Bain, Joseph Jacobs, Robert Schmidt, Colonel Sam W. Wilkes, and Benteen's closest friend: Joseph Nash. At Westview, five lieutenant colonels took charge of the casket, aided by Benteen's old comrade from the Fort Rice days: (Major) Blair D. Taylor.

In November 1902, Benteen's body was moved to Arlington National Cemetery. Kate Benteen lived until 1906, spending most of her years as a widow with friends from the military service — especially her "adopted" daughter, Violet Norman Ladd. She was granted a widow's pension through the efforts of several of Benteen's old associates such as General James H. Wilson and Majors Ezra B. Fuller, Luther R. Hare, and Thomas M. McDougall. Freddie married, served 17 years in the Regular Army and another decade on active service as a "retired" officer. He had three daughters, none of whom ever saw their grandfather.

There are no monuments to Frederick William Benteen today. He remains as he lived: a rather obscure supporting actor who appeared briefly on center stage in a well-known American history drama and then quietly faded away. It was his misfortune to live largely unknown and to die largely misunderstood.

APPENDIX A

10th MISSOURI CAVALRY, 1862-1865

Colonel

Florence M. Cornyn	4 Dec 1862	killed 10 Aug 1863 by Lt Col Bowen
Andrew J. Alexander	22 Sept 1863	(never joined)

Lieutenant Colonel

William D. Bowen	(1 Oct 1861)	dismissed 14 Oct 1863 by GCM
Frederick W. *Benteen*	14 Feb 1864	mustered out 30 June 1865

Major

Thomas Hynes	4 Dec 1862	dismissed 28 May 1864 by GCM
Frederick W. *Benteen*	4 Dec 1862	prom. to Lt Col 14 Feb 1864
William H. Lusk	4 Dec 1862	mustered out 30 June 1865
Martin H. Williams	14 Feb 1864	tr. to 2 Mo Cav 26 June 1865
Frederick R. Neet	8 Aug 1864	mustered out 30 June 1865 as Capt

Adjutant (1Lt)

Jeremiah F. Young	(20 Aug 1862)	prom. to Capt 5 April 1864
John L. Walsh	30 April 1864	mustered out 30 June 1865

Regimental Quartermaster (1Lt)

Albert E. Hall	11 Dec 1862	resigned 9 July 1864
Robert Swain Jr.	3 Aug 1864	mustered out 30 June 1865

Commissary of Subsistence (1Lt)

Michael Ravold	11 Dec 1862	resigned 1 April 1864
Thomas B. Hunter	1 July 1864	mustered out 30 June 1865

Surgeon

Edward L. Feehan	6 Dec. 1862	dismissed 12 March 1864 by GCM
William L. Tollman	13 March 1864	mustered out 30 June 1865

Assistant Surgeon

William L. Tollman	(6 Sept 1862)	prom. to Surgeon 13 March 1864
Herman Elgass	10 Aug 1864	(commission not delivered)
James E. Marshall	10 Aug 1864	(commission declined)
James E. Ruley	8 Oct 1864	mustered out 30 June 1865

COMPANY A

Captain

John W. Stephens	(9 Oct 1861)	resigned 17 Dec 1862
William J. DeGress	18 Dec 1862	(commission declined)
Duncan McNicol	26 Dec 1862	died 15 Aug 1863 of disease
Peter Joyce	16 Aug 1863	mustered out 11 July 1865

1st Lieutenant

Charles A. Williams	(11 Oct 1862)	resigned 18 Dec 1862
Peter Joyce	23 Jan 1863	prom. to Capt 16 Aug 1863
Robert Swain Jr.	16 Nov 1863	apptd. RQM 3 Aug 1864
Edmond Bates Kanada	19 Sept 1864	prom. to Capt (D Co) 29 Nov 1864
William P. Edgar	29 Nov 1864	mustered out 30 June 1865

2nd Lieutenant

Henry Treece	26 Dec 1862	prom. to 1Lt (D Co) 10 Aug 1864
Edmond Bates Kanada	10 Aug 1864	prom. to 1Lt 19 Sept 1864

COMPANY B

Captain
Amos P. Curry	(1 Oct 1861)	mustered out 5 Aug 1864
William J. DeGress	26 Aug 1864	mustered out 30 June 1865

1st Lieutenant
E.S. Dickinson	(1 Aug 1861)	mustered out 9 Aug 1864
William J. DeGress	15 Aug 1864	prom. to Capt 26 Aug 1864
Samuel Pruitt	26 Aug 1864	mustered out 30 June 1865

2nd Lieutenant
Benjamin Joel	(3 Nov 1862)	prom. to 1Lt (C Co) 26 Dec 1862
Silas J. Whitcraft	26 Dec 1862	mustered out 5 Aug 1864
Samuel Pruitt	19 Aug 1864	prom. to 1Lt 26 Aug 1864

COMPANY C

Captain
Frederick W. *Benteen*	(1 Oct 1861)	prom. to Major 4 Dec 1862
Albert E. Hall	8 Dec 1862	(commission annulled 11 Dec 1862)
William J. DeGress	16 Dec 1862	(commission annulled 19 Dec 1862)
Daniel W. Ballou	26 Dec 1862	mustered out 5 Aug 1864
John B. Roe	23 Jan 1865	tr. to 2 Mo Cav 26 June 1865

1st Lieutenant
Daniel W. Ballou	(1 Oct 1861)	prom. to Capt 26 Dec 1862
Benjamin Joel	26 Dec 1862	mustered out 1 Aug 1864
Walter J. Cripps	10 Aug 1864	tr. to 2 Mo Cav 26 June 1865

2nd Lieutenant
John B. Roe	(24 Oct 1862)	prom. to 1Lt (H Co) 7 Dec 1864

COMPANY D

Captain
Martin H. Williams	(25 Sept 1861)	prom. to Major 14 Feb 1864
John Dysart	15 Feb 1864	resigned 20 June 1864
Edmond Bates Kanada	29 Nov 1864	tr. to 2 Mo Cav 26 June 1865

1st Lieutenant
Mortimer R. Flint	(25 Sept 1861)	tr. to 1 Ala Cav 19 Nov 1863
Henry Treece	10 Aug 1864	mustered out 30 June 1865

2nd Lieutenant
John Dysart	(8 Nov 1862)	prom. to Capt (D Co) 15 Feb 1864

COMPANY E

Captain
William H. Lusk	(1 Sept 1862)	prom. to Major 4 Dec 1862
Patrick Lanigan	26 Dec 1862	resigned 1 Aug 1863
H.C. McCullough	2 Aug 1863	mustered out 24 June 1865

1st Lieutenant
H.C. McCullough	(1 Sept 1862)	prom. to Capt 2 Aug 1863
Stephen Andreon	3 Aug 1863	mustered out 30 June 1865

2nd Lieutenant
Patrick Lanigan	(11 Oct 1862)	prom. to Capt 26 Dec 1862
Stephen Andreon	26 Dec 1862	prom. to 1Lt 3 Aug 1863

COMPANY F

Captain
Frederick R. Neet   8 Sept 1862   prom. to Major 8 Aug 1864

1st Lieutenant
Michael McDonald   8 Sept 1862   mustered out 22 June 1865

2nd Lieutenant
Van Buren Stoddard   8 Sept 1862   mustered out 22 June 1865

COMPANY G

Captain
Henry G. Bruns   10 Sept 1862   died 7 July 1863 of wounds
John Walsh Rice   8 July 1863   dismissed 12 Sept 1864 by GCM
John B. Moyer   28 Sept 1864   mustered out 24 June 1865

1st Lieutenant
John Walsh Rice   10 Sept 1862   prom. to Capt 8 July 1863
John B. Moyer   9 July 1863   prom. to Capt 28 Sept 1864
George P. Brill   28 Sept 1864   mustered out 24 June 1865

2nd Lieutenant
John B. Moyer   10 Sept 1862   prom. to 1Lt 9 July 1863
Joseph C. Huber   21 Dec 1863   (never joined)

COMPANY H

Captain
Patrick Naughton   13 Sept 1862   resigned 10 July 1864
Jerome T. Kelly   3 Dec 1864   mustered out 27 June 1865

1st Lieutenant
Horace Wilcox   13 Sept 1862   resigned 2 June 1863
Jerome T. Kelly   3 June 1863   prom. to Capt 3 Dec 1864
John B. Roe   7 Dec 1864   prom. to Capt (C Co) 23 Jan 1865
E.H. Ringgold   15 March 1865   (never joined)

2nd Lieutenant
Jerome T. Kelly   13 Sept 1862   prom. to 1Lt 3 June 1863
Miles Reilly   13 Nov 1863   mustered out 27 June 1865

COMPANY I

Captain
Robert B.M. McGlasson   20 Oct 1862   mustered out 30 June 1865

1st Lieutenant
Ferdinand Owen   22 Oct 1862   mustered out 30 June 1865

2nd Lieutenant
John S. Hazard   20 Oct 1862   tr. to Invalid Corps 25 Aug 1863
Martin C. Auld   25 May 1864   dismissed 29 May 1865 by GCM

COMPANY K

Captain
Sherman Underwood   20 Oct 1862   resigned 17 March 1864
Jeremiah F. Young   5 April 1864   mustered out 30 June 1865

1st Lieutenant
Elisha M. Jennings   20 Oct 1862   resigned 1 Feb 1864
Elisha Bedwell   21 June 1864   mustered out 30 June 1865

2nd Lieutenant
Nicholas B. Klaine   20 Oct 1862   resigned 14 May 1863

COMPANY L

Captain

Robert H. Ruhl	28 Oct 1862	resigned 22 July 1863
Charles F. Hinricks	1 Aug 1863	mustered out 30 June 1865

1st Lieutenant

Charles F. Hinricks	28 Oct 1862	prom. to Capt 1 Aug 1863
Jacob Greenwood	1 Aug 1863	dismissed 25 March 1864 by GCM; revised to hon. discharge 1 July
Leslie R. Norman	8 Aug 1864	resigned 23 May 1865

2nd Lieutenant

Jacob Greenwood	28 Oct 1862	prom. to 1Lt 1 Aug 1863

COMPANY M

Captain

David Cain	31 Oct 1862	dismissed 23 Nov 1864 by GCM
Thomas F. Hayden	23 Jan 1865	mustered out 30 June 1865

1st Lieutenant

Thomas F. Hayden	31 Oct 1862	prom. to Capt 23 Jan 1865
John A. Hayden	23 Jan 1865	mustered out 30 June 1865

2nd Lieutenant

Charles H. Barton	31 Oct 1862	dismissed 30 Aug 1863 by GCM
John A. Hayden	16 Nov 1863	prom. to 1Lt 23 Jan 1865

APPENDIX B

9th MISSOURI CAVALRY (October 1862)
Lt. Col. William D. Bowen

A Co.
Capt. John W. Stephens
1Lt. Edward Madison
 Charles A. Williams
2Lt. Lloyd D. Robinson

B Co.
Capt. Amos P. Curry
1Lt. E.S. Dickinson
2Lt. Benjamin Joel

C Co.
Capt. Frederick W. *Benteen*
1Lt. Daniel W. Ballou
2Lt. Edwin M. Emerson
 John B. Roe

D Co.
Capt. Martin H. Williams
1Lt. Mortimer R. Flint
2Lt. John Dysart

Adj: 1Lt. Daniel P. Parsons

Surgeon: Horace Newell

E Co.
Capt. Robert B.M. McGlasson
1Lt. Ferdinand Owen
2Lt. William J. DeGress
 John S. Hazard

F Co.
Capt. Sherman Underwood
1Lt. Elisha M. Jennings
2Lt. Nicholas B. Klaine

G Co.
Capt. John Ing
1Lt. Philip Florrich
2Lt. Henry Stephens
 Charles T. Hartman

H Co.
Capt. John D. Crabtree
1Lt. Francis M. Hyatt
2Lt. James E. Baker

Qm: 1Lt. Albert E. Hall

Asst. surgeon: D.H. Law

APPENDIX C

1st BATTALION, MISSOURI CAVALRY — 1861
(Subsequently known as BOWEN'S BATTALION)
Major William D. Bowen

A Co.
Capt. John W. Stephens
1Lt. Edward Madison
2Lt. Pierre F. Bushnell

B Co.
Capt. Stanford Ing
1Lt. E.S. Dickinson
2Lt. Amos P. Curry

Adj: 1Lt. Charles A. Williams

C Co.
Capt. Frederick W. *Benteen*
1Lt. Daniel W. Ballou
2Lt. Edwin M. Emerson

D Co.
Capt. Martin H. Williams
1Lt. Mortimer R. Flint
2Lt. John D. Crabtree

Qm: 1Lt. Milton Santee

Surgeon: D.H. Law

APPENDIX D

138th USCT (UNITED STATES COLORED TROOPS) INFANTRY — 1865
Colonel Frederick W. *Benteen*
Lt. Col. George Curkendall
Major John A. Pickler

A Co.
Capt. Hiram B. Bates
1Lt. Andrew S. Rush
2Lt. Lewis A. Berryhill

B Co.
Capt. Byron W. Worden
1Lt. Garrett V. Johnson
2Lt. Lewis J. Tucker

C Co.
Capt. John C. Gammill
1Lt. John H. Lawson
2Lt. William H. Page

D Co.
Capt. Willard Fales
1Lt. Joshua Shuey
2Lt. James P. Miller

E Co.
Capt. Joseph W.T. Deupree
1Lt. Alexander Collins
2Lt. Alpheus Picken

Adj: 1Lt. John L. Walsh

Surgeon: Thomas J. Maxwell

F Co.
Capt. Howard Shackelford
1Lt. Romaine S. Hough
2Lt. John C. Gristy

G Co.
Capt. William H.H. Rogers
1Lt. James W. Paxton
2Lt. William J. Garvin

H Co.
Capt. James L. Mathieson
1Lt. John A. Kirkpatrick
2Lt. John A. Roberts

I Co.
Capt. Dan W. Lyon
1Lt. John M. Ryan
2Lt. John C. Welch

K Co.
Capt. Albert L. Goslin
1Lt. John L. Brown
2Lt. Martin M. Mitchell

Qm: 1Lt. William W. Thompson

Asst. surgeon: Caleb Sweazey

APPENDIX E

THE ORIGINAL 7th CAVALRY (Organized 10 Sept. 1866)
(Fort Riley)

Colonel: (vacant)
Andrew J. Smith (arr. 26 Nov. 1866)

Lieutenant Colonel: (vacant)
George A. Custer (arr. 3 Nov. 1866)

Major: John W. Davidson, 2 Cav
Alfred Gibbs (arr. 6 Oct. 1866)

Major: (vacant)
Wickliffe Cooper (arr. 25 Feb. 1867)

Major: (vacant)
Joel H. Elliott (arr. 20 May 1867)

Adj: Capt. William H. Harrison, 2 Cav
17 Nov. 66: 2Lt. William W. Cooke
(see D Co.)
21 Feb. 67: 1Lt. Myles Moylan (arr. 20 Feb. 1867)

Rqm: 1Lt. Cyrus McC. Allen, 2 Cav
3 Dec. 66: 1Lt. Thomas W. Custer (see A Co.)
10 March 67: 1Lt. Thomas B. Weir (see RCS)

Rcs: (vacant)
24 Feb. 67: 1Lt. Thomas B. Weir (see H Co.)

A Co. (Organized 10 Sept. 1866; Riley)
Capt: Henry E. Noyes, 2 Cav
Louis McL. Hamilton (arr. 9 Jan. 1867)
1Lt: (vacant)
Thomas W. Custer (arr. 16 Nov. 1866)
2Lt: James N. McElroy, 2 Cav
10 March 67: William W. Cooke (see D Co.)

B Co. (Org. 10 Sept. 1866; to Lyon 27 Nov. 1866; to Dodge 26 April 1867)
Capt: (vacant)
William P. Robeson (arr. 14 Nov. 1866; resigned 8 June 1867)
William Thompson (arr. 28 April 1867)
1Lt: Oliver O.G. Robinson, 2 Cav ————
2Lt: Henry M. Bragg, 3 Cav ————

C Co. (Organized 10 Sept. 1866; to Lyon 27 Nov. 1866)
Capt: (vacant) ————
1Lt: Oliver O.G. Robinson, 2 Cav
Matthew Berry (arr. 16 Nov. 1866)
2Lt: (vacant) ————

D Co. (Organized 10 Sept. 1866; Riley)
Capt: (vacant) ————
1Lt: Elijah R. Wells 2 Cav
Samuel M. Robbins (arr. 9 Jan. 1867)
2Lt: (vacant)
William W. Cooke (arr. 16 Nov. 1866)

E Co. (Organized 10 Sept. 1866; to Fletcher 23 Oct. 1866; which became Hays 11 Nov. 1866)
Capt: (vacant)
Albert P. Morrow (arr. 11 Dec. 1866)
promoted to Maj. 9th Cav Apr. 1867
Edward Myers (arr. 22 May 1867)
1Lt: James N. Wheelan, 2 Cav ————
2Lt: (vacant)
David W. Wallingford (arr. 17 Jan. 1867)
Frank Y. Commagere (arr. 20 Feb. 1867)

F Co. (Organized 10 Sept. 1866; to Ellsworth 18 Oct. 1866; which
     became Harker 11 Nov. 1866)
Capt: Henry E. Noyes 2 Cav   —————
1Lt: (vacant)   —————
2Lt: (vacant)   Henry J. Nowlan (arr. 12 Dec. 1866)

G Co. (Organized 17 Sept. 1866; to Ellsworth 18 Oct. 1866; which
     became Harker 11 Nov. 1866)
Capt: Henry E. Noyes, 2 Cav   Albert Barnitz (arr. 21 Feb. 1867)
1Lt: (vacant)   —————
2Lt: (vacant)   Henry Jackson (arr. 4 Dec. 1866)

H Co. (Organized 17 Sept. 1866; Riley)
Capt: (vacant)   Frederick W. *Benteen* (arr. 29 Jan. 1867)
1Lt: Samuel Hildeburn, 3 Cav   Thomas B. Weir (arr. 19 Feb. 1867)
2Lt: James N. McElroy, 2 Cav   —————

I Co. Organized 30 Sept. 1866; to Wallace 30 Nov. 1866)
Capt: Henry E. Noyes, 2 Cav   Myles W. Keogh (arr. 16 Nov. 1866)
1Lt: (vacant)   —————
2Lt: (vacant)   James M. Bell (arr. 16 Jan. 1867)

K Co. (Organized 30 Sept. 1866; to Dodge 27 Nov. 1866)
Capt: (vacant)   Robert M. West (arr. 16 Nov. 1866)
1Lt: Cyrus McC. Allen, 2 Cav   —————
2Lt: (vacant)   Charles Brewster (arr. 1 Feb. 1867)

L Co. (Organized 30 Sept. 1866; to Morgan 31 Dec. 1866)
Capt: (vacant)   Michael V. Sheridan (arr. 26 Nov. 1866)
1Lt: Elijah R. Wells, 2 Cav   Lee P. Gillette (arr. 29 Dec. 1866)
      Cyrus McC. Allen, 2 Cav
2Lt: (vacant)   Henry H. Abell (arr. 7 Jan. 1867)

M Co. (Organized 22 Dec. 1866; Riley)
Capt: (vacant)   —————
1Lt: Elijah R. Wells, 2 Cav   Owen Hale (arr. 19 Dec. 1866)
2Lt: (vacant)   21 Feb. 1867: William W. Cooke (see
                                                    D & A Cos.)
                                               James T. Leavy (arr. 20 May 1867)

APPENDIX F

THE "HISTORIC" 7th CAVALRY REGIMENT
(May 1876 through January 1878)

Individuals present at major engagements during this period are indicated by the following abbreviations:

 LBH = Little Big Horn, 25-27 June 1876
 CC = Canyon Creek, 13 September 1877
 BP = Snake Creek in the Bear Paw Mts., 30 Sept.-5 Oct. 1877

Home stations of record appear in parenthesis after company designations; home station of regimental staff & headquarters was Ft. Abraham Lincoln, Dakota Terr.

Colonel: Samuel D. *Sturgis* — after 1 Oct. 1874 Superintendent of General Mounted Service Recruiting; joined regt. 18 Oct. 1876; CC (cmdg.)

Lieutenant Colonel: George A. *Custer* — killed 25 June 1876; LBH (cmdg)
 Elmer *Otis* — joined regt. 21 Feb. 1877; sick at Rice after 31 July 1877

Major: Joseph G. *Tilford* — leave of absence 28 Oct. 1875-27 Oct. 1876; DS cmdg Ft. Lincoln 2 May-22 Oct. 1877
 Lewis *Merrill* — DS at Philadelphia until 10 Feb. 1877; CC
 Marcus A. *Reno* — LBH; court-martialled 8 Mar. 1877; undergoing a 2-year suspension from 8 May 1877

Adjutant (1Lt): William W. *Cooke* — killed 25 June 1876; LBH
 George D. *Wallace* — relieved 6 June 1877 (see G Co.)
 Ernest A. *Garlington* — (see G Co.); CC

Quartermaster (1Lt): Henry J. *Nowlan* — (see I Co.)
 Winfield S. *Edgerly* — relieved 20 Oct. 1876; unassigned until 14 Nov. 1876; (see L Co.)
 Charles A. *Varnum* — (see A Co.); CC

A Company (Ft. Lincoln until Sept. 1876; Ft. Rice thereafter)
Captain: Myles *Moylan* — LBH; BP
1st Lieutenant: Algernon E. *Smith* — killed 25 June 1876 (TDY — cmdg E Co.); LBH
 Andrew H. *Nave* — rejoined regt from sick leave 22 Sept. 1876; DS at Ft. Lincoln after 2 May 1877
2nd Lieutenant: Charles A. *Varnum* — LBH
 Ezra B. *Fuller* — joined regt 26 Sept. 1876; CC (TDY — cmdg H Co.)
 William H. *Baldwin* — joined regt 4 Jan. 1878

B Company (Ft. Lincoln)
Captain: Thomas M. *McDougall* — LBH
1st Lieutenant: William T. *Craycroft* — rejoined regt from leave 28 Sept. 1876; DS at St. Paul after 2 May 1877
2nd Lieutenant: Benjamin H. *Hodgson* — killed 25 June 1876; LBH
 William W. *Robinson* Jr. — joined regt 20 Sept. 1876; transferred to F Co. 9 Oct. 1876
 William J. *Nicholson* — joined regt 18 Oct. 1876; transferred to G Co. 19 May 1877
 Thomas H. *Barry* — joined regt 15 Dec. 1877

C Company (Ft. Lincoln until Sept. 1876; Ft. Totten thereafter)
Captain: Thomas W. *Custer* — killed 25 June 1876; LBH
  Henry *Jackson* — rejoined regt 28 Sept. 1876 (from DS at Washington)
1st Lieutenant: James *Calhoun* — killed 25 June 1876 (TDY — cmdg L Co.); LBH
  Charles A. *Varnum* — made acting rqm 20 Oct. 1876
  Winfield S. *Edgerly* — transferred from L Co. in Jan. 1877
2nd Lieutenant: Henry M. *Harrington* — killed 25 June 1876; LBH
  George O. *Eaton* — never joined; transfer revoked 30 Sept. 1876
  Horatio G. *Sickel* Jr. — joined regt 1 Oct. 1876

D Company (Ft. Lincoln until Sept. 1876; Ft. Rice thereafter)
Captain: Thomas B. *Weir* — LBH; died 9 Dec. 1876 at New York
  Edward S. *Godfrey* — BP
1st Lieutenant: James M. *Bell* — (see F Co.)
  Edwin P. *Eckerson* — joined regt 30 July 1876; BP
2nd Lieutenant: Winfield S. *Edgerly* — LBH
  Daniel C. *Pearson* — never joined; transfer revoked 7 Nov. 1876
  Edwin P. *Brewer* — joined regt 19 Dec. 1876; CC (TDY — I Co.)

E Company (Ft. Lincoln)
Captain: Charles S. *Ilsley* — DS at Leavenworth (adc for Brig Gen John Pope)
  since 1869
1st Lieutenant: Charles C. *DeRudio* — LBH (TDY — A Co.); DS at Crow Agency
  2 Aug.-25 Oct. 1877
2nd Lieutenant: William van W. *Reily* — killed 25 June 1876 (TDY — F Co.); LBH
  Hugh L. *Scott* — joined regt 30 Sept. 1876; transferred to I Co. 6 Dec. 1876
  James D. *Mann* — joined regt 30 Dec. 1877

F Company (Ft. Lincoln until Nov. 1876; Ft. Abercrombie until April 1877; Ft. Lincoln)
Captain: George W.M. *Yates* — killed 25 June 1876; LBH
  James M. *Bell* — CC
1st Lieutenant: Henry *Jackson* — (see C Co.)
  William W. *Robinson* Jr. — transferred from B Co. 9 Oct. 1876;
  TDY — B Co. after 29 May 1877
2nd Lieutenant: Charles W. *Larned* — DS at West Point until 25 July 1876, when
  transferred to Military Academy staff
  Charles B. *Schofield* — never joined; transfer revoked 30 Sept. 1876
  Herbert J. *Slocum* — joined regt Nov. 1876; CC

G Company (Ft. Lincoln)
Captain: John E. *Tourtellotte* — DS at Washington (adc to Gen Sherman) since 1870
1st Lieutenant: Donald *McIntosh* — killed 25 June 1876; LBH
  Ernest A. *Garlington* — joined regt 1 Aug. 1876; made adj 6 June 1877
  George D. *Wallace* — transferred from adj 6 June 1877
2nd Lieutenant: George D. *Wallace* — LBH
  John W. *Wilkinson* — joined regt 10 Sept. 1876; promoted to 1Lt of
  L Company in Dec. 1876
  William J. *Nicholson* — transferred from B Co. 19 May 1877; CC

H Company (Ft. Rice)
Captain: Frederick W. *Benteen* — LBH; CC
1st Lieutenant: Francis M. *Gibson* — LBH; DS at Tongue River 12 Aug.-25 Oct. 1877
2nd Lieutenant: Ernest A. *Garlington* — never joined company (see G Co.)
  Albert J. *Russell* — joined regt 3 Oct. 1876; CC

I Company (Ft. Lincoln)
Captain: Myles W. *Keogh* — killed 25 June 1876; LBH
 Henry J. *Nowlan* — CC
1st Lieutenant: James E. *Porter* — killed 25 June 1876; LBH
 Luther R. *Hare* — CC (TDY — regimental engineer officer)
2nd Lieutenant: Andrew H. *Nave* — sick leave until 22 Sept. 1876; (see A Co.)
 George F. *Chase* — never joined; transfer revoked 16 Oct. 1876
 Hugh L. *Scott* — transferred from E Co. 6 Dec. 1876; TDY — E Co.
  4 Aug.-25 Oct. 1877

K Company (Ft. Lincoln)
Captain: Owen *Hale* — recruiting until Sept. 1876; killed 30 Sept. 1877; BP
 Edward G. *Mathey* — joined company 30 Dec. 1877
1st Lieutenant: Edward S. *Godfrey* — LBH
 Charles *Braden* — disabled; on limited duty (recruiting at St. Louis) 1874-79
2nd Lieutenant: Luther R. *Hare* — LBH
 Edwin P. *Andrus* — never joined; transfer revoked 30 Aug. 1876
 J. Williams *Biddle* — joined regt 28 Sept. 1876; killed 30 Sept. 1877; BP
 Heber M. *Creel* — joined regt 26 Dec. 1877

L Company (Ft. Lincoln)
Captain: Michael V. *Sheridan* — DS at Chicago (adc to Lt. Gen. Sheridan) since 1869
1st Lieutenant: Charles *Braden* — (see K Co.)
 Edward S. *Godfrey* — joined company 26 Sept. 1876; returned to K Co. 20 Oct. 1876
 Winfield S. *Edgerly* — joined company 14 Nov. 1876; transferred to C Co. in Jan. 1877
 John W. *Wilkinson* — transferred from G Co. in Jan. 1877; CC
2nd Lieutenant: Edwin P. *Eckerson* — never joined company; (see D Co.)
 Loyd S. *McCormick* — joined regt 10 Sept. 1876; returned sick to
  Ft. Lincoln 25 May 1877

M Company (Ft. Rice)
Captain: Thomas H. *French* — LBH; CC
1st Lieutenant: Edward G. *Mathey* — LBH; leave 25 Oct. 1876-25 May 1877; "absent
  without leave" until 21 Sept. 1877; (see K Co.)
 Ezra B. *Fuller* — joined company 2 Jan. 1878
2nd Lieutenant: James G. *Sturgis* — killed 25 June 1876 (TDY — E Co.); LBH
 John C. *Gresham* — joined regt 21 Sept. 1876; CC

APPENDIX G

BENTEEN'S 9th CAVALRY, 1883-1888

Colonel: Edward Hatch   (regtl. hdqs: Fts. Riley, McKinney, Robinson)

Lt. Col.
Nathan A.M. Dudley
James S. Brisbin

Adjutants
1Lt. Clarence A. Stedman
John F. Guilfoyle
Joseph Garrard

Majors
1) Guy V. Henry
2) Thomas B. DeWees (d. 5 July 1886)
3) Frederick W. *Benteen* (Riley, Sill,
    McKinney, DuChesne)
   James F. Randlett
   Adna R. Chaffee (FWB's replacement,
    1888)

Quartermasters
1Lt. Millard F. Goodwin
Charles W. Taylor

A Trp. (Elliott, Niobrara)
Capt. Michael Cooney
1Lt. John Conline
John F. McBlain
2Lt. Matthias W. Day
Gonzalez S. Bingham

B Trp. (Hays, McKinney,
    Robinson, DuChesne)
Capt. Byron Dawson
1Lt. Martin B. Hughes
George R. Burnett
2Lt. Alton H. Budlong
Eugene F. Ladd

C Trp. (Sill, Robinson,
    DuChesne)
Capt. Charles D. Beyer
Gustavus Valois
John Conline
1Lt. Ballard S. Humphrey
2Lt. Philip P. Powell
Edmund S. Wright

D Trp. (Riley, McKinney)
Capt. John S. Loud
1Lt. John F. Guilfoyle
Philip P. Powell
2Lt. George R. Burnett
James H. Benton

E Trp. (Lyon, Riley, McKinney,
    Washakie, DuChesne)
Capt. J.A. Olmsted
1Lt. Frank Beers Taylor
Montgomery D. Parker
2Lt. Robert T. Emmet
Eugene F. Ladd
Harry G. Trout

F Trp. (Reno, Robinson)
Capt. Henry Carroll
Clarence A. Stedman
1Lt. David J. Gibbon
John F. Guilfoyle
2Lt. Charles W. Taylor
William McAnany

G Trp. (Sill, Niobrara)
Capt. John M. Bacon
Patrick Cusack
1Lt. Patrick Cusack
Robert T. Emmet
2Lt. Walter L. Finley
Grote Hutcheson

H Trp. (Riley, McKinney)
Capt. George A. Purington
Eugene D. Dimmick
1Lt. Thomas C. Davenport
David J. Gibbon
2Lt. John H. Gardner

I Trp. (Reno, Niobrara,
    Robinson)
Capt. Frank T. Bennett
    Martin B. Hughes
1Lt. Jerrauld A. Olmsted
    Matthias W. Day
2Lt. Charles J. Stephens

K Trp. (Supply, Robinson)
Capt. Charles Parker
1Lt. Henry H. Wright
2Lt. Montgomery D. Parker
    Philip A. Bettens

L Trp. (Riley, McKinney,
    Leavenworth)
Capt. Francis Moore
1Lt. Eugene D. Dimmick
    Walter L. Finley
2Lt. Charles M. Schaeffer
    Alfred B. Jackson

M Trp. (Riley, Washakie,
    DuChesne)
Capt. Louis H. Rucker
1Lt. Gustavus Valois
    Montgomery D. Parker
    Frank Beers Taylor
2Lt. John F. McBlain
    John H. Alexander

APPENDIX H

BENTEEN'S COMMANDS AND COURT-MARTIAL BOARD

FORT HARKER, KANSAS   3 May 1868 - 19 October 1868
C.O: Capt. Frederick W. *Benteen*, 7 Cav
Adj: 1Lt. Mason Carter, 5 Inf.   Qm: Capt. Henry Inman, qmd
C/s: Capt. William H. Bell   Surg: Dr. Blencowe Eardley Fryer
    B/5 Inf: John W. Craig
    H/5 Inf: Capt. David H. Brotherton; 2Lt. George P. Borden
    H/7 Cav: 1Lt. William W. Cooke
    M/7 Cav: 1Lt. Owen Hale; 2Lt. Donald McIntosh

FORT RICE, DAK. TERR.   20 September 1875 - 5 May 1876
C.O: Capt. Frederick W. *Benteen*, 7 Cav
Adj. 2Lt. James G. Sturgis, 7 Cav   Qm: Capt. James W. Scully, qmd
    Surgeon: Dr. Blair D. Taylor
    D/17 Inf: 1Lt. James Humbert; 2Lt. James Brennan
    H/7 Cav: 1Lt. Francis M. Gibson; 2Lt. Charles C. DeRudio (dept. Feb. 1876)
    M/7 Cav: Capt. Thomas H. French; 1Lt. Edward G. Mathey

FORT SILL, INDIAN TERR.   21 May 1884 - 5 April 1885
C.O: Major Frederick W. *Benteen*, 9 Cav
Adj: 1Lt. Charles J. Crane, 24 Inf   Surgeon: Dr. Jefferson R. Kean
    1Lt. William H.W. James, 24 Inf
    C/24 Inf: Capt. Bethel M. Custer; 2Lt. Charles N. Clinch
    E/24 Inf: Capt. John W. Clous; 1Lt. Henry F. Leggett
    I/24 Inf: Capt. Alfred C. Markley; 1Lt. Ammon A. Augur
    K/24 Inf: Capt. James N. Morgan; 1Lt. William H.W. James; 2Lt. William Black
    C/9 Cav: Capt. Charles D. Beyer; 1Lt. Ballard S. Humphrey; 2Lt. Philip P. Powell
    G/9 Cav: Capt. Patrick Cusack; 2Lt. Grote Hutcheson

FORT DuCHESNE, UTAH TERR.   23 August 1886 - 18 December 1886
C.O: Major Frederick W. *Benteen*, 9 Cav
Adj: 1Lt. Joseph W. Duncan, 21 Inf   Surgeon: Dr. Robert B. Benham
    1Lt. Willis Wittich, 21 Inf
    1Lt. Harry L. Bailey, 21 Inf
    B/21 Inf: Capt. Stephen P. Jocelyn; 1Lt. Willis Wittich; 2Lt. Henry D. Styer
    F/21 Inf: 1Lt. Joseph W. Duncan; 2Lt. John S. Parke
    I/21 Inf: 1Lt. Harry L. Bailey; 2Lt. Lawrence J. Hearn
    K/21 Inf: 1Lt. Charles M. Truitt; 2Lt. Edward S. McCaskey
    B/9 Cav: Capt. Byron Dawson; 1Lt. George R. Burnett; 2Lt. Harry G. Trout
    E/9 Cav: Capt. Jerrauld A. Olmsted; 2Lt. Eugene F. Ladd

COURT-MARTIAL BOARD, 1887

Col. August V. Kautz, 8 Inf (Pres.)
Col. Henry C. Merriam, 7 Inf
Lt. Col. Nathan W. Osborne, 6 Inf
Lt. Col. Robert H. Offley, 17 Inf
Lt. Col. Joshua S. Fletcher, 2 Inf (excused)
Major Andrew S. Burt, 8 Inf
Major James S. Casey, 17 Inf

Major Edmond Butler, 2 Inf
Major John N. Andrews, 21 Inf
Major William J. Lyster, 6 Inf
Major Alfred T. Smith, 7 Inf
    (absent sick)
Capt. Allan H. Jackson, 7 Inf
    judge advocate

APPENDIX J

BENTEEN ASSOCIATES

1) Benteen, Frederick Wilson "Freddie" — Benteen's son
   b. 27 March 1867, Atlanta, Georgia   Army Officer
Commissioned 1899, though overage; m. Maria Louisa Cassanova y del Canan 1899; three daughters: Anna Louisa Maria "Anita Cassanova" (m. Stephens Mitchell), Katherine Elvira Maria "Katherine L..", Maria Luisa (m. Myron F. Steves); retired 23 May 1916, but served in France 1918 and as ROTC instructor for another decade.
   d. 20 July 1956, Atlanta, Georgia

2) DeGress, William John — recipient (and publisher) of Benteen's letter on Washita
   b. 19 October 1834, Cologne, Germany   Insurance broker
Served in Regular Army 1856-1861; commanded B Co. 10th Missouri Cavalry 1864-65; moved with wife and children to South America 1871; resided in Mexico City from 1874 until just prior to his death.
   d. 30 December 1905, St. Louis, Missouri

3) Gobright, Lawrence Augustus "Larry" — Benteen's cousin
   b. 2 May 1816, Baltimore, Maryland   Journalist
Based in Washington D.C. from 1841; co-founder of New York Associated Press; only reporter accredited to sit in on Lincoln Cabinet meeting; considered "dean" of Washington newsmen.
   d. 22 May 1879, Washington D.C.

4) Ladd, Eugene Frederick — married Benteen's "adopted" daughter
   b. 19 September 1859, Thetford, Vermont   Army officer
Graduated from West Point 1884; served under Benteen in 9th Cavalry; m. Violet Norman 30 May 1888; daughter Katharine Louise; rose to full colonel (in adjutant general's department); retired 1915; recalled to active duty WWI; resided in Cohasset, Massachusetts after the war.
   d. 23 April 1927, Boston, Massachusetts; posthumously promoted to Brigadier General in the Regular Army.

5) Nash, Joseph van Holt — Benteen's closest friend
   b. 8 July 1834, Petersburg, Virginia   Book publisher
Graduate of University of Virginia; served in Confederate Army during Civil War, a major on staff of General Fitzhugh Lee by 1865; *may* have been Benteen's orderly in 7 Cav on ride to Ft. Harker in 1868; arrived in Atlanta with wife and three children in 1878 as regional representative for D. Appleton Publishers; made President of American Book Company in 1894; one of Benteen's pallbearers.
   d. 17 November 1900, Augusta, Georgia

6) Norman, Leslie R. — Benteen's brother-in-law
   b. 1843, Philadelphia, Pennsylvania
Appointed 1st Lieutenant of L Co. 10th Missouri Cavalry in 1864; arrested 8 April 1865 in Selma, Alabama for being drunk on duty and threatening to shoot E.F. Winslow; allowed to resign three weeks later; returned to St. Louis; m. Mary J. Willis 14 April 1867; resided at 3311 St. Vincent Ave. (St. Louis).
   d. 19 January 1905, St. Louis, Missouri

7) Wilson, James Harrison — Benteen's mentor
  b. 2 September 1837, Shawneetown, Ill.   Army Officer/Railroad exec.
Graduated from West Point in 1860; promoted to brigadier general of volunteers by October 1863; commanded Cavalry Corps, Military Division of Mississippi 1864-65; Military Governor of Georgia 1865-66; m. Ella Andrews 3 January 1866 — three daughters; resigned from Regular Army in 1870; railroad executive for next 25 years; made major general of volunteers during Spanish-American War; retired in 1901; made major general in the Regular Army by special act of Congress in 1915.
  d. 23 February 1925, Wilmington, Delaware

8) Winslow, Edward Francis — Benteen's Civil War commander
  b. 28 Sept. 1837, Augusta, Maine   Railroad engineer/exec.
Commanded 4th Iowa Cavalry in Civil War (and brigade which included Benteen's 10th Missouri Cavalry); Military Governor of Atlanta 1865-66; m. Laura-Laseur Berry 24 September 1860 (no children); vice-president of Burlington, Cedar Rapids & Northern Railroad; president of the St. Louis & Santa Fe, the Atlantic & Pacific, and a New York railroad company before retiring at the turn of the century for ill health; furnished railroad passes for Benteen in 1880s.
  d. 22 October 1914, Canandaigua, New York

OFFICERS WHO SERVED UNDER BENTEEN IN H CO. 7th CAV

1(1Lt. Thomas B. Weir, 1867
2) 1Lt. William W. Cooke, 1867-1869
3) 1Lt. Charles Brewster, 1869
4) 2Lt. Charles C. DeRudio, 1869-1876
5) 1Lt. Francis M. Gibson, 1871-1880
6) 2Lt. Albert J. Russell, 1876-1881
7) 1Lt. Charles A. Varnum, 1880-
8) 2Lt. William H. Baldwin, 1881-

Benteen's predecessor: 1Lt. Samuel Hildeburn, 3rd Cavalry
Benteen's successor: Capt. Charles C. DeRudio, 7th Cavalry

BIBLIOGRAPHY

I. PRIMARY SOURCES
A. Manuscripts, Letters, Diaries, etc.

001. Benteen, F.W., Letters to David F. Barry, 1888-1898
Copies of originals owned by Eastern Montana College Special Collections/Custer Collection as transcribed by CKM; John Carroll's transcriptions also consulted.

002. Benteen, F.W., Letters to Catharine L. Benteen, 1871-1888
Originals in Univ. of Georgia (Athens) Special Collections; some transcribed in Graham (040), balance in *Camp Talk* (009); letters are from Benteen to his wife, cited by date of letter.

003. Benteen, F.W., Letter to Mrs. Henrietta Fairbanks, 24 Aug. 1882
Mrs. Fairbanks was Benteen's older sister; original in Univ. of Georgia (Athens) Library Special Collections.

004. Benteen, F.W., Letter to Capt. Edward Field, 8 Feb. 1886
Citations based on typescript owned by U.S. Army Military History Institute (Carlisle Barracks, PA) Archives.

005. Benteen, F.W., Letter to Capt. Edward S. Godfrey, 3 Jan. 1886
Location of original unknown; copy from Graham (040) p. 334 cited.

006. Benteen, F.W., Letter to Capt. Edward S. Godfrey, 19 Aug. 1892
Original in Univ. of Georgia (Athens) Library Special Collections.

007. Benteen, F.W., Notations in margins of Custer's *Life on the Plains*, undated
Original "annotated" copy of Custer's book owned by the Myron F. Steves family (Benteen's granddaughter).

008. Carroll, John M. (ed.), *The Benteen-Goldin Letters on Custer and His Last Battle*. Liveright, 1971
Transcriptions of letters from Benteen to Theodore W. Goldin from 1891-1896; originals in Gilcrease Institute of Amer. History, Tulsa, OK.
NOTE: Benteen's second narrative of the battle of the Little Big Horn is contained in this book (pp. 176-187).

009. Carroll, John M. (ed.) *Camp Talk*. J.M. Carroll & Co., 1983
Letters from Benteen to his wife Kate 1871-1888; not cited (see 002).

010. Godfrey, Edward Settle., Letter to J.A. Shoemaker of Billings, Montana, 2 March 1926
Original's location unknown; copy cited from Goldin (008) pp. 16-17.

011. Hinricks, Charles F.,   Diary, 1863-1865
     Hinricks was an officer in Benteen's 10th Missouri Cavalry; original
     lost; copy cited from Western Historical Manuscripts Collection, Univ.
     of Missouri (Columbia).

012. Jennings, Elisha Middleton,   Letters to Mary E. Elders, 1863
     Jennings was an officer in the 10th Missouri Cavalry; Mary Elders
     was his fiance; original letters lost; typescript copy cited from Uni-
     versity of Missouri (Columbia).

013. McDougall, Thomas Mower,   Letters to David F. Barry, 1900-1909
     Location of originals unknown; cited from J.M. Carroll's publication
     of Barry letters (pp. 23-29).

                         B. Government Documents

014. Annual Report of Adjutant General of Missouri for year ending 31
         Dec. 1864. Emory S. Foster (public printer), 1866.
     Page 182 under "Historical Memoranda" contains a single letter
     written by Benteen (27 July 1864).

015. Annual Report of Adjutant General of Missouri for year ending 31
         Dec. 1865. Emory S. Foster (public printer), 1866.
     Pages 365-370 contain a section, "Historical Memoranda," written
     (probably) by Benteen and Capt. Jeremiah F. Young.

016. Annual Report of Secretary of War, 1876. (House Ex. Doc. #1, Pt. 2;
         44th Cong. 2d Sess., vol. 2; Serial Set 1742).

017. Annual Report of Secretary of War, 1877. (House Ex. Doc. #1, Pt. 2;
         45th Cong. 2nd Sess., vol. 2; Serial Set 1794).

018. Benteen, Frederick William,   Military, medical & pension records.
     National Archives, Adjutant General's Record Group 94.
     NOTE: Same records for the following individuals also copied:
     William D. Bowen, William W. Cooke, Florence M. Cornyn, William
     J. DeGress, Charles C. DeRudio, Arthur W. DuBray, Joel H. Elliott,
     Ezra B. Fuller, Owen Hale, Thomas Hynes, Thomas M. McDougall,
     Robert B.M. McGlasson, Leslie R. Norman, Robert M. West, Martin
     H. Williams.

019. Benteen, Frederick William,   Official Court-martial Transcript, 1887.
     Original ms. in National Archives, Old Army Branch RR 2327; page
     numbers cited are from transcription by John M. Carroll, though
     Carroll transcriptions were verified against copy of original.

020. *Fair Play* Files. National Archives.
     Files are of documents pertaining to compensation of owners for
     loss of Steamboat *Fair Play*.

021. French, Thomas H.,   Official Court-martial Transcript, 1879.
     Original in National Archives; page numbers cited are from John
     M. Carroll's transcription.

022. Fuller, Ezra Bond, Letter to Commissioner of Pensions, 28 November 1904.

Original in Benteen's pension records folder in Record Group 94.

023. Hare, Lieut. Luther Rector, Report to Chief Engineer, Dept. of Dakota, 24 January 1878.

Contained in Secretary of War Report (1878), vol. 2, Appendix QQ, pp. 1672-1680.

024. U.S. Dept. of Navy, *War of the Rebellion: A Compilation of the Official Records of the Union and Confederate Navies.* Govt. Printing Office.

Series I, vol. 23: "Naval Forces on Western Waters" only.

025. U.S. War Department, *War of the Rebellion: A Compilation of the Official Records of the Union and Confederate Armies 1861-1865.* 129 volumes. G.P.O. 1880-1901.

Abbreviated OR; all citations refer to Series I; all are Part I volumes except where otherwise specified.

NOTE: also from National Archives microfilm:

a) Post Returns of: Atlanta, Dodge, Duchesne, Harker, Hays, Lincoln, McKinney, Meade, Nashville, New Orleans, Niobrara, Randall, Riley, Rice, Rolla, Sill.

b) Regimental Returns of: 7th Cavalry & 9th Cavalry.

C. Newspapers

026. Atlanta *Constitution* 22 June 1898 (notice of Benteen's death).

027. Atlanta *Constitution* 25 June 1898 (Benteen's obituary and notice of funeral arrangements).

028. Atlanta *Journal* 24 May 1897 ("Brave Old Benteen: A Southern Federal" – interview with Benteen on 24 May 1897).

029. Missouri *Democrat* 8 Feb. 1869 (letter on Washita from Benteen to DeGress).

030. Kansas City *Times* 3 Jan. 1887 (article datelined "Fort Leavenworth" dealing with events at Fort DuChesne, U.T.).

031. The *Weekly Atlanta Intelligencer* 9 May 1866 ("Outrageous Attempt at Murder – Horse Stolen").

D. Books

032. Brininstool, Earl A., *Troopers With Custer.* Bonanza Books, 1952.

Chapter III (pp. 67-92) entitled "Benteen's Own Story" is mosaiced from Benteen's second narrative of the battle of the Little Big Horn and his 1879 Court of Inquiry testimony.

033. Carroll, John M. (ed.), *Cavalry Scraps: The Writings of Frederick W. Benteen.* Guidon Press, 1979.
   Consists of 11 short shories written by Benteen, covering events in his career from 1867-1885.

034. Carroll, John M. (ed.), *I, Varnum: An Autogiography.* Arthur H. Clark, 1982.
   Consists of two brief beginnings of an autobiography by Colonel (retired) Charles Albert Varnum.

035. Custer, Elizabeth B., *Boots and Saddles.* Univ. of Okla. Press, 1961.
   Elizabeth B. Custer was the wife of George A. Custer; originally written in 1885, the book covers the Dakota years (1873-1876).

036. Custer, Elizabeth B., *Tenting On the Plains.* Harper & Bros., 1893.
   Covers the Kansas years (1867-1871).

037. Custer, George Armstrong, *My Life On the Plains.* Univ. of Nebraska Press, 1966.
   Custer was commanding officer of the 7th Cavalry 1866-1876; book covers the years 1867-1869.

038. Finerty, John Frederick, *Warpath and Bivouac.* Univ. of Oklahoma Press, 1961.

039. Godfrey, Edward Settle, *Field Diary.* Champoeg Press, 1956.

040. Graham, Colonel William A., *Abstract of the Reno Court of Inquiry.* Stackpole, 1954.

041. Graham, Colonel William A., *The Custer Myth: A Source Book of Custeriana.* Stackpole, 1953.
   Some parts of the book, admittedly, are *not* primary source materials, but most of it consists of first-hand accounts of the battle of the Little Big Horn and related subjects.
   NOTE: Benteen's first narrative of the battle (pp. 177-182).

042. Hammer, Kenneth M. (ed.), *Custer in '76: Walter Camp's Notes On the Custer Fight.* Brigham Young Univ. Press, 1976.
   Slightly edited publication of the field notes of amateur historian Walter Mason Camp (1867-1925), recording his interviews with surviving participants of the battle of the Little Big Horn.

043. Hunt, Frazier & Robert, *I Fought With Custer: The Story of Sergeant Windolph.* Charles Scribner's Sons, 1947.
   An "as-told-to" autobiography of Charles Windolph, last 7th Cavalry survivor of the battle of the Little Big Horn.

044. Jocelyn, Stephen Perry II, *Mostly Alkalai.* Caxton, 1953.
   Capt. Stephen P. Jocelyn of the 21st Infantry was at Ft. DuChesne under Benteen 1886-1887; book is by his son, based on diaries and letters from the period.

045. Libby, O.G. (ed.), *The Arikara Narrative.* Rio Grande Press, 1976.
Recollections of Arikara (Ree) Indian scouts.

046. Mulford, Ami Frank, *Fighting Indians in the 7th United States Cavalry.*
P.L. Mulford, 1879.
Mulford was trumpeter in M Company, 7th Cavalry in 1877.

047. Scott, Hugh Lenox, *Some Memories of a Soldier.* Century Pub. Co.,
1928.
Autobiography of Major General (ret.) H.L. Scott, who served in
the 7th Cavalry 1877-1897.

048. Schofield, John McAllister, *Forty Six Years in the Army.* Century Pub.
Co., 1897.
Autobiography of General (ret.) J.M. Schofield.

049. Terry, Alfred Howe, *Field Diary.* Old Army Press, 1972.
Notations in journal of Brigadier General A.H. Terry covering
17 May to 22 August 1876.

050. Utley, Robert M. (ed.) *Life in Custer's Cavalry: Diaries and Letters
of Albert and Jennie Barnitz.* Yale Univ. Press, 1970.
Selections from diaries and correspondence of Albert Barnitz, from
1867 to 1870 the commanding officer of G Company, 7th Cavalry.

E. Articles

051. Ediger, Theodore A., "Some Reminiscences of the Battle of the Washita." *Chronicles of Oklahoma,* vol. xxxiii, no. 2, Summer 1955,
pp. 137-141.
Recollections of two aged Cheyenne women who survived the
Washita fight.

052. Ellis, Horace, "A Survivor's Story of the Custer Massacre on the
American Frontier" *Journal of American History,* 2d Quarterly,
1909, pp. 227-232.
Recollections of service in the 7th Cavalry by Jacob Adams of H Co.

053. (Hamilton) "In Memoriam: Captain Louis McLane Hamilton" *Chronicles of Oklahoma,* vol. xlvi, Winter 1968-69, pp. 362-385.
Reprint of memorial written by Custer and Capt. Robert M. West
in December 1868 for Hamilton, who was killed at the Washita.

054. Johnson, Roy P., "Jacob Horner of the 7th Cavalry" *North Dakota
History,* vol. 16, 1949, pp. 75-100.
Recollections of Jacob Horner of K Company.

II. SECONDARY SOURCES
A. Manuscripts

055. Bentley, Charles Allen, *The Military Career of Frederick W. Benteen:
The Indian Wars.* (unpub. Master's thesis) Univ. of Georgia,
1975, 118 pp.
Work of Benteen authority C.A. "Pete" Bentley.

056. Bentley, Charles A., "Notes" (unpublished) n.p.
  Pete Bentley is a researcher who interviewed Mr. and Mrs. Stephens Mitchell (Benteen's granddaughter) on 12 November 1974 and 15 September 1975; citations from copies of those notes.

057. Jamieson, Perry D., *The Development of Civil War Tactics.* (dissertation for PhD in History) Wayne State Univ., 1979.

058. Lee, Bob, *The Reno Courts-Martial* (unpublished speech text), n.d. 16 pp.

059. Steves, Myron F. Jr., "Notes" (unpublished) 9 pp.
  "Buddy" Steves (Benteen's great-grandson) recorded recollections of Stephens Mitchell (husband of Benteen's granddaughter) of conversations with Frederick Wilson Benteen (Benteen's son) in the early 1950s.

B. Books

060. Asay, Karol, *Grayhead and Longhair: The Benteen-Custer Relationship.* J.M. Carroll & Co., 1983.
  Analytical work of Benteen authority Karol Asay; draft (46 pp) of booklet used for citations.

061. Beal, Merrill D., *I Will Fight No More Forever: Chief Joseph and the Nez Perce War.* Univ. of Wash. Press, 1966.

062. Brady, Cyrus Townsend, *Indian Fights and Fighters.* McClure & Phillips, 1904.

063. Buresh, Lumir F., *October 25th and the Battle of Mine Creek.* Lowell Press, 1977.

064. Byrne, Patrick E., *Soldiers of the Plains.* Minton, Balch & Co., 1926.

065. Carroll, John M. (& Byron Price), *Roll Call On the Little Big Horn.* Old Army Press, 1974.

066. Catton, Bruce, *This Hallowed Ground.* Doubleday, 1956.

067. Chandler, Melbourne C., *Of Garryowen In Glory.* Turnpike Press, 1960.

068. Cullum, George Washington, *Biographical Register of the Officers and Graduates of the U.S. Military Academy.* Houghton, Mifflin, 1891-1940.

069. Dustin, Fred, *The Custer Tragedy.* Edward Bros., 1939.

070. *Dictionary of American Biography.* Charles Scribner's Sons, 1958.

071. Dyer, Frederick H., *A Compendium of the War of Rebellion.* Yoseloff, 1959.

072. Edwards, William B., *Civil War Guns.* Castle Books, 1962.

073. Fougera, Katherine Gibson, *With Custer's Cavalry.* Caxton Printers, 1940.
  Often regarded as primary source material, this book is in fact the

work of the daughter of Katherine Garrett Gibson (wife of Francis M. Gibson of the 7th Cavalry), based (loosely) on her mother's diary and notes; there are some errors of fact.

074. Frost, Lawrence A., *The Court-Martial of George Armstrong Custer*. Univ. of Okla. Pess, 1968.

075. Frost, Lawrence A., *General Custer's Libbie*. Superior, 1976.

076. Gray, John S., *Centennial Campaign*. Old Army Press, 1976.

077. Grinnell, George Bird, *The Fighting Cheyennes*. Univ. of Okla. Press, 1956.

078. Heitman, Francis B., *Historical Register and Dictionary of the United States Army*. Univ. of Illinois Press, 1965.

079. Hoig, Stan, *The Battle of the Washita*. Univ. of Nebr. Press, 1976.

080. Jackson, Donald, *Custer's Gold: The United States Cavalry Expedition of 1874*. Univ. of Nebr. Press, 1972.

081. Johnson, Barry C., *Benteen's Ordeal at Ft. DuChesne*. Johnson-Taunton Military Press, 1893.

082. Jones, James Pickett, *Yankee Blitzkrieg: Wilson's Raid Through Alabama and Georgia*. Univ. of Georgia Press, 1976.

083. Leckie, William H., *The Buffalo Soldiers*. Univ. of Okla. Press, 1967.

084. Longacre, Edward G., *Union Stars to Tophat*. Stackpole, 1972.
     A biography of Benteen's mentor, James Harrison Wilson.

085. Merington, Marguerite, *The Custer Story*. Devon-Adair, 1950.

086. Miller, Francis Trevelyn, *Photographic History of the Civil War*. (Vol. 4: Cavalry) Yoseloff, 1957.

087. Mills, Charles K., *Charles C. DeRudio*. J.M. Carroll & Co., 1983.

088. Monnett, Howard N., *Action Before Westport: 1864*. Westport Hist. Soc./Lowell Press, 1964.

089. *National Cyclopedia of American Biography*. James T. White & Co., 1898-1926.

090. *Official Army Register*. Govt. Printing Office, 1892-1947.

091. *Outline Descriptions of the Posts of the Military Division of the Missouri*. U.S. Army, 1876.

092. Packe, Michael St. John, *Orsini: The Story of a Conspirator*. Little, Brown, 1957.
     Contains factual data on the early life of DeRudio not found elsewhere.

093. Rickey, Don, *Forty Miles A Day On Beans and Hay*. Univ. of Okla. Press, 1963.

094. Sefton, James E., *The United States Army and Reconstruction, 1865-1877*. Louisiana State Univ. Press, 1967.

095. Starr, Stephen Z., *Jennison's Jayhawkers*. Louisiana State Univ. Press, 1973.

096. Stewart, Edgar I., *Custer's Luck*. Univ. of Okla. Press, 1955.

097. Terrell, John Upton (& Colonel George Walton), *Faint the Trumpet Sounds: The Life and Trial of Major Reno*. David McKay Co., 1966.

098. Utley, Robert M., *Frontier Regulars*. Macmillan, 1973.

C. Articles

099. Anderson, Harry H., "The Benteen Baseball Club: Sports Enthusiasts of the Seventh Cavalry" *Montana: the Magazine of Western History*, July 1970   pp. 82-87

100. Kennan, Jerry, "Wilson's Selma Raid" *Civil War Times Illustrated*, January 1963   pp. 37-44

101. Johnson, Lamont, "Benteen of the Seventh" *Zane Grey's Western Magazine*, August 1949   pp. 67-76

102. Julian, Colonel Allen P., "Brevet Brig. Gen. Frederick W. Benteen" *Atlanta Historical Bulletin* xi   June 1966   pp. 19-31

103. Langsdorf, Edgar, "Price's Raid and the Battle of Mine Creek" *Kansas Historical Quarterly* xxx   Autumn 1964   pp. 281-306

104. Rector, William G., "Fields of Fire: The Reno-Benteen Defense Perimeter" *Montana: the Magazine of Western History*   Spring 1966   pp. 65-72

105. Stewart, Edgar I., "The Reno Court of Inquiry" *Montana Magazine of History* vol. ii, July 1952, no. 3   pp. 31-43

106. Stone, Melville E., "Some Things Seen: V. Still Digressing: Carlo di Rudio" *Colliers Weekly*   15 May 1920   pp. 7, 34, 36

107. Walton, Lt. Col. George H., "The Tart-Tongued Bomb Thrower of the Seventh Cavalry" *Army*   August 1964   pp. 62-66
Biographical sketch of Charles C. DeRudio.

Notes

The number in (parentheses) following the quoted phrase
refers to the bibliography item so numbered.

page

12 "Petersburg Military Institute"
(019) p. 87

13 "war was started" (028) 14 May
1897

14 "sight-seer" (059) p. 2

14 "setting up" (019) p. 86

16 "It was then decided..." (025) III
p. 90

16 "Dutch troops" (056) 12 Nov 1974

17 "retreat was undoubtedly..." (048)
p. 46

18 "demanded a change" (025) II p. 95

18 "Major Sturgis, in compliance..."
(025) II p. 95

18 "A man with my views..." (019)
p. 86

19 "many and many" (019) p. 86

19 "When Benteen told..." (056)
12 Nov 1974

19 "who brought pressure to bear"
(059) p. 2

19 "horrified" (059) p. 2

19 "the Union deserved..." (059) p. 2

19 "the prayers of my..." (019) p. 87

20 "mounted units performed tactical..."
(057) p. 170

20 "Cavalry was often used..." (057)
p. 170

20 "cavalry units were sometimes
held..." (057) p. 171

20-1 "Mounted troops were sometimes
used..." (057) p. 171

22 "in great confusion" (025) III p. 240

23 "commenced in rapid retreat" (025)
III p. 240

23 "embarrassed" (025) III p. 241

24 "Please receive my thanks..." (025)
X p. 510

27 "Will you please inform..." (025)
VIII p. 37

27 "quarter in Rolla" (018 — Benteen)
— endorsement to letter 29 Dec 1861

27 "I have a sister..." (018 — Benteen)
— letter 29 Dec 1861

27 "almost infant" (019) p. 86

29 "on a heavy picket..." (025) VIII
p. 269

29 "After two rounds..." (025) VIII
p. 269

29 "concealed by the brush" (025)
VIII p. 270

29 "they fled" (025) VIII p. 270

31 "efficient" (008) 22 Feb 1896

33 "persevere" (025) VIII p. 200

33-4 "withstood three separate..." (019)
p. 87

35 "disrespectful behavior towards..."
(018 — Benteen)

35 "conduct prejudicial to..." (018 —
Benteen)

35 "courtly" (060) p. 5

35 "Corporal Weaver declines..." (018
— Benteen)

35 "Adjutant, Corporal Weaver cannot..." (018 — Benteen)

36 "the finest cavalry charge..." (025)
VIII p. 122

37 "a good amount of negative..." (025)
VIII p. 124

37 "The scout was very hard..." (025)
VIII p. 124

37 "The army and navy..." (025) VIII
p. 240

41 "some wood in the furnace" (020)
— Waggener's Affidavit

41 "Charley, how much steam..." (020)
— Plummer's Affidavit

41 "There is not enough..." (020) —
Plummer's Affidavit

41 "pursued them rapidly..." (025)
VIII p. 243

42 "about 40" (025) VIII p. 245

42 "a few shell..." (025) VIII p. 243

42 "then proceeded to destroy..." (025)
VIII p. 243

page
70 "The Tenth Missouri was..." (025)
XXX p. 811
71 "as being valuable and gallant..."
(025) XXX p. 811
71 "the conduct of curious personages..." (025) XXX p. 811
71 " I have been ordered to report..."
(018 – Hynes) letter 21 Oct 1863
72 "driven immediately from..." (025)
XXXII, p. 248
72 "advancing at a gallop..." (025)
XXXII p. 249
73 "The 10th Missouri, it was said..."
(066) p. 306
73 "Meridian was thoroughly sacked"
(066) p. 306
73 "sent two messengers eastward"
(025) XXXII p. 250
73 "a drumhead court-martial was
held..." (086) p. 200
74 "Splendid, Benteen!..." (019) p. 89
74 "it got to be said..." (019) p. 89
74 "with the celerity and ease..." (019)
p. 89
74 "books, papers and records..." (014)
p. 182
74 "refused to send them" (014) p.
182
75 "In view of the fact..." (025)
XXXIX p. 96
75 "for prompt assistance rendered..."
(025) XXXIX p. 314
76 "for efficient discharge..." (021)
XXXIX p. 315
76 "That Forrest is the very Devil!"
(025) XXXIX Pt. 2 p. 121
76 "I am sorry to have to say..." (025)
XXXIX p. 146
76 "and in fifteen minutes..." (014)
p. 182
76 "wagon train, much quartermaster..."
(014) p. 182
76 "their being ordered to St. Louis..."
(018 – Benteen) letter 31 July 1864
83 "Marmaduke had stationed..." (063)
p. 51
85 "by dint of great urging..." (025)
XLI p. 331
85 "wild wave" (088) p. 115
85 "the grayclads ceased their resistance..." (088) p. 115
85 "Rebels! Fire! You damned asses!"
(088) p. 116

85 "I took the responsibility..." (025)
XLI p. 331
86 "battle raging" (025) XLI p. 331
86 "there was work to be done" (025)
XLI p. 331
86 "the enemy far beyond the battleground..." (025) XLI p. 331
87 "That day we marched..." (025)
XLI p. 331
87 "broke and gave promise..." (025)
XLI p. 332
87 "I at once determined..." (025)
XLI p. 332
88 "for God's sake" (025) XLI p. 332
88 "fatal blunder" (025) XLI p. 332
88 "thick grove of trees" (103) p. 296
89 "Again and again, Benteen
ordered..." (041) p. 159
89 "Then began a fierce..." (025) XLI
p. 332
89 "I cut eight rebels..." (025) XLI
p. 336
89 "Bonny Brown Bess..." (019) p. 90
90 "The rebel line was routed..." (103)
p. 287
90 "The thousands of Confederates..."
(063) p. 129
90 "In the bend in the creek..." (103)
p. 297
90 "Eight artillery..." (103) p. 297
91 "The enemy, not mounted riflemen..." (103) p. 303
91 "Felt it should be more..." (025)
XLI p. 333
95 "I met a great many stragglers..."
(025) XLI Pt. 4 p. 302
95 "very much jaded" (025) XLI Pt. 4
p. 302
95 "in writing" (025) XLI Pt. 4 p. 318
95 "improper to continue a pursuit..."
(025) XLI Pt. 4 p. 318
95 "as long as horses can stand..." (025)
XLI Pt. 4 p. 333
95 "a portion of the forces..." (025)
XLI Pt. 4 p. 445
95 "I have had the cooperation of..."
(019) p. 91
96 "has at all times been..." (019) p. 92
96 "I visited his regiment..." (019) p.
92
96 "I have made him a Brigadier
General..." (019) p. 92
96 "a horse to St. Louis" (025) Pt. 2
p. 36

page
124 "reconciled" (035) p. 21
127 "a post consisting..." (075) p. 157
127 "an orphan and unknown" (008) 12 Feb 1896
129 "abounded in bluster..." (001) 28 Sept 1895
129 "that Genl. Wilson wrote..." (001) 28 Sept 1895
129 "They must, after reading..." (001) 28 Sept 1895
129 "the impression made on me..." (008) 12 Feb 1896
130 "Now, Autie..." (001) 28 Sept 1895
130 "all friendship has got to cease..." (001) 28 Sept 1895
131 "bad management" (050) p. 97
132 "$30,000" (008) 5 Feb 1896
132 "accredited..." (008) 31 Jan 1896
133 "a prettily made..." (033) p. 39
133 "couldn't stand the clanking..." (033) p. 39
133 "There is an unwritten law..." (033) p. 39
133 "watched the situation with..." (033) p. 40
134 "We got no wine from him..." (033) p. 40
136 "good shots, good riders..." (077) p. viii (Vestal's Intro)
137 "I cannot say..." (019) p. 100
137 "I think if the management..." (041) p. 214
137 "I noticed, too..." (033) pp. 35-36
137 "We should treat the Indians..." (041) p. 214
137 "When I accepted a captaincy..." (008) 5 Feb 1896
138 "who were at one time..." (013) 27 Dec 1905
138 "I am not an indian hater..." (001) 11 Jan 1895
140 "I think the Indians promised..." (033) p. 14
140 "The Cheyennes had not time..." (033) p. 15
140 "They had some idea..." (033) p. 15
141 "upon a series of islands..." (050) p. 34
141 "Every Cheyenne had..." (033) p. 15
141 "The Indian men..." (036) p. 578
141 "Well... we slaughtered..." (033) p. 16
141 "But I really hadn't..." (033) p. 16

141 "Custer didn't like..." (033) p. 16
142 "When Custer reached the Smoky Hill..." (098) p. 118
142 "doubtless they thought that hate..." (033) p. 15
142 "General Custer has become bilious..." (050) p. 46
142 "Everytime that a new officer..." (050) p. 46
143 "Capt. Benteen, Wallingford, Nowlan..." (050) p. 49
143 "Things are very unpleasant here..." (050) p. 50
143 "shot himself — suicide — because..." (008) 12 Feb 1896
144 "were shot while begging..." (008) 12 Feb 1896
144 "one of the deserters was brought..." (008) 12 Feb 1896
145 "received a great awakening..." (008) 12 Feb 1896
145 "spreadeagled on the plain..." (008) 12 Feb 1896
145 "men of the command..." (008) 12 Feb 1896
145 "a distinguished man, but given at time..." (008) 12 Feb 1896
145 "hadn't the time" (008) 12 Feb 1896
146 "We were free of Custer" (008) 12 Feb 1896
147 "mess of seven" (008) 20 Oct 1891
147 "bite the dust" (008) 20 Oct 1891
149 "I simply exchanged some horses..." (033) p. 7
150 "ran into the hospital..." (050) p. 178
150 "quite severely in a number..." (050) p. 178
150 "but it scared Thompson pissless..." (008) 22 Feb 1896
150 "Around ten o'clock on the morning of..." (079) p. 46
151 "with the cock-and-bull story..." (033) p. 1
151 "confronting about fifty braves" (033) p. 2
151 "were into that gang..." (033) p. 2
151 "almost trampling on..." (033) p. 2
151 "my men, as well as..." (033) p. 3
151-2 "They were scared by us..." (033) p. 5
152 "doubtless" (033) p. 4
152 "engaged in howling..." (033) p. 4
152 "trounced" (033) p. 5

page
177 "Mrs. Benteen's baby..." (050) p. 241
178 "an exceedingly comely squaw..." (037) p. 415
178 "lived with her" (008) 17 Feb 1896
178 "seen many times in the very..." (008) 14 Feb 1896
178 "Custer slept with her..." (007) p. 249
178 "issue" (008) 17 Feb 1896
178 "a simon-pure Cheyenne..." (008) 17 Feb 1896
178 "Mona" (007) p. 249
178 "had a hellish temper" (007) p. 249
178 "gave him the marble heart..." (008) 17 Feb 1896
181 "Custer heap good!" (008) 17 Feb 1896
181 "Isn't that awful?" (008) 17 Feb 1896
181 "Why, Tom..." (008) 17 Feb 1896
181 "My dear Friend... (DeGress Letter)..." (029) 8 Feb 1869
183 "belittling" (008) 22 Feb 1896
183 "cowhide" (008) 22 Feb 1896
183 "General Custer..." (008) 22 Feb 1896
184 "Colonel Benteen, I'll see..." (008) 22 Feb 1896
184 "no tears from whipping!" (008) 22 Feb 1896
184 "Custer wilted like..." (008) 22 Feb 1896
184 "Sheridan gave Custer a piece of..." (008) 22 Feb 1896
184 "cared but little for..." (008) 22 Feb 1896
184 "evidently knew whom to whip!" (008) 22 Feb 1896
184 "I had far too much pride..." (008) 14 Feb 1896
184 "I always surmised..." (008) 10 Nov 1891
186 "undergoing their mummeries and..." (033) p. 27
187 "signalled them that..." (033) p. 27
186 "they obeyed" (033) p. 27
186 "in full paraphernalia of war..." (033) p. 27
186 "A cyclone couldn't have scattered..." (033) p. 28
186 "ample time to shuffle..." (033) p. 28

186 " 'Tis scarcely necessary..." (033) p. 28
187 "exhorted their friends..." (033) 28
187 "not much before the going down..." (033) p. 29
187 "He and his troop..." (008) 17 Feb 1896
187 "still owed" (008) 17 Feb 1896
187 "Custer paid me off..." (008) 17 Feb 1896
188 "still remember the fiendish gleam..." (008) 17 Feb 1896
188 "never said good-bye even..." (008) 17 Feb 1896
188 "Not by a damned sight!" (008) 17 Feb 1896
188 "Well... I'll fix this up..." (008) 17 Feb 1896
188 "At your old business..." (008) 17 Feb 1896
188 "Yes... I can't keep out..." (008) 17 Feb 1896
189 "I gave three hearty cheers!" (008) 17 Feb 1896
192 "seduced" (092) p. 246
192 "to save her mother's shame" (092) p. 246
192 "had never seen a family..." (092) p. 246
192 "about seven inches long..." (107) p. 63
192 "like a clutch of monstrous bird's eggs..." (092) p. 249
192 "gas fixtures" (106) p. 34
193 "in his anxiety to obtain..." (092) p. 260
193 "as by a miracle" (018 – DeRudio) Smedberg Memorial
193 "I am in contact with some..." (107) p. 64
194 "Custer, in particular..." (107) p. 65
194 "I treated him as a gentleman..." (001) 1 April 1898
194 "his piercing eyes, his witty..." (107) p. 62
194 "The 'Count' was always..." (001) 23 March 1898
194 "That fall a memorial..." (042) p. 83
195 "made a haul at Jenison's..." (008) 17 Feb 1896
195 "I coolly returned on..." (008) 17 Feb 1896
195 "After that... you can imagine..." (008) 17 Feb 1896

page
212 "the highest opinion of his..." (008) 12 Feb 1896
212 "skinned" (008) 12 Feb 1896
212 "those damned cormorants" (008) 12 Feb 1896
213 "putting temptation in his way" (008) 12 Feb 1896
213 "on all the inspections..." (008) 12 Feb 1896
213 "genteel sufficiency of that clique" (008) 19 Jan 1896
213 "A something I look on..." (008) 19 Jan 1896
213 "a small pool of water..." (008) 10 Nov 1891
213 "I always knew he was one..." (008) 10 Nov 1891
214 "Of all the nonentities..." (008) 10 Nov 1891
214 "would have no regimental officer..." (008) 23 March 1896
217 "My husband urged that it..." (035) p. 114
217 "cold-blooded" (001) 15 Oct 1895
217 "just about the most penurious..." (001) 25 June 1897
217 "about as avaricious and..." (001) 29 March 1897
217 "As everyone visited us..." (035) p. 114
217 "not sufficiently cordial" (035) p. 114
217 "a burlesque imitation" (035) p. 114
217 "advancing coldly, extending the tips..." (035) p. 114
217-8 "I believe her objection to me..." (001) 29 March 1897
218 "Custer never killed anything but horses..." (001) 29 March 1897
218 "had it ever occurred" (001) 29 March 1897
218 "gold at the grass" (096) p. 65
219 "He threw his arms around..." (008) 22 Feb 1896
219 "Custer... at the time..." (008) 22 Feb 1896
220 "got after" (008) 22 Feb 1896
220 "She doubtless was a nympho-maniac" (008) 19 March 1896
220 "Taking into consideration the fact..." (099) p. 84
222 "My conscience was never wholly at ease..." (033) p. 18

222 "heartfelt thanks and everlasting gratitude" (043) p. 45
222 "for their unremitting..." (043) p. 45
222 "the gallant commander..." (043) pp. 45-46
224 "The times were just against him" (033) p. 38
225 "leaving laundresses and heavy baggage behind" Post Returns, Fort Rice, May 1876
225 "had to trudge 3 times daily..." (001) 1 April 1898
225-6 "and in a word, set him on..." (001) 1 April 1898
227 "swing clear" (096) p. 138
228 "Yes... we've been very..." (008) 22 Feb 1896
228 "hold my own like a man" (008) 22 Feb 1896
228 "preferment" (008) 22 Feb 1896
228 "some such influence" (008) 22 Feb 1896
228 "I then began to scent out..." (008) 22 Feb 1896
230 "behind playing Wagon Master" (049) 31 May 1876
230 "left the column..." (049) 31 May 1876
230 "swing clear" (096) p. 138
232 "Also sent Gibson..." (049) 10 June 1876
232 "No one likes to serve..." (002) 12 June 1876
232 "Thence we start..." (002) 14 June 1876
232 "Many of us are of..." (002) 14 June 1876
232 "I don't run around much..." (002) 14 June 1876
232 "Reno gave him no reason..." (049) 19 June 1876
235 "engaged in some personalities..." (042) p. 247
235 "twitted" (042) p. 247
235 "hoped he would be..." (042) p. 247
235 "It was plain to be seen..." (042) p. 247
235 "Everything packed — ready..." (002) 15 June 1876
237 "Trumpets sounding, horses prancing..." (008) p. 176
239 "These directions were wholly..." (008) p. 176

page
261 "saved the command..." (028) 24 May 1897
261 "Major, the men were pretty..." (040) p. 43
261 "No, that was a cavalry..." (096) p. 378
262 "Reno and Weir were never..." (008) 10 Nov 1891
262 "engaged in a hot exchange..." (096) p. 396
262 "went up to where Reno..." (042) p. 70
262 "inquired as to the whereabouts" (041) p. 181
262 "in a fit of bravado" (032) p. 81
262 "to show his smartness" (008) 10 Nov 1891
263 "Reno did not appear..." (042) p. 70
263 "It was impossible..." (073) p. 269
264 "in a pile of stones..." (008) 1 March 1892
264 "myriads of howling..." (008) 1 March 1892
264 "we then showed our full force..." (002) 4 July 1876
264 "The reason for this is..." (008) p. 187
264 "concluded that he had gone..." (073) p. 269
264 "that there was no necessity...' (008) 1 March 1892
265 "take a position on the point" (008) 1 March 1892
265 "French weakened..." (008) 1 March 1892
265 "gathered the procession in..." (008) 1 March 1892
265 "I don't know how many..." (041) p. 181
266 "the other companies laid down..." (104) p. 72
269 "gossiping away like an old..." (002) 10 July 1876
269 "cussing out" (008) 16 Jan 1892
269 "broad Saxon" (008) 16 Jan 1892
269 "I never felt more like..." (002) 10 July 1876
269 "That fellow is about..." (002) 10 July 1876
270 "Fred, I think you'd better..." (042) p. 71

270 "We'll have to abandon..." (010) 2 March 1926
270 "I won't do it" (010) 2 March 1926
270 "If there should be a conflict..." (010) 2 March 1926
270 "Benteen's." (010) 2 March 1926
271 "Close call; try again." (042) p. 101
271 "Benteen was on his feet..." (042) p. 136
271 "encouraging the men..." (042) p. 136
271 "Men, this is a ground hog case..." (042) p. 136
271 "drawing the fire" (042) p. 96
271 "Well, they fire about..." (042) p. 96
271 "Benteen was the only..." (042) p. 62
272 "Falstaffian crowd" (041) p. 182
272 "must hold" (004) 8 Feb 1886
272 "no matter what became..." (004) 8 Feb 1886
272 "I think in desperate..." (041) p. 259
272 "Though I'm rather fond of..." (041) p. 182
272 "plump him thro' his spinal" (041) p. 182
272 "so confoundedly mad..." (041) p. 182
272 "I was so tired..." (041) p. 182
272 "getting mad" (041) p. 182
272 "Why of course we hustled..." (004) 8 Feb 1886
272 "they somersaulted and vaulted..." (041) p. 182
273 "rather impressed the Indians..." (004) 8 Feb 1886
273 "a hail of bullets at them" (042) p. 67
273 "smiled and said: If..." (042) p. 67
273 "Benteen was unquestionably..." (062) p. 404
273 "Too much cannot be said..." (041) p. 247
273 "Benteen was really the only..." (042) p. 62
274 "this won't do" (041) p. 145
274 "a damned chucklehad" (034) p. 94
274 "Benteen saved the command..." (042) p. 114
275 "He did not reply for..." (034) p. 94

page
294 "I saw Reno's sentence..." (002)
    17 May 1877
294 "slip" (002) 17 May 1877
294 "a day or so" (002) 29 May 1877
294 "Captain Benteen started out..."
    (046) p. 89
295 'Now, all this amounts to..." (002)
    14 June 1877
296 "drunk and perfectly stupid" (002)
    30 June 1877
296 "I believe French expects to..."
    (002) 30 June 1877
296 "He was in arrest..." (002) 30 June
    1877
296 "He'll get dropped..." (002) 9 June
    1877
296 "Mathey isn't out here..." (002) 30
    June 1877
296 "very prejudicial to Fred's..." (002)
    1 July 1877
297 "so much for seeking..." (002) 4
    Aug 1877
297 "Glad to know you are..." (002) 30
    June 1877
297 "If you don't exercise..." (002) 3
    July 1877
297 "For Christ's sake — or..." (002) 3
    July 1877
297 "It is feared should..." (002) 11
    Aug 1877
297-8 "I suppose DeRudio's Co. ..."
    (002) 11 Aug 1877
298 "Chases after Indians..." (002) 11
    Aug 1877
298 "Have just returned from General..."
    (002) 11 Aug 1877
299 "Tomorrow we move..." (002) 2
    Sept 1877
299 "All my spare time..." (002) 2 Sept
    1877
299 "He loved to fish..." (054) p. 99
299 "We are in a small valley..." (002)
    5 Sept 1877
299 "If the Nez Perces..." (002) 5 Sept
    1877
300 "We may corral the Nez P's..."
    (002) 6 Sept 1877
300 "pumped" (008) 17 Nov 1891
300 "told him that he was..." (008) 17
    Nov 1891
300 "there is only one pass..." (008) 17
    Nov 1891

300 "when you know where..." (008)
    17 Nov 1891
300 "Some of the more weary..." (054)
    p. 90
300 "going to have a hell..." (008) 17
    Nov 1891
300 "you'll find an abandoned..." (008)
    17 Nov 1891
303 "The ignorance of the guides..."
    (023) p. 1679
303 "I fear you will be..." (017) p. 73
303 "council of war" (008) 17 Nov
    1891
303 "Mine was Cambronne's..." (008)
    17 Nov 1891
303 "Why in the name of..." (008) 17
    Nov 1891
303-4 "got as red as a turkey..." (008)
    17 Nov 1891
304 "Colonel Benteen, that is..." (008)
    17 Nov 1891
304 "Well, they are gone now..." (008)
    17 Nov 1891
304 "if necessary" (008) 17 Nov 1891
304 "I'll guarantee that it..." (008) 17
    Nov 1891
304 "Sam D. Sturgis should..." (008)
    14 Sept 1895
305 "deep cut with precipitous..." (023)
    p. 1679
305 "blowing a gale" (054) p. 92
305 "The other officers moved..." (054)
    p. 91
306 "some unfortunate blunder" (017)
    p. 570
306 "misapprehended" (017) p. 570
307 "They had never lost..." (008) 14
    Sept 1895
307 "I can recall no more..." (008) 19
    Oct 1894
307 "Sturgis was never very..." (008) 17
    Nov 1891
307 "a hullabaloo of a report" (008) 17
    Nov 1891
307 "abandoned in pursuit" (017) p. 571
307 "conspicuous gallantry" (017) p. 572
307 "I do not believe a more..." (022)
    28 Nov. 1904
307 "Benteen was one of..." (054) p. 99
308 "You may possibly surprise..." (002)
    2 Oct 1877
308 "has got his hands full" (002) 3
    Oct 1877

page

321 "as brave an officer as ever..." (041)
p. 244

322 "The grand old Mount Hood..."
(002) 23 April 1879

322 "cares only for himself" (002) 2
May 1879

322 "a nice fellow, I like..." (002) 2
May 1879

322 "Now... I wouldn't give the damned
thing..." (002) 3 May 1879

323 "quite a broth of a boy" (002) 5
May 1879

323 "read such books as Aesop's..."
(002) 5 May 1879

323 "This is too rapid a town..." (002)
3 May 1879

323 "and so the damned town and country..." (002) 3 May 1879

324 "it has been my misfortune..." (058)
p. 12

324 "a schemer from the head of the
creek" (001) 1 May 1889

324 "was so frightened" (058) p. 11

324 "was very pale and loked..." (058)
p. 11

324 "would be shot" (058) p. 11

324 "must have feelings against..." (058)
p. 11

324 "deplored" (006) 19 Aug 1892

324 "to twist him around so" (006) 19
Aug 1892

325 "It would be a matter of deep
regret..." (058) p. 12

325 "I mean by this that he did not
express..." (058) p. 12

325 "It should have been not guilty..."
(058) p. 13

325 "merciful consideration" (058) p. 13

325 "performed the painful duty..."
(058) p. 13

325 "manifestly excessive" (058) p. 13

325 "claim any great extent of lenity"
(058) p. 13

325 "respectfully recommended" (058)
p. 13

325 "five files in the list of..." (058)
p. 13

325 "deficient in that respect to..."
(058) p. 13

326 "Every officer of the post..." (097)
p. 299

326 "The exception was Fred Benteen."
(097) p. 300

326 "Sturgis treated Reno like..." (008)
20 Feb 1896

326 "Poor a soldier as Reno was..."
(008) 20 Feb 1896

326 "the most frivolous of charges"
(008) 22 Feb 1896

326 "Reno was a far better soldier..."
(008) 20 Feb 1896

326 "I am as confident as I can be..."
(001) 29 Aug 1895

327 "Tom Thumb" (008) 17 Feb 1896

327 "Tom Custer and Cooke were sent..."
(008) 17 Feb 1896

327 "might have prevented his being
killed..." (008) 17 Feb 1896

328 "flame" (003) 24 Aug 1882

328 "I could tell you things that
would..." (010) 2 March 1926

328 "Don't you think it is just as..."
(010) 2 March 1926

329 "I am sorry... but I cannot..." (003)
24 Aug 1882

329 "I should like to" (003) 24 Aug 1882

329 "in a first class state..." (003) 24
Aug 1882

329 "as is usual" (003) 24 Aug 1882

329 "hanging about" (003) 24 Aug
1882

329 "had the proprietor of..." (003) 24
Aug 1882

329 "Something or other..." (003) 24
Aug 1882

333 "aches from falling" (002) 28 Sept
1883

335 "The first thing that attracted..."
(033) p. 36

336 "Ole-Tanke, Ole-Tanke!" (033)
p. 36

336 "in the long ago" (033) p. 36

336 "Here was this three hundred fifty
pound..." (033) p. 36

336 "would make a coward of him..."
(033) p. 35

339 "a more thorough lying scoundrel..."
(back of letter, Hatch-to-Benteen)
25 Feb 1885

339 "After getting the 'Boomers' in a
fair..." (033) p. 43

339 "every creek was a river..." (033)
p. 43

340 "shrieked with delight" (033) p. 44

340 "boss time" (033) p. 44

341 "sick in quarters" (Post Returns, Ft.
McKinney, March-April-May 1886)

page
364 "and exposing his person" (019) p 70
364 "The Court does therefore sentence him..." (019) p. 70
364 "a conceited kind of pup..." (002) 11 May 1887
364 "he received some discipline for his..." (019) p. 71
364 "remission of sentence" (019) p. 71
364 "reasons given in the..." (019) p. 71
364 "in view of his long and honorable service..." (019) p. 72
365 "base of operations for..." (002) 11 May 1887
365 "it cost me $10,000 more than..." (008) 20 Oct 1891
365 "city blocks in perspective" (008) 20 Oct 1891
365 "been testing my urine, shoving his fingers..." (002) 21 April 1888
365 "booked" (002) 21 April 1888
365 "rather than stay with the crowd Hatch..." (006) 19 Aug 1892
366 "in getting away from Hatch..." (002) 27 April 1888
366 "with an unusually warm reception" (002) 28 April 1888
366 "sick in quarters" (Post Returns, Ft. Niobrara, April-May 1888)
366 "the step alluded to" (002) 2 May 1888
366 "I couldn't afford to let his mother..." (006) 19 Aug 1892
366 "he will be very well off..." (008) 3 April 1892
366 "why should his life be wasted..." (008) 3 April 1892
366 "feel less dependent" (002) 3 May 1888
366 "The poor girl, I fear..." (002) 3 May 1888
367 "incapacitated for active service because..." (018 — Benteen) medical records
370 "after 19 years of waiting, the U.S. has..." (008) 3 April 1892
370 "his mother is perhaps unduly..." (008) 16 Jan 1892
371 "threw the $100 to the dog." (001) 1 April 1898
371 "Those were pretty rollicking gay days" (008) 17 Nov 1891

371 "I don't regret a day..." (008) 17 Nov 1891
371 "It does rather brace one up to..." (008) 10 March 1896
372 "not command good English" (008) 25 April 1896
372 "pretty twaddy and uninteresting" (008) 25 April 1896
372 "pretty near the ludicrous" (008) 25 April 1896
372 "from making a further damned fool..." (008) 25 April 1896
372 "I think the dummy is spieling..." (008) 25 April 1896
372 "The lecture abounded in..." (008) 26 May 1896
372 "in a measure of brain..." (008) 25 April 1896
372 "Gen. Miles would have been..." (008) 3 April 1896
372 "too much circus, too little brain!" (008) 3 April 1896
372-3 "I've been a loser in a way..." (008) 17 Nov 1891
373 "must have been on his 'high horse' ..." (001) 10 March 1897
373 "the game not worth the candle" (001) 10 March 1897
373 "showed the white feather" (008) 10 Nov 1891
373 "Godfrey... now that pretty near all..." (008) 16 Jan 1892
374 "I sent word to Godfrey to..." (008) 16 Jan 1892
374 "There is nothing he dislikes more..." (028) 24 May 1897
374 "General Benteen is very popular..." (028) 24 May 1897
374 "The newspapers killed Custer..." (028) 24 May 1897
374 "could I only have been President..." (001) 1 April 1898
374 "there is no log-chain strong enough..." (001) 1 April 1898
374 "I'm going to give you a commission..." (056) 12 Nov 1974
374 "Chances of his recovery were..." (026) 22 June 1898
375 "harvest of barren regrets" (019) p. 86
375 "I fought for Old Glory..." (056) 12 Nov 1974
375 "Where he hoped for pearls..." (008) 3 April 1896

Index